The ISLE OF MAN RAILWAY

Volume III

THE BRITISH NARROW GAUGE RAILWAY No.2C

The ISLE OF MAN RAILWAY

Volume III

An outline History of The Isle of Man Railway

including

The Manx Northern Railway and

The Foxdale Railway

J.I.C. Boyd

by

James I.C. Boyd

THE OAKWOOD PRESS

First published 1962 as one volume

ISBN 0 85361 479 2

This edition is published in three volumes.

Printed by The Witney Press, Witney, Oxon.
Repro by Ford Graphics, Ringwood, Hants.
Typeset by Oakwood Graphics.

Published by
The Oakwood Press
P.O. Box 122, Headington, Oxford OX3 8LU

Contents

Abbreviations

Beyer, Peacock & Co. Ltd.	BP&CL
British Railways, British Rail.	BR
County Donegal Railways Joint Committee.	CDRJC
Coras Iompair Eireann.	CIE
County Donegal Railways Joint Committee.	CDRJC
Department of Tourism & Transport.	DTT
Douglas & Laxey Coast Electric Tramway Ltd.	D&LCETL
Douglas, Laxey & Ramsey Railway Co. Ltd.	DL&RRCL
Douglas, Laxey & Snaefell Railway.	DL&SR
Douglas Southern Electric Tramways Ltd.	DSETL
Foxdale Railway (St John's & Foxdale Railway).	FR
Great Western Railway.	GWR
Institution of Civil Engineers.	Inst CE
Institution of Mechanical Engineers	Inst ME
Isle of Man Department of Tourism & Transport.	IOMDTT
Isle of Man Mining Co. Ltd.	IOMMCL
Isle of Man National Transport.	IOMNT
Isle of Man Passenger Transport Board.	IOMPTB
Isle of Man Railway Co. (Ltd.)	IOMR
Isle of Man Road Services.	IOMRS
Isle of Man Steam Packet Co. Ltd.	IOMSPCL
Isle of Man Steam Railway (Ailsa I).	IOMSR
Isle of Man Steam Railway Supporters' Association.	IOMSRSA
Isle of Man Tourist Board.	IOMTB
Isle of Man Tramways & Electric Power Co. Ltd.	IOMT&EPCL
Isle of Man Victorian Steam Railway Co. Ltd. (Ailsa II).	IOMVSRCL
London, Midland & Scottish Railway.	LMSR
London & North Western Railway.	LNWR
Manx Brick & Tramway Co. Ltd.	MB&TCL
Manx Electric Railway.	MER
Manx Electric Railway Board.	MERB
Manx Northern Railway.	MNR
Manx Steam Railway Society.	MSRS
Member of the House of Keys.	MHK
Midland Railway.	MR
Ministry of Transport.	MOT
Navy, Army & Air Force Institutes.	NAAFI
Officer Cadet Training Unit.	OCTU
Royal Air Force.	RAF
Royal Naval Air Service.	RNAS
Speaker of the House of Keys.	SHK
St John's & Foxdale Railway	SJ&FR
Steam Railway.	SR
'Steam Railway News' (organ of IOMSRSA).	SRN
Transport & General Workers Union.	T&GWU
West Clare Railway (section of CIE).	WCR

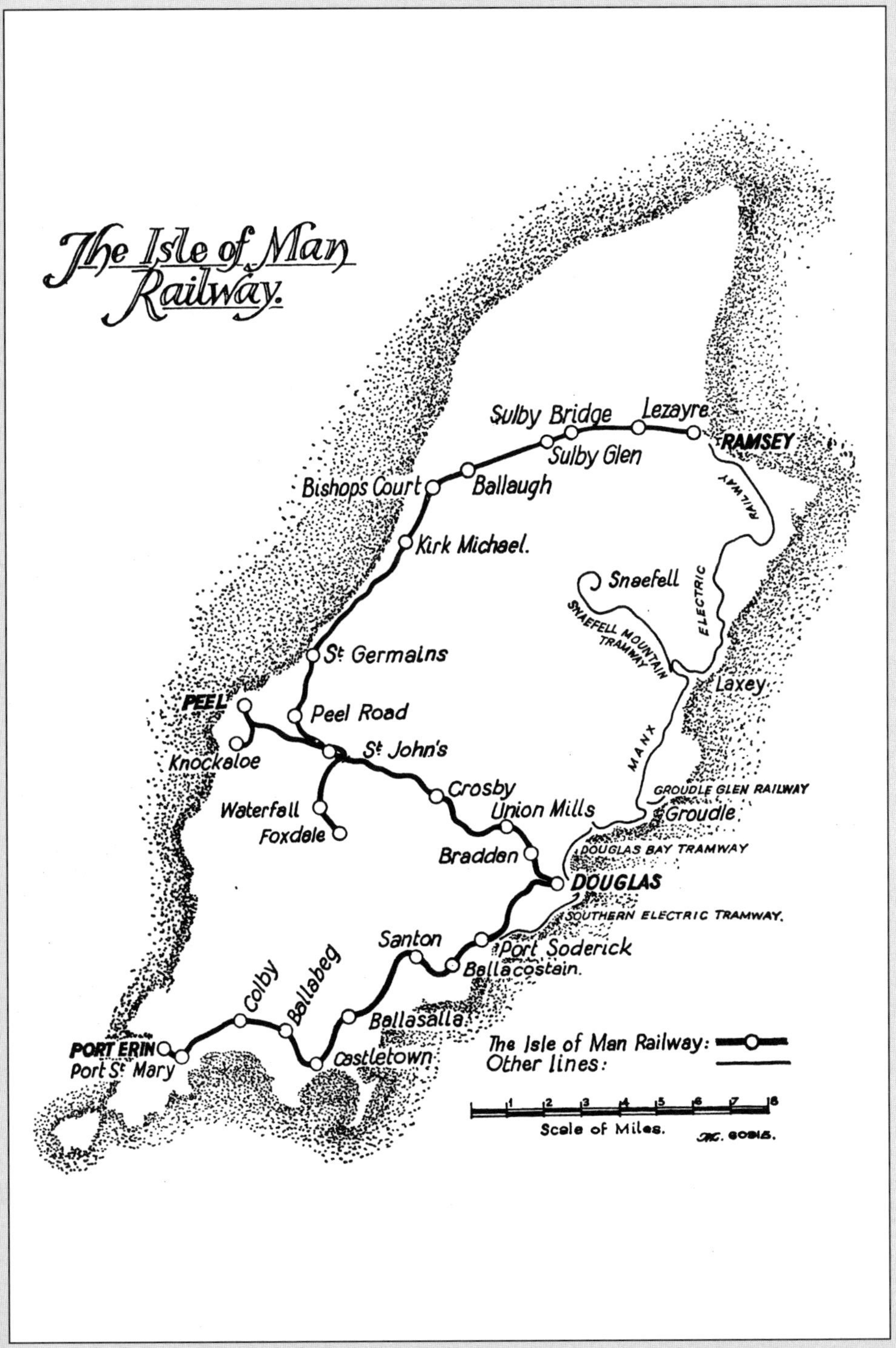
The Isle of Man Railway.
Sulby Bridge
Lezayre
RAMSEY
Sulby Glen
Bishops Court
Ballaugh
RAILWAY
Kirk Michael.
Snaefell
ELECTRIC
SNAEFELL MOUNTAIN TRAMWAY
St. Germains
Laxey
PEEL
Peel Road
MANX
Knockaloe
St. John's
Crosby
GROUDLE GLEN RAILWAY
Waterfall
Union Mills
Groudle
Foxdale
DOUGLAS BAY TRAMWAY
Bradden
DOUGLAS
SOUTHERN ELECTRIC TRAMWAY.
Santon
Port Soderick
Ballacostain.
Colby
Ballabeg
Ballasalla
The Isle of Man Railway:
PORT ERIN
Castletown
Other lines:
Port St. Mary
1 2 3 4 5 6 7 8
Scale of Miles.

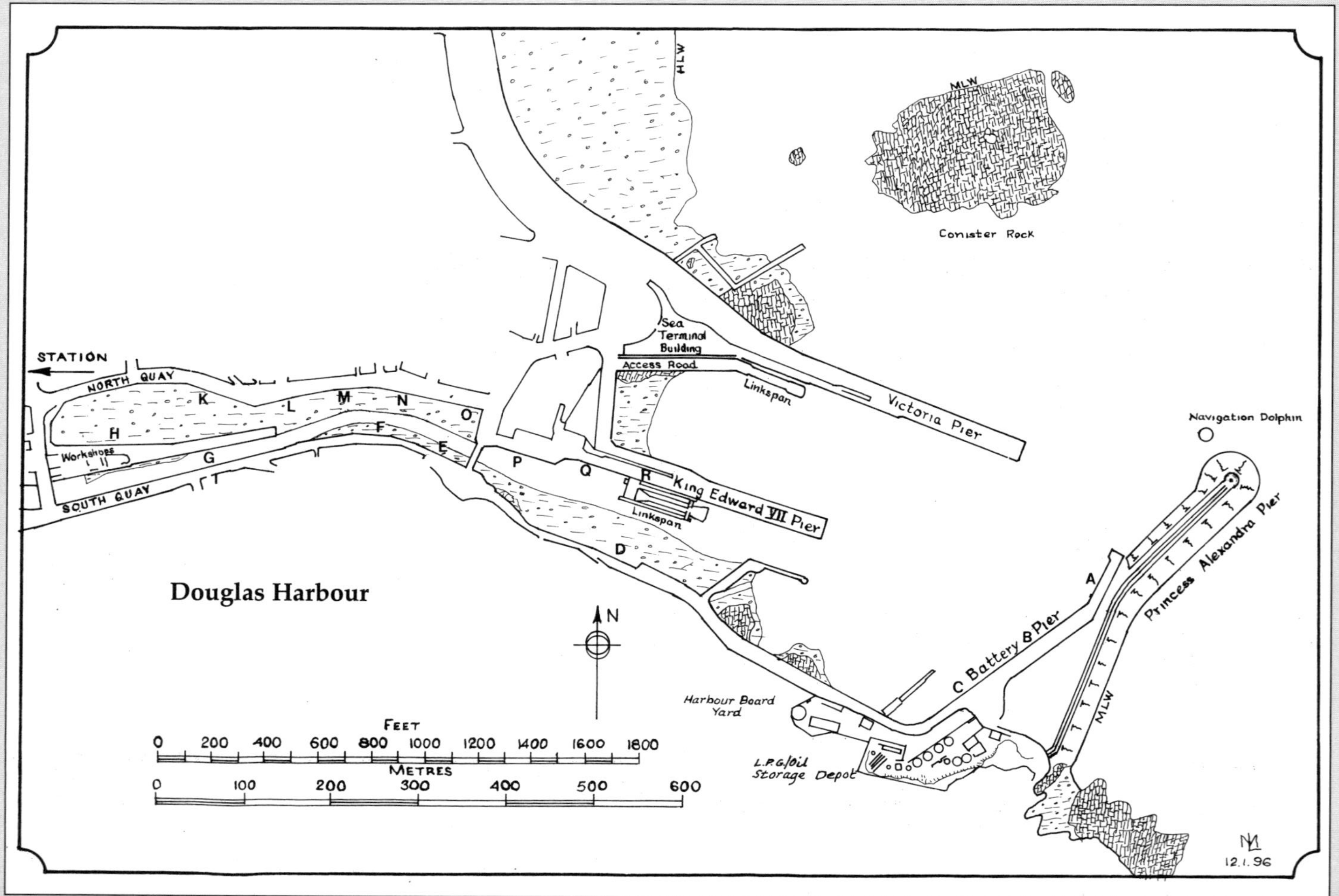
Douglas Harbour
STATION
NORTH QUAY
SOUTH QUAY
Workshops
H
K
L
M
N
O
G
F
E
P
Q
R
D
A
B
C
Sea Terminal Building
Access Road
Linkspan
Victoria Pier
King Edward VII Pier
Linkspan
HLW
MLW
Conister Rock
Navigation Dolphin
Princess Alexandra Pier
MLW
Battery Pier
Harbour Board Yard
L.P.G./Oil Storage Depot
N
FEET
0 200 400 600 800 1000 1200 1400 1600 1800
METRES
0 100 200 300 400 500 600
12.1.96

Douglas Harbour

The drawing of the Harbour (*opposite*) shows the position in 1991. Facilities here have been of the utmost importance to the IOMR since 1873, both in supply of materials for construction and since, and the ensuing arrival and departure of native and holiday-makers which followed. Whilst Ramsey was essentially linked to the MNR and its importance must not be underestimated, Douglas was the premier seaport and Harbour facilities have been extended since the 1860s. Though traffic has been diminished by the coming of air travel, Douglas now has the added feature of shipping road transport.

The IOMR station is at the west end of the North Quay.

	Name of Berth	*Historic Use*
A	Light House	
B	Woodwork	Cattle. Vessel 'painting up'
C	25 ton steam crane	
D	Fort William	Tankers discharging Kerosene
E	Anglo	Esso spirit
F	Wigan	Coal
G	South Quay	General
H	Inner Tongue	Passenger Vessel lay up
J	Outer Tongue	Motorised Fishing Vessels, Gas Tankers
K	Queen Street (above Bell's Ferry)	Timber
L	St Matthew's Church	General
M	British	General
N	Market	General
O	Coffee Palace	General
P	Office	Original passenger berth. Latterly IOMSPCL container berth
Q	Watch House	Originally, passenger berth
R	Original 'Red Pier'	

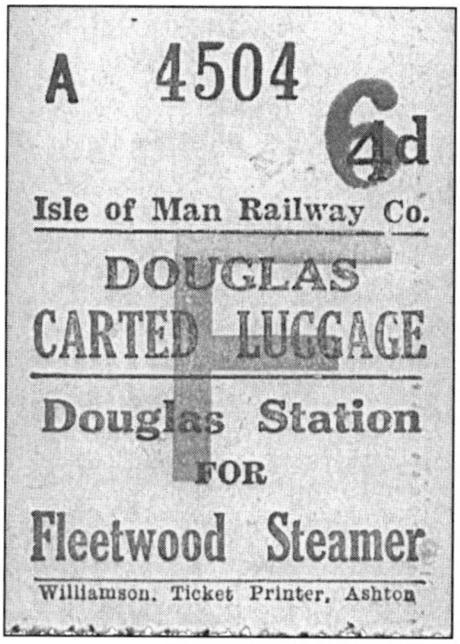

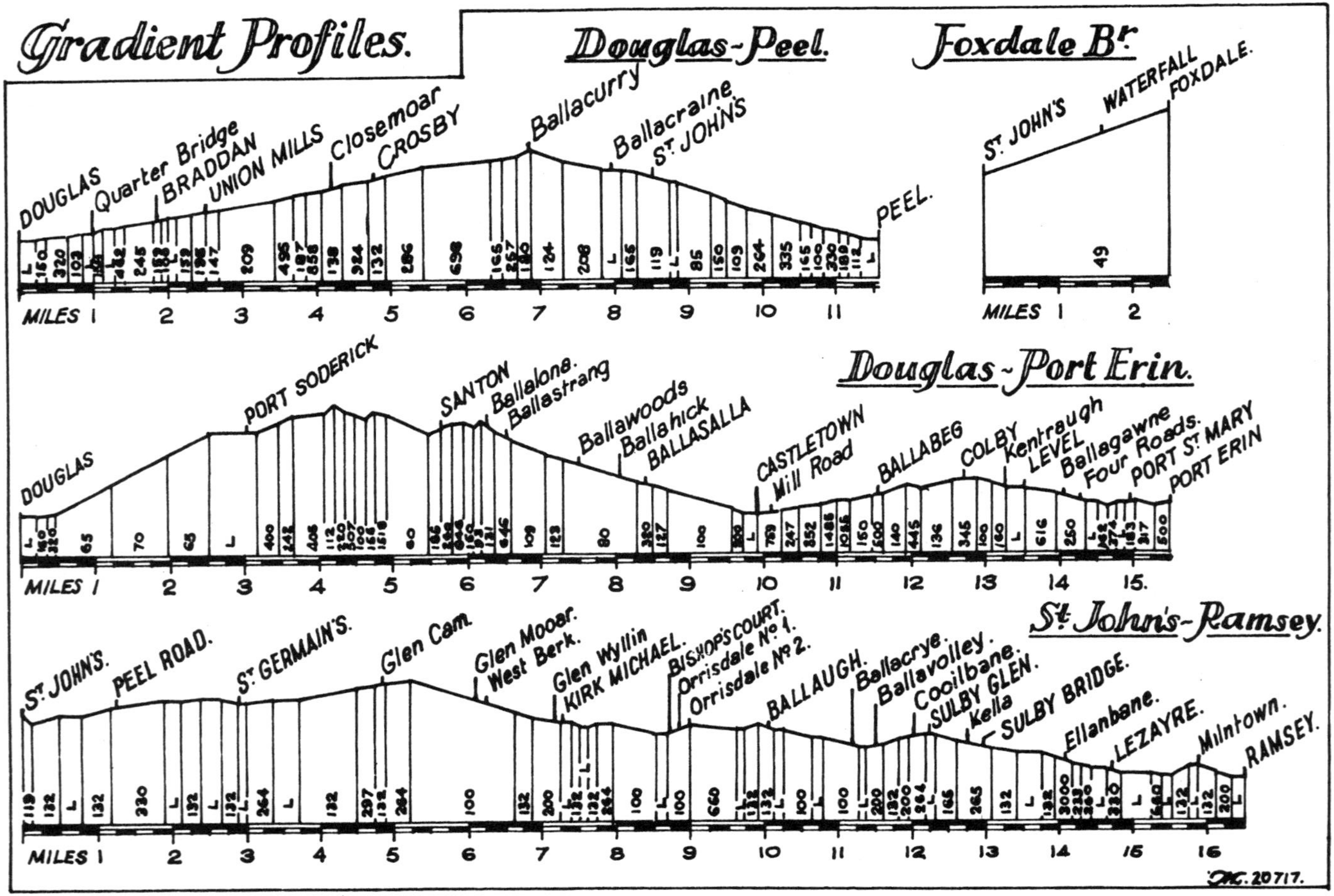
Gradient Profiles.
Douglas-Peel.
DOUGLAS
Quarter Bridge
BRADDAN
UNION MILLS
Closemoar
CROSBY
Ballacurry
Ballacraine
St JOHN'S
PEEL.
Foxdale Br.
St JOHN'S
WATERFALL
FOXDALE.
Douglas-Port Erin.
DOUGLAS
PORT SODERICK
SANTON
Ballalone.
Ballastrang
Ballawoods
Ballahick
BALLASALLA
CASTLETOWN
Mill Road
BALLABEG
COLBY
Kentraugh
LEVEL
Ballagawne
Four Roads.
PORT St MARY
PORT ERIN
St John's-Ramsey.
St JOHN'S.
PEEL ROAD.
St GERMAIN'S.
Glen Cam.
Glen Mooar.
West Berk.
Glen Wyllin
KIRK MICHAEL.
BISHOP'S COURT.
Orrisdale No 1.
Orrisdale No 2.
BALLAUGH.
Ballacrye.
Ballavolley.
Cooilbane.
SULBY GLEN.
Kella
SULBY BRIDGE.
Ellanbane.
LEZAYRE.
Milntown.
RAMSEY.
MILES
JC. 20717.

Gradients and heights quoted in the following description of routes

Gradients quoted are those supplied by the IOMR for the purpose of the original edition of this title in the mid-1950s.

Gradient figures also appear in L.T. Catchpole's notes made in the mid-1930s; these may have been taken from the gradient posts. They have an 'official' atmosphere about them and are very complete.

An official Gradient Survey of all IOMR lines was made by Allott in 1925 (then Engineer to the Company); this survives in the Reference Library of the Manx Museum. (Ref: No. R/41).

Not all these sources concur precisely: the Gradient Diagram herein is taken from the First Edition and has not been amended. Between Peel Road and Kirk Michael, Orrisdale No. 2 and Ballaugh, Cooilbane and Ellenbane, (all on the ex-MNR section) IOMR official figures differ from those of Allott - some of these variations may be due to subsidence.

Heights are taken from IOMR records and may not agree with current figures.

[This description makes no mention of Sheadings, the electoral divisions into which the Island is divided: these are again divided into parishes.]

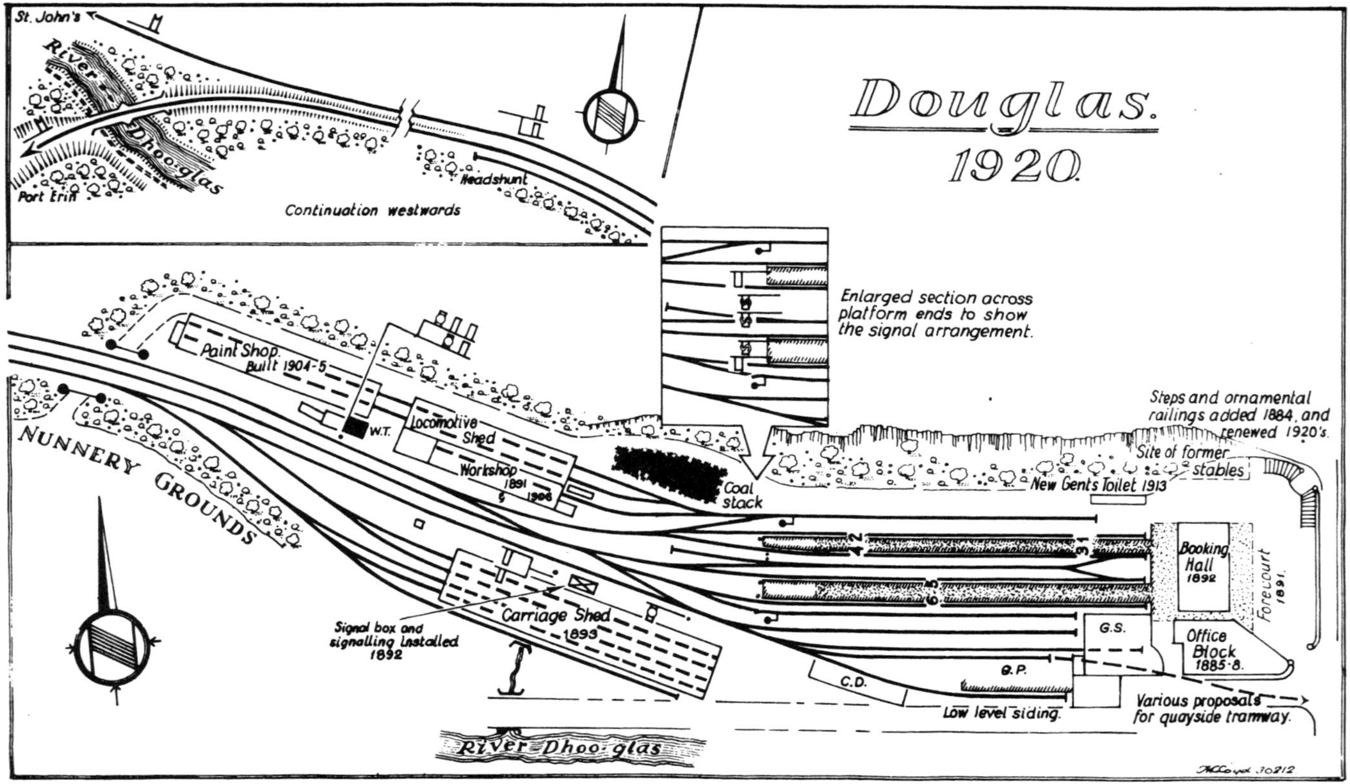
Douglas.
1920.
St. John's
River Dhoo-glas
Port Erin
Continuation westwards
Headshunt
Enlarged section across platform ends to show the signal arrangement.
Paint Shop Built 1904-5
W.T.
Locomotive Shed
Workshop 1891 & 1906
Coal stack
NUNNERY GROUNDS
Signal box and signalling Installed 1892
Carriage Shed 1893
Steps and ornamental railings added 1884, and renewed 1920's.
Site of former stables
New Gents Toilet 1913
Booking Hall 1892
Forecourt 1891
Office Block 1885-8.
G.S.
G.P.
C.D.
Low level siding.
Various proposals for quayside tramway.
River Dhoo-glas
1
2
3
4
5
6

The Railway Routes Described

Since the early 1950s the IOMR route system has fallen into decline so that today (1995) only the Douglas-Port Erin Line survives. Parts of the abandoned lines have been dedicated as footpaths and/or bridleways, but the surroundings of these courses are changing rapidly and losing the appearance of their railway origins.

The object of the ensuing descriptions is to record the railway as if in being, and a period of the late 1940s has been chosen as appropriate for the purpose. The use of the present tense in regard to currently abandoned courses does not therefore imply the survival of any features existing in the late 1940s.

Douglas Station

It has already been explained how Douglas station came to be built on the site of The Lake at the mouths of the combined rivers Dhoo and Glas. To the south the hills which culminate in Douglas Head rise sharply; to the north there is an even steeper bluff on top of which runs the Peel road and rising behind, carries that portion of the town which was built in the latter part of the last century.

The terminal building is but a street's width away from the top of the Inner Harbour (the original 'port of Douglas'), around which the oldest parts of the town are to be found. The visitor may well be disenchanted however, by the distance between the present-day point of disembarkation and the station; with truth it may be conceded that the fall in usage of the railway is in some measure due to a lack of railway connection to the modern piers: this shortcoming has been fully aired in Volume I.

The station has an impressive frontage with concourse standing on the site of a former timber yard and saw mill. Administration buildings with verandah flank one side, and the imposing stairway and clock tower gateway the other. Handsome railings and the predominance of red brick provide an architectural livery and unify the whole. Under the office block in the upper floors of the administration building the ground floor was, until recently, given over to a large Refreshment & Coffee Room, Bar and the like. It is often said that even Athens has no station of this quality.

It has been commented that the architect of these brick station buildings thought that to impress the traveller - which they certainly do - he would embody all the styles he knew. Thus:

> The booking hall is characterised by heavily-built shaped gables, liberally supported with pilaster strips; three gables to the platform side and two to the street where the third bay is occupied by a massive square tower. The hall is lit by two large roundheaded windows, the doorway between carrying a Dutch gable feature

on its lintel with below, another round-headed arch of Romanesque style.

The main office block to the south, and the work done in the early 1920s on the site of Quiggins' property, incorporates another square tower which like that just described, has a French Gothic roof carrying cast iron cresting on its ridge. On the north-west corner there is a turret with a candle-snuffer cap and to the west a pedimented bay with three lights, again supported by pilaster strips.

The clock tower at the head of the stairway on the north flank bears a clock in an aedicule with faces north and south, flanked by gilded towerlets and Norman blank arcading.

And in 1994, whilst not every building is in occupation of the Railway any longer, it is all there for the examination!

(A close study of all the original wooden stations including Douglas with its timber platforms of that time, suggests that American practice in style and construction was closely followed, especially of transcontinental lines. This was particularly noticeable in the appearance of Douglas, Peel and Port Erin stations.)

The interior circulating area would do justice to any minor railway and is arguably the finest of narrow gauge railway stations in the British Isles. There is no hint of horse-tramway up-marketed into railway here, or of an English Light Railway built under the 1896 Act, with corrugated iron accommodation throughout. Pass through the fine Booking Hall (with its separate windows for North and South Lines and an additional office on an island site in the centre) and the wide and lengthy platforms reach out before one, adequately protected from the weather by generous steel and glass roofing. All this makes some recompense for any inconvenience (such as parting with one's heavy luggage and leaving it to the offices of an official Porter - not a railway employee - whose services will soon be found to be utterly reliable) experienced between ship and railway station.

The very length of the platforms reflects the extent of trains required to carry the thousands of visitors who cram this station in the summer; imagine a day when the evening excursion to Port Soderick returns or, even more chaotic, when the Tynwald Day excursionists flock back in hundreds.

Each platform face is capable of holding two average-length trains coupled together: each is numbered, the eastern end faces of the northern platform are Nos. 1 and 3, and the whole length of the faces of the southern platform being Nos. 5 and 6. Platforms 2 and 4 are not now marked as such, but were formerly the western end faces of the northern platform, 2 being the extension of 1 and 4 the extension of 3. This arrangement allows the use of platforms as follows: the northern to be used for Peel and Ramsey trains where it is often convenient to marshal two distinct trains (though actually coupled together) for each destination at the same platform face. Thus the combined train is announced as standing with its leading portion for Ramsey in either platform 2 or 4, and its rearmost portion for Peel in platform 1 or 3. This arrangement can lead to confusion among passengers who, though the train be clearly marked by painted boards hung from the handrails of the Guard's brake, would entrain in the wrong portion. A more recent and improved arrangement is to marshal the two halves, one on each side of the northern platform, and run the Ramsey section out of the station, then back it on to the Peel portion as departure time nears. This also makes luggage loading more convenient.

Both flanks of the southern platform are commonly used for Port Erin line trains, but no platform face is specifically reserved for a destination and northern line trains do use the south platform occasionally. Incoming trains use the inner faces of the two platforms; these are the only ones giving access to the engine release road and coal stage.

But at this moment the station is empty; note the three-track area between the platforms, allowing the engine of the arriving Port Erin train (left) or arriving Ramsey/Peel train (right) to be released from the front of the train without delay; in fact, the slick manner in which an engine (now brought to a stand) is detached from its train, runs forward whilst the fireman - who has jumped to the ground - operates the ground levers of the pointwork, is impressive. No less notable are the Yucca plants and Palm trees which grow between each set of tracks, evidence of the temperate climate on the Island.

To the extreme left (south) of the station runs a long wall; it marks the edge of railway property. Behind this wall lie the rope works of Quiggin & Co., now no longer in use as such. Immediately left and in front, comes the goods station, goods yard, cattle bank, sunken siding giving wagon-height loading facilities and, further away, the long three-road corrugated iron Carriage Shed with the attractive signal box in front of it. Beyond that Shed can be seen further sidings in which wagon repairs are often carried out in the open. A backdrop of the trees in The Nunnery Estate completes the scene.

In the middle distance the tracks converge and curve to the right, so out of sight. Prominently visible are the platform starter signals, the water column and a small platform with attendant wicker baskets, whereby engines on the release road can be quickly prepared for their next journey.

Now, to the right and beyond: here the station is bounded by wooded ground rising quickly from the trackside; it is surmounted by the back of shops on Peel Road, and further along, by a row of houses. This is that portion of the site which was excavated by the Railway Company when further land from the Taubman Estate was purchased. It is also the area where the Douglas, Laxey & Snaefell Railway portion of the station might have been had that railway come into being.

Beyond the platform on the right is the coaling area (approximately 400 tons of coal may be stacked here against emergency) with a mechanical excavator used for that purpose (or civil engineering work for which it is carried on a special wagon). The stone-built workshops are to the left (south) side of these buildings: beyond them, across a yard, is the carpenter's shop and paint shop. On the right is a long Engine Shed - all these buildings appear as one entire block from the station platform. Works' administration offices are in the left-hand section, nearest the station - this was the last extension of the Works to be built. A mess hut formed from the body of a Manx Northern carriage does duty in the foreground of the buildings. Prominent in front of the Workshop complex is the long row of wheelsets stored between the tracks.

Walk to the end of a platform and enjoy the embracing nature of this fine railway terminus, with its wide-ranging facilities. There is much use of white distemper on exterior walls: it keeps its colour well in the clean atmosphere so that the impression of shining brass on clean locomotives and carriage furniture, the glint of copper against cheerful foliage, leaves a happy impression.

For a narrow gauge railway, note the lavish signalling - passing mention is given of it as such matters are covered elsewhere in this volume. But best of all, see the station on a busy summer's day and experience the intensity of working, the to-ing and fro-ing of the station shunting engine, the quick turn-round of light engines from in-coming to out-going trains, the engines on shed, ready steamed for turn of duty, and the impressive rakes of carriages which at times, are insufficient to carry all those offering.

Goods traffic is dealt with to the south side of the premises and is largely hidden from view as the intervening sidings are full of standing trains. The covered Goods Sheds are extensive and give road/rail interchange under cover.

There may be one or more complete locomotive boiler with fittings, standing on the trackside near the Shed, or loaded in an open wagon. Such a boiler may be destined for installation in a locomotive or have been removed from one as being past its useful life in service: it may be being held for further use as the steam supplier for the Workshops.

The foregoing description with its emphasis on the adequacy of equipment makes a Report by Trevithick of May 1874, all the more noteworthy. A diagram of the exact layout at this date has not survived, but its general form is hinted at, being a series of six parallel passenger and goods roads 'without connection save at the outer end', and with a wagon weighbridge at the far end of the southernmost siding. The whole reflects almost total lack of practical knowledge as to what a railway layout should be!

1. There was no means of releasing engines on arriving at Douglas.
2. The weighbridge was sited in such a position that it was blocked off from the station by storing stock behind it; wagon empties could not be attached to a train and loaded wagons could not be weighed.
3. Consequent on 2, it took half an hour to assemble six wagons [*sic*] in a train with only one engine in steam for a large part of the year. This had to be accomplished between the running of trains.
4. An average of half an hour was needed to coal and water an engine between trips.
5. 'Simple country folk look on with more of curiosity than annoyance at the engine rushing about all over the station . . . we are pushed now with only 8 light trains per day: what will it be like in the season when 32 are running?'

Trevithick enclosed three 'alternative plans' for consideration: these embodied -

PLAN 1

a. Sunken siding for minerals (being part of Foxdale Mines contract so to provide)
b. Siding for empty carriages
c. Separate sidings for goods and minerals, these to be separated from the siding to the goods shed
d. A siding on which to marshal goods trains
e. A siding for empty wagons
f. 'The carriages now standing out in the open should have a covered shed; presently they are completely exposed to weather on one side'
g. A small workshop for repairs

PLAN 2

a. 'The present station being circumscribed by the limit of the land acquired, and positioned so that it was approached by a sharp curve to the effect that the "distance signal cannot be seen if clear", should be altered by the purchase of more land, and developed therefrom'
b. 'A wooden carriage shed is needed'
c. 'An addition to the present Locomotive Shed is required'
d. The workshops should be of masonry construction. [Trevithick commented that even this "plan was pinched and confined, and would require extending again"]

PLAN 3

This would require even more land being acquired; the station 'would be larger but by no means magnificent. Land could be got now and buildings and sidings added as needed.'

A footnote explains that all these Plans have the strictest economy in mind; that the recently-completed contract with the Foxdale Mines would involve the annual carriage of *c.* 6,000 tons of timber; that conveyance of lime from Ballasalla could be forecast at *c.* 10,000 tons per year. (There was presently no accommodation for timber and lime at Douglas.)

For operating purposes today (*c.* 1948) the tracks within the station are numbered, north to south, Nos. 1-11. As the two independent routes enter the station it will be noted that though they branch out into other lines their only actual connection is a facing crossover which permits northern line trains to pass on to the southern line - there is, of course, a common connection by means of the engine release road but this cannot be used for train operating. The northern line gives connections to the Engine Shed and Workshops; the southern line to the goods yard, carriage sidings and Goods Shed. A long shunting neck is carried out of the station beside the Port Erin line. There thus appear to be three lines leading from the premises.

Railway Workshops

The Workshops are remarkably self-sufficient, carrying out work for the road undertaking as well as the railway. Viewed from the front of the Locomotive Department the single road on the left runs the length of the Workshop; this is divided from the Engine Shed alongside by an inner wall. The machinery was driven by a horizontal stationary engine, steamed from an ex-locomotive boiler working at reduced pressure. Heavy lifting is done by a 15-ton travelling crane which operates over part of the Workshop only. The single road has a full-length inspection pit. Before mains electricity reached the Works, the premises were lit by an old train dynamo driven off the shafting.

It is customary to strip down only one engine at a time for heavy repairs - the boiler is lifted off the frames and run away on a wooden bogie (mounted on railway wheels); the wheels are taken from the frames for tyring, etc. and a further bogie used to carry the frames and cylinder assembly up the Workshop for attention.

The building containing two roads lying across an open yard beyond the Engine Shed proper, can also be used as a Repair Shop, mainly for work on carriages: there is equipment here and elsewhere for all types of woodwork repair, upholstering and painting, and rolling stock of all types can be stored here over the winter.

[The Manx Northern had its own small Workshop at the north end of the Ramsey Engine Shed. It is still to be seen as are other outbuildings surrounding it, formerly used in connection with repairs. Latterly it was used as a Wagon Repair Shop. All these are now vacant and repairs are concentrated at Douglas.]

The mounted water tanks supplied by Ransomes & Rapier on the south-west face of the building feed the Works complex and take their water from the river by arrangement with The Nunnery Estate. Certain window openings are supported by old rails as beams, and considerable variety in weight is revealed thereby.

In 1938 the contents of the Fitting Shop included: *†

15 ton Travelling Crane
Wheel Lathe
Two Screw Cutting Lathes
Radial Drill and Boring Mill
Shaping and Planing Machine
Smith's Shop: Two Furnaces.

The Shop was powered by a single-cylinder double-acting horizontal steam engine supplied by an old locomotive boiler at reduced pressure. It was built by John Chadwick & Sons Ltd., Prince's Bridge Ironworks, Manchester and purchased by the IOMR in December 1919. Installed in February 1920 it came from an Accrington cotton mill per Thomas Mitchell & Son Ltd., Engineers & Merchants of Edgar Street, Bolton. Lighting was at 100 v. DC by dynamo and batteries.

Douglas (excl.) - Peel

The more northerly of the two lines leaving Douglas side-by-side is the original, or Peel, line. From the outskirts of the station they at first share the valley of the Douglas River, but while the Peel route climbs imperceptibly at 1/320, that for Port Erin climbs steeply beside it at 1/65, part of the steepest length on the whole IOMR system. At times when trains for each destination leave simultaneously, the Peel train is able to show a clean pair of heels as it swings right and northwards through the small factory estate which has grown up here since World War II. With the River Dhoo (by now separated from the Glas and on the left side), the course passes under Pulrose Bridge, provided in 1938 to replace a level crossing.

Down in the bottom of the valley, the rural nature of The Nunnery Estate which marks the initial stages of the journey on the left side, is replaced by the harsh Pulrose Housing Estate and the Generating Station (opened 1929 - coal fired - and extended in 1948 when the Station on the North Quay was closed down; a second diesel-operated Station alongside was opened in 1989). The railway next passes through King George V Park, developed for sports and athletic events and replacing, in part, the Douglas Race Course site of years gone by. These playing fields were laid out using material from the Foxdale Mines' waste tips, brought down during the depression of the

*Taken from L.T. Catchpole's records.

†Among the above-mentioned tools (but not specifically listed) would be a lathe built by Smith & Coventry of Manchester for the opening of the railway. This was removed from the premises as recently as autumn 1992.

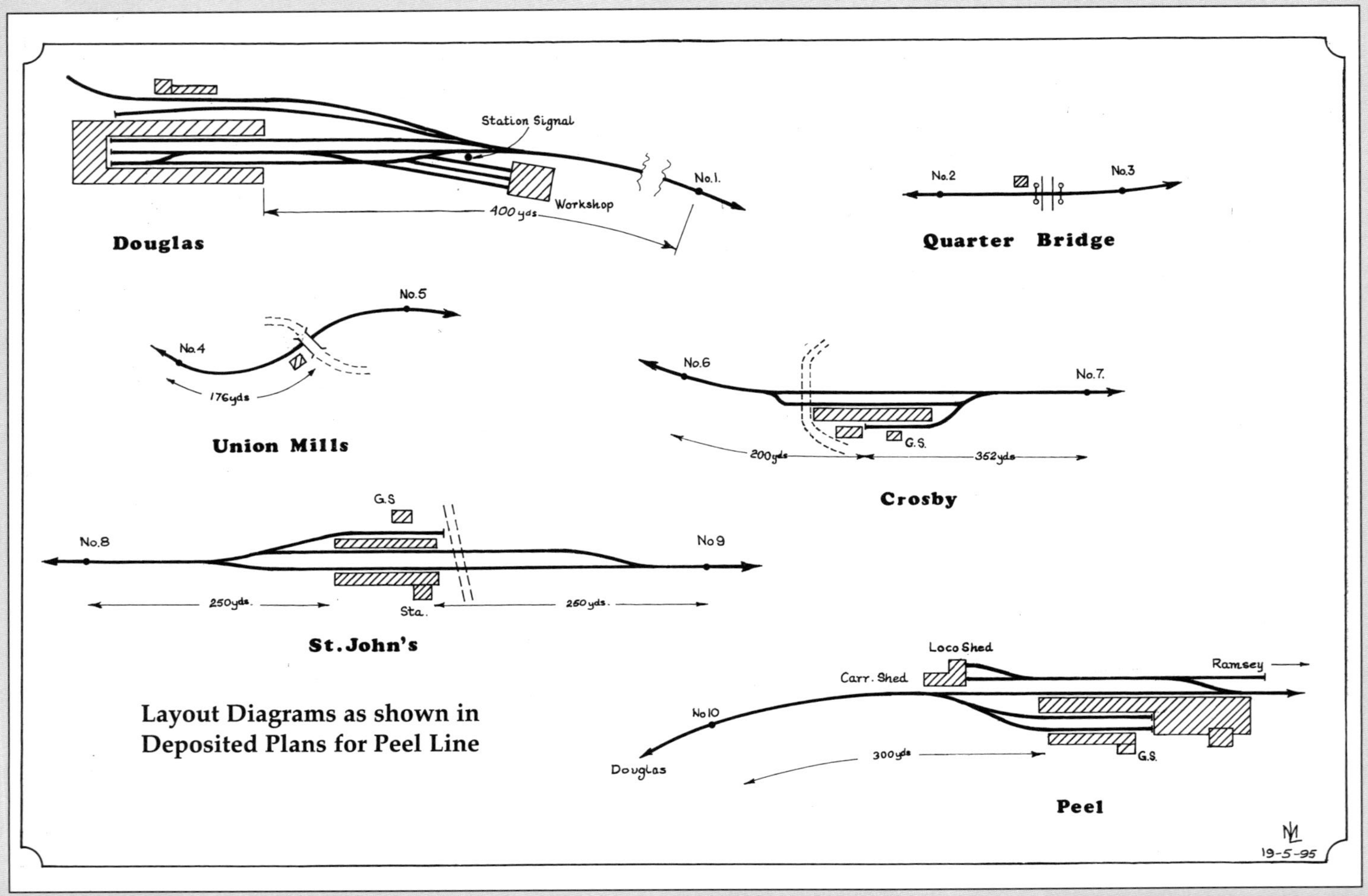

Layout Diagrams as shown in Deposited Plans for Peel Line

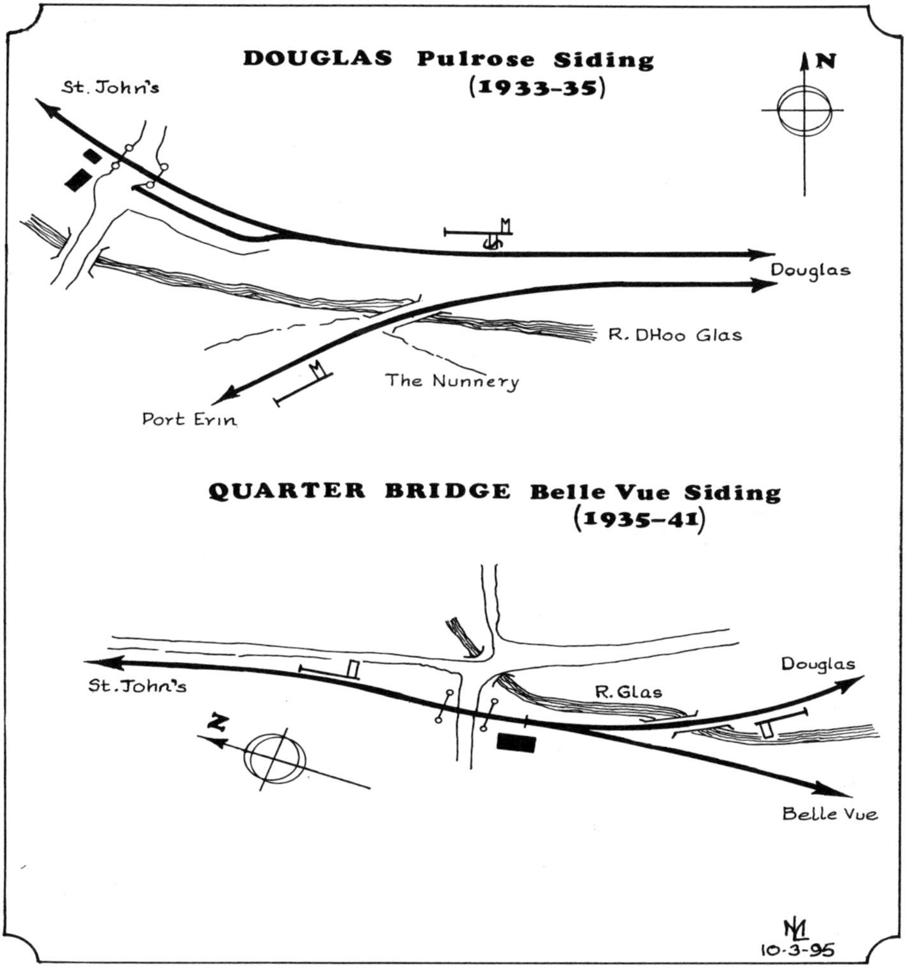
DOUGLAS Pulrose Siding
(1933-35)
N
St. John's
Douglas
R. DHoo Glas
The Nunnery
Port Erin
QUARTER BRIDGE Belle Vue Siding
(1935-41)
St. John's
Douglas
R. Glas
N
Belle Vue
10-3-95

1930s to assist unemployment in the winter. A siding was laid down for spoil trains and a special shunt arm was affixed to the Home signal for Up trains coming in from Peel. Siding and signal have now been removed.

Immediately before Quarter Bridge (1 m.) the River Glas is spanned by an 86 ft. lattice girder bridge which replaced the initial structure in 1902 (Vol. I, p. 244). There follows a gated crossing over the main highway to the south of the Island.* The nearby junction of roads is a well-known point on the Tourist Trophy Racing Circuit. The crossing keeper's lodge is still occupied (there being no nearby station to provide staff for opening and closing the gates). There was a Halt on the far side of the crossing for a short period in the late 1920s, and also found are the remains of a cattle bank used formerly in connection with Agricultural Shows held on the adjacent Kirby House Estate.

There follows a straight stretch of line; the Dhoo accompanies it on the left and the road is behind a wall on the right - this section of road was straightened during the building of the railway: the line is flanked by an avenue of trees and climbs at 1/105 for a short distance, then the adjacent road turns left and crosses the line close beside the twin churches of Kirk Braddan, the older being rebuilt in 1773 and the newer replacement built in 1876. The railway being beneath the road bridge, passengers are almost denied a view of either church: emerging from the bridge, there is a fine wood of conifers on the left. In a widening of the lineside on the right is a small wooden hut standing at the Halt used for Sunday open air church services and for which a special service of trains runs in high season.

River and railway now run side by side in the valley bottom, the countryside on either hand being of that indeterminate variety which concedes that sooner or later it will be swallowed up by a growing urban sprawl. In the past this would have been a pleasant stretch: it enjoys the curious title of Snugborough, and milepost Two marks the site of the

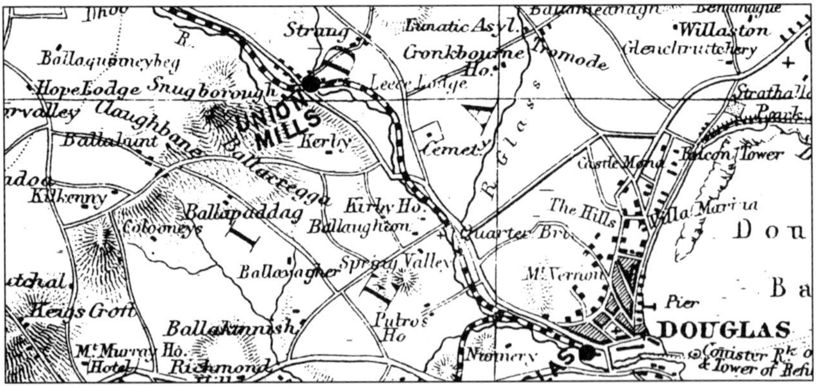

Note: the maps in this section are reproduced from Bacon's Large Scale Map of the Isle of Man, 1909.

*This is not the ancient route, which lies further south and runs through Oakhill.

stopping place used by passenger specials for the Strang Racecourse (Vol. I, p. 54). The climb from Kirk Braddan is never more than 1/100. Immediately, a long slow curve begins to the left and the Dhoo is crossed by Snugborough Bridge, installed to reduce danger from flooding. This curve continues into Union Mills station. Union Mills, (2½ m.: 7 mins.) is surrounded by an attractive coppice of conifers, planted by the Company. For at least the first thirty years of the station's life, it stood on almost bare ground but the planting of these quick-growing trees has changed its appearance completely. There is a passing loop and a platform on the Down side only; a siding at the south end serves a cattle dock. Half-way along the station the track curves to the right. The station gardens were, until recently, the pride and joy of an enthusiastic Station Master and the winner of annual competitions. The nearby main road, which crosses the railway at the north end of the station, has robbed it of local traffic to increasing degree. The station building is unlike any other on the system, being of horizontal timber planking with single pitch roof; it stands at the north end of the Up side with a flagpole beside it.

Once under the stone overbridge the line immediately crosses the Dhoo on its way towards Douglas; the bridge is of 30 ft steel span built on the skew:

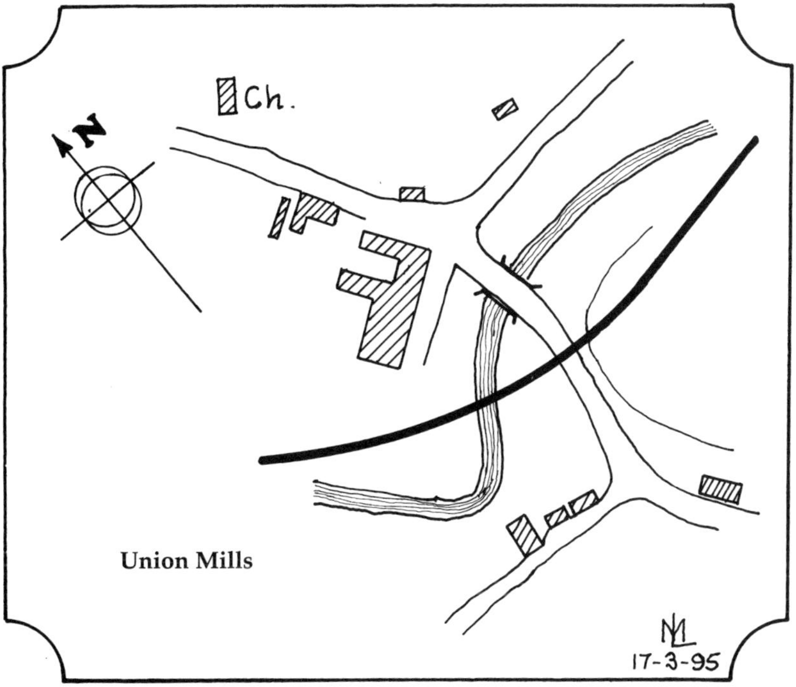

Union Mills is much as was built; the large shaded area is the mills' building from which the locality is named.

for a short distance river (on the left) and railway run side by side, the historic woollen and corn mills (now much altered) beside it on the other side. On low embankment the line curves further to the right, the river moves away to the south and the country opens out into the Central Valley; the railway climbs steadily, here at 1/132. To the south, whilst the immediate ground is low and swampy, farmland extends towards the low hills beyond and on the north flank rising fields climb up towards the Douglas-Peel road which the track follows at some distance all the way to Peel.

Low embankments, shallow cuttings and gentle curves take the railway south of Glenlough and with a long right-hand curve, over a 12 ft embankment and through a cutting of similar depth. Milepost 3 is now passed and the site more closed in by scrubland, so hiding the nearby river: the ground now rises more steeply to the north and a considerable cutting 15 ft deep is followed by an occupation crossing leading from Glenlough and down to the Dhoo. To the left the countryside is pastoral, with attractive hills beyond, leading upwards towards Braaid and St Patrick's Chair; the marshy nature of the land between however, remains. Now opens up a long straight length (4 m.), with woodland on the right and a small sheet of water: Closemooar crossing is reached, having its original keeper's lodge beside it. The water mill and disused mine chimney at Glen Darragh (Glen of Oaks) can be picked out to the south.

Once over the crossing a right-hand curve through a cutting brings the line within reach of the outskirts of Crosby, and after a short run through fields behind the village, a left-hand curve brings it below Marown Church perched on the hillside above. Running along a shelf, the railway enters woodland with the Dhoo a little distance to the left and the main road higher up above on the right and this continues until Crosby station is reached, but first the Braaid road is crossed on the level (the keeper's lodge survives here also), the station passing loop beginning on the Douglas side of this road.

Crosby (4¾ m.: 15 mins) has undergone several changes, not every one of which can now be identified but being near the main road it has lost much of its local traffic; it is well known as a starting point for ramblers as the hills on either side are delightful. The station is a wooden one and until 1960 had a small elderly goods shed beside it and off the passing loop on the Up side a facing turnout leads to two sidings, one with a cattle bank, the other, partially obscured by an advertisement hoarding, is a disused manure siding (Vol. I, p. 228) where crippled wagons are now stored - all these features are on the north of the station. The south side is girt by a plantation of deciduous and conifer trees and behind them, the Highway Board's roadstone quarry where steam road rollers maybe lurking.

The river now running beside us on the left is the Greeba, a tributary of the

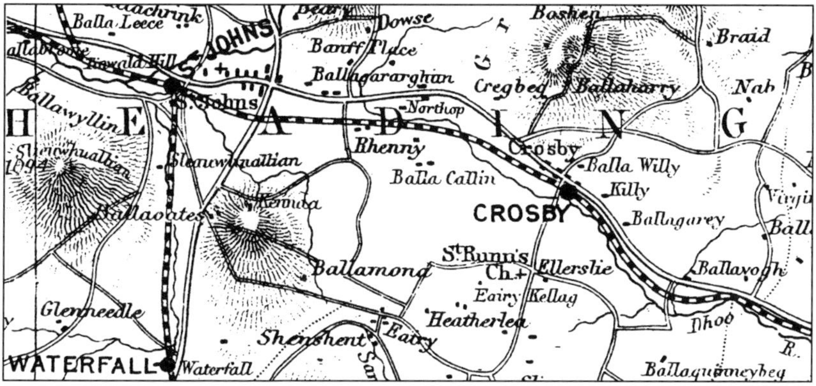

Dhoo which veered away from the railway a little way back to find its source in the hills to the south behind Glen Darragh. The Greeba's path is becoming more and more marshy until, like the railway, at 5¼ miles it enters woodland. Meanwhile the railway has earlier passed through a cutting and taken up a shelf-like site to the south of the 'Wagon & Horses' Inn on the road above (Halfway House, as it is called). To the left and up on the hillside - now closing in on the railway - stands the farm Cooil Ingle (the spelling varies) in an attractive fold in the slopes: soon the hillside to the south comes in alongside the route, the Greeba flowing at its foot to our left. The line runs on a low embankment and to the right the ground is wet and marshy, with squat birch trees and rushy meadow: thus the view is hidden to the north from the traveller, for just beyond runs the main road, winding its way along the foot of the wooded slopes of Greeba Mountain (1,384 ft), a prominent height.

Cooil Ingle crossing (5¾ m.) is reached and crossed, and with a slight curve to the left, the skewed Cooil Ingle Bridge carries the track over the Greeba river by steel spans on stone parapets; here the river is only 10 ft wide.*

The line is now in the narrowest section between Douglas and Peel, the steep slope of Archallagan coming right down to lineside and pinching road and railway between its foothills and those of Greeba opposite. Past milepost 6 this hillside to the left is at its steepest; the rough boscage to the right is part of The Curragh (more exactly hereabouts, Curragh Glas - The Grey Bog) and in older days was a lake with an ancient habitation. Now the line reaches the most extreme portion of the swampy surroundings with birch, ash and dwarf oak which have accompanied it almost since Crosby and within that scrub to the right is found the source of the Greeba. Shortly, Rhenny level crossing is reached; it is another minor road (6¼ m.), and was initially known as Northop.

Almost straight now, the course threads through woodland but beyond the trees can be seen open pastureland as the hills on either side recede and,

*The bridge is not the original one.

with a slow curve to the right, the view opens out on either side to lush fields. Another slow curve to the left and Ballacurry crossing is reached; a few houses and a farm mark the hamlet of that name: in the past, requests have been made for a station here and it has been a loading point for mine traffic.* Just beyond the crossing, where the hills close in tightly once more on the left side, comes a small bridge over the Darragh which issues from a narrow, wooded glen (Glion Darragh not to be confused with the earlier-mentioned Glen Darragh) to the south. This marks the summit of the line between Douglas and Peel, 185 ft above sea level and almost 7 miles from Douglas. The final climb at 1/180 does not tax the engine too much, and the train gathers speed as it descends at 1/124 - although heavy trains for Peel were often banked as far as St John's, it was also a practice for a banking engine to drop back from the train here, and return, light engine, to Douglas. It is a feature here that only at this point can the north and south of the Island be connected by land without crossing a river or stream. The hamlet once boasted a chapel (now gone) while the road leading north joins the main road at Greeba and crosses fertile, low-lying fields.

Once over this watershed, the Greeba and Dhoo rivers cease to provide a route for the railway now entering the valley of the Neb which it follows to Peel: descents of 1/203, 165 and 119 follow. About milepost 7 the proposed junction for the IOMR branch to Foxdale would have been sited and the steep flank of the hill to the left would have carried a contour-hugging course through Kennaa; the claim that a specially-powerful locomotive would have been needed is easy to endorse. There is an occupation crossing at Kerrow Garrow (7¼ m.) up to which woodland either side of the line has resumed: this soon becomes pasture with coppices here and there. To the left open farmland reaches up towards the hills around Foxdale, and the mouth of the Foxdale valley is prominent. This change in the surroundings is quite a sudden transformation, and the line, now almost straight, reaches Ballacraine crossing (134 ft) just short of milepost 8; this place was originally named Curragh Road and the site of an erstwhile stopping place for Glen Helen (Vol. I, p. 226). The crossing lodge survives.

It is now possible to see the arched bridge carrying the branch to Foxdale crossing our route a little way ahead; this bridge is soon reached but first comes a disused sand and gravel pit to the left, immediately before the Foxdale overbridge. This working was opened up by the Company in 1919 when similar materials were no longer obtainable from Latham's nearby pit. The Foxdale bridge has an 11 ft 9 in. clearance from track to apex of arch, and a 25 ft span, sufficient for double track. Immediately the elongated station of St. John's is reached (8½ m.: 25 mins).† At one time and another, there have

*It was an early practice to leave wagons standing on the main line here, in connection with the Cornelly Mine (op. 1837). The mine was abandoned in September 1886.

†Once the crossroads of the Manx railway system, the Foxdale line is now virtually closed completely though an unforeseen need to collect mine refuse from time to time has ensured the track remains *in situ*. At this end of the branch the course is overgrown, but higher up, due to mine waste containing lead being used for 'ballast', it is clear of boscage.

been three stations here, together with numerous changes of track layout. A long timber footbridge spanning all lines at the western end was demolished in 1945, but on Tynwald Day in 1920 most of the 24,103 passenger journeys made in one single day used this station and the footbridge was essential!

The present station is an enlargement of the original one when the IOMR first reached Peel, it was then but a passing loop, there being no expectation of any local traffic. There was, however, a station building on the north side (later moved over to the south) and to accommodate Manx Northern traffic it was enlarged north and east from 1879. Its present format is entirely due to MNR intrusion, and the later junction with the Foxdale Railway. At this most important phase, the traffic passing off the Foxdale system and continuing by MNR to Ramsey, by-passed the IOMR station altogether! The lesser-revenue-earning passenger connections between MNR and IOMR were carried out by some remarkable shunting movements which were witnessed by the Government Inspector, Col. Rich, when travelling as a passenger . . . he warned the two Companies (not on the best of terms) that they should parley and 'get their act together' before a serious accident took place (Vol. I, p. 166).

The present station may be seen to have three platforms, that on the southside being used for St John's - Peel trains which may or may not be the train to or from Douglas . . . The two centre roads either side of the middle island platform are for through running. (It will be noted that in the ex-MNR signal box frame, the levers for the Up starting and Down splitting signals can only be pulled 'off' when the points are set for the northernmost line of the island platform. As Ramsey trains frequently use the northerly *loop* instead of platform line, because of the convenient proximity to the water tank, flag signalling has to be resorted to. The signal locking confirms that the original intention was that all trains should use the platform lines, and the loop merely for shunting.) A Peel-bound train does not take water here

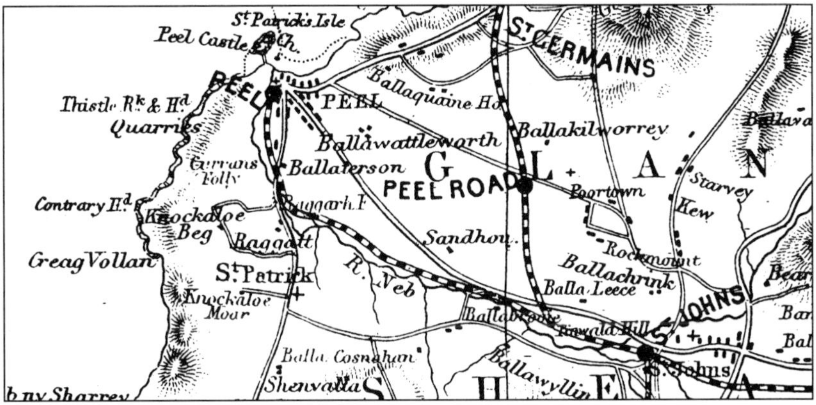

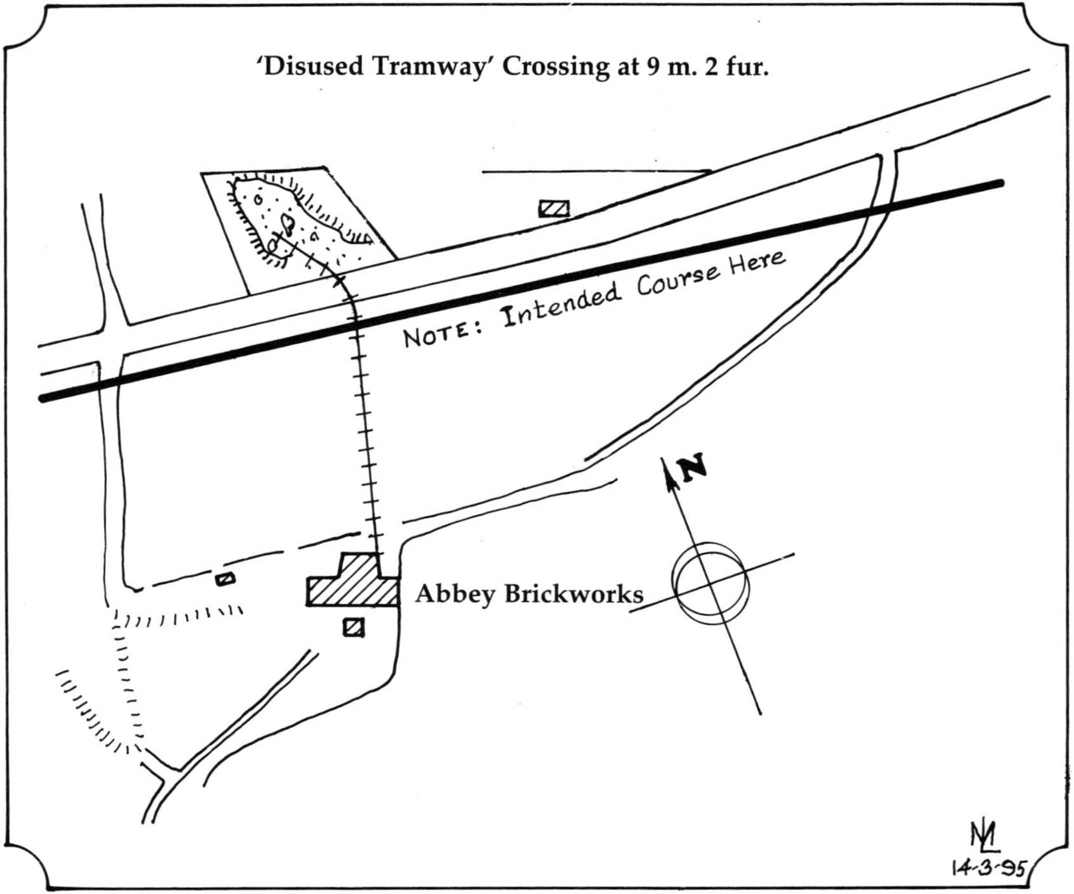
'Disused Tramway' Crossing at 9 m. 2 fur.
NOTE: Intended Course Here
N
Abbey Brickworks
ML
14-3-95

and continues over the double-tracked level crossing, the independent Peel and ex-MNR Ramsey lines running side by side for some distance west of St John's until the latter bears away and begins to climb, curving over the Douglas-Peel road as it does so. 'Races' between trains leaving westwards simultaneously may enliven the journey.

The afore-mentioned crossing requires double-gates and the Darragh River is crossed by two independent spans just beyond; these are of 25 ft span and replaced the original single bridge for the IOMR installed by Watson & Smith. Just beyond the level crossing, the remains of the Foxdale Railway station can be seen on the right. Shortly the physical junction with the Foxdale branch (still extant) may be noticed, running into the Ramsey line from the east. At the point where the two routes divide, the Peel line falls sharply at 1/80 and sheers away from the Ramsey track. Though there are steep hills rising suddenly to Slieu Whallian (1,092 ft) to the left, the valley bottom where runs the railway, is flat and is mainly of sand and gravel. At 8¾ m. the Neb is crossed (by single girder bridge) on its way from Glen Helen to the sea at Peel and the railway continues to fall towards Peel at 1/100, 109 and 112: only in Peel itself does the route become level.

The view to the left is dominated by Corrin's Hill which bars any view of the coast, and the hill is topped by a Tower on the summit (502 ft), Corrin's Folly;* to the right hills tumble down gently towards the sea and numerous gravel workings appear and disappear on each side; the historic Abbey Brickworks was connected to the claypit by a tramroad and fortunately for the railway promoters, by 1872 this tramway was disused: it would have had to be crossed on the level - or tunnelled beneath at the IOMR expense - the exact arrangement of crossing (or even if the tramway resumed operation later) is not known.

At milepost 10 and as the line passes along the edge of Peel Golf Course to the right, the land to the left has undergone change where the river has been diverted, then the Neb valley narrows sharply and where its diversions ends, resumes its original course in wooded gorge towards Glenfaba Bridge. The sharp-eyed may discern, on the left, an embankment leading away from the railway, to cross the narrow valley bottom and the course of the old river: this branch began at a junction hereabouts and went southwards, carrying the former Knockaloe Aliens' Camp branch (in use 1915-20) to the foot of its steepest upgrade section.

Now curving to the right the route is carried by a stone embankment through the wooded defile of the Neb, past Glenfaba Mill on the right (a feature which comes and goes very quickly, and so under the Peel-Patrick road bridge - the river occupies an adjacent arch. This is a very picturesque section of railway and beyond the bridge the line is carried along the north side of the defile on walling: this was part of the section of railway diverted

* See ISLE OF MAN (Canon E. H. Stenning) p. 341.

to prevent a recurrence of flooding by the river which caused the accident of 1874 (Vol. I, p. 72).

Next, river and railway curve from west to north together, and the valley opens out quickly; between them runs the leat to the former Peel ropeworks, the site of its long building all but gone. The Electricity Generating Station (left side: now under construction, opened 1950) comes into view. The remaining buildings between rail and river have had varying uses as shipyards, engineering works and corn mill. Though now gone, behind the rising Generating Station, along the river bank once lay a 3 ft gauge plateway which connected the Peel brickworks' quarry pit with the Works itself (the quarry is still visible). A light bridge crossed the river to gain the quarry; the system was horse-worked and by means of a sharp, right-angled bend, left the riverside and crossed over the IOMR, so into the brickworks on the right of the line.

The brickworks' premises on the right are followed by Moore's Kippering Sheds whose smell still permeates the district: then comes the erstwhile chemical works and finally the Gas Works (historic, and still in use), all these premises are divided from the station by Mill Street, where by level crossing, Peel station is entered (11½ m.: 36 mins.). Note how narrow is the station site, how tidal the river and steep the slope of the hill opposite. It is hemmed by the river to the right and Mill Street on the other and to obtain more land when the station was rebuilt, Mill Street was moved. Thus the terminus was the nearest to the sea of any point on the former IOMR and during World War I a temporary harbour connection was extended from it; it did not survive the peace. However, again in the period prior to 1914, Peel's position on the west coast had led to a limited passenger steamer service with Belfast, for which special trains were run, but it was not an especially profitable enterprise - in fact, the proximity of the station to the harbour has not given the railway at Peel any special advantage.

The river beside the station is tidal, and in previous times it was not unusual for much of the Peel fishing fleet (comprising 'Nickies' tied rail-to-rail*) to occupy the river wall alongside the old station - an arresting sight for visitors from the mainland. (Unfortunately this east bank of the river is not sufficient for latterday needs and to protect the mouth of the river a breakwater extension was projected from the west bank; here, larger ships can berth in safety.) In 1884 a West Quay tramway was considered, linked to the station at one end and passing under the pile at the harbour entrance on which stands the formidable Peel Castle. This fortification commands not only the defence of the town, but also the view, the eye travelling along the river fetches up on this impressive ruin.

Entering the station, the train first passes the engine shed on its left. Its unattractive extension - largely of corrugated iron sheeting - is seldom

*Manx Nickies - a copy of the west Cornish lugger. Used for driftnet fishing - fine sea boats found making their way round coasts of British Isles. Peel was principal fishing port in Island, Port St. Mary coming second, having 125 vessels registered there is 1880s. [WEST COAST SHIPPING. (M. K. Stammers). 1976. p. 29].

required today and is wrongly reputed to have been built to house the engine used on the Knockaloe branch. Whatever timber it contained burned down some time ago, and the engine in the shed behind was rescued heroically. A large water tank alongside stands on a stone plinth; engines may take water from either side of it.

The station rebuilding of 1907/8 was in the manner of a superior village hall with a white stucco finish. The station interior is notable; the ample circulating area has a 'chapel' atmosphere especially in the roof trusses. The doors are teak with scumble finish, having frosted glass panels in the lavatory examples and where the 'Simplicitas' ware has fluted matching columns to lavatory and hand basin pedestals. Lavatory seats with brass furniture are in mahogany. Though today it is a little time-worn, it is still quite splendid. The Goods Shed is of kindred design to the station and is on the right when entering by train, together with cattle bank and goods platform. The long island platform has a run-round loop on the harbour side, and a carriage siding; until recently there were further carriage sidings here but they were usurped for road improvements.

During World War I the extended harbour siding was a projection of one of these carriage sidings along the side of the station building and along the quayside for about 200 yards: thus for a time, with that at Ramsey, the

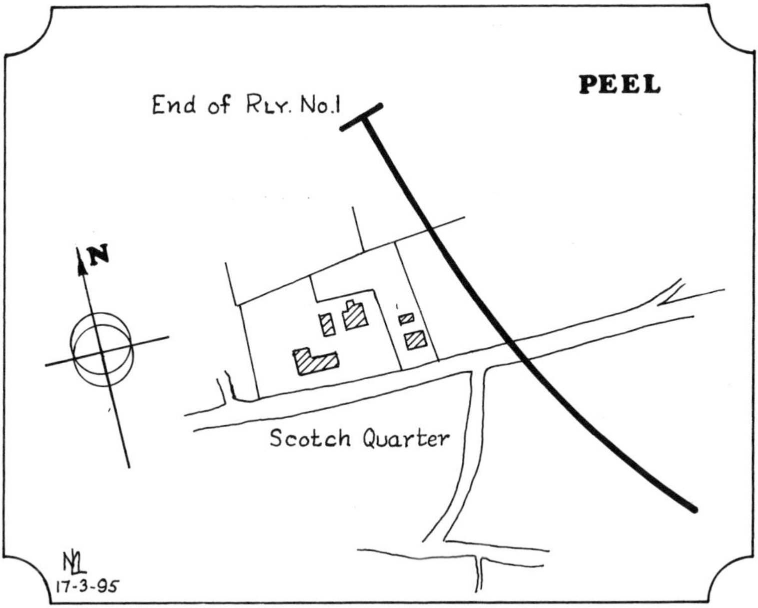

Plans & Sections for original RAILWAY No. 1 showing proposed end of the line on the high ground above Peel enabling the railway to be continued to Ramsey without involving a steep gradient from Peel Harbour onto a Ramsey extension; with abandonment of the Ramsey projection, this plan was not adopted.

railway system enjoyed two harbour links. German and other prisoners were taken straight off vessels into wagons and by rail to Knockaloe. This line was lifted after 1920 when the Camp was disbanded.

Before the coming of the railway, the site of Peel station was a waste of tidal land known as The Bank, between river and Gas Works. Had the original proposition to continue to Ramsey been carried out, Peel station would have been of through pattern; with engine and carriage sheds up on the hillside above the town; its intended layout appears on the proposed Signalling Plans of 1872. [In August 1872 the present site was obtained, far more convenient for the town, but it suffered from instability and before the rebuilding took place, thousands of tons of material had to be spread over the area in order to reclaim it completely from tidal effect.]

It may be mentioned that opposite the station, above the west river bank, rose an incline for a tramway which climbed Corrin's Hill and served a stone quarry; this course may still be discerned.*

St John's

The station of today is an elongated junction and is basically a place of interchange, there being little call for a station in terms of local need as the main Douglas-Peel road is a matter of but yards away; however, on one day in the year (5th July) Tynwald Fair Day, the station witnesses passengers in astronomical numbers.

As before-mentioned, the three platforms serve the Douglas-Peel line on the south side; Douglas-Ramsey trains prefer the north loop giving them access to the water tank on the south side; the northernmost platform is normally used by Ramsey-Douglas trains. The timetable allows that four trains may occupy the station at once and passenger interchange for the three main terminals may, ideally, be done in a few hectic moments before the trains depart, virtually simultaneously. Through trains to and from Ramsey (only) are offered the facility of water for the engine at each end of the north platform. It is impossible to be dogmatic about regular train movements as such convenience as running two trains coupled together from Douglas (sometimes with the engine of the second train sandwiched in the middle) and splitting them short of the station, so detachment of the second portion may take place; each portion will then run forward separately, one for Peel and the other for Ramsey. Meanwhile trains from Ramsey and Peel may have arrived, and so every track is occupied. (Diagram p. 34.)

To meet the Inspecting Officer's requirements, a considerable length of wooden fencing once railed off the ends of the platforms at the west end, and funnelled passengers over an impressive timber footbridge carried on stone

*See THE ISLE OF MAN RAILWAY (Boyd) [Fourth Edition Appendix 5.]

piers; otherwise it was all too easy for the unwary passenger, taking a short-cut in order to change trains, to step off the nine-inch-high platform and be struck by an incoming train. Especially was this bridge desirable on Tynwald Day when over 13,000 people might be carried each way in the morning (the festivities were over by early afternoon). Today the train service has lessened due to Tynwald visitors using the road. The by-now unsafe footbridge has disappeared and the attractive wooden fencing is replaced by ugly tubular posts and chains.

At the east end is the long corrugated iron shed built to house additional carriages when the Company's business increased to the point where the Douglas and Ramsey sheds could not hold them all (there are no sheds at Peel and Port Erin). The yard on the north side contains a cattle bank and goods platform. There have been at least two Goods Sheds here but there is no sign of either today: from Vol. I it may be envisaged how different the yard was before the Foxdale Railway was built, and how storage on the ground was provided for mining materials and output. Although the siding accommodation is small, before 1911 it would have been almost entirely given over to Foxdale requirements.

On the west of the road crossing stands to the north, the disused Foxdale line station, a superior structure in brick which reveals the ambitions and confidence of its promoters. The IOMR station building of 1873 is a poor cousin to the foregoing.

The signalling still betrays its origin - the simple ground-worked points and signals reveal IOMR ancestry, and some - but not all - of the remainder were provided by the MNR, including the signal box at the east end. An open lever frame on the Foxdale station platform covered movements on MNR and FR metals only.

It remains to mention the principal local source of traffic, the sand and gravel industry - even today, in and around the station area can be defined the abandoned workings:

1) to the northwest of the Foxdale station
2) in the area surrounding both sides of the Foxdale branch on the east side of the St. John's - Castletown road overbridge (immediately under that bridge may yet be seen branches running off either side of the branch)
3) that already mentioned adjacent to the main line, immediately prior to the Foxdale branch overbridge on its east side

Temporary portable tracks of 'Jubilee' type, along with side tipping wagons, were used in all these pits* and each of them had 3 ft gauge rail access suited to locomotive working.

The diagrams show how the station has developed into its present form: it will be realised by noting the dates just how short was the period when the

*Efforts to complete a list of the commercial names / owners / lessees / dates of working these pits have been unsuccessful.

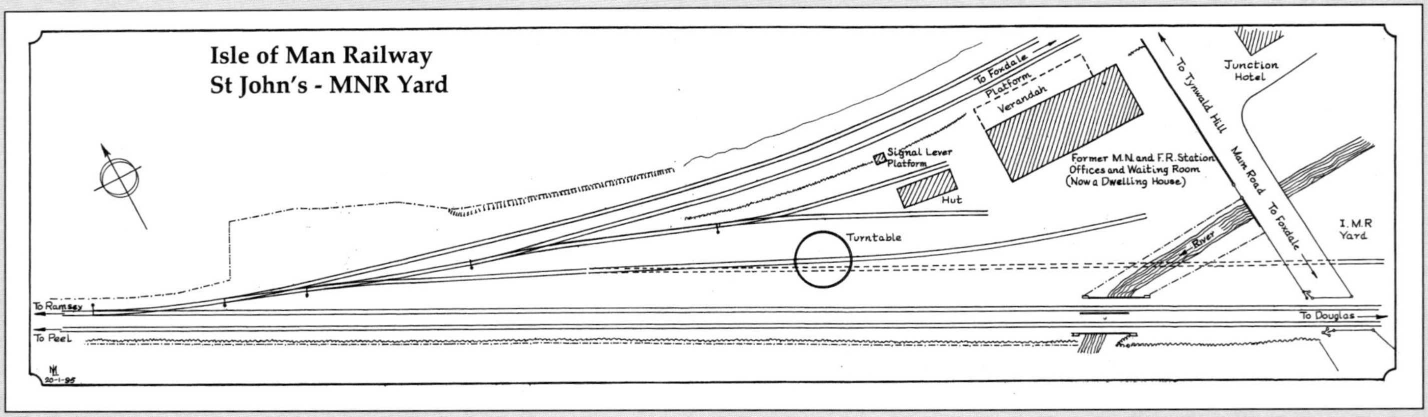
Isle of Man Railway
St John's - MNR Yard
To Foxdale
Platform
Verandah
Signal Lever Platform
Hut
Former M.N. and F.R. Station Offices and Waiting Room (Now a Dwelling House)
To Tynwald Hill
Main Road
To Foxdale
Junction Hotel
I.M.R Yard
River
Turntable
To Ramsey
To Peel
To Douglas
20-1-95

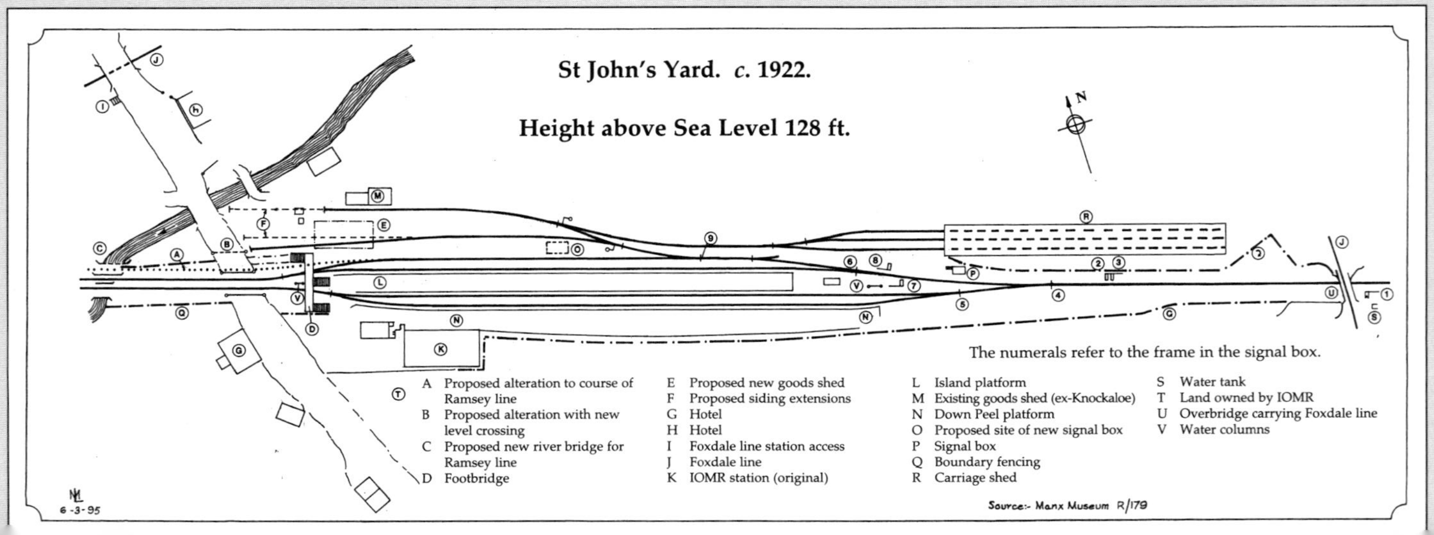
St John's Yard. c. 1922.
Height above Sea Level 128 ft.
N
The numerals refer to the frame in the signal box.
A Proposed alteration to course of Ramsey line
B Proposed alteration with new level crossing
C Proposed new river bridge for Ramsey line
D Footbridge
E Proposed new goods shed
F Proposed siding extensions
G Hotel
H Hotel
I Foxdale line station access
J Foxdale line
K IOMR station (original)
L Island platform
M Existing goods shed (ex-Knockaloe)
N Down Peel platform
O Proposed site of new signal box
P Signal box
Q Boundary fencing
R Carriage shed
S Water tank
T Land owned by IOMR
U Overbridge carrying Foxdale line
V Water columns
Source:- Manx Museum R/179
6-3-95

layout had to deal with the independent movements of trains of the three companies before rationalisation together with the Inspecting Officer's wise advice, brought these luxuries to an end. The initial ritual of bringing MNR trains which had arrived at the Foxdale Railway site (between 1879 and 1886, the site of the MNR terminus alone, but between 1886 and 1897 also used by both MNR and FR) would have made St John's a most interesting place.

Arising from these changing practices, the detailed appearance and surroundings of the MNR terminus (one could hardly accord it the title of 'station') 1879-86 have regrettably, escaped notice.

It remains to note the station lighting is now done by electricity, using the original oil-lamp standards and surmounted by what are humourously thought to be fish-tanks - a unique feature on the railway system. Finally, note how the station nameboards differ in their lettering: 'St John's Change for --------' is lettered appropriately to face the various trains.

Douglas (excl.) - Port Erin

The immediate environs on leaving Douglas are as has been described for the Peel Line. Whilst running parallel to that Line the track begins to rise at 1/150, eases to 1/320 and then steepens to 1/65.* Trains leave Douglas smartly in order to have impetus for the bank: fallen leaves as the line passes through the grounds of the wooded Nunnery Estate will cause wheelslip. The blast of a steam engine's exhaust will echo among the trees which line the banks of the river here.

Peel and Port Erin Lines part company in about a mile and the latter passes over the lattice girder span of the Nunnery Bridge, installed in 1894/5 to replace the pioneer 2 span wrought iron girder structure. This section all lies on a 10 chain radius left-hand curve; a steep-sided cutting ensues and the Up distant signal is passed. Though invisible from the train, the track over the bridge (though flat-bottomed) is held in chairs with wooden keys - a feature of some other bridges on the system. This initial start for Down trains is a severe test for the locomotive; a combination of curve and gradient coming so soon after a 'cold start' can pull an engine's fire to pieces before the top of the gradient is reached; much paper and ink has been expended by the Company in calculating the wear and tear on locomotives working on this steep length of the South Line. Trains make a brave sight and sound as they pound up the cutting and echo in the woodland!

Visitors frequently remark on this initial sylvan setting of the journey, the train heaving its way painfully up the hill with an almost intentional desire to allow the newly-arrived to savour the loveliness of the place. Shrubbery brushes the side of the carriages and, if the smoke from the engine's exhaust is not offending the passengers by percolating into the compartments, the

*In 1945 an attempt was made by the IOMR. Company to ascertain the steepest gradient on the system, existing surveys showing both 1 in 60 and 1 in 65. From a source not disclosed, they advised Beyer, Peacock (in connection with a specification for new locomotives), the figure was 1 in 63.

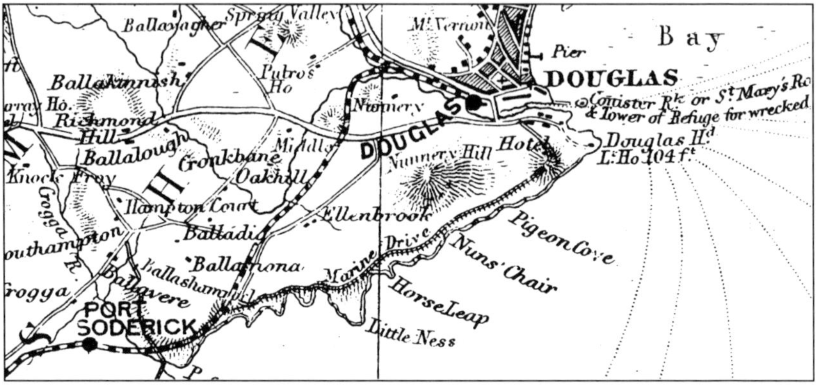

windows can be opened, the bark of the blast made louder, and leafy smells may overcome those of hot machinery. A well-remembered cleric used to take advantage of this slow-moving, struggling progress to scatter seeds of wild flowers from a window.

The cutting ends with a curve to the right and the line leaves the woodlands: now ¾ mile from Douglas, we are out in the country* and high above the fields to either side on an embankment. The town, with the Pulrose Housing Estate and the Generating Station, is below and behind on the right, and a broad sweep of hill and mountain rises in the background. The uphill gradient continues without a break and there is a long straight stretch of route: but once out of the cutting and off the curves, the engine's job is easier. There is an unattended occupation level crossing at the White Hoe Isolation Hospital (the scene of many a scrape between road and rail vehicles). (1 m.) With the northern slopes of Douglas Head on the left, the valley narrows; following up the Kewaigue stream the railway crosses the road at Kewaigue by a stone-arched bridge; the building alongside was once a flax mill.

After running parallel to the old Castletown road on our left for some time, the line passes under it at Oakhill where a long cutting begins (2 m.). Oakhill Road was the second bridge to cross a highway on the South Line. The act of Tynwald specifically stated what size of arch must be built and because the first bridge at Kewaigue had held up progress, the contractors used temporary wooden bridges to cross over/under so as not to delay work on the Douglas-Castletown length. The temporary bridge at Oakhill was simplified by throwing it at right angles across the railway - and presumably a similar tactic was employed at Santon and Blackboards further on - but when the permanent structure was built, Watson & Smith incurred the displeasure of the Highway Board by building it in the same alignment, alongside. They were forced to rebuild it on the skew, and thus widen the

*An environment now utterly spoilt by inappropriate industrial building (1994).

extreme narrowness of the roadway. Here the grade eases slightly to 1/70 (but later increases to 1/65) but the cutting, now only 12 ft wide and rock-walled for a considerable distance, is damp and enginemen must exercise skill in bringing the train to the top of the hill; the summit is reached after a curve to the right (*c.* 200 ft). To the left there is a brief but delightful view of the sea and cliffs encompassing Port Soderick below; this is Keristal, once served by the Douglas Southern Electric Tramways Ltd. which connected Douglas Head with Port Soderick via the Marine Drive. This viewpoint, high above Port Soderick which is hidden below, continues for less than half a mile before the line turns right, inland and northwards and into cutting (3 m.), emerging from this, on a left-hand curve, Port Soderick station lies ahead, the railway levelling off at the Keristal summit.

The station is almost hidden by trees and stands on a shelf cut into the hillside. There is a passing loop, the facing points being entered carefully at reduced speed; the steep road from Ballaveare down into Port Soderick is crossed by an impressive masonry bridge (3⅛ m.: 11 mins). The station layout lies on a left-hand curve; the building is on the right, a substantial two-storey affair with concrete facing: it replaced a wooden building in 1896. The intensive Douglas-Port Soderick excursion traffic* is alluded to elsewhere, as is the growth of the station facilities which were necessary to accommodate it. Despite the impact of the seasonally-operated Marine Drive Tramway (opened to Keristal in 1896 and fully in 1897) such was the increase of tourism that right up until the start of World War II (September 1939) this short-haul business by railway was very considerable; unfortunately, it did involve the operating expense of working the heaviest section of the *entire* IOMR system (save the Foxdale Branch) i.e. between Douglas and Port Soderick. The passing loop is presently out of use and Port Soderick itself is in rapid decline nowadays; the station is now an Unstaffed Halt, there being no local traffic hereabouts. A former siding has disappeared; the Down side has a platform, the Up, none. A peep into the past is supplied by a Minute of 1894 (the time of tramway competition):

> The only way this station can be improved is by purchasing more land . . . and building a house . . . doubtful if plants would grow here . . . much exposed to prevailing winds.

The climb resumes after Port Soderick but more easily, gradients are 1/400, 242 and 405, and milepost 4 is passed. This is another delightful stretch of country, the line passing along Crogga Glen, a narrow wooded valley along the bottom of which the little Crogga River finds it way into the sea at Port Soderick.† As to Crogga itself, this distinctive house was built by the Quayle family.

The next summit comes at the watershed (4¼ m.), at 230 ft: this is the

*Port Soderick, developed by the Forrester family in the late 1890s.

†Geologically, the Crogga Gorge: the river may formerly have discharged at Port Grenaugh.

highest point between Douglas and Port Erin, attained after another uphill stretch of 1/112. Gradients into Port Erin are now almost all in favour of Down trains as the line falls at 1/220, 507 and 100, but then comes an interruption with a rise at 1/155, but the fall that follows is a problem for Up trains; its inclination has been recorded variously as between 1/60-65.

Between the above summit and the second rise, and on the Port Erin side of a small road overbridge, is the overgrown Halt at Ballacostain (4¼ m.) (sometimes known as Pistol Castle). Lying to the right hand of the train, being almost at ground level, it requires a sharp eye to detect it; it is merely a low platform edged with timbers, and having a small gate in the hedge behind, giving access to the footpath to the road leading to Pistol Castle beyond. The Halt was used in connection with a nearby Rifle Range and was latterly used by King William's College OTC, the only consistent users down the years. The 'platform' is only 10 yds long and 1½ ft high (see Vol. I, p. 241).

There is a momentary fall from the 'platform', and then a climb of 1/100 commences which lifts the railway out of the head of the Crogga Valley and provides a seascape over the Plain of Malew to the south, over Port Grenaugh and away to Derbyhaven and Langness. The track begins to rise on embankment, crosses a small stream issuing from woodland below Ballaquaggin Farm on the hillside to the right, and passes the 4½ milepost. [This site gives us an opportunity to compare the somewhat limited width of embankment crowns and cutting bottoms with the rather more generous measurements of the MNR.] Still rising and beginning a northward curve a second underbridge allows a farm track from Ballaquaggin to reach fields to the left of the line. Now 15 ft above the pasture comes the beginning of a curving cutting which becomes 15 ft deep. A lesser summit is passed and there begins a long fall which, with slight interruption, continues until Ballasalla is reached. A farm road crosses the line at the cutting's end and there comes a short, high embankment, its glen running down towards Port Grenaugh and giving a delightful view of the coast. In past days, the long curve just traversed was known as Beehive Curve, but those days (and the hives) have gone.

We are 5 miles from Douglas here; we pass under the old Castletown road, falling mostly at 1/60 and remain in cutting for quite ¼ mile; this is 20 ft deep and all views are lost. A left-hand curve at its end is marked by a minor road's overbridge and emerging, the fall ceases as a high embankment (5½ m.) carries the track left-hand on a short climb into Santon station. Immediately before that station, there comes a bridge over a stream and minor road, providing a marked 'hump' in the line. Santon is reached (5⅝ m.: 10 mins.). The correct spelling should be Santan (a corruption of St Sanctain) though at first it was intended to be named Ballavale: it stands in a most pleasant fold of countryside.

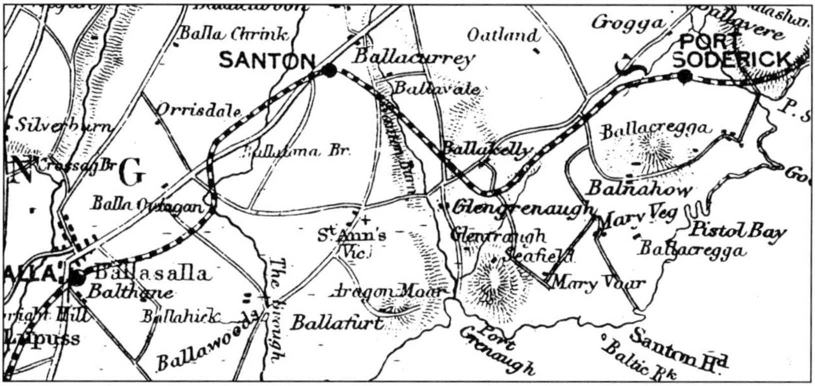

Whilst not on the original list of stations, it was decided before the railway opened that a station both here and at Port Soderick would be desirable, the site and layout being then undecided. Within a year or so, a drawing prepared for Santon carried the footnote 'A large number of trains cross at this station'; the passing loop was then an accomplished fact. The accommodation was initially a small sentry box [*sic*] but the box was sent to Port Soderick in 1875 when Santon acquired its present building which is similar to the structure at Colby. There is a 'manure siding' (hidden from passengers' view by an advertisement hoarding), an old wheel-less 'E' van for a goods store, cattle bank and a row of lonely lampposts, but there are no platforms. The west end is in steeply-sided cutting and conifers are prominent along its slopes. The loop converges under the Douglas-Castletown road bridge, notable for its tall arch. At the present time, Santon has disappeared from the timetables altogether, not an uncommon situation: trains continue to stop by request and doubtless the station will re-appear in print again. For the time being, the loop is out of use and trains use the Up side: pointwork is padlocked for security as no one is on duty here - the frequent bus service on the nearby main road syphons local business from the railway.

From Santon the line curves leftwards along a tall embankment carrying the line over the Santon Burn until it runs above and parallel to the road, travelling south-westwards. Road and railway follow the valley of the Burn, the line falling at 1/150; two level crossings follow each other in a short distance, first comes Ballalonna (6¼ m.) and then Ballastrang (6½ m.). Road and railway are now in close proximity and at Blackboards Bridge* (7 m.) the line passes under the main road near the point where it is joined by the old road (which runs nearer the coast from Douglas to this junction). To the left the passenger is rewarded with a wide land and seascape stretching from Santon Head, southwards to Derbyhaven and Langness Point with its

*So named because of the board fence formerly provided.

lighthouse. Below and on the seaboard lies Castletown and nearby, King William's College with its prominent tower: Ronaldsway Airport is on the nearer level ground. Ballaquaggan Farm is passed on the right, a small bridge giving access to it is crossed, once renewed with the discarded wrought iron spans from the original Nunnery Bridge. All the while the railway is descending to the Coastal Plain at 1/109.

Now comes Ballawoods level crossing (7¼ m.); the fall continues for a mile at 1/80 then eases to 1/320, and all the time coastal views obtain to the left, and as the slopes to the right recede, a fine range of upland stretches inland to the north; both aspects of the Island's geography are therefore in view.

We are now in limestone country and the approaching station, Ballasalla, was once an important loading point for lime, used both for agriculture and more importantly, consigned to Douglas for building purposes. Again, on our left and about ½ mile away, may be seen the extensive Turkeyland Quarry; in 1878 it was intended it should be connected to the railway at Castletown by a branch tramway and earthworks were begun at the quarry end. An isolated length of embankment may yet be seen. Unfortunately, the IOMR Co. would not countenance a junction nearer the quarry but failure of the scheme was put down to the refusal of the adjoining landowner to allow the line to cross his land.*

Another level crossing follows, Ballahick (8¼ m.): it is almost in Ballasalla station; both this crossing and the previous one at Ballawoods serve minor roads, Ballawoods having a cement-rendered crossing house and Ballahick a wooden hut. Then comes the station itself (8⅜ m.: 27 mins.), having a loop which has always been the most convenient place at which to pass trains on the South Line. The original wooden building with corrugated iron roof still survives, though there are no platforms. Connected to the Up loop are two sidings, one serving a wooden goods store and the other a high level loading dock with cattle bank at one end. At the west end is a major road level crossing, one of the busiest on this Line. A water tank serves Down trains.

Leaving Ballasalla, of which little is seen from the train, the line enters a cutting and falls at 1/100: after a further length falling at 1/200, level track is reached. Immediately beyond the level crossing at Ballasalla the railway enters a curved cutting which ultimately ends by the line taking up a position by the Silver Burn on its right. Passengers who have been following the railway's progress by means of an Ordnance Survey map will have received a surprise when about a quarter of a mile beyond Ballasalla, the train passes under a stone overbridge which is not marked on any map! Neither does the bridge itself seem to serve any useful purpose today.

One item which only informed passengers will appreciate is that from the first rail-joint on the west side of the level crossing the track is laid with rails bought second-hand from Ireland. Not every one is marked but all are 30 ft

*Further reference to lime traffic will be given later: it was first used in the Island as a manure *c.* 1642.

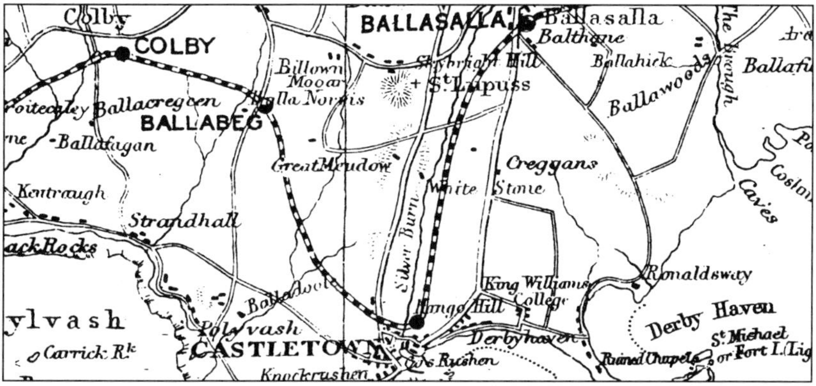

long and fish-jointed by unusual plates having bolt holes with paired holes near each end, and a longer plain section between them. Some rails carry 'WEST CUMBERLAND. STEEL. 1882 GNR'. Known to generations of railwaymen as 'The Irish Rails', they still have plenty of life in them. These rails extend as far as the entry to Castletown, the next station.

Soon the line is in open ground: the fields to the right are threaded by the Burn and broken here and there by glacial moraines which have long been studied by geologists. The land to the left is marred by growing industry beside the Ronaldsway Airfield, the site of a battle in 1250 and a heart of economic revival today.* In the right distance, the hills have now fallen away and the Plain of Rushen will carry the railway for most of its remaining distance. How much easier for the railway builders was this section than the Douglas-Ballasalla length . . . . !

A minor road overbridge marks the entrance to Castletown (9⅞ m.: 33 mins.), the station is a large one by Manx standards as only five years before the railway was opened, it was the historic capital of the Island. Castle Rushen dominates the little town today, just as it did in the past. Fishing, general merchandise and the famous Castletown Brewery all contribute to goods traffic, and wagons on the rear of a mixed train will usually be 'fly shunted' into the goods yard without the passenger portion at the front of the train coming to an intermediate stand, and should such wagons fail to have sufficient momentum to enter the yard, a good push from the station employees is all-sufficient.

Something of the story behind the situation of the station has already been told:† the existing site is a compromise between feuding local factions; the earliest conception would have taken the line even further away from the town to the north, with a station somewhere near Great Meadow. A glance at the map will show the wide sweep the railway makes in its passage between Ballasalla and Ballabeg in order to accommodate Castletown.

*A Halt is now provided for the Airport here. (1994).
†Vol. I, p. 36.

Quarries of the Castletown District

Castletown Quarries
1 Billown - Limestone (Jefferson's, later Creggan's)
2 Ballahot - Limestone (Jefferson's)
3 Turkeyland - Limestone (Jefferson & Moore, later Jefferson's
4 Scarlett - Limestone (Proctor's, later Bridson's)
5 Copper Mine

See text for proposals for links with IOMR at Castletown or Ballasalla.

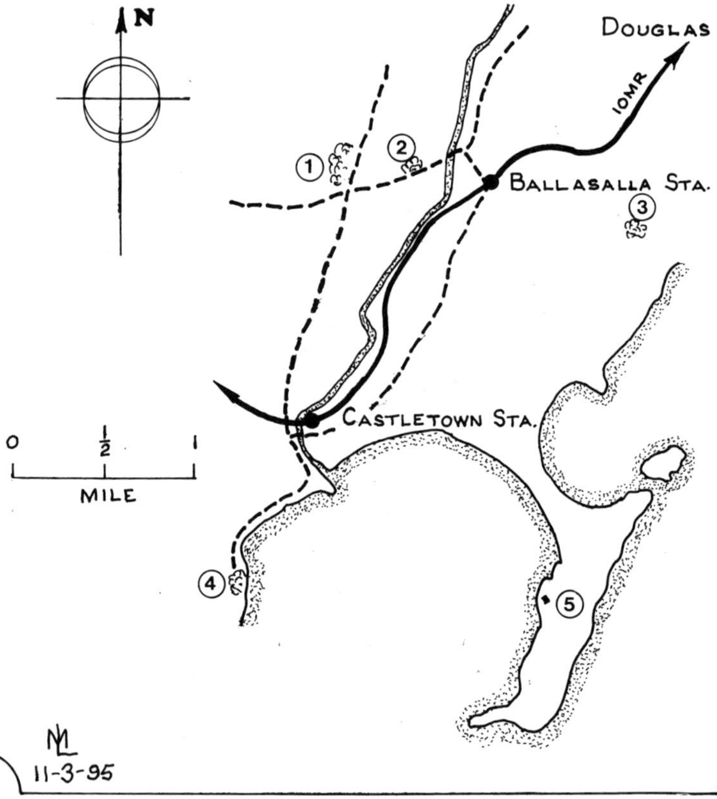

There are two sidings off the Down loop, entered by facing points at the east end; one serves a large Goods Shed of dressed slab with brick string courses and quoins and the other is a long road which passes behind that Shed towards the back of the station building. There are no raised platforms; the stone building, made of carboniferous limestone from the quarry on Scarlett Point, is to the south of the line and the north side of the layout is bordered by a row of trees and a water tank, filled by handpump from a well below, is sited for Up trains.

The substantial station building, with its twin gables, and wooden verandah supported on pillars which was added to the frontage in 1902, is a handsome edifice and quite unlike any other on the Island railways . . . in fact, variety in station architecture is notable everywhere.

Leaving the station the railway is lined with large mature trees; the Silver Burn is crossed by a masonry bridge of three arches (the central one having a 26 ft span). Curious are the remains of a former water tank on the bridge, believed to precede that provided at Ballasalla but found to be too far from Douglas and so causing anxiety to engine crews. A right hand curve ensues; to the left the town is partially screened from sight by trees. To the right open fields lead the eye northwards to the slopes of South Barrule (1,585 ft) in the distance, a bare hill which dominates the south-west end of the Island.

There is a level crossing here (Mill Road: 10¼ m.) and entering cutting, the line passes under the Castletown-St John's road as that road begins northwards towards Foxdale - one of the longest near-straight roads on the Island. Passengers can see nothing at this point but it is of historic interest as being the chosen position for Castletown station in 1873 . . . that is, until influential townspeople living on the east side of the river, had the site changed to the existing one (there was more than a hint that shares would not be taken up in the Railway Company if the promoters were foolish enough not to read the writing on the wall). What *can* be seen however, (and on the right) is a considerable widening of the cutting where Watson & Smith extracted many tons of material during building of the line.

The track curls away in a north-westerly direction out from the cutting and across a low-lying area of ground. Much to the surprise of many passengers, the view recently seen from the right-hand windows now appears on the left - the wide mouth of Bay ny Carrickey, a long sandy shore and beyond, the promontory of Gansey Point with Port St Mary Bay behind. Bringing up the rear and southwards is a long peninsula crowned by Mull Hill: this ends seaward in Spanish Head, the most south-westerly point on the Island. (Out of sight and beyond, is The Sound which separates the main land from the Calf of Man.) As the eye moves northwards, Mull Hill drops to sea level and the roofs and chimneys of Port Erin can be discerned, lying at the foot of a shallow 'U' having Mull Hill to the south and Bradda Hill to the north.

Conspicuously, the Milner Tower* atop Bradda Head, catches the eye. However, approaching Ballabeg the railway swings left again - in due course some of this passing scene will again be visible from the right side . . . but not yet.

And so we near Ballabeg (11½ m.) a hamlet to the right of the train whose principal building is the church, and here the railway curves to the left and the line runs for a mile or two along the foothills of Slieau Earystane (1,020 ft). A stopping place once existed here; not only does it appear and disappear from timetables but in this year of our journey there is little physical or printed evidence. [The writer recalls a small wooden hut on the east side of the Arbory-Castletown road overbridge nearby in the late 1920s, a station so ephemeral that it was worth walking over our fellow travellers' feet to reach the window and lean out to see if by some miracle, it had survived.] Its early history can only be determined from the Minutes; the presence of flowering shrubs and tree planting suggests its former position (11½ m.: 37 mins.).†

Trains do not stop at Ballabeg today, and work up quite a fair turn of speed on this slight climb; it is quite usual to reach 45 mph.# The Port Erin road, making its way also to the west, follows our course on its right, about a field's distance. There comes a climb at 1/140, a short downward slope and then a rise again at 1/136; there is then a slight fall at 1/346 on which slope Colby station is situated: this is the summit of the line between Castletown and Port Erin, but it would be difficult to recognise it as such.

Colby (13 m.: 47 mins.) resembles Ballasalla in some ways, having a similar weather-board and corrugated iron building, passing loop and Down side fringed with trees, including palms. White wooden paling, a feature of most IOMR stations, is in typical use - and there are no platforms. There is a loop turnout with an occupation crossing at the west end, an even lesser one at the east and a single siding off the Up loop; this has a cattle bank against it.

There is a rapid fall from Colby and trains work up some fine speeds, whistling almost continuously in warning of their approach to level crossings at Kentraugh (13¼ m.), Colby Level (13½ m.), Ballagawne (14 m.), Four Roads (14⅜ m.) and Port St. Mary (14¾ m.). The foremost is another occupation crossing and the scene of a nasty smash between train and farm cart many years ago. Colby Level retains its stone-built crossing lodge. From Colby the line falls at 1/100, followed by 1/165; then comes a length which ends at Level road crossing formerly a Halt with a name board hanging from the gutter of its small wooden building and reading 'Level-Colby-Halt'. (The term 'Level' was taken from the adjacent drainage sough from the Ballacorkish Lead, Zinc and Copper Mine (220700).) The Halt is now in use again (1994).

Although only half a mile from the sea, low rising ground prevents a

*The Milner Tower, erected to commemorate the connection between Port Erin and William Milner, the famous Liverpool safe-maker, who had residence there and was known as its 'godfather'. The Tower is said to be in the shape of the earliest safe-key!

†Vol. I, p. 75 etc.

#Ballabeg is now re-opened. (1994).

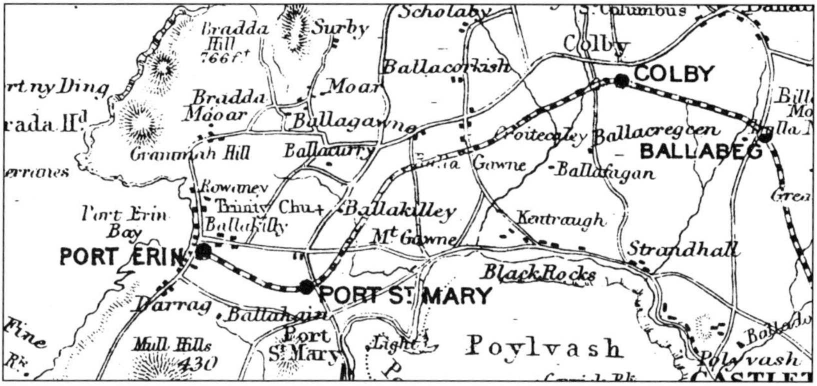

continuous view of the coast between here and Port St Mary. At Ballagawne crossing (another extended, original stone crossing lodge) the railway turns south-west and performs a smaller version of the sweep it made into Castletown - this time to serve Port St Mary. Running through the fields Four Roads crossing is reached; here the old stone lodge survives (disused) on the left and there is a newer crossing bungalow built in dressed slabs with red brick string courses [and red tiles in 1964] to the right here: the Castletown-Port Erin road via Gansey is crossed.

In no time at all, a right hand curve in shallow cutting makes a slight rise and leads to the crossing prior to Port St Mary station: there is a cottage (railway property) but opening and closing of the gates is done by station staff. Port St Mary itself is a little distance from the station and what is seen of it is only the unlovely backs of boarding houses on the Promenade.

The size of the station building is breath-taking and is second only to Douglas (14¾ m.: 48 mins.): Welsh (Ruabon) red brick is dominant. The adjacent road links Four Roads with Port St Mary and is a very busy one: when closed the gates caused considerable congestion. The original timber building was replaced by the present one in 1898 when a raised platform was also provided. At the west end, two sidings face Port Erin, one entering the Goods Shed similar to that at Castletown and the other serving the cattle bank. The Gas Works nearby provides a little business in coal for the railway.*

From Port St Mary the line runs north-west to Port Erin, into which there is a slight fall; the low plain between the two places has geographical interest in that it separates the southern upland massif from the isolated Mull Hill Peninsula. No sooner is the curve out of Port St Mary completed than Port Erin station can be discerned ahead - the intermediate ground is uninteresting and rapidly filling with new domestic construction of dull uniformity. The terminus is approached over a small level crossing, preceded by a bijou wooden hut wherein the crossing keeper may shelter

*Note the incidence of building the Gas Works and new station in the same year.

and also work the Home signal protecting it.

Before the station was rebuilt completely, the existence beside the line at this entrance to the station of a complete engine boiler, smokebox and mountings is recalled: its use as a temporary water tank to serve whilst water was cut off in 1911, seems likely.

Port Erin station building (15⅜ m.: 50 mins.) is built of materials akin to Port St Mary and is now far from the description given to it in 1877: 'a pretty, Swiss-cottage-like station, with its tall flagstaff . . . in view of the village from most points.' [And what of this original stone building and the first station in general? Whilst there are numerous early photographs of Port Erin (showing that it was even then, hardly more than a village), the station site was unfortunately masked by a row of terrace houses from the high point south of the place where pictures were conventionally taken. In consequence no close-up view of the building has come to light. However, distant views reveal a building very similar to the present one, though much smaller. There were two bays as now, but of the same size and outline, and the ornamental timbering in the gable ends was similar to that used on Manx Northern stations. The west end of the building had an open-sided glass-roofed lean-to shelter across the wall, and the right end a small building, possibly a porters' room or such like. The western bay had had a Swiss-style porch added to its front, and this may have been of 'rustic effect'. Between the bays, the verandah and seating were much as in the present building.

The Engine Shed occupied the same site as the present one*. It was exactly the same in style as that at Peel, with two louvre smoke ventilators in the roof; these had replaced two chimneys. Four windows were in each side: a stone plinth at the south-east corner supported a large water tank with pumphouse beside it - that which had upset residents with its noise at night. This tank was replaced by a smaller one fitted with a gabled roof. Inspection of this building and its roofline today, will indicate where later rebuilding took place.

The Douglas-bound train in a photograph on which these details are visible shows the Port Erin-based engine (chimney-facing Douglas) with an open wagon next to the engine, followed by brake van and three bogie coaches.]

The long island platform with a level crossing bisecting it, is notable: trains may not be stabled so as to block this crossing. Behind it lie (right) three tracks, one a carriage siding, representing the extensions built in 1911; this extra provision is essential in a busy summer. To the left, as the train enters, is a long locomotive release line, and another siding off it is known for some reason as the 'Birkenhead Siding' (probably built in 1911). Continuing towards the buffer stops, there is the Engine Shed on the left, water tank tower, and Goods Shed, each built in stone and the buffer stops come right up beside the main road from Douglas. It is but a few moments' walk to the

*In 1994 this Shed is out of use as such: a newer building alongside the Museum houses the locomotive.

seafront. The double-gabled station premises might have a rather institutional appearance but for the embellishments of a useful awning added at a later date. An architectural description of the building has been given as 'a single storey red brick building with matching tiled roof, the centre flanked by gable-ended pavilions: one of these is larger than the other and projects forward onto the platform area to close an end of the awning which is carried on cast iron columns with folliated brackets. The gable ends have attached timber framing carried on dentils, and decorated barge boards. On the larger pavilion the roundheaded windows have terra cotta hood moulds with projecting key-blocks, joined by a band of fluted terra cotta to form a continuous string course. There is a decorative string course at eaves level too, while the smaller gable has a band of stepped, projecting brickwork below the dentils.' Bricks were supplied by Monk & Newell of Ruabon; woodwork was in pitchpine, a material also used in the rebuilt Peel station. Originally it was intended to provide an upper floor to house the Station Master, but this was never carried out. Major alterations took place in 1914 whereby the office was enlarged and new lavatories provided. The water column at the platform end was part of the 1914 improvements.

The width of the platform is considerable, but when one notices that the station lorry frequently stands in readiness upon it (just outside the Waiting Room door), and prepared to be loaded with luggage from the train for distribution to boarding houses and hotels in the town, the space is not excessive . . . in fact, in consideration of the journey from Douglas just completed, it is interesting how many station 'platforms' are occupied by the Company's road vehicles, which can be driven right up beside the luggage van when the train comes to a stand.

Tradition has it that in promotional times, Port St Mary was to be the terminus and Port Erin served '*en route*': no evidence has been found to support this legend.

Though on the edge of the town, the station is well-placed for business and its proximity to the shore and local shops make Port Erin a popular venue for day visitors. The left (south) side of the station layout is bounded with trees and hedges which struggle for survival in winter against the strong westerly gales: the right (north) side still has some rural qualities about it . . . but even now there are whispers of building developments in this large triangular field. The Highway Authority too, is anxious to widen the roadway outside the station, and if this is done, the nice and useful forecourt will disappear.

If you have a few minutes in hand before your returning train to Douglas, wander down to the Promenade and consider the proposition of 1873, that the railway might be extended down to the new breakwater . . . what an experience that would have been! And on the return journey, make note of the variety in station architecture . . . no monotony here!

St John's (excl.) - Ramsey

(Distances are measured from St John's: times from Douglas.)

General Note

Compared with the routes already described which were built by the IOMR, the MNR was of more robust construction. With a ruling gradient of 1/100 and minimum curve radius of 20 chains (IOMR 1/*c*. 65 and 10 chains) and repeated gradients of 1/132 and 1/264 to give an easy configuration, plus ample earthworks unlike the skimpy right-of-way of the IOMR, gave the IOMR a 'second cousin' aspect. But the MNR had weaknesses which the IOMR never experienced.

The North Line's civil engineering together with the well-maintained track - ballasting was a little variable but all over was sufficient - contained the customary 'Speed Section' or 'Lezayre Straight', part of ganger Norman Lace's No. 14 length Sulby-Ramsey. It was 1¾ m. long and was the scene of driver A.H. Caine's exploit with No. 11 which had been re-boilered in 1959-60; a speed of 60 mph was claimed on a Douglas-Ramsey working, a perfectly possible figure at this location; in fact, the MNR men, with their original engines which had a reputation for haste, would close the regulator at Lezayre and allow the train to coast the remainder of the journey into Ramsey.*

Westwards out of St John's (128 ft) the Ramsey Line parallels the Peel Line for 800 yards; at 150 yards west of St John's road crossing the Foxdale line trails in on the right side - it is noteworthy that no rail connection exists between the ex-MNR and IOMR on this side of the level crossing, the post-1905 usefulness of such a link being apparently non-existent.

In the triangle of land between the rear of the disused Foxdale station building (now a house for the St John's Station Master) and the Ramsey route along which we now travel, there are no-relics of the former 1897 interchange platform, but the Island's only railway turntable survives there, albeit looking disused. Two overgrown sidings lie beside it, one leading into a small wooden storage shed: on these sidings stands a melancholy line of crippled wagons, but at one time they stored stock used between here and the Foxdale Mines.

The Ramsey-bound line crosses the Neb on a 30 ft span double wrought iron bridge some feet above and parallel to a similar one carrying the Peel Line beside it: Immediately beyond, Ramsey trains veer towards the north-west and climb the embankment through open country, making for the foothills east of Peel and rising at 1/132. The main Douglas-Peel road is crossed by a 50 ft span wrought iron plate girder bridge and at the top of this ascent stands, on the left and in cutting, Peel Road station - now a Halt - (152 ft), opened on 18th June, 1883† and having the only raised platform on the MNR system other than that at Ramsey (1¼ m.: 34 mins.). Names for this station were intended as Poortown Bridge or Poortown#: the latter was chosen but

*This and other exploits recalled by Julian Edwards. SRN No. 53, July 1979, p.5. MANX NORTHERN RAILWAY CENTENARY.

†Other sources give 1st November.

#Poor was the landowner's name.

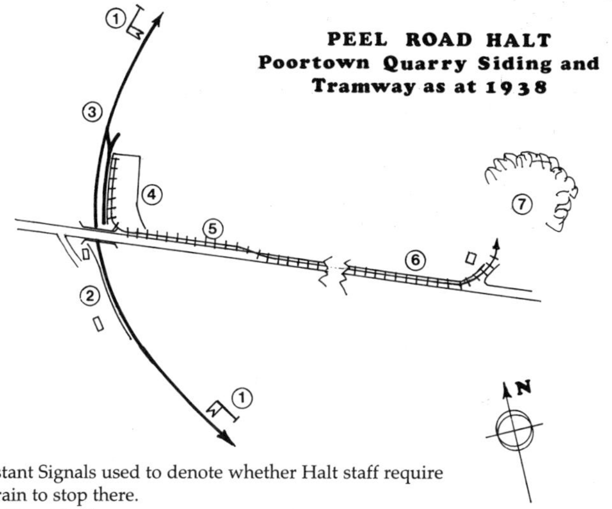

1 Distant Signals used to denote whether Halt staff require a train to stop there.
2 Peel Road Halt.
3 Siding of 1885 to serve high-level loading bank.
4 Loading Bank with 2 ft gauge tramway wharf.
5/6 Tramway of 1886 off/on road.
7 Poortown Quarry.

'Peel Road' was adopted in May 1885. On its low platform stands a wooden building with corrugated iron roof and looking very much the worse for wear, but there is a pleasant fringe of trees; though not in the timetable now, trains will stop if required. A visit here in summer can be quite misleading, as it is a fearful situation on a winter's day, notorious for its exposure to south-west gales and for the blockage of its cutting by snow.

Over the many years the writer has used the railway, he has never known his train to stop here, but when it was opened it was well-used by Peel passengers - it was quicker (and cheaper) to alight here from Ramsey and walk into Peel, rather than continue down to St John's and wait for an IOMR connection. It was the MNR practice to send newly-employed staff here for their initial baptism of railway work. A small IOMR 'E' van, placed here in 1911, does duty as a store shed under the lee of the adjacent Poortown-Peel road overbridge formed of cast-iron beams, 21 yds long.

Beyond the bridge, on the right hand, is a siding (lifted in 1948) facing Ramsey and serving a high-level loading bank capable of holding eight open wagons, and the point is controlled by Annett's Key, a physical part of the single line staff between St John's and Kirk Michael; this equipment did duty

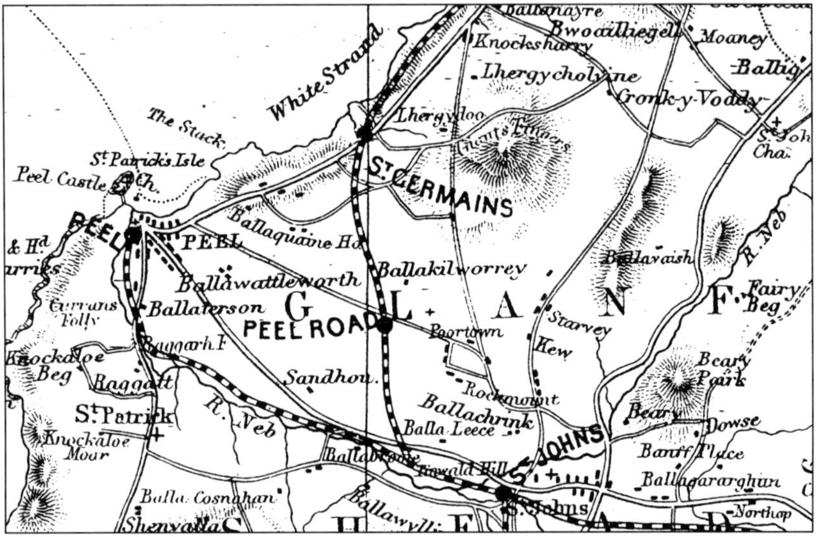

formerly at Knockaloe Junction, Glenfaba. The siding was installed in 1885-6 to serve a roadside 2 ft gauge tramway leading down from the Highway Board's quarry at Poortown and worked by horsepower; its open wagons were supplied through A.S. Nelson & Co. Ltd. (see Vol. I, p. 190) and the MNR, being shipped into Ramsey in November 1886.* [The Board now sends most of its products by road and the siding is disused: the course of the tramway follows the roadside and drops steeply on curve onto the top of the loading bank where it ends at wagon-top height on the IOMR. In 1936 the quarry extracted approximately 100,000 tons of stone, but the railway only took a fraction of this tonnage.]

After Peel Road the climb eases to 1/200 but shortly increases to 1/132 again; now the upland countryside is much wilder and hereabouts on the left would have been the first turnout of the triangular junction of the proposed Peel Railway (Vol. I, p. 188) with the second junction a few yards further on. The Lhergydoo-Peel road passes overhead on one of two cast-iron bridges on this MNR section; here the high ground of the north end of the Island closes in on the right side and the Irish Sea comes into view on the left.

A quarter mile before St Germain's Halt comes a summit and level crossing with the Ramsey-Peel road: the Halt follows, with buildings on the right (2⅞ m.:

*The quarry extracts 'grabbo' as aggregate for roads. This is an appropriate point to define this material. Unfortunately for the builders of the railway it comes in several qualities: though some is extremely hard much is also very soft. Houses built of it in Peel have proved to be of varied value. When the stone-built MNR buildings were examined at IOMR takeover in 1905, much of their stonework was found to be in a near dangerous condition and certain lintels were replaced by rails. However, many buildings were left to disintegrate and today some stations' stone is so weathered it can be pulled off in the hand. [Further detail: 'THE ISLE OF MAN: Celebrating a sense of place.' (Robinson & McCarroll). p. 38.]

40 mins.). This is the first MNR building proper and is constructed in Peel red sandstone and variously altered over the years. We do not stop here for the fortunes of this station have long gone into decline: the countryside surrounding it is hardly likely to create much traffic although at the outset (1879) this was the nearest MNR station to Peel, an awkward 175 ft below us. Though too early in the journey to assess the position, it soon becomes clear how similar to each other were MNR stations compared with those on the IOMR. St Germain's has the traditional double gables and tall chimneys; there is no platform but the loop and siding are still in place - the latter on the left side, and there is also a disused goods and cattle platform.

In bygone years a great tonnage of sand for building was loaded into wagons here; it came by horse cart from The White Strand. As early as 1890 the siding was removed - it seems the loop disappeared then (or shortly thereafter). In 1926 the track materials from the siding at Lezayre were dumped here; the loop was restored in 1926 and the siding and loading bank re-appeared in 1929. The need for sand was such that the loading bank was further extended in 1931; this traffic ceased but the installation remained for wartime emergency use, loop and siding being lifted finally during 1954.

The station disappeared from the timetable on 3rd July, 1961 but tickets were still being issued in the following August . . . another instance of the fallibility of that publication. (References elsewhere to operation and traffic will reveal the curious circumstance of this place, including a decision in 1890 to close the station except on Saturdays.)

The railway now enters quite a different terrain - falling slightly it moves closer to the west coast, comes out along the clifftops and clings to their edges then, moving inland again, only to return to the fringe of the land once more. All this is due to following the contours to reduce the gradients as the summit of the Ramsey Line is approached: here and there small dells are crossed (such as Glen Broigh) and this length throughout provides a fine panorama of seascape from Peel now moving away behind us on the left, to occasional views of the coast north of Kirk Michael, with low sandstone cliffs and beaches, so different from anywhere else the railway reaches in the Island. Thus, from Peel Castle and breakwater to the south, to Jurby in the north, the train commands the view - only recently did the RAF, flying from Jurby, cease to mock-bomb targets in the sea off this coast. This is a most unstable coast and the sea hungrily chews away the foot of the cliffs, and so endangers the railway above.* Some distance above the railway, the Ramsey-Peel road keeps us company on the right.

The situation and variety of the next few miles makes for more detailed description. Leaving St Germain's the railway is now about 200 ft above the shore, which lies to the left and below cliffs. The third milepost is passed and track runs along a low embankment, falling slightly and curving right and

*Further detail: Robinson & McCarroll p. 77

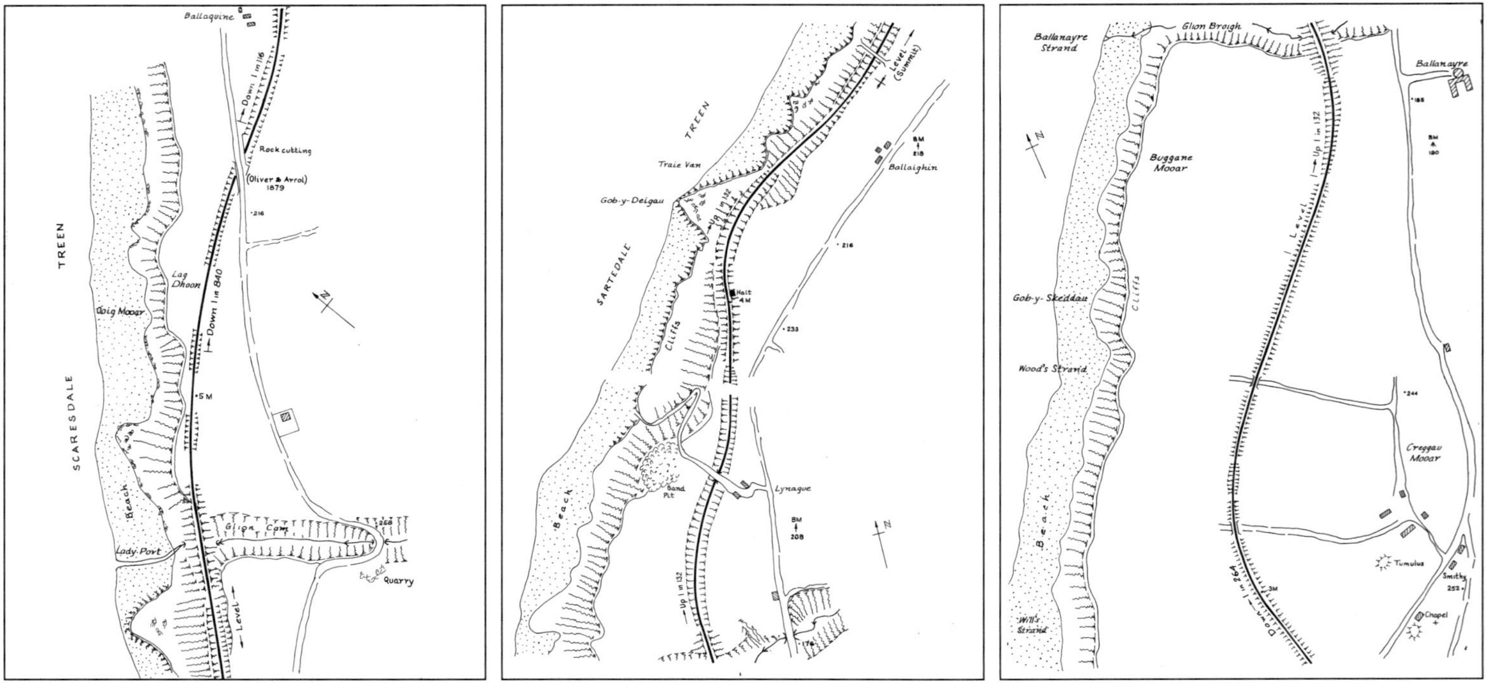

Route of ex-MNR between Ballaquine (northern extremity) and St Germain's (southern extremity) on the west coast, including section of railway at Gob-y-Deigan liable to subsidence. Gradients subject to reservations expressed in the text. *Michael Lloyd*

crossing the fields which stretch between the cliff-tops and the adjacent road. Beyond the road, the land to the right rises sharply, sometimes near and sometimes withdrawn from the right hand of the road. After an occupation underbridge comes a shallow cutting and then a longish, straight embankment and a second underbridge; the rails are about 22 ft above the fields, but fall to about 15 ft as the embankment ends. For some yards, the line is level but ahead can be seen a change in the character of the land and with a left hand curve, the line enters cutting and the long slog up past Goby-Deigan and along The Donkey Bank ensues, 1/132 for almost a mile until the summit prior to Glen Cam is reached. Both the embankment just traversed and the cutting now entered display the ample generosity of the MNR works: the embankment top is 15 ft wide and the cutting 18 ft wide at the bottom.

The pace of the train slows noticeably as the full length reaches the gradient: the cutting is deep but ends suddenly with an embankment over 45 ft high which crosses the wooded Glion (or Glen) Broigh, and finishes just as suddenly when cutting resumes again. We have just passed Ballanayre on the right. Within the cutting the railway takes up a right-hand curve: with a depth of 20 ft, all view of the coast is now lost to the passengers as a minor road to serve a sandpit at Lynague crosses the line by a typical MNR stone overbridge, 18 yds long. The cutting deepens and the railway curves westwards; with a depth of 40-80 ft the proximity of the clifftops to the left is quite undisclosed until with remarkable suddenness the train emerges from the cutting to find itself on a spectacular embankment, the most breathtaking site on all the Manx railway system.

Rather than the track being placed on a terrace here, it is sited on embankment, clear of the cliff-face, some distance below the summit on which it now finds itself. For since Glion Broigh the geology has changed, and the route now has to traverse a falling coastline formed of gravel and sand and with constant instability throughout. It is therefore necessary to uphold the line on embankment away from the cliff-face.

That embankment ending, and a fine view of the beach below terminated, the track starts another right-hand curve and passes a permanent way hut to the left, from where a look-out would be posted from time to time to monitor any cliff falls due to heavy rain etc., for the whole of this section is falling down towards the sea. For many years it has been suggested that both the road (above) and the railway (below) be moved further inland, but the expense would be tremendous.

Beneath the floor of our carriage the wheels are running on rails held in chairs, one of several MNR lengths so treated to ensure the track was stiffened-up. Trains are limited to a speed of 12-20 mph but a Ramsey-bound train would find it difficult to exceed this as the upgrade of 1/132 continues unbroken. The position of the permanent way hut marks the headland behind it, known as Gob-y-Deigan: a few yards south of the hut, but on the opposite side of the line, the MNR introduced a stopping place on 13th July, 1887 and provided an open-fronted timber shed for shelter; this was served by a footpath from the road above, and from it there led another path to the beach. Whilst the whole length of line from 3¾ m. to 4½ m. climbs at an unbroken 1/132, The Donkey Bank foot hereabouts is dubbed The Gob-y-Deigan Bank, though in fact they are both one. Between its opening in 1887 and closure at the onset of World War I in 1914, a leaflet of 1895 stated:

> Parties of four persons First Class or six persons Third Class can be set down except on Sundays by train ex-Ramsey 11.20 a.m. and picked up by the train due to pass at 4.40 p.m. When booking, notify Station Master of intention.

Note that only passengers originating in Ramsey were to be cultivated; no one off the IOMR was being given the privilege.

As if this exciting locale was insufficient, a short distance beyond the cutting which commences at the permanent way hut, passengers are fortunate to enjoy a second, longer but similar stretch of track, also chaired, on an even higher embankment and, looking back to the left, can see the headland of Gob-y-Deigan with Peel Castle and harbour beyond.* With the ending of this second embankment, The Donkey Bank is almost conquered for the long straight Ballakaighin cutting is now entered and within it comes the summit of the MNR system (5¼ m.: 229 ft). It will be noted that on the Gradient Profile of the North Line (see p. 10) the summit is not shown until a point nearly half a mile on the Ramsey side of Glen Cam is reached. This is entirely due to subsidence along this length which today appears to be accelerating. The profile reproduced is based on the survey done by Allott in the mid-1920s. Across it is thrown a timber occupation bridge on stone pillars; this is the summit length and there is a nominally level interval. The line then emerges to cross the considerable embankment at Glen Cam, formed of 50,000 cu. yds of material from the previous cutting, which is 70 ft high and notable for its instability; it has tended to slip down onto the shore from the time of building, and given much anxiety and expense: annual surveys are made and the site is pegged to record the degree of movement both vertically and laterally.† It was one of three points on the MNR which required constant attention. A speed limit of 12 mph is currently in force and is another of the several stretches of track along here where the flat-bottomed rail is laid in chairs to give it stability; furthermore, in the recent past rails from the Baldwin Reservoir contract have found their way into this section.#

* In the years following closure of the line in 1968, these embankments have subsided about 4-5 ft. in the interim.

† An elderly 'local' insisted that subsidence etc. had so changed the appearance of the railway between St. Germain's and Kirk Michael, that parts of The Donkey Bank embankment, were once cutting; this seems a little hard to accept!

See elsewhere for detail Baldwin Reservoir materials.

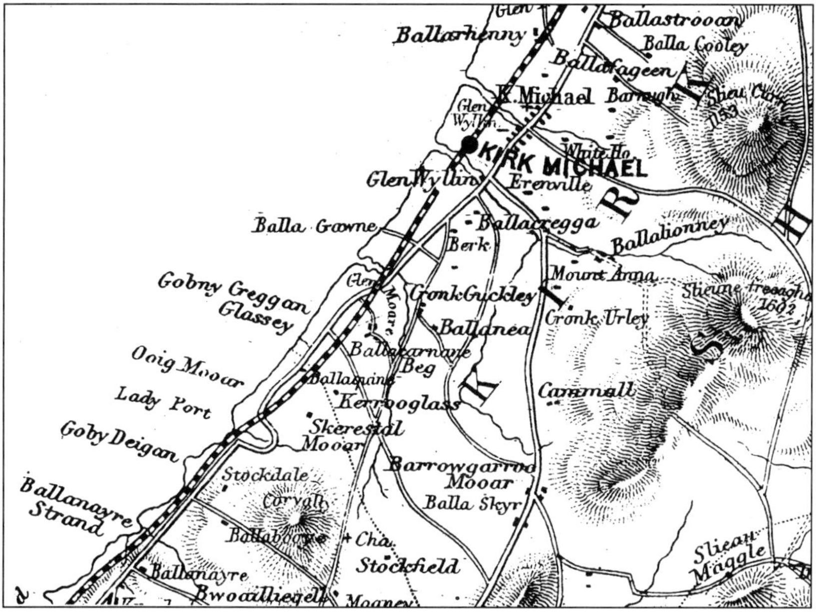

Tradition has it that the MNR locomotive CALEDONIA was considered something of a liability hereabouts, and that chaired curves were put in to prevent the gauge from spreading and the effects of subsidence.

Then the railway falls at an average of 1/100 (there being several changes) as it comes to Ballaquine Bridge, a skew structure by Oliver & Arrol, carrying the Peel-Ramsey road over the line, now in narrow rock cutting: it is 37 yds long of wrought iron camber deck plates and rolled girders. Next, three farm roads are crossed, Ballaquine, Ballacarnane Beg and Ballacarnane Mooar.

Ballaquine Farm nestles within a left-hand curve which brings the railway closer to the road under which it has just passed.* Now out of cutting and on low embankment, the sea spreads away to the west and the line emerges on a slow right-hand curve, all the while on low embankment, an open site highly susceptible to winds off the sea. Farmland surrounds, the land rising slowly upwards to the hills on the east. Clearly ahead can be discerned the sandy-cliffed coast reaching north-westwards towards Jurby, and nearer, the huddle of Kirk Michael and its prominent church tower. Adjacent farm gates still survive of the MNR pattern, all of them securely padlocked with 'standard' railway fittings, recalling the special bench in Douglas Workshops which is put aside for the repair of broken padlocks and twisted keys.

Continuing along this slowly-turning curve, the roadway almost within hailing distance on our left, the rails are carried on tall embankment, crossing

*Erronously given as the summit in ENGINEERING (12 September 1879).

the aforementioned lanes leading eastwards up to the farms at Ballacarnane Beg and Ballacarnane Mooar respectively: these bridges have long been formed of rolled steel joists which replaced the timber members of the MNR period. Abutments are usually of Manx slate with Peel stone quoins. The falling grade is now at 1/116 and the embankment quite 50 ft high: the line has now curved eastwards so much that on a clear day the coast of Galloway is visible less than 40 miles away, whilst almost due west and in the clearest atmosphere, the Mourne Mountains are easily discernible. With the last of the three underbridges behind us, the train continues its right-hand passage whilst prominent on a hill closely adjacent on our right, the projecting 'Keeil Stone' is to be seen. A short cutting at the hill's foot terminates precipitately where the line reaches the edge of Glen Mooar: for this last stretch the fall has increased to 1/100.

This deep glen suddenly appears and the train crosses on an impressive viaduct: as built it consisted of three wrought iron lattice girders each of 60 ft span and 75 ft above the river bed, but it was another weak point in the construction of the railway and was rebuilt in 1921 with lattice steel girders. Falling still, the railway drops at 1/100 from the viaduct and meets West Berk level crossing (an occasional Request Stop) with its attendant lodge which had been built to make it convertible into a station proper. Curving northwards and westwards the railway enters a deep cutting through soft drift gravel with unstable results so that sleepers have been inserted to shore up the sides where necessary. There is a widening on the west side where a ballast hole was situate. This wet cutting carries the course under the Peel-Ramsey road (diverted and improved) and the bridge is of wrought iron 12 ft spans 48 ft wide. The railway still curves but now north-eastwards in a dreary cutting when suddenly a second deep glen is crossed by a viaduct, a notable structure. This is Glen Wyllin with the river 55 ft below. This viaduct is also a reconstructed one, of 1915, the original having been condemned as early as 1909, when Greenbank, the IOMR Civil Engineer, proposed to dismantle both Glen Mooar and Glen Wyllin bridges and substitute embankments; his alternative plan was to rebuild them in masonry with three arches, each having a 30 ft opening - in the event, neither scheme was carried out.*

The large village of Kirk Michael is reached through a shallow cutting and the line now levels out. There is a locomotive water tank on the left side used to replenish engines which have worked turn-back trains either from Ramsey or Douglas; they have to block the running line to take water. A level crossing precedes the station; the loop here was extended over the crossing in 1883, making it the longest on the MNR section. The station (7¼ m.: 50 minutes: 137 ft) is a popular excursion venue for day trippers; Glen Wyllin was purchased by the IOMR in 1935 and its amusements developed

*More detail of these viaducts and their rebuilding will be found on page 79-81.

into a form so beloved of an unsophisticated decade which was content with simple pleasures - there were swings and roundabouts, a Boating Lake, Bandstand and Cafe; the Minutes of the time refer to the purchase of rowing and motor boats! The Cafe used crockery of slightly differing form from the station Refreshment Rooms, but all bore the Company's crest. Open-air concerts were a feature of the summer season. The station is connected to the glen by a footpath which leads down to an attractive sandy shore. Here the sea is encroaching annually.

Back to the station; the building is on the right and similar to St Germain's. The stone-built goods shed of 1923 replaced the original of 1883 in the same material - not of brick, as is sometimes suggested. To accommodate excursions terminating here, the line through the goods shed is extended into a carriage siding.

Onward from Kirk Michael the straggling village is passed on the right: the shore is out of sight but beyond the sea spreads out in an increasing sweep and soon it will disappear from view as the railway turns ever more eastward. To the right the heights of the north make an impressive ridge; from north to south Slieau Curn (1,148 ft), Slieau Dhoo (1,417 ft) and Slieau Freoghane (1,601 ft) beckon climbers in summer and deter in the winter - mist often covers their summits. Falling at 1/100, a little way out of Kirk Michael the line crosses the small Glen Ballyre (or Glion Balleira) (7½ m.) by a 48 ft span plate girder bridge of wrought iron, supplied by Oliver & Arrol of Edinburgh (these were originally 40 ft spans): this has a strange strengthening abutment on the south pier; even after the IOMR took over the MNR in 1905, its safety was always held in deep suspicion. A 12 ft high embankment ensues.

A slight rise of 1/100 then takes place; after a long cutting spanned by three overbridges (each subtly different from the other) a long fall at 1/100 begins. There is an occupation crossing at Rhencullen. Bold hills to the right still require us to gaze upwards to see the skyline as the railway, moving now almost in an easterly direction, clings to their foothills. A large building with a chapel on the right marks Bishop's Court, the official residence of the Bishop of Sodor and Man: there is a seat beside the line here marking the private Halt, lying in a dip of 1/100 in each direction. Over the road to the right the small Bishop's Glen is passed. [The fish-tailed semaphore signal facing Ramsey-bound trains here is *not* connected with the trains calling at the Halt, but protects the forthcoming level crossing.] From Rhencullen we traverse a long curving embankment 12 ft high, threaded by two farm underbridges.

The use of the Halt and irregularities connected thereto have been the subject of many hours of discussion in Board Meetings; various Managers have always been unhappy about the right of a Bishop to hold up a train at a place where there is no official surveillance; in 1922 the Bishop's rights were further restricted when only Ramsey-bound trains were permitted to stop. Between 1930 and 1935 the facility covered only the Monday train bound for Ramsey Mart.*

The land conveyed by the Diocese of Sodor & Man to the MNR included an area at Bishop's Court [*sic*] and parts of the parishes of German [*sic*] and Michael. The arrangement required the Diocese to make annual application to use a Halt provided for it near the Court, and state the times of the trains it wished to use. In practice, the application took virtually the same form each year. The land was acquired under the MNR Act of 1878 and the Railway Compensation Act 1881; the regulations governing the investment of monies are set out in The Bishop's Court & Vicarages (Railway Purchase Moneys) Act 1880 by which the Episcopal Trustees were to have a sum not exceeding £100 for the erection of a stone wall 'in lieu of the existing fence between the MNR and the garden and pleasure grounds . . .' Royal Affirmation to the last-named as to the opening date of a Halt has been seen.†

Rising still at 1/100, Orrisdale No. 1 level crossing comes next with its 18 ft single gates: here in 1882 the making of a platform for a sum of £5 was investigated and from 2nd March a service of two trains daily on Wednesdays and Saturdays, was permitted to use it. Tickets were printed but after about a year the experiment was deemed disappointing; what had become a Halt was reduced to a Request Stop. A singular piece of relaying here in 1885 saw chairs put into the track. Until the mid-1890s there was a siding before No. 1 was reached: this served the Court and brought coal etc. to the premises. There is no trace today.

Hereabouts the railway forms a geological boundary: to the south rises the imposing and rounded northern upland massif escarpment while to the north the coast is now rapidly moving away - masked by a series of low moraine ridges formed in glacial times, and now heavily farmed. Yet on a still day, the sound of waves falling on the shore is clearly to be heard.

For the first time since St John's there will follow a goodly length of straight track - it extends almost as far as the next station, Ballaugh; but meanwhile Orrisdale No. 2 level crossing is reached. The curved cutting between the two crossings prevents clear sighting of the gates as between one and the other; the distance is but 250 yards, and mostly in cutting so each crossing is signalled from the other.

Parallel with the main road, before reaching Ballaugh, the railway crosses Ballaugh Mill stream and then, Ballaugh river, the latter by a bridge of two spans (one of 30 ft and the other 33 ft - originally 25 ft each) of wrought iron plate girders giving 12 ft clearance between spans. Already the scenery on the left of the train is beginning to change completely as the alluvial plains of Ayre appear and stretch away from the lineside; in contrast with the highlands to the right, the land becomes flat and almost featureless. This

*The subject is covered in more detail under 'Traffic'.

†Diocesan Collection: Accession No. 9309. 'Sherwood's case, list No. 1'. (Diocesan Records now held in the Manx Museum.)

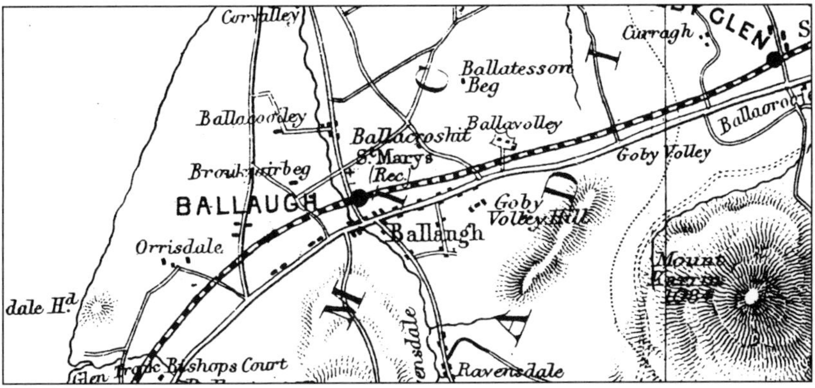

area makes Ayre utterly different from any other part of the Island; at its northern tip stands Point of Ayre lighthouse and on the best of days, the coasts of Ireland, Scotland, England and Wales can be seen: the colour of the fields on Galloway may be visible.

Ballaugh ($10\frac{1}{8}$ m.: 58 minutes) is the principal station between Kirk Michael and Ramsey and its building is of 'standard' MNR style and on the right hand; entry is made over a road crossing which carries an extension of the passing loop, necessitated in 1883. Opposite the building is a stone goods shed and a 1922-built siding leads off the Down side of the loop and forms an outer loop to it; on this is the loading bank and cattle platform, and the goods shed is served by a siding leading off it. There is a small and attractively-kept garden, and the station area is fringed with well-cut hedges. Trains cross each other here, and the 1950 timetable shows an occasional exchange of locomotives whilst doing so.

Over the next mile comes 'Teare's Crossing' [occupation] and there is a steady fall, mostly at 1/150 and 1/100; at the foot of this slope lies The Curragh, the larger of two on the Island, a boggy tract of scrub and marsh lying to the left of the track. Road and railway now run side by side all the way to Ramsey, tucked in below the foothills to the south and the northern plain to the north.

Along this length come three level crossings, Ballacrye (11 m.), Ballavolley ($11\frac{3}{8}$ m.) and Cooilbane ($11\frac{7}{8}$ m.),* all with minor roads. Ballavolley (crossing lodge on the right) is preceded on the same side by the earthwork of a siding facing Ramsey which was laid in 1882 to serve the foot of an incline which ran steeply up the adjacent hillside to serve Clarke's stone quarry.† At its foot it crossed the Kirk Michael - Ramsey road on the level and entered a coppice in which was a high-level loading bank which served the MNR siding at its wagon-top height. Young boys were said to have been stationed to protect such road traffic as there was; output was consigned to Ramsey for the use of a builder, McCulloch. The working appears to have been abandoned by the

*IOMR official mileages are $10\frac{1}{8}$ m., $11\frac{5}{16}$ m. and 12 m.

†Producing slab lintels for doors, fireplaces etc.

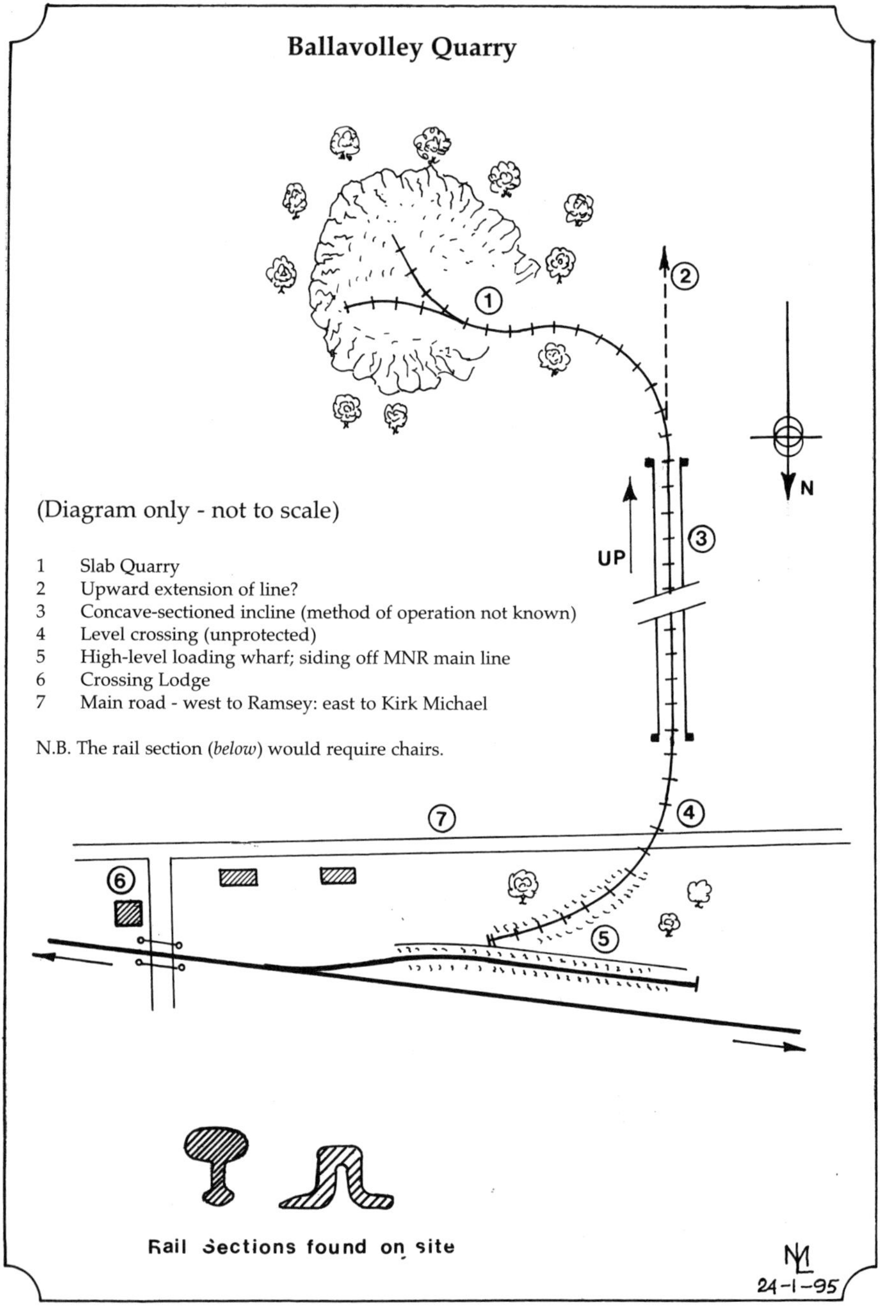
Ballavolley Quarry
(Diagram only - not to scale)
1 Slab Quarry
2 Upward extension of line?
3 Concave-sectioned incline (method of operation not known)
4 Level crossing (unprotected)
5 High-level loading wharf; siding off MNR main line
6 Crossing Lodge
7 Main road - west to Ramsey: east to Kirk Michael
N.B. The rail section (below) would require chairs.
1
2
3
4
5
6
7
UP
N
Rail Sections found on site
24-1-95

early 1890s. The main line at this point, and for several miles thereafter, tends to be on low embankment. The working of this siding and its necessary pointwork, seems to have been somewhat casual: the points were operated by the daughter of the nearby crossing keeper or, in her absence, by the train crew . . . one wonders what Col. Rich had to say about this!

Cooilbane comes next, with a crossing lodge contracted in May 1881, is, like Kella (which follows), different from all the other lodges/ cottages on the MNR. The line continues on a most direct course which it follows from Ballaugh; very shortly Sulby Glen station appears on the right after a climb of 1/150 and 1/200 (12¼ m.: 65 minutes). This marks the last small summit on the Ramsey Line; it was intended that the station be named Sulby Siding but this was not adopted. The 1880 crossing lodge here was at first of unusual design; it was close to the track and was demolished in 1910 when it and the station were completely reconstructed, making for a feature quite unlike any other on the line: the small wooden goods shed, of MNR origin, survives. There is a raised platform and the station building boasts an unglazed awning forming half the gable of the full roof span. There is a siding on the south side, facing the Down trains, beside which is a cattle and goods bank; this siding continues along the rear of the platform.

The level crossing just beyond the station carries the road to Jurby. The locals prefer using Sulby Glen to Sulby Bridge station although the latter is slightly nearer the village which lies mainly between them; the former station's conveniences are used by villagers and visitors alike, Sulby Bridge having no such facilities, and these give Sulby Glen an importance quite beyond its primary function!

A little way further on, Kella crossing is passed; notable is the somewhat different and bijou gate house, built in November 1880 to accommodate the then-Permanent Way Inspector, John Cameron (later Manager of the MNR). The line is falling at 1/200 and 1/204 here; Sulby Bridge (13 m. : 68 minutes) comes next, a typical MNR structure with building on the south side of the line and palm trees fringe its northern boundary. Milepost 13 stands beside its passing loop and there is a siding off that loop serving a cattle bank. It was a loading point for the West Craig brickworks' traffic whose products were not of highest quality due to the high calcium carbonate content of the local clay. The level crossing on the east end of the station carries the road to the north-east of the Island and the bridge, after which the station is named, is a fine one on the adjacent main road.

The railway now passes through a relatively uninteresting stretch of country until Ramsey is reached. One mile east of Sulby Bridge station comes a crossing with a minor road to the Point of Ayre at Ellenbane (originally Ellanbane): the usual lodge building is on the right hand. Continuing, hills to the south have retreated somewhat and although The

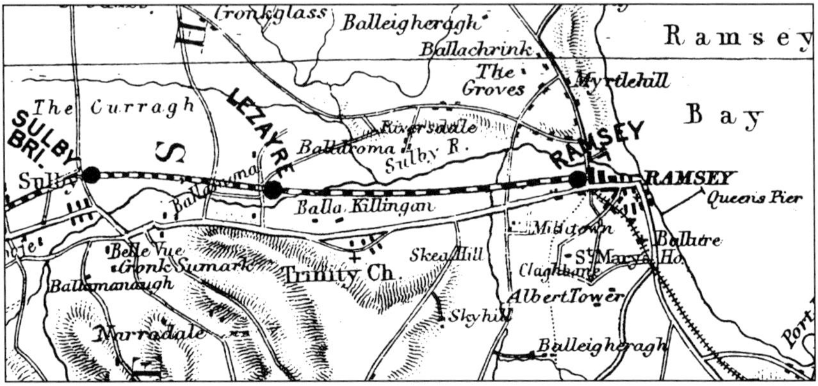

Curragh is left behind, the line now passes through flat meadowland virtually devoid of outstanding features. Just prior to Lezayre level crossing (14¾ m.: 73 minutes) the little station of that name is reached - again, on the right side. The Sulby River has followed us on the right ever since Sulby Bridge, and Lezayre can only be reached from the south by road by passing through a ford - a causeway serves for pedestrians.

Lezayre received its 1880 masonry building after it opened and a siding was added mainly to serve the nearby Ballakillingan Estate in 1884: the original intention was to name it Garey, after a nearby farmstead. Its telegraph instrument was removed in 1884 as the MNR was so short of cash that another (to install at its new St John's station terminus on the Foxdale line), could not be afforded. The gate signal is on the Ramsey side only and worked from the foot of the post, and the crossing lodge is on the north side; the building is alike to no other and has decorative quoins in yellow brick. Its siding (mainly used for lime traffic) was lifted in 1926 and the materials taken to St Germain's (q.v.). Last used by school trains, it has 'enjoyed' a status quite common on the IOMR, of being of the 'Now you see me, now you don't' category in the timetables. At this time of our journey it is treated as being closed and is not in the timetable but the courteous guard will stop the train by request without having his palm crossed by silver!

Lezayre station served a mainly rural area and was about half a mile from the parish church and a small collection of houses built around it; the church is a large building which has lost some of its congregation to the later Chapels of Ease at Sulby (St Stephen's) and west at Ramsey (St Olave's). The Parish of Kirk Khris Lezayre includes the village of Sulby and formerly, half of Ramsey. Along the route of the railway were corn and/or cloth mills at Sulby, Lezayre and at Milntown on the Glen Auldyn River. The scene today gives little evidence of past industry.

The accompanying Sulby River to our right changes course half a mile

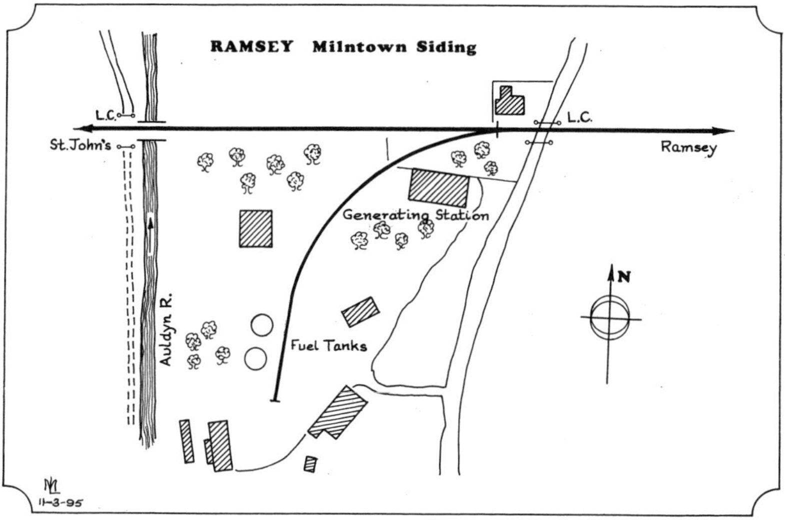

Milntown siding was used for oil traffic and had a short life. It was brought into use in August 1968, but had been lifted by October 1969. Not to scale.

beyond Lezayre and turns north-east so obliging the railway to cross it; since 1914 the bridge is of steel lattice girder type, when it replaced an older 80 ft 'bow-string' construction having a loop-shaped member over the track to connect the two side spans; it was known as The Basket Bridge from the appearance of this 'handle'. The present structure has an 84 ft span and as old names die hard, it still retains the nickname of its predecessor.* As with the other original MNR bridges, the incoming IOMR of 1905 regarded it with strong dislike.

Almost half a mile further along comes the bridge over the Auldyn River; it is a 40 ft span plate girder affair in wrought iron. After passing Milntown level crossing (Gardeners Lane) and lodge, the environs of Ramsey are reached - Milntown was an erstwhile Halt for a military camp.

Ramsey terminus (16½ m.: 77 minutes) is, (station buildings apart - these have some character) a dismal situation. Once situated on the western fringe of the town, the surrounding area is now being covered by municipal and commercial property, and housing estates: the station area stands immediately to the south bank of the river, and its long, prominent corrugated iron carriage shed 'to hold two trains' does nothing to improve its appearance. Like other stations on the Ramsey Line, its approach is protected by a fish-tailed semaphore signal.

Entering the station premises, ahead lies the passenger terminus and, to the

*MANX MUSEUM: R/177 drawing of 1879 bridge.

left the goods yard, goods and lead ore shed, and carriage shed. Beside the buffer stops at the platform end, stands the 2-engine-shed-cum-workshop: to the right, behind the main platform, 100 yds long, is a bay line (the 'New Road' of the early 1880s). The platform starts at ground level but in front of the station building (on the right) the original raised section survives.

The station building in Italianate style is unlike the now-familiar MNR type in red sandstone; it is of local stone, cement rendered and cream-painted, and having some architectural merit; it is, of course, far too ambitious in size for today's requirements, and its past importance as the administrative centre of a railway company, is entirely faded. Additional accommodation had been built onto the east end in the 1880s and there was once a considerable Refreshment Room. There is a run-round loop and alongside its headshunt is the interesting stone-built engine shed; evidence of its extension to house CALEDONIA in 1886 is clear from a difference in the walling and behind it, a long lean-to is used for stores. At the farthest end is a small workshop where overnight miracles were often performed. A 'Tank & Coke Stage' (to quote an old Plan) stands outside the shed doors, the tank being a wooden one on a brick plinth; the whole is quite derelict.

Returning now to the point where our train enters the station: a cattle bank and goods platform can be seen against the boundary wall on the extreme left, and this wall can be followed to the north-east corner of the site where it runs south and clockwise along the side of Bowring Road, so down and bordering the east edge of the premises. It returns to run west, and form a southern boundary wall to the station building: this last length becomes the frontage to Station Road and here the main entrance is to be found. This considerable stone wall encloses a triangle of ex-MNR land; along Bowring and Station Roads its appearance has been upgraded by cement rendering and bright yellow paint.

The main block is made up of two gable-ended pavilions with a recessed central entrance sheltered on the south face by an extension of the main roof. The slate-covered roofs have substantial overhang supported by brackets at the eaves and decorative barge boards at the gable ends; the chimneys have round-headed stone slabs functioning as pots. Roundheaded windows in the pavilion gables have ornamental cills supported on brackets, making for an all-together eye-catching building, intimating that a railway of some pride lay behind it.

In the north-east corner of the yard, the most northerly siding continues through a gate in the wall and crosses Bowring Road on a right-hand curve (there are no gates to protect the road) and becomes the start of the Harbour Tramway. Between this siding and the passenger station there stands (in order):

a) an open area once the site of J.R. Cowell's timber yard*
b) a siding with stockaded coal stack and the currently-used water tank, built in 1920

*J.R. Cowell was a director of the MNR: the firm later became Cowell & Wattleworth, regularly referred to, and mis-spelt as just 'Cowle's'.

Plate 1: Douglas, with the railway station in its proudest days in the centre of the picture. Looking further eastwards and beyond, are the inner and outer harbours. In foreground lies part of the wooded Nunnery Estate. *Manx Technical Publications*

Plate 6: Signalman's view of THE VIKING as it rumbles into Douglas from Port Erin, carrying 'express' headlamps (an obviously fresh mainland-inspired publicity innovation). *Peter Dobson*

Plate 6: Signalman's view of THE VIKING as it rumbles into Douglas from Port Erin, carrying 'express' headlamps (an obviously fresh mainland-inspired publicity innovation). *Peter Dobson*

Plate 4: A morning working bound for the North Line awaits 'Right-away' in the arrival platform at Douglas. It is almost 10.15 am and the safety valves on Nos. 3 & 5 are lifting. The train will divide at St John's; No. 3 will run ahead there and when No. 5 with the first pair of coaches bound for Peel has gone forward, will back down on the remainder and make for Ramsey. April 1957. *J.I.C. Boyd*

Plate 5: A spirited duo exits from Douglas, with No. 4 on the nearer South Line and No. 12 *en route* for St John's. Always a fine double-act, with musical accompaniment from chimneys and cylinder drain cocks. 1936. *C.E. Box*

Plate 2: Douglas station concourse was a fine structure, giving access to trains for cars and vans in its ample capaciousness. February 1967. *D.A. Robinson*

Plate 3: Looking towards Douglas terminal buildings, the nearer rake of carriages occupies the South Line arrival platform. Other stock is stabled in the run-round loop. 1962. *J.I.C. Boyd*

Plate 1: Douglas, with the railway station in its proudest days in the centre of the picture. Looking further eastwards and beyond, are the inner and outer harbours. In foreground lies part of the wooded Nunnery Estate. *Manx Technical Publications*

Plate 7: Westward the tracks reach out from Douglas terminal; the lines leading to the Carriage Sheds on the left are served by a headshunt. May 1961. *J.I.C. Boyd*

Plate 8: A Peel-bound train leaves the environs of Douglas and passes beneath Pulrose bridge. Traces of the former level crossing can be seen. April 1960. *J.I.C. Boyd*

Plate 9: A Sunday morning at Kirk Braddan Halt, and worshippers from the nearby church - dressed to conform with Sunday habits before the Second War - rejoin the special train to return to Douglas. July 1933. *H.C. Casserley*

Plate 10: The Peel Line approaches Union Mills (out of sight in the trees) at Snugborough river bridge, itself rebuilt to cope with flood waters. To the right stood the erstwhile Racecourse Halt. May 1961. *J.I.C. Boyd*

Plate 11: Crosby station seen from the west and looking towards Douglas and showing the considerable length of the loop. March 1962. *J.I.C. Boyd*

Plate 12: Seen from the north-east and the road over the Foxdale Branch station at St John's, a Peel train stands in the distance. Half-hidden is a Ramsey train, its engine detached to take water. May 1961. *J.I.C. Boyd*

Plate 13: The sand and gravel pit in the land between the main line and the Foxdale Branch, St John's. There was a temporary 3 ft gauge siding off the Branch into the pit (*extreme right*). 1936.
C.E. Box

Plate 14: Beyond the west end of St John's station, and looking towards Peel, could be seen the left track bound for Peel and the right (ex-MNR) heading for Ramsey; there was no connection between the two except at the east end of the station. From off the ex-MNR line, is the junction for the Foxdale Branch, and its squat semaphore signal. 1936.
C.E. Box

Plate 15: No. 4 approaches Peel with a mixed train; it has just passed Glenfaba Mill and under the bridge, and traverses that section of railway which was diverted to avoid floods. The telegraph/telephone lines are duplicated. *J.I.C. Boyd Collection*

Plate 16: From off the riverside along the last few yards into Peel, a horse and wagon might appear unexpectedly to cross the line on the level and enter the Glenfaba brickworks. The tramway was 'metalled' with discarded bricks to assist the horse. 1935. *J.I.C. Boyd Collection*

Plate 17: The horse drawing its loaded wagon from the Glenfaba 'quarry' along the riverside towards the railway crossing. The plain wheels of the vehicle and tram-plates are conspicuous. *c.* 1935. *J.I.C. Boyd Collection*

Plate 18: A heavy morning train drifts into Peel with steam to spare. The first three coaches have succumbed to sagging. Only the bare bones of the engine shed extension remain. 9th July, 1959. *J.I.C. Boyd*

Plate 19: The exterior of Peel station contrasts markedly with the ancient sandstone-built warehouse on the right of the picture; one of the most attractive buildings to grace any narrow gauge railway, it reflects the good taste of the IOMR Company. October 1992. *J.I.C. Boyd*

Plate 20: Seen from the slopes of St Patrick's Isle, work is in hand to widen the causeway across the head of Fenella Bay connecting Peel Castle with the West Quay. In the centre right is a row of narrow gauge tip wagons on a timber staging and a reversing neck leads back to the foot of the incline on Corrin's Hill. *J. Valentine*

Plate 21: Taken at the same time as *Plate 20* but viewed from the other direction, the causeway construction is part-hidden on the left. In the centre foreground is the tramway engine shed with the upperworks of the vertical boiler locomotive apparent: a staging with another vertical boiler steam unit is

Plate 22: Along the South Line: looking west at Map Ref. 320714 on the Port Erin side of 'Beehive Curve', the overbridge at Ballaquaggin carries the old Douglas-Castletown road, close by milepost 5. April 1993. *J.I.C. Boyd*

Plate 23: A brilliant evening at Santon with its venerable building, viewed towards Douglas. The last train of the day has gone; only the motor-caravan despoils the timelessness. May 1993. *J.I.C. Boyd*

Plate 24: Port Erin-bound, No. 4 hustles its morning train through Santon road bridge.

J.I.C. Boyd

Plate 25: The former station building at Ballasalla, seen here in April 1966, has been replaced; the semi-rural background is now entirely commercial. '*Et nova et vetera*'. *J.I.C. Boyd*

Plate 26: The period of the Ailsa Régime is evidenced by the ex-British Rail containers mounted on carriage underframes at Castletown: August 1968 - but not many passengers in sight. *J.I.C. Boyd*

Plate 27: A wintry landscape at Colby in February 1901, showing immaculate trackwork; the Mull Hills show on the left and the engine house and chimney of the abandoned Ballacorkish Mine appear on the right-hand skyline. *J.I.C. Boyd Collection*

Plate 28: Port Erin is approached, shrouded in sea mist during a hot August 1947. The Port St Mary Home signal stands left; that for Port Erin, on the right. The permanent way suffers from wartime neglect. *J.I.C. Boyd*

c) a siding ending beside the stone-built goods and lead ore shed ('The Lead Stores'). Its history in connection with the Isle of Man Mining Co. has already been described (Vol. I). It is a multi-doored building with a siding on each side, partially protected either side by an awning of corrugated iron projecting from the building
d) the long double-road carriage shed in corrugated iron which would hold the entire coaching stock of the MNR: protection from the salt-laden atmosphere was most desirable. Standing opposite much of the main passenger platform as it does, it is a gloomy backcloth for the waiting passenger and is in strong contrast even to the goods shed, which though of mundane purpose, has pleasing features

Personal approval of the shelter from wind and room afforded by a timber and glass porch standing in front of the station building on the platform side is to the credit of a place so exposed to the elements: it is equally acceptable on hot gusty days when the wind blows clouds of dust and grit from off the surface of the yard.

The Ramsey Line received a continuing programme of minor alterations to its signalling and point operation; detailed examination of Ramsey station photographs reveals small changes in pointwork, and elimination of the original cast-iron box-type point levers by more modern pattern. Presumably these are due to the life-expiry of equipment.

An official Civil Engineering Survey of the MNR in 1894 made summary of its construction:

> . . . several heavy cuttings through boulder clay on the West Section . . . two viaducts with lattice girders having three spans of 60 ft each mounted on splendid native stone piers: the ironwork of each weighs 50 tons . . . twenty-four bridges of varying span 20-50 ft, the latter a bow-string over the Sulby River . . . platforms are dispensed with save at three important stations, and then those are only 12 in. high . . . along the route there are nine stations and eleven gatekeeper's houses. The Ruling Gradient is 1/100 and the sharpest curve of 20 chains radius . . .

On our journey between St John's and Ramsey we should have been extremely fortunate to distinguish all of these!

****

Note: much of the foregoing railway has now been designated an official footpath but the passage of same is not always easy in places. In particular it should be noted that owing to subsidence, track formation between St. Germain's and Glen Mooar has been materially affected and the Gradient Diagram should be used to determine the original situation. (1994).

The article in ENGINEERING 1879 (ii) p. 211 describing the route contains dimensions of bridges which are no longer pertinent as all these and similar structures had been rebuilt at the period of this description i.e. late 1940s.

ST JOHN'S

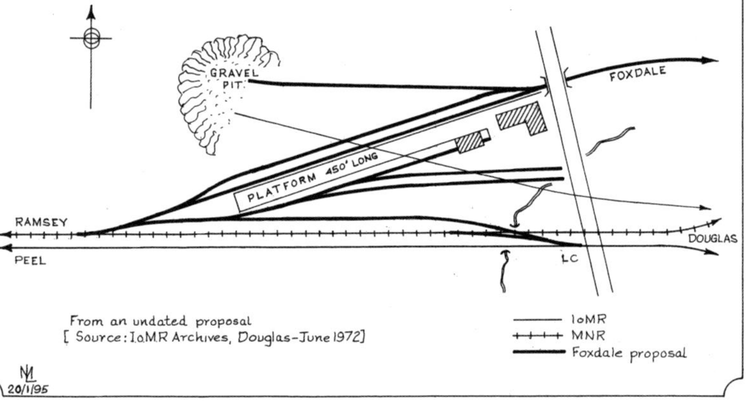

St.JOHN'S
Sand & Gravel Pit Sidings as at 1938

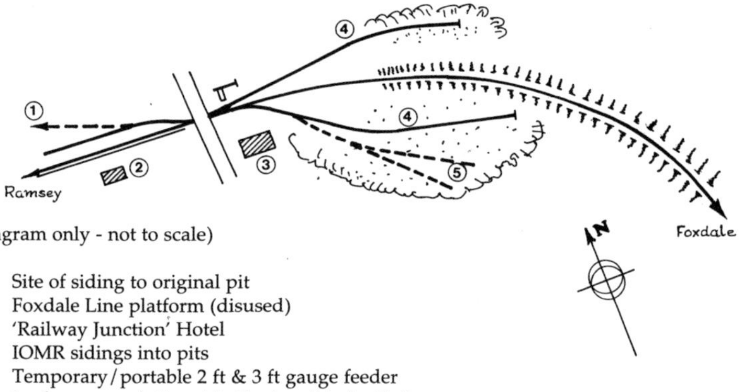

(Diagram only - not to scale)

1 Site of siding to original pit
2 Foxdale Line platform (disused)
3 'Railway Junction' Hotel
4 IOMR sidings into pits
5 Temporary / portable 2 ft & 3 ft gauge feeder tracks accomadating side-tipping skip-bodied wagons

Note: the siding into the IOMR Company's pit east of the Foxdale Line overbridge, is omitted.

St John's (incl.) - Foxdale

The Foxdale Branch (formerly the Foxdale Railway itself) begins at a junction facing towards Ramsey and veering away from the main IOMR Peel-Douglas line as it approaches St John's, 12 chains west of St John's level crossing. This unusual arrangement has its origins in the history of the independent Manx Northern and Foxdale Railways (Vol. I). Leaving the junction the Branch enters a separate St John's station at first used as a temporary terminus for MNR trains from Ramsey known as St John's (New) and opened in July 1884. The permanent station has a low platform, not an original feature, and a red brick building with yellow quoins on the south side; on the opposite side stands a water tank on a brick plinth, water being pumped by means of a large handwheel. This station dates from the opening of the FR in 1886 and is but a slight modification of the 1884 situation - its wooden building was transferred to Waterfall. There is a run-round loop and over the boundary to the north side is a considerable excavation, the site of Dumbell's sand and gravel pit, once served by a siding from the IOMR and latterly from off the run-round loop. Beyond the platform the Castletown-St John's road plate girder bridge crosses the line, being that same road as forms a level crossing with the IOMR/MNR single lines lower down the hill. A flight of steps from it descends to the platform; there are some mature trees around. At the west end of the platform is a 9-lever open ground frame, virtually derelict these days. Almost under the bridge a turnout serves various sand and gravel pits closed in the late 1930s. The Branch begins a climb of 1/48.6 here; it continues almost without break into Foxdale, and the minimum curve is 10 chains radius.

It will be recalled that the FR was opened to the occasional (but not regular) mineral train from June 1886 and that that Company had been leased to, and was worked by, the MNR under Agreement commencing on 3rd January, 1885, so that from the initial junction the route was actually the property of a third Island railway company. Passing beside the Railway Junction Hotel and sandpits on left and right, the line climbs on by a sweeping 22 chain right-hand and curved embankment to pass over the IOMR almost at right angles by means of a stone and Maughold-brick arched bridge. To comply with IOMR complaints the arch is wide enough to contain two parallel tracks, though in fact advantage was never taken of it.

This high embankment carries the line, now straightening out, over a bridge comprising of two steel plate girders of 47 ft 6 in. span each with a central pier 5 ft wide, and it crosses both the St John's-Castletown road and the Foxdale River; it is well-buttressed and evidence of that trouble with the contractor (Vol. I, p. 183) is clearly seen in the north abutment.

This viaduct, (Gill's Bridge) is the main civil engineering feature of the

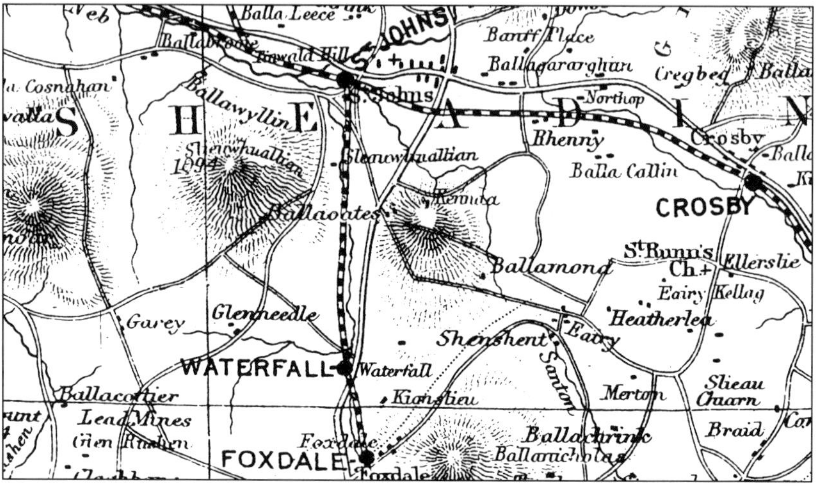

Branch although there are considerable earthworks all the way to Foxdale. At first the railway uses the west side of the river, the road being on the other, and with the river in the bottom, all three thread the valley with its steep west side. The slopes of Slieau Whallian (1,092 ft) rise sharply above the railway track which runs on a shelf above the river; this lower part of the valley is quite unspoilt by the mining which takes place a little way beyond. The early part of the route is partially in cutting and passes through considerable afforestation. The present-day course now joins the proposed route of 1882, having followed the revised 1884 scheme up to here. The first mile ends with a straight section within cutting, followed by a curve beside an old mine (west side) on a considerable embankment and the gradient now eases slightly to 1/50 for the remainder of the way. The line, though seldom used, is clear of weed due to the use of waste material from the mines containing lead as a form of 'ballast'. The track is as first laid, using chairs to support the flat bottomed rails.

Another curve through a short cutting brings the railway nearer the river and road on the opposite bank; habitation appears and grows more insistent as Lower Foxdale is reached. A minor road to Ballanass leaves from opposite, crosses the river near waterfalls and climbs up to pass over the Branch by a steel bridge with concrete abutments. After crossing a stream by a small two-span bridge the railway reaches Waterfall Halt (1m. 73 ch.) - which was first intended to be Hamilton Waterfall or alternatively, Lower Foxdale. During its active life, it was variously termed Waterfalls or Waterfall, both titles being used by its owners and operators. Within weeks of being opened, its agent was dismissed and the Foxdale Station Master was given the additional responsibility. By 1898 its loop had been lifted and the ground frame taken out, the station being de-rated to an unstaffed Halt. The station building (ex-St John's of 1884) was removed by 1905 and by the date of this account a small wooden shed (more at home in a garden) does duty . . . perhaps the ganger's tools are kept therein?

An overbridge carries a farm road to Ballamore and after another reverse curve the line passes over the road by a 30 ft span plate girder bridge on the skew, (the Hamilton or Luke Bridge) supported on concrete abutments. The temptingly bare surfaces of the girders caused the IOMR to paint/advertise its 'Two Day 5/- Go as you please' (introduced August 1927!) runabout tickets thereon: whilst the lettering remained constant, the figure showing the fare was amended (upwards) by repainting each successive year. There was a wooden fence between road and railway on the south side which did not please Greenbank in 1905.

Foxdale is almost reached, heralded by the straggling village on each side of the road, more in keeping with a Welsh mining community. The railway now uses a section of embankment supported each side by stone retaining walls.

As the terminus is neared, the immense piles of 'arisings' from the mines, and dumped hereabouts, rear their heads which are quite bare of any vegetation and though plundered from time to time (latterly to make runways during the recent war) they are still formidable in size.* [The original intention was to curve eastwards here, cross the river and terminate on its east bank, on the south side of the Foxdale-Braaid road.] A final length of straight line heads to the terminus (2¾ m.: 14 minutes from St John's). The station and low platform are to the west of the line and have features similar to St John's: the platform was raised 'at the last minute', and a water tank on it was of wood. The reduced fortunes of the station building are clear enough: from time to time it is let off and since May 1926 when it was leased to the guard of the Branch train @ 3s. a week, it has ceased to have railway usage.

The materials of the building are similar to the Company's station at St John's, using red brick with yellow quoins and string course, the chimney stacks being of the same materials. The frontage had a recessed shelter provided with a wood and glass screen; and recently, the south end has been rendered to make it weatherproof.

As with most other stations on the Island, the Inspector had insisted on a prominent clock but here and at St John's there was the additional luxury of a wall-mounted drinking fountain.

The water tank was carried on a brick tower built by John Glen, and in similar style to the station - originally carrying a rectangular tank, it now supports a cylindrical metal one. The 9-lever ground frame on the platform has been removed and all pointwork has ground levers.

*Reduction of this material has taken place 1886-1911 and 1936-1953.

There is a run-round and traces of temporary tracks used to clear the dumps - spoil trains ran infrequently until 1943 and the last trains of all operated on 22nd and 26th January, 1960. There is now no trace of FR signalling at either Waterfall or Foxdale, but that at St John's is complete though out of use. The running line continues for a few yards beyond the platform and finally buries itself in a dead-end supported by shoring. There is a high-level loading platform on its east side and here narrow gauge trolleys from the mines unloaded their bags of ore into low-sided MNR (or) vehicles. The Foxdale-Braaid road passes within feet of the Branch end.

A singular feature of the small siding layout to the north-west of the station was a space-saving scissors crossover.

The mines were reached by a connection which led off behind the station building and climbed steeply, crossing the aforesaid road on the level (no gates): beyond the roadway the track has been lifted and its arrangement can only be deduced from old maps - this connection is now dismantled, but it passed the FR Co.'s corrugated iron goods shed, inconveniently situated on the steep gradient (about 1/12), and there was a transfer platform: wagons passing in and out of the mine area would be held up by wagons standing at that platform. Two separate 3 ft gauge tracks debouched from the mine premises by gateway and shed door respectively, each crossed the road and converged on the wharf at the high-level platform where two MNR wagons could be accommodated. The peak output from these mines was achieved before the arrival of the railway though the peak output of lead was reached in 1892 and a lesser tonnage of copper in 1882. Along a 'line' of about 2½ miles, there were thirteen mine shafts; the workings around the Branch terminus were the most successful.

It is timely to speculate on the short life-expectancy of many mine-connected railways in Great Britain; that to Foxdale proved to be no exception. Looking back, every mine in the area had been abandoned by 1819 but the Foxdale Mine itself was leased from the Duke of Atholl in 1823 by one, Knott of Kendal. His tenure was short but by 1830 the district was said to be 'flourishing' again and the Foxdale Mining Co. was set up in 1853. Hindsight comes easily, and by the time the railway reached Foxdale, things might have been different if the promoters had realised that the high-noon of Foxdale was passing.

The Knockaloe Branch

Apart from the extension along Peel Harbour,* a Knockaloe Branch was opened on 1st September, 1915 as a wartime measure to serve 20,000 persons in the Alien Detention Camp on the south side of Corrin's Hill, above and west of the village of Patrick. From its junction (which faced Peel) on the east side of the road bridge at Glenfaba, the line curved sharply south and over the River Neb. The junction point was locked by the patent 'Annett's Key' on the single line staff, the equipment being used later for the quarry siding laid in at Peel Road station. After the bridge the Branch climbed at a remarkably steep inclination, parallel to but east of the road to Glen Maye, which it crossed on the level by a sharp curve and entered the camp precincts which lay on the west side of the road. It continued to climb on the south side of the Camp road, still very steeply, and ended about ½ mile from the level crossing. The whole Branch was right-angular in shape, each arm being about ½ mile in length. Buildings have now obliterated the roadside section, and alterations to the river (now channelled into the original Glenfaba Mill sluice) have removed part of the banking near the junction, but the abutments for the wooden Neb bridge and some cutting may still be discerned.

It would seem that the up grade here was at least 1/20. Engine No. 15 CALEDONIA was used on the line.

This Branch brought much-needed troop, alien and supplies traffic to the IOMR. On the curve between the junction and the Neb bridge there was a passing loop; here the engine ran to the rear of the train which it propelled up the bank for safety reasons. There was a long siding alongside the Patrick road and to the left of ascending trains, entered by a facing point, serving the laundry; the track then curved away in order to swing to the right hand over the road, and on this curve was another loop and a goods shed. After crossing the road (Patrick church is immediately beside the crossing place) it entered the Camp proper, passing the Guard Room and Construction Office. Climbing up the main Camp road there was a facing siding on the left serving the Quartermaster's Stores; a short loop, then a long loop followed, serving Hospital, further Guard Room, Catering Store and Bakery: also two sidings marked the terminus within the Administration Block, these served the Power House to which coal was brought, Anthracite Store, Canteen Store, etc.

Omitted from this semi-official list of buildings, compiled no doubt when the Camp was completed, is the Engine Shed. It is possible to give this building an air of mystery for the official Plan of the site (see p. 72) does not list one, but the Shed, which survives, *is* shown on the Plan yet without any rails leading into it. Perhaps the building was not yet commandeered when the Plan was prepared?

*The Peel station commencement of the siding can be seen on left of illustration in RAILWAY MAGAZINE, July 1923, p. 5.

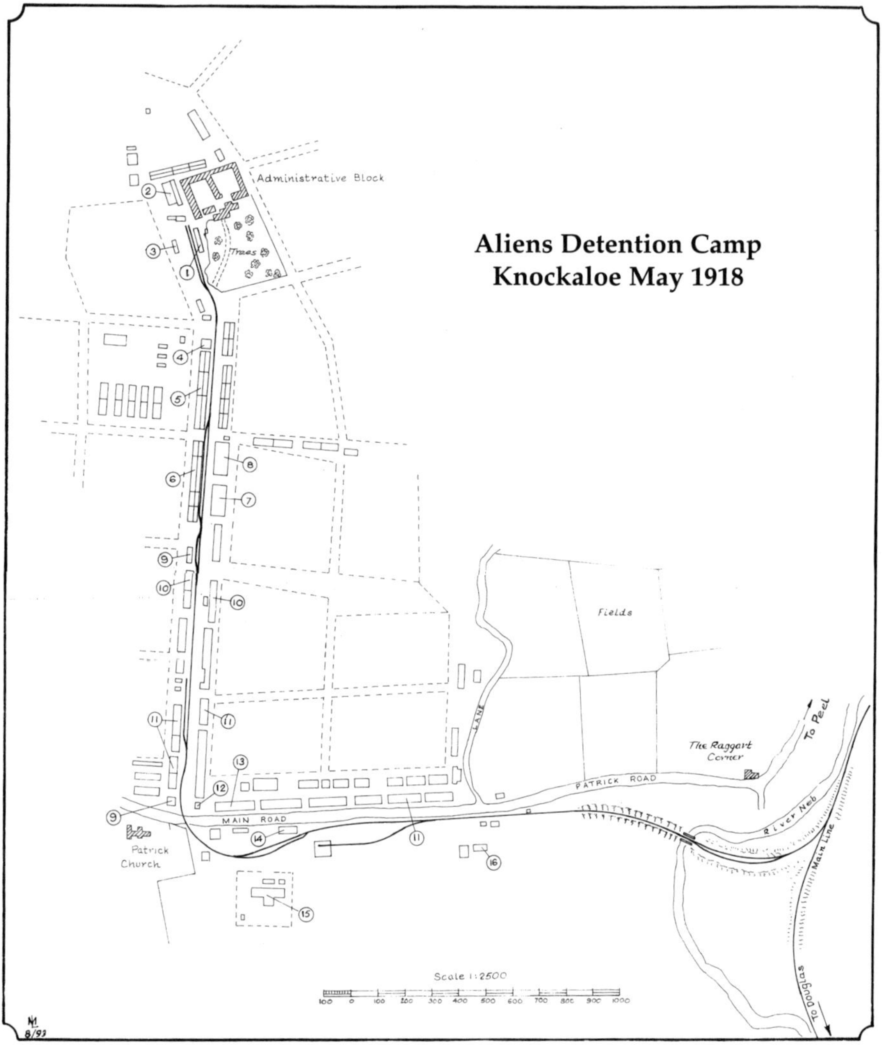
Aliens Detention Camp
Knockaloe May 1918
Administrative Block
Trees
Fields
LANE
The Raggart
Corner
PATRICK ROAD
MAIN ROAD
Patrick
Church
River Neb
Main Line
To Peel
To Douglas
Scale 1:2500
100 0 100 200 300 400 500 600 700 800 900 1000

To complete the mystery one must refer to the Engine Shed at Peel where an extension built in timber and corrugated-iron has long been assumed to have been built to house No. 15 during its service at Knockaloe. 'Housed' at Peel the engine may have been, but the extension was not put up until the Camp had been abandoned, and with surplus materials from huts.

To return to the Shed at Knockaloe; this is a longish low building built in stone with a door at the east end; the original roof was possibly of corrugated-iron. It probably housed farm implements and is un-necessarily long for but one engine. However, the roof trusses at the east end have been modified in simple fashion to give more clearance, as at that time the chimney of CALEDONIA was a tall one.

Tradition has it that the engine was usually kept at Peel . . . without shelter. Human nature being what it is, it was stabled there because it was more convenient for the train crew. Equally, legend has it that, when required, No. 15 was shedded at Knockaloe. There is a good case for both to be correct.

This was a most unusual system, and on account of the gradient, and the amount of traffic it carried, it had operating problems quite outside the normal experience of the Company. Built on behalf of the British Government - as was the associated Peel Quay line - by Baldry, Yerburgh & Hutchinson Ltd., it was closed on 14th October, 1920 and lifted 1923-24. Today only the Administration Block remains, forming part of the Agricultural Station.

Map Key

1	Locomotive Shed (no track shown on official plan)
2	Canteen Store
3	Power House, Anthracite & Coal store
4	Guard Room
5/6	Hospital (buildings opposite 4-5 are Canteen?)
7/8	Bungalows
9	Guard Room
10	Catering Stores & Bakery
11	Quartemaster's Stores & Laundry
12	Guard Post
13	Construction Office
14	(Not known)
15	Patrick Church
16	(Not known)

The purpose of all buildings is not recorded e.g. sleeping quarters for aliens. Identification is needed. Some erections must be living quarters etc. for the military.

Civil Engineering

(In this Section more-extended detail and / or earlier reference is made of the following features):

Feature	*Date*
Turntables (proposed)	1876 & 1961
Turntable (installation)	1923-25
'Basket' Bridge	1879
Foxdale River Viaduct	1886
Glen Mooar Viaduct	1879
Glen Wyllin Viaduct	1879
Nunnery Bridge	1895 & 1978
Other principal bridges	
Stations & Halts	
Level Crossings	
Structure Gauges	

Turntables

Some discussion had taken place in 1876 and correspondence survives* regarding the desirability of installing turntables at the three terminii (Vol. I pp.94-95, 99), following some cogent demonstration by Hunt about the amount of flange wear caused by bunker-first running to the driving wheels under the cab. In consequence the Board, in an effort to keep down expense, compromised by agreeing to a turntable at Douglas but for reasons unexplained such was never obtained, much to the bitterness of Hunt. He wrote'. . .If we had only one turntable at Douglas we should be in the same position as now as the engines perform half their work in hauling trains attached to either end . . . Thus the trailing wheels running first have not only the friction caused by the contact of their flanges against the outside rail of a curve but also the additional strain caused by the action of the train in its tendency to assume a straight line.' An explanatory diagram accompanied his observations but knowing the composition of the Board and the financial stringency then obtaining, it did not bring Hunt's desired effect.

A second attempt to install a turntable was more successful. In 1923 negotiations were begun with Messrs Ransome & Rapier Ltd. of Ipswich to purchase a 35 ft diameter (loading 55 tons) turntable manufactured for the 3 ft gauge West Clare Railway delivery of which had not been taken owing to that Railway being a target for destruction during the Irish Civil War. After haggling over a price and a suitable site on the IOMR, the table was placed on the south side of the ex-Foxdale Railway station at St John's, its use being

*In Tower Collection

mainly for turning stock - but not locomotives - to ensure even exposure to weathering and extend the life of paintwork. Little use was made of it after 1955. (For full account see Vol. II pp.65-70.)

The matter of yet another turntable comes under the heading, 'Now you see one, now you don't' for this was a piece of equipment much needed, sought-after, quoted-for and finally turned down by the IOMR. And despite everything, the turntable in question *was* bought, shipped into Douglas and secreted away until in the mid-1970s when the Company decided to clear out the buildings in Douglas. At this abysmal stage, smaller items were loaded into an Empress Van and larger ones - almost all being rolling stock in an advanced state of dereliction - moved out to Ballasalla yard for sale etc. (see Vol. II p.189). The larger items were dragged from behind the Douglas Carriage Shed where some had stood in a jungle of natural and man-made carnage for more years than could be recalled. Those which could still run on wheels made their exit with some decency but the wrecks were loaded haphazardly on any suitable cripple to make the journey; it was the forerunner of Ethnic Cleansing in a railway context.

Among this collection of vintage junk was an item which had hitherto escaped notice; Shaw had bought 'some parts for a turntable' at the CDRJC auction in March 1961(see Vol. II p.152). From correspondence following this event, Shaw's instructions were to buy two railcars and two turntables. The IOMR wrote to The Hammond Lane Metal Co. Ltd., Dublin on 29th April, 1961 explaining that they had intended to buy the railcar turntable at Killybegs but found it had already been bought by Hammond. It still lay at Killybegs; could the IOMR buy it, and if so, would the CDRJC dismantle and ship it? Hammond offered to sell for £85 *in situ* but on 13th May, the IOMR wrote, 'having regard to the difficulty and cost of transport we have decided not to do business on this occasion'. So just what was the origin of the turntable which emerged from the shambles at Douglas in November 1974, purchased by Manx Metals along with other redundant material, for scrap? It was decidedly not the re-incarnation of 'some parts for a turntable' (for which labour was not available).

The turntable itself was unusual as it was constructed around the cut-down frames of a Donegal Railway's Class '2' 4-6-0 tank engine, said to be the last of a class of six engines built in 1893 by Neilson & Co. Ltd. of Glasgow, and the forerunner of a type built later by other makers for the Letterkenny & Burtonport Extension Railway and the West Clare Railway. The last of this class were No.4 MEENGLAS and No. 8 FOYLE which are recorded as being 'dismantled' in 1937, and possibly No. 8's frame was the one in question. (No reliable account or description of the re-incarnation of locomotive to turntable has been published, but information given to the Author in March 1951 at Killybegs has been used.)

Sulby River Bridge
15 m. 26 ch.

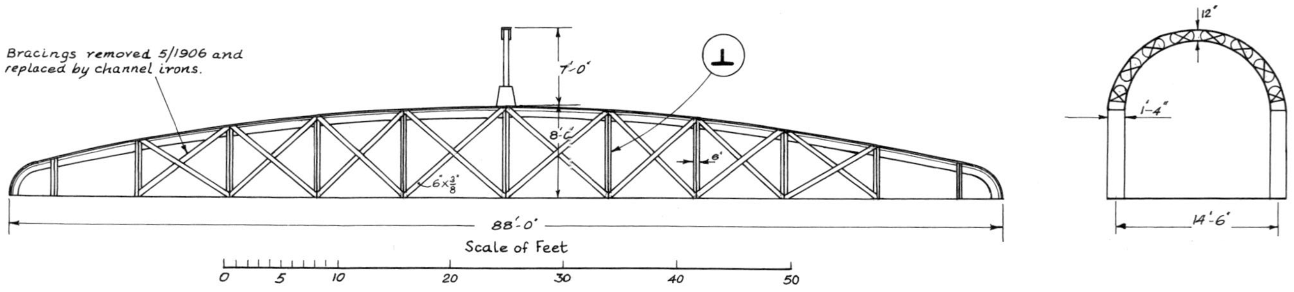

Drawing based on incomplete drawing in Manx Museum. Ref:- R177.

NL
17-4-95

The table itself was made by modifying the frames and cutting off the projections of the hornguides below the mainframe. Extensions to table length were made by simple cantilevers made from old rails (which were somewhat lightweight) and rollers to revolve the table were placed under the modified buffer beams of the original locomotive. Economy of construction was the keyword.

When so much IOMR history can be gleaned from extant paperwork, the full story of 'The turntable that never was' will only be known if the records are located.*

Paradoxically, at the present time the Railway is seeking a turntable for precisely the same purpose as declared in the early 1920s (see Vol. II p.65).

Sulby ('Basket') Bridge

The bridge at 15 m. 26 ch. from St John's over the river near Sulby was that ex-MNR structure which caused the most concern to the IOMR. As already noted, Allott was employed to make inspection of ex-MNR bridges, this taking place on 10th November, 1913; he confirmed the weakness of this and the two viaducts over Glens Wyllin and Mooar respectively. The IOMR agreed to renew all three and employ Allott as Consulting Engineer in place of the elderly Henry Greenbank who was now unfitted for such tasks†. The existing truss-girder bridge had already been strengthened in May 1906 when the cross bracings were replaced with channel iron girders. The truss span was 88 ft long with a height of 8 ft in the centre tapering down completely at each end. A head-stay arched over the centre line of the trusses, giving 6 ft clearance headroom below; the width between side members was 13 ft 2 in. (it was the basket-handle appearance of the head-stay which gave rise to the nick-name)#.

The new bridge was of different design giving 13 ft 6in. clear in width between the side members. Seven firms tendered for the work, Francis Morton & Co. Ltd. being the most competitive and chosen (despite an expression of dissatisfaction with them in replacing the bridge at Quarter Bridge in 1902-03 with a lattice girder span supplied by The Phoenix Foundry), lattice girder spans and Hobson's Patent Flooring were to be used again, being chosen for Nunnery and Quarter Bridge bridges previously.

It was intended to complete the work for the Summer Timetable of 1914 but so heavy was traffic that replacement did not take place until Sunday

*A postscript to this matter comes in the discovery of a crude sketch on the reverse of a piece of scrap paper; dated 30th May, 1961 it gives the overall length of the table as 36 ft 2 in., which included the cantilevers, each 6 ft 0 in. long. It ran on a circle of rails 22 ft 6 in. diameter. Another entry says Shaw 'bought the turntable seen at Strabane' (where all items for auction had been collected).

†See Vol. II pp.39-40

#Drawing Ref: R/177 Manx Museum.

Drawings for the new bridge: 87 ft girders, 79 ft 9 in. span: dated 7th April, 1914.
Ref: R/95/6/7/8. R/231 Manx Museum.

PLATE 7. GLEN WYLLIN VIADUCT.

RECONSTRUCTION OF GLEN WYLLIN VIADUCT.

Fig. 1

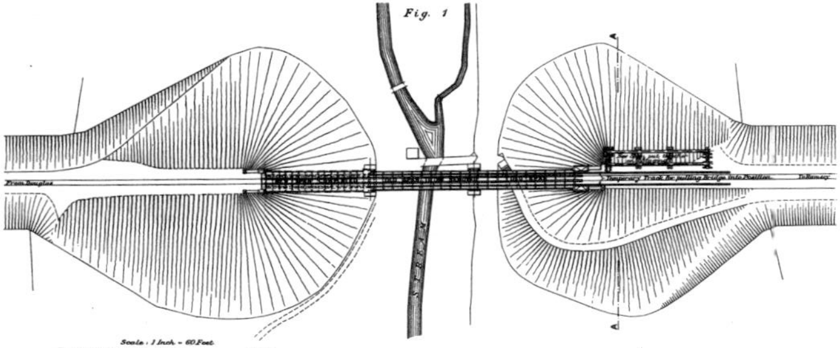

Scale: 1 Inch = 60 Feet.

PLAN OF SITE.

Fig. 2.

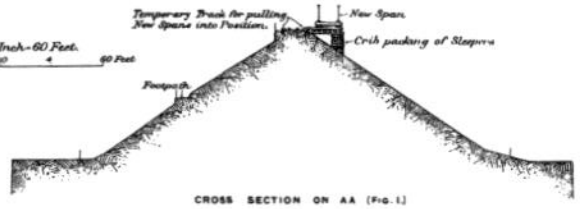

Scale: 1 Inch = 60 Feet.

CROSS SECTION ON AA (Fig. 1)

Fig. 3.

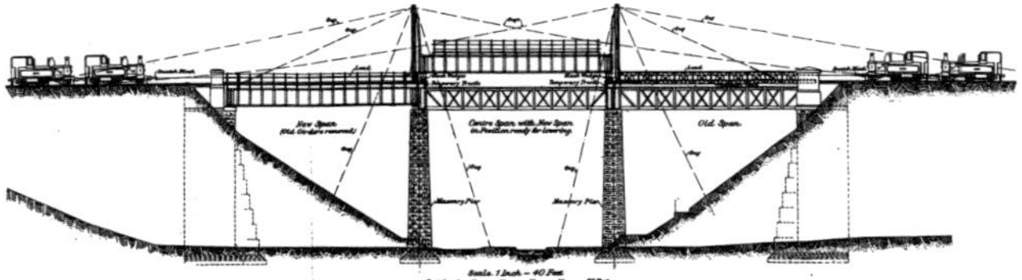

Scale: 1 Inch = 40 Feet.

ELEVATION SHOWING METHOD OF LOWERING NEW SPAN INTO POSITION.

Fig. 4.

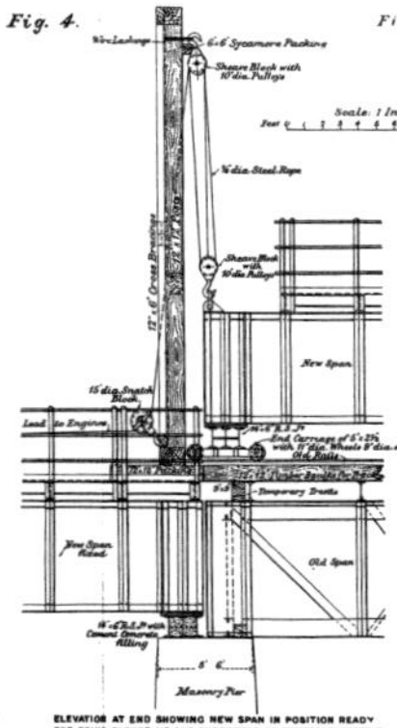

ELEVATION AT END SHOWING NEW SPAN IN POSITION READY FOR BEING PACKED UP AND SUPPORTED ON TEMPORARY TRESTLE

Fig. 5.

Scale: 1 Inch = 8 Feet

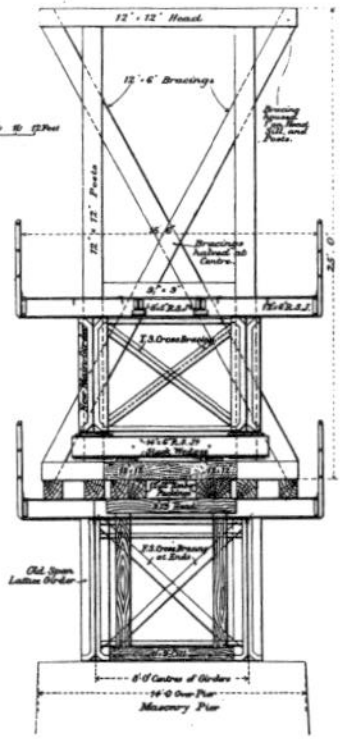

CROSS SECTION SHOWING NEW SPAN SUPPORTED ON TEMPORARY TRESTLE PREVIOUS TO OLD GIRDERS BEING MOVED OUT

Fig. 6.

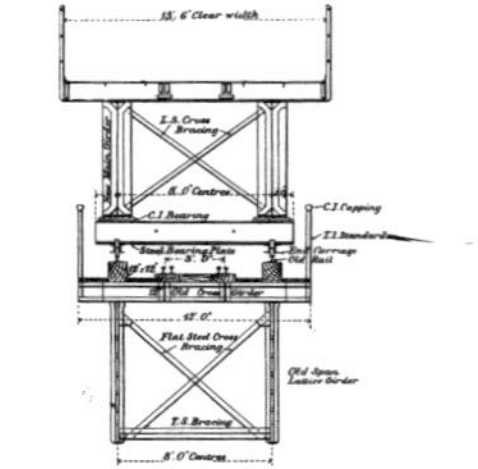

CROSS SECTION AT CENTRE SHOWING NEW SPAN ON OLD SPAN

Fig. 7.

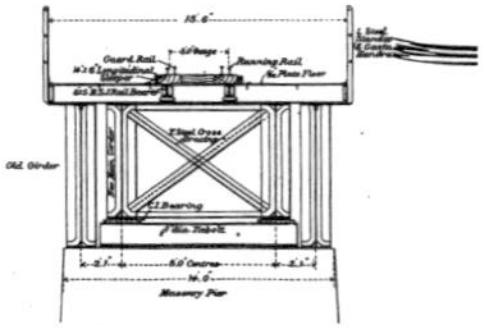

CROSS SECTION SHOWING NEW SPAN LOWERED INTO POSITION AND OLD GIRDERS MOVED OUT.

29th November; it was accomplished by mounting the new spans to the south of, but alongside the old, on timber beams supporting old rails. The old bridge was slid bodily sideways northwards onto wooden beams, the new spans taking its place and allowing a test train to occupy the new work by afternoon. The whole was done in atrocious weather conditions under the eyes of Henry Allott and James Bradshaw (Locomotive Superintendent).

The locomotives used in the test were DERBY, MAITLAND, THORNHILL, and CALEDONIA and the last two-named (ex-MNR engines) were still working chimney-first out of Ramsey as they had always done.

Glen Mooar Viaduct (Phase 1 - 1914)

The IOMR Board had agreed to have wind bracings and other strengthening fitted despite the continuing of bad weather which had marked the substitution of Sulby Bridge. Francis Morton completed the work by the year-end; it was minor but essential, yet only costing £98. Allott allowed the speed limit to rise to 15 mph over it.

Glen Wyllin Viaduct

Urged by the IOMR for such, Allott intended to replace the existing work with an arched masonry structure for which drawings were prepared in December 1913 but, on finding the ground unsuited to take the weight, made fresh plans in May 1914 for a three-span plate girder bridge which would utilise the same piers as the existing bridge. The 1879 bridge consisted of three lattice-girder iron spans each 65 ft long x 7 ft 6 in. deep; examination showed extensive corrosion due to the salty atmosphere. Bracing to counteract side sway was minimal.

The new work was fully described in Paper No. 4247 read before the Institution of Civil Engineers, extracts of which mention:

> . . . .height of 55 ft above bell-shaped valley . . . original of very light construction, imperfectly braced laterally . . . design of the old structure did not allow use of additional girders or . . . means of partial reconstruction . . . main girders of new work are about 6 ft deep . . . weight of each span is about 40 tons . . . a staging to reconstruct the work in steel would have cost the same amount as the value of steel work when erected . . .

A timber staging was erected on the slope of the embankment at the north-west end of the bridge. Suitably floored, the three span units were assembled thereon with the aid of the IOMR 8-ton crane, the parts having been brought to the site in wagons. A temporary rail track resting on 12 in. square timbers was then laid over the bridge. The crane was used to erect a pair of lifting legs at one end of the span and the permanent track over that span was removed.

The new span was drawn sideways off the staging, two-wheeled trolleys fastened either end, and with the attachment of a long wire rope to a locomotive on the Ramsey side embankment, the new span was drawn along the temporary track.

The second pair of lifting legs was then removed to the south end of the new span. With two locomotives on the embankment at each end, and using suitable tackle, the new span was lifted by the legs and then lowered onto temporary packing on top of the masonry piers. The old girders (all track etc. from within being removed) were slid out on greased strips to the extreme edge of the piers and the new girderwork was lowered to permanent position as the four locomotives reversed towards the bridge with the span suspended by the wire ropes.

Each span required possession of the line from 1 am Sunday to 5 am Monday, during which time the track would be replaced.

At first, dismantling of the old spans proved to be frustrating and time-consuming. They were 'very weak laterally, and of light construction and being laid on tarred felt, when the time came to slide them out, much of the felt had stuck to the underside and caused a lot of friction': they had to be lashed to the new spans owing to their weakness, so that they could be safely slid out. The final two spans created problems but the men became used to the drill and results were more quickly obtained. It was necessary to raise the track to a new level to cross the bridge.

The last old girder was slid more easily on a sandwich of grease between steel plates. The obsolete girders were suspended from the floors of the new spans, cut at the centre by acetylene flame and removed in halves by the 8 ton crane which carried them, suspended, to Kirk Michael station goods yard to be dismantled later.

Francis Morton & Co. Ltd. did the work under Allott's supervision; the Sundays on which the three new spans were lifted were 13th June, 11th July and 25th July, 1915: Lord Raglan the Governor witnessed the second phase. Tests did not occur until 19th September when DERBY, CALEDONIA and LOCH were involved.

Glen Mooar Viaduct

The opportunity was taken to verify the probable condition of this bridge by using portions of the dismantled Glen Wyllin structure for testing. This resulted in Allott forbidding double-heading and imposing a speed limit of 10-12 mph: further inspection took place in Spring 1916 but it was deemed unwise to begin improvements owing to a shortage of materials due to the First War. Faults in the piers, and misalignment, were found and attributed to poor construction.

In 1919 , among other schemes for lessening the slippage on The Donkey Bank, Allott suggested removing 20,000 tons of material above the track and so lighten the weight bearing down; this could be used to form an embankment and so replace the bridge. Dismayed at the estimated cost of this and other schemes involving Gob-y-Deigan, The Donkey Bank and Glen Mooar, more modest plans were evolved. The existing bridge was of three 60 ft long wrought-iron lattice members 7 ft 6 in. deep 75 ft above the bed of the river, with a girder deck. There was 65 ft between the piers and 12 ft between handrails. A new viaduct in steel and a culvert between two of the piers to check earth movement was less expensive and the IOMR approved Allott's ideas and costings in June 1919. Work began on the culvert in May 1920 while Morton again won the contract for the bridge which, due to rising costs and the War, would be more than three times the cost of Glen Wyllin. The first new span was placed between Sunday 29th May and Wednesday 1st June, 1921 and atrocious weather made it a hazardous undertaking. The other new spans went in on 19th-20th June and 10th-11th July and again the old spans were taken to Kirk Michael for dismantling in due course. A final test took place on 4th September; MAITLAND, KISSACK and THORNHILL coupled together were involved, THORNHILL still running chimney-first from Ramsey and without chimney numerals.

This time plate girder spans were not used in the renewal: delay in delivery of the new ones was due to the number of post-war strikes and they were of similar construction to the existing members save the new were of steel. Alterations to the tops of the piers exposing the plate-work at the ends of the new spans took place, and the original stonework encasing the ends was not replaced; this was to assist the movement of air and prevent corrosion inside the stonework.

[IOMR archives contain; 1. Morton's drawings of the Glen Wyllin contract. 2. Allott's blueprints dated 19th July, 1920 for Glen Mooar giving detail of the 8 ft gauge track used to draw the new spans into position, and a Plan of the ground.]

Foxdale River Bridge

The Foxdale Railway had two overbridges in close proximity shortly after leaving St John's and they shared the same embankment to carry FR

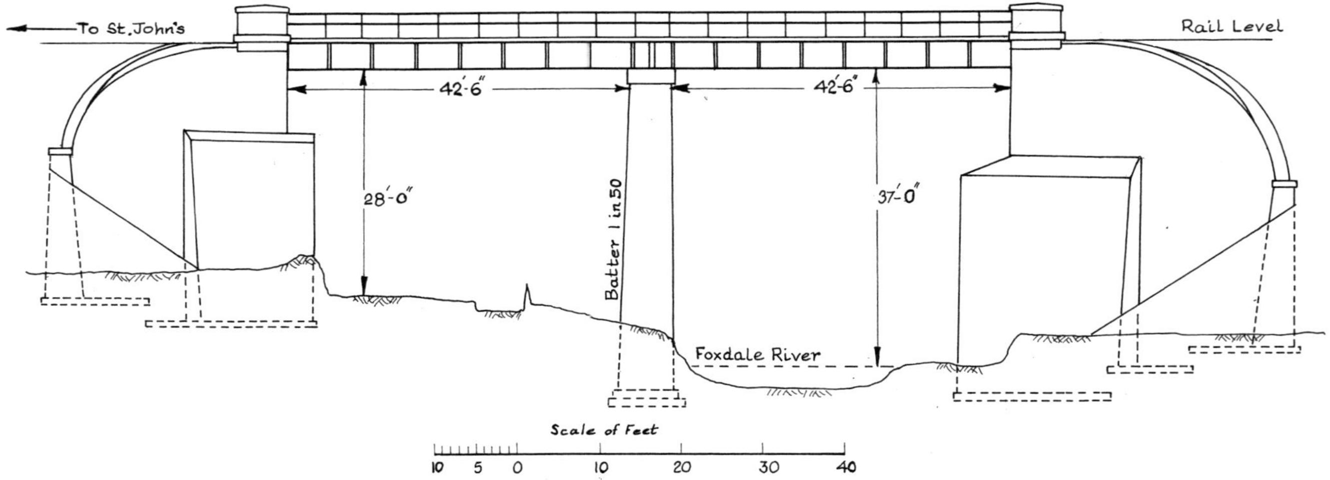

FOXDALE RAILWAY
Bridge No. 3 at 0 Miles 47 Chains

tracks above the IOMR and the Foxdale River respectively. The building of the latter has already been noticed (Vol. I p.182) and even today the additional buttresses may be seen. There were two 47 ft 6 in. steel plategirder spans, the one bridging the river 37 ft above the water to the underside of the span and the other giving a 28 ft clearance over the adjacent road; each had a span clearance of 42 ft 6 in. The abutments and central pier were of masonry with some concrete.

Nunnery Bridge

This bridge, 72 ch. from Douglas, was the first major work encountered when travelling on the South Line. Situated entirely within The Nunnery Estate, it crossed the combined rivers Dhoo and Glas and was subject to flooding. It had capped masonry approaches pierced by short spans to give pedestrian passage to Estate workers etc., and ease floodwater pressure. In all, four wrought iron spans carried the railway; the side spans were 10 ft long and the two central spans 24 ft long met on a 6 ft central masonry pier. When this structure was demolished the spans found further life in various pieces of equipment in Douglas Workshops. Partial demolition had been achieved by a mighty flood on 7th November, 1894 which swept away the Douglas bank abutment but did not damage the spans which were dislodged. It was agreed that the bridge was unsafe and after repairs were alleged to have been started it was decided that The Phoenix Foundry Co. Ltd. should supply a new steel bridge with 80 ft and 85 ft lattice girders. (Vol. I p.222). Temporary use of the repaired bridge and a restriction on speed imposed, came into force on 15th November. In April 1895 the new girders were fitted; they cost £550. [Curiously, the drawings of the old bridge in the Manx Museum state 'steel span' but the contemporary description is 'iron'.]

After much debate during which the bridge was alleged to have further life and, almost in the same breath to be only fit for demolition, a sudden decision saw its demolition in October 1978. This took place during a period when the railways of the Island were being administered by some who were unfitted for the task and many activities of dubious portent took place. There was controversy about the bridge, but little was permitted to be known save that there was, among other defects, serious corrosion in those pockets of the steelwork where the paintbrush had failed to penetrate. However, the present bridge consists of lattice spans supplied by Messrs Wilson & Collins, an Island firm, and passed its first train on 23rd March, 1979. (The second and third bridges can be compared in *Plates 32 & 33* in Vol. II and the second bridge when new in *Plate 70* in Vol. I.)

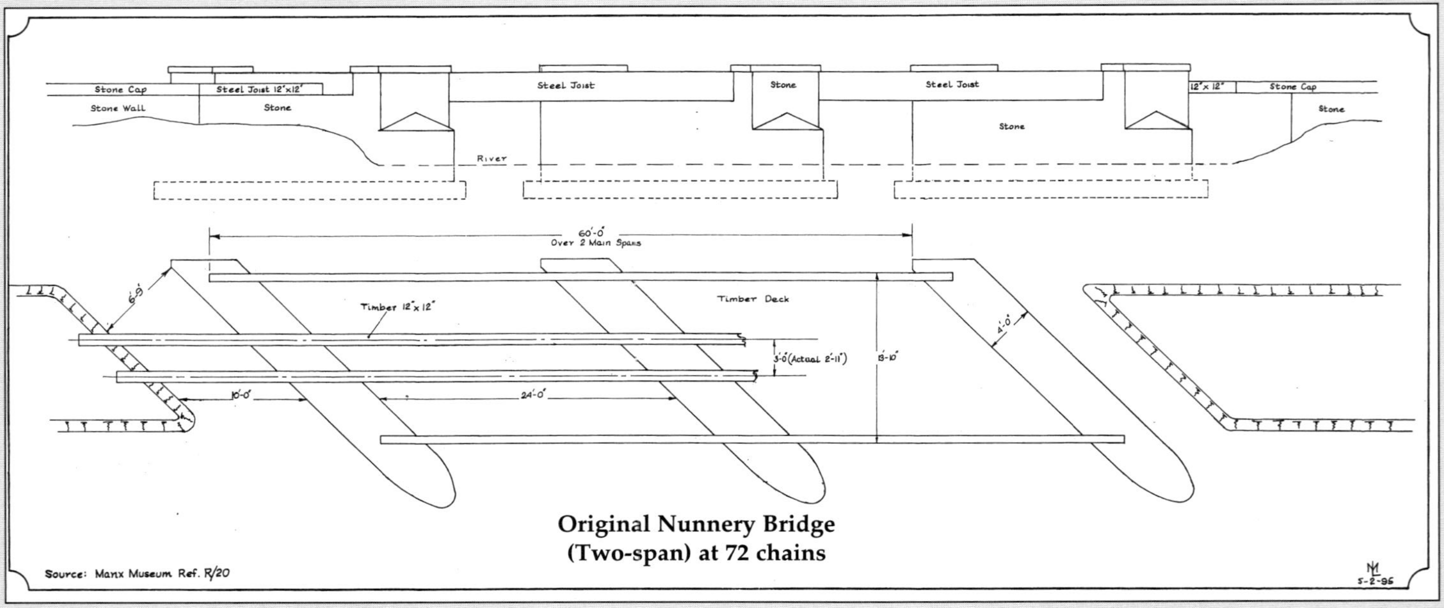

Original Nunnery Bridge (Two-span) at 72 chains

Source: Manx Museum Ref. R/20

Original bridges structures - non-masonry

In the lists of bridges which follow, the Peel and South Line items show the structures as rebuilt (where this applies) but in an effort to confine the lists to reasonable length certain lesser ones are omitted e.g. the overbridges at Oakhill and at Peel Road to mention two of many. Those omitted are mentioned in the description of Routes.

The Manx Museum houses many bridge drawings and these should be consulted for individual cases.

The IOMR list shows bridges as *rebuilt;* in general bridges were first built with economy using longitudinal timber baulks suitable for 18 ft-20 ft span, later to be replaced by rolled wrought iron beams 12 in.-15 in. deep. In time, steel girders 2 ft 6 in. took the place of iron. (These dimensions are only a rough guide and the whole question of structure strength is mentioned in connection with innovations in motive power.)

The MNR and Foxdale Railway lists show bridges *as built.*

List of Principal Bridge Structures

Site	*Purpose*	*Structure as re-built*
Peel Line		
Kirk Braddan	Road	Masonry arch: underbridge
Quarter Bridge	River Glas	86 ft span lattice girder: overbridge
Snugborough	River Dhoo	(see footnote)*: overbridge
Union Mills	River Dhoo	30ft span steel girder: skewed-overbridge
Cooil Ingle	Greeba River	34ft span steel girder: skewed-overbridge
St John's	Foxdale Railway	Masonry arch: 25 ft high x 11 ft 9 in. wide underbridge
St John's	River Darragh	25 ft span steel girder: overbridge
Ballaleece	River Neb	36 ft x 2 spans steel girder: overbridge
Glenfaba	Peel-Patrick road	Masonry multi-arch: underbridge 40 ft length x 15 ft high x 12 ft wide

*Replaced by two wrought iron spans in 1903 and latterly of two steel, 36 ft 6in. and 32 ft long, and infilled with concrete.

Port Erin Line		
Kewaigue	Secondary road	Masonry arch: overbridge
Port Soderick	Secondary road	Masonry arch: overbridge
Santon	Douglas-Castletown road	Masonry arch: underbridge
Blackboards	Douglas-Castletown road	Masonry arch + concrete span extension: underbridge*
Castletown	Silver Burn	3 spans in masonry: central span 26 ft: overbridge

*Stone arch 34 ft length x 12 ft 2 in. wide extended by concrete slab 19 ft length x 13 ft wide - skewed due to road widening.

Site	*Purpose*	*Structure as built*
Ramsey Line		
St John's	River Darragh	(no record of orig.construction)
Ballalleece	River Neb*	30 ft x 2 spans wrought iron: overbridge
St John's	Douglas-Peel road	50 ft span wrought iron: overbridge
Ballaquine	Ramsey-Peel road	110 ft.span wrought iron: underbridge
Glen Mooar	Spanning glen	60 ft x 3 spans of lattice wrought iron: overbridge
Glen Wyllin	Spanning glen	60 ft x 3 spans of lattice wrought iron: overbridge
Glen Balleira	Spanning glen	40 ft span wrought iron: overbridge
Ballaugh	Dhoo River	25 ft x 2 spans wrought iron: overbridge
Lezayre	Sulby River	80 ft† span bowstring: overbridge
Milntown	Auldyn River	40 ft span wrought iron: overbridge

*Girders 36 ft + 31 ft as rebuilt
†Bowstring girder length 88 ft.

Foxdale Line		
St John's	Spanning IOMR	Masonry arch: overbridge
St John's	Foxdale River	42 ft 6 in. span plate girder: overbridge
Foxdale	Foxdale-St John's road	30 ft span plate girder: underbridge

Stations & Halts

Peel Line

m.	*c.*	*Location*	*Opened*	*(Last) Closed*
1	0	Quarter Bridge Halt	25.6.1928	15.5.1929
1	40	(Kirk) Braddan Halt	1895	8.9.1968
-	-	Strang Racecourse Platform	No official record	
2	40	Union Mills	1.7.1873	8.9.1968
4	60	Crosby	1.7.1873	15.11.1965
			Re-opened: 3.6.1967	8.9.1968
8	0	Ballacraine Halt*	6.1876	1.7.1879
			Re-opened: 6.1927	15.5.1929
8	40	St John's	1.7.1873	15.11.1965
			Re-opened: 3.6.1967	(Pass.) 8.9.1968
				(Goods) 24.4.1969
11	40	Peel	1.7.1873	15.11.1965
			Re-opened: 3.6.1967	(Pass.) 3.9.1968
				(Goods) 29.4.1969

* Crossing Lodge used as temporary Halt in season only and named Glen Helen.

Port Erin Line

m. c.	*Location*	*Opened/Re-opened*	*(Last) Closed*	*Notes*
3 10	Port Soderick	1.8.1874	15.11.1965	
		11.7.1967	1975-76	
		1977		(SO)
4 25	Ballacostain Halt* (Pistol Castle Rifle Range)	5.5.1902	16.5.1929	Used intermittently since; not in public use
5 50	Santon	1.8.1874	26.5.1958	
		11.7.1967	1975-76	
		1977		(SO)
8 30	Ballasalla	1.8.1874	15.11.1965	
		11.7.1967	1968	Trains from Douglas-Castletown (SO) Trains Castletown-Port Erin (SO)
		4.1969		(SO)
		1975		Specials Douglas-Castletown only
		1976		Trains Ballasalla-Port Erin (SO)
		1977-on		(SO)
8 60	Ronaldsway Halt			Intermittently open from 11.7.67-on. Seasonal timetables refer.
9 70	Castletown	1.8.1874	15.11.1965	
		11.7.1967		Terminus from Douglas (SO)
		2.6.1968		Castletown-Port Erin (SO)
		4.1969		(SO)
		1975		Specials Douglas-Castletown only
		1976		Trains Ballasalla-Port Erin (SO)
		1977-on		(SO)
11 40	Ballabeg	4.6.1876	4.10.1948	
		5. 5.1980		Nominally open at various intermittent (SO): not always advertised
13 0	Colby	1.8.1874	15.11.1965	
		2. 6.1968		(SO)
		4.1969	1975	(SO)
		1976		(SO)
		1977-on		(SO)
13 14	Colby Level Halt	19.3.1928	early 1930	
14 60	Port St Mary	1.8.1874	15.11.1965	
		2.6.1968		(SO)
		4.1969	1975	(SO)
		1976		(SO)
		1977-on		(SO)
14 60	Port Erin	1.8.1874	15.11.1965	
		2.6.1968		(SO)
		4.1969	1975	(SO)
		1976		(SO)
		1977-on		(SO)

(SO) Summer only.

Notes with reference to Port Erin Line

To avoid minutiae, Port Erin Line dates are outline only. Nominal closures in early 1975 were followed by August re-opening later that year. All stations nominally open for Winter 'Shoppers' Trains' 1981-82. (see Vol. II for detail). Stations (open for Summer traffic only) are closed at all other seasons, the same practice applying each ensuing year unless a formal closure (as noted above where applicable) has taken place previously.

North Line (Mileages from St John's)

m. c.	*Location*	*Opened/Re-opened*	*Closed*
1 20	Peel Rd*	28.6.1883	2.6.1952
2 70	St Germain's†	23. 9.1879	3.7.1961
4 10	Gob-y-Deigan Halt	13.7.1887	1914
7 20	Kirk Michael	23.9.1879	13.9.1965
		4.6.1967	7.9.1968
8 40	Bishop's Court Halt	As required	1950
10 10	Ballaugh	23.9.1879	13.9.1965
		4. 6.1967	7.9.1968
11 40	Ballavolley Halt#	19.7.1965	13.9.1965
		4.6.1967	7.9.1968
12 10	Sulby Glen	1880	13.9.1965
		4.6.1967	7.9.1968
13 0	Sulby Bridge	23.9.1879	13.9.1965
		4.6.1967	7.9.1968
14 60	Lezayre (Garey)	pre-9.1879	2.10.1961
		4.6.1967	7.9.1968
16 40	Ramsey	23.9.1879	13.9.1965
		4.6.1967	7.9.1968

*Intended to be 'Poortown Bridge', and initially named 'Poortown'
†Intended as station for Peel
#For Wild Life Park

Foxdale Line (Mileages from St John's)

m. c.	*Location*	*Opened/Re-opened*	*Closed*
0 0	St John's (Branch sta.)	(Goods) 6.1886	
		(Pass.) 17.8.1886	*
1 73	Waterfall(s)†	(Goods) 6.1886	16.6.1940
		(Pass.) 17.8.1886	#
2 60	Foxdale	(Goods) 6.1886	16.6.1940
		(Pass.) 17.8.1886	§16.6.1940

*Passenger trains transferred to using the IOMR station at a later date and Branch station abandoned (see Vol. II)
†Original intention to be named 'Hamilton Waterfall' or 'Lower Foxdale'
#Closed at various dates as status diminished (see Vols. I & II). (See also SRN No. 19 pp.20-21)
§Spoil trains continued until 1.1960 but station not in use as such (see Vol. II)

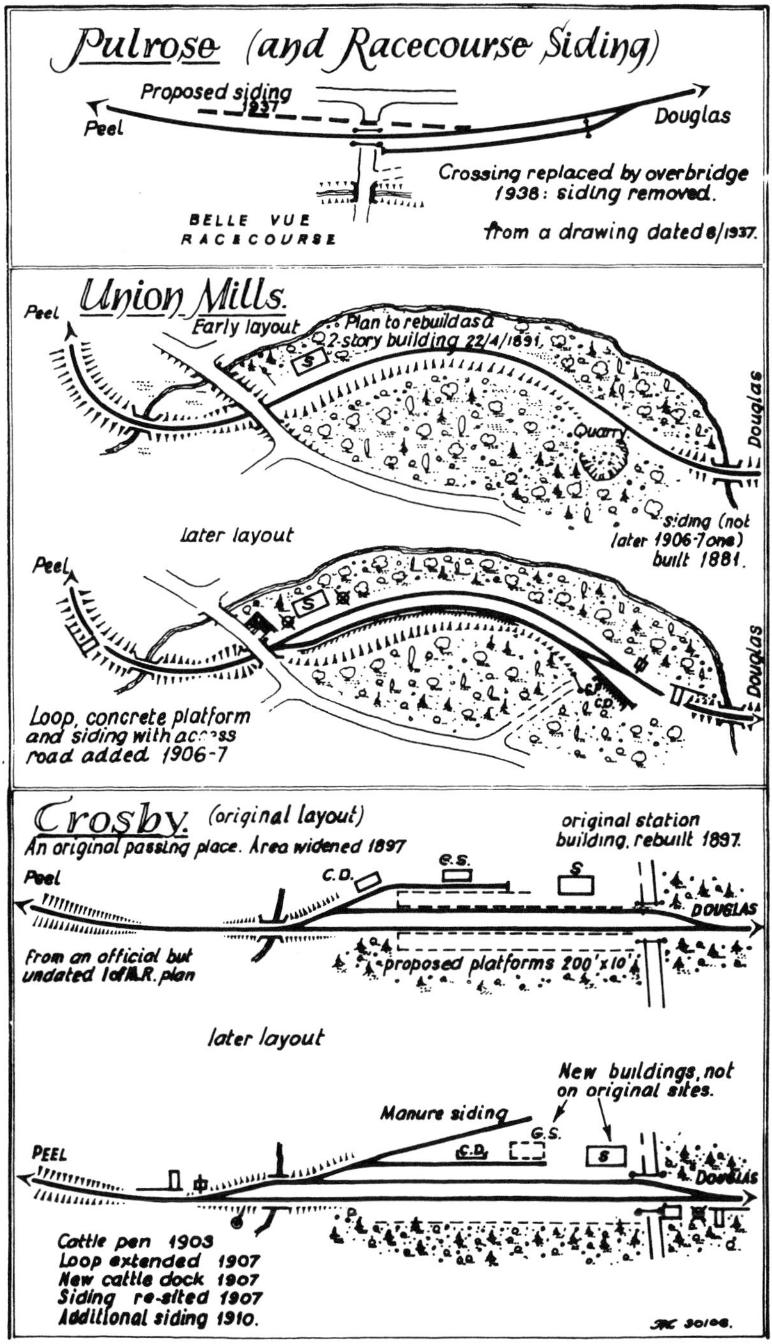
Pulrose (and Racecourse Siding)
Proposed siding 1937
Peel
Douglas
Crossing replaced by overbridge 1938: siding removed.
BELLE VUE RACECOURSE
from a drawing dated 8/1937.
Union Mills.
Peel
Early layout
Plan to rebuild as a 2-story building 22/4/1891.
S
Quarry
Douglas
siding (not later 1906-7 one) built 1881.
later layout
Peel
S
C.D.
Douglas
Loop, concrete platform and siding with access road added 1906-7
Crosby. (original layout)
An original passing place. Area widened 1897
original station building, rebuilt 1897.
Peel
C.D.
G.S.
S
DOUGLAS
From an official but undated IofM.R. plan
proposed platforms 200'x10'
later layout
New buildings, not on original sites.
Manure siding
G.S.
C.D.
S
PEEL
DOUGLAS
Cattle pen 1903
Loop extended 1907
New cattle dock 1907
Siding re-sited 1907
Additional siding 1910.

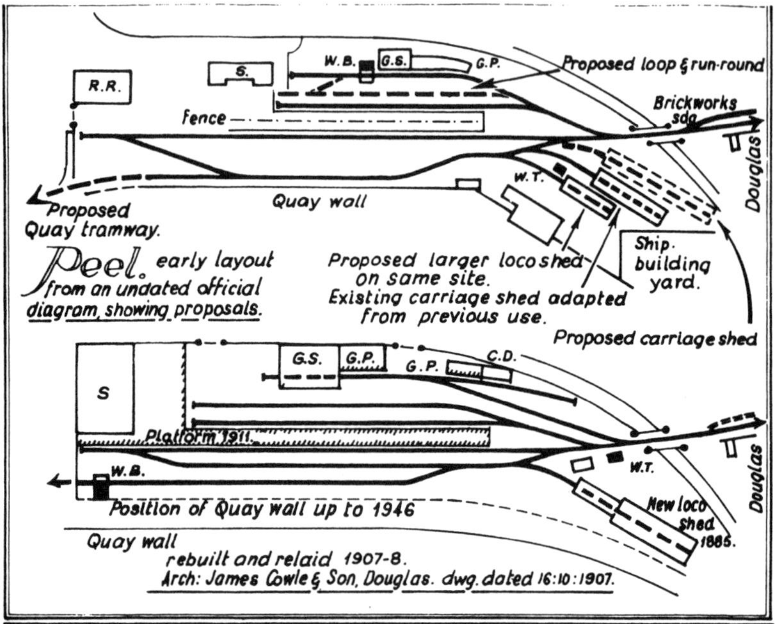
Peel. early layout
from an undated official
diagram, showing proposals.
R.R.
S.
W.B.
G.S.
G.P.
Proposed loop & run-round
Fence
Brickworks sdg.
Douglas
W.T.
Proposed Quay tramway.
Quay wall
Proposed larger loco shed on same site.
Existing carriage shed adapted from previous use.
Ship-building yard.
Proposed carriage shed
S
G.S.
G.P.
G.P.
C.D.
Platform 1911
W.B.
W.T.
Douglas
New loco shed 1885.
Position of Quay wall up to 1946
Quay wall
rebuilt and relaid 1907-8.
Arch: James Cowle & Son, Douglas. dwg. dated 16:10:1907.

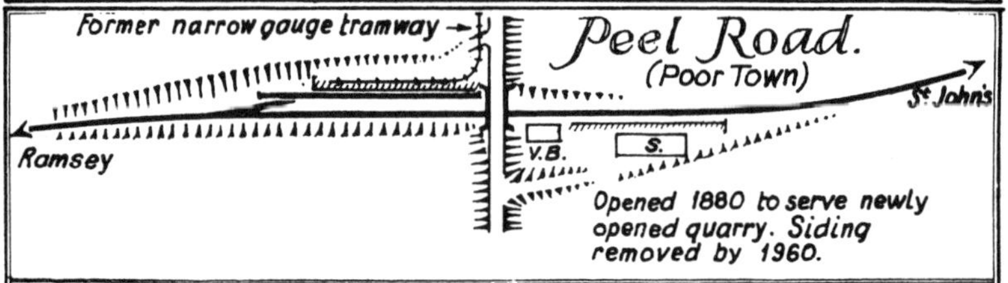
Peel Road.
(Poor Town)
Former narrow gauge tramway
St John's
Ramsey
V.B.
S.
Opened 1880 to serve newly opened quarry. Siding removed by 1960.

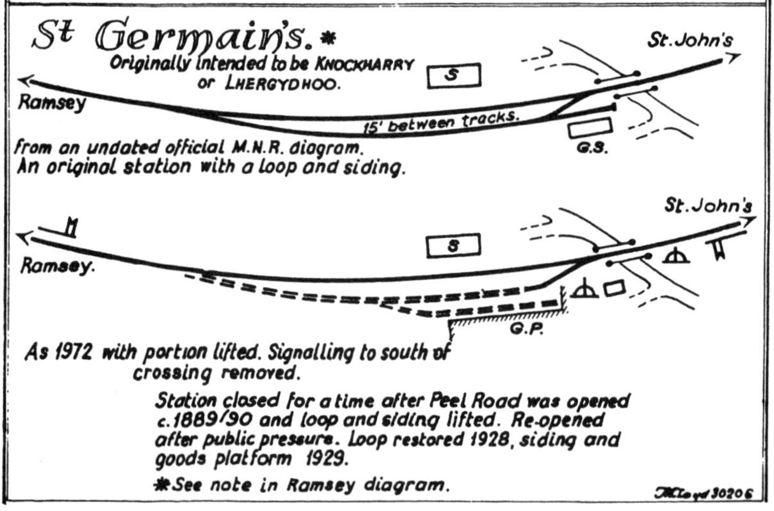
St Germain's.*
Originally intended to be KNOCKHARRY or LHERGYDHOO.
St. John's
S
Ramsey
15' between tracks.
G.S.
from an undated official M.N.R. diagram.
An original station with a loop and siding.
St. John's
S
Ramsey.
G.P.
As 1972 with portion lifted. Signalling to south of crossing removed.
Station closed for a time after Peel Road was opened c.1889/90 and loop and siding lifted. Re-opened after public pressure. Loop restored 1928, siding and goods platform 1929.
*See note in Ramsey diagram.
JICLloyd 30206

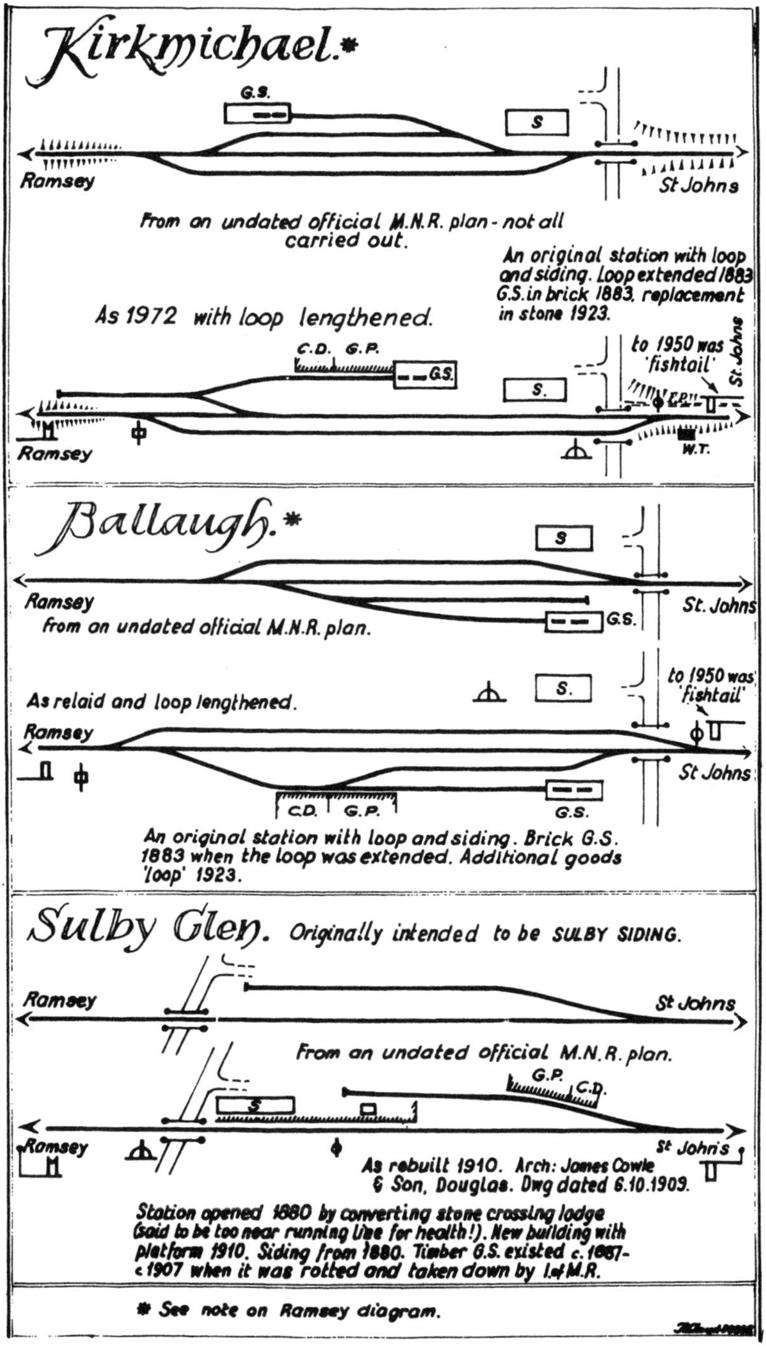
Kirkmichael.*
G.S.
S
Ramsey
St Johns
From an undated official M.N.R. plan - not all carried out.
An original station with loop and siding. Loop extended 1883 G.S. in brick 1883, replacement in stone 1923.
As 1972 with loop lengthened.
C.D. G.P.
G.S.
S.
to 1950 was 'fishtail'
St. Johns
W.T.
Ramsey
Ballaugh.*
S
Ramsey
from an undated official M.N.R. plan.
G.S.
St. Johns
As relaid and loop lengthened.
S.
to 1950 was 'fishtail'
Ramsey
St Johns
C.D. G.P.
G.S.
An original station with loop and siding. Brick G.S. 1883 when the loop was extended. Additional goods 'loop' 1923.
Sulby Glen. Originally intended to be SULBY SIDING.
Ramsey
St Johns
From an undated official M.N.R. plan.
G.P. C.D.
S
Ramsey
St John's
As rebuilt 1910. Arch: James Cowle & Son, Douglas. Dwg dated 6.10.1909.
Station opened 1880 by converting stone crossing lodge (said to be too near running line for health!). New building with platform 1910. Siding from 1880. Timber G.S. existed c. 1887-c. 1907 when it was rotted and taken down by IofM.R.
* See note on Ramsey diagram.

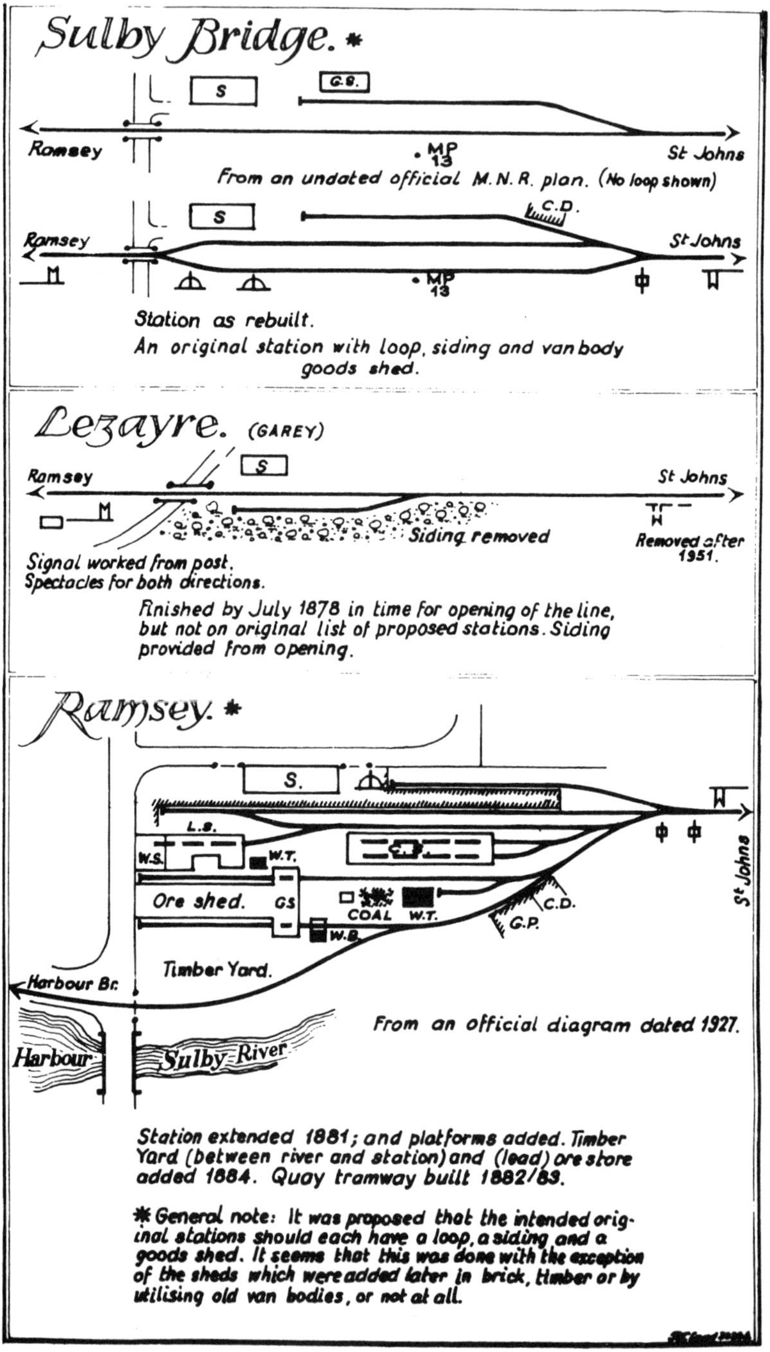
Sulby Bridge. *
S
G.S.
Ramsey
MP 13
St Johns
From an undated official M.N.R. plan. (No loop shown)
S
C.D.
Ramsey
St Johns
MP 13
Station as rebuilt.
An original station with loop, siding and van body goods shed.
Lezayre. (GAREY)
S
Ramsey
St Johns
Siding removed
Removed after 1951.
Signal worked from post.
Spectacles for both directions.
Finished by July 1878 in time for opening of the line, but not on original list of proposed stations. Siding provided from opening.
Ramsey. *
S.
L.S.
W.S.
W.T.
Ore shed.
GS
COAL
W.T.
W.B.
C.D.
G.P.
St Johns
Timber Yard.
Harbour Br.
Harbour
Sulby River
From an official diagram dated 1927.
Station extended 1881; and platforms added. Timber Yard (between river and station) and (lead) ore store added 1884. Quay tramway built 1882/83.
* General note: It was proposed that the intended original stations should each have a loop, a siding and a goods shed. It seems that this was done with the exception of the sheds which were added later in brick, timber or by utilising old van bodies, or not at all.

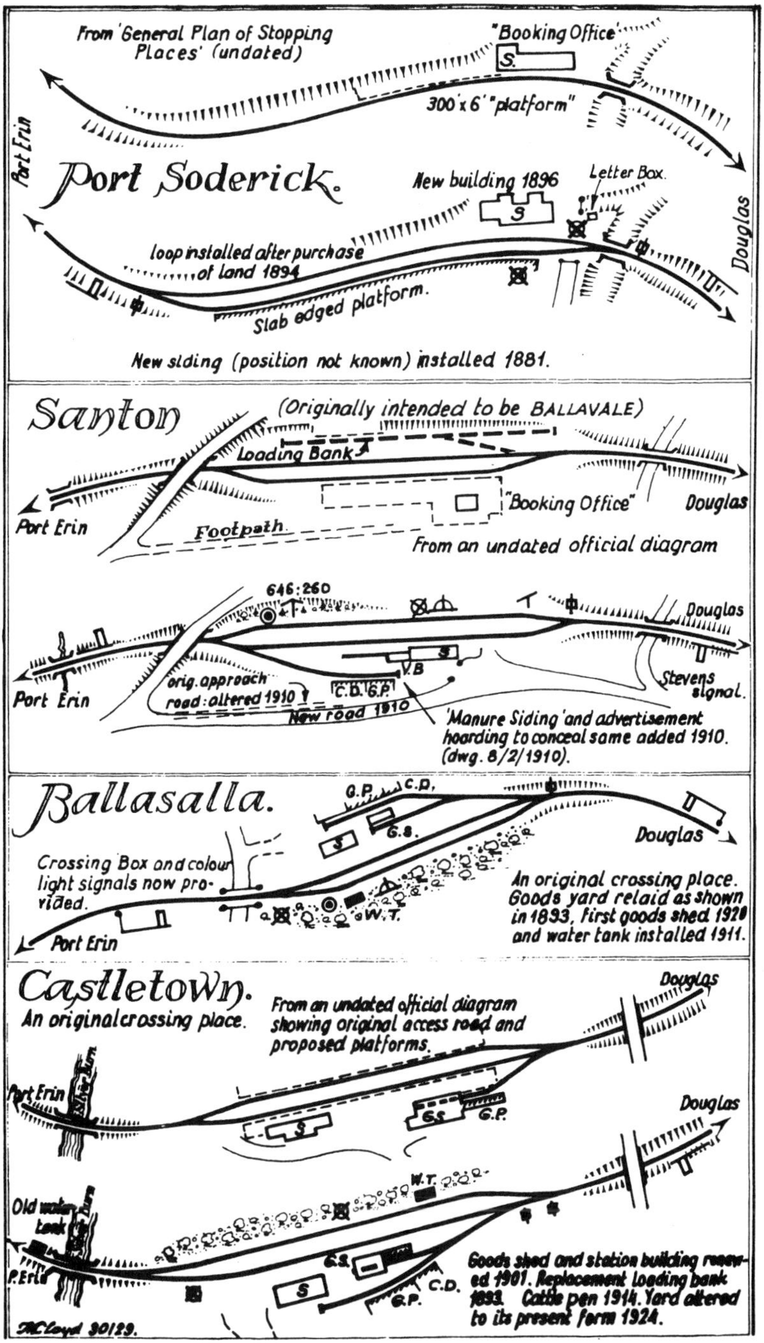
From 'General Plan of Stopping Places' (undated)
"Booking Office"
300' x 6' "platform"
Port Erin
Port Soderick.
New building 1896
Letter Box.
Douglas
loop installed after purchase of land 1894
Slab edged platform.
New siding (position not known) installed 1881.
Santon
(Originally intended to be BALLAVALE)
Loading Bank
"Booking Office"
Douglas
Port Erin
Footpath
From an undated official diagram
646:260
Douglas
Port Erin
orig. approach road: altered 1910
C.D. G.P.
New road 1910
V.B
Stevens signal.
'Manure Siding' and advertisement hoarding to conceal same added 1910. (dwg. 8/2/1910).
Ballasalla.
G.P. C.D.
G.S.
Douglas
Crossing Box and colour light signals now provided.
W.T.
Port Erin
An original crossing place. Goods yard relaid as shown in 1893, first goods shed 1920 and water tank installed 1911.
Castletown.
An original crossing place.
From an undated official diagram showing original access road and proposed platforms.
Douglas
Port Erin
G.S
G.P.
Douglas
W.T.
Old water tank
P. Erin
G.S.
S
C.D.
G.P.
Goods shed and station building renewed 1901. Replacement loading bank 1893. Cattle pen 1914. Yard altered to its present form 1924.
J.I.C. Boyd 30/29.

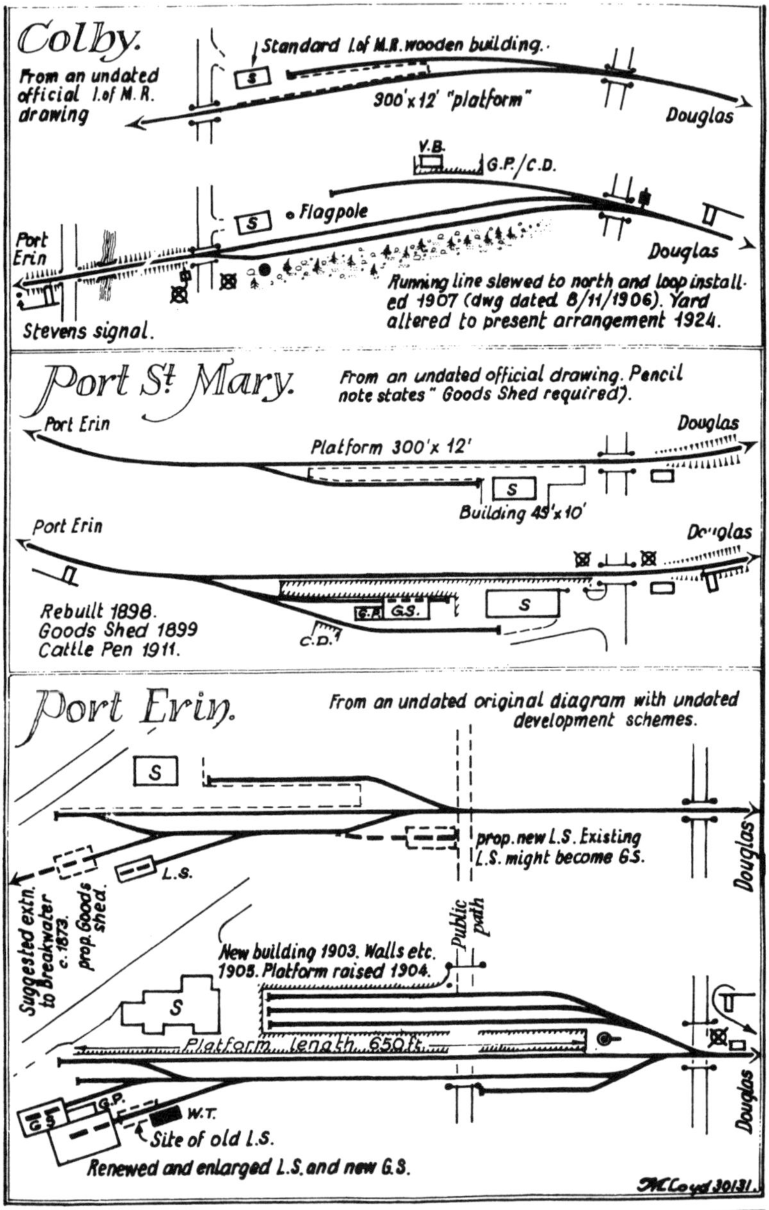

Station plans and layouts are in diagram form only and are not drawn to scale.

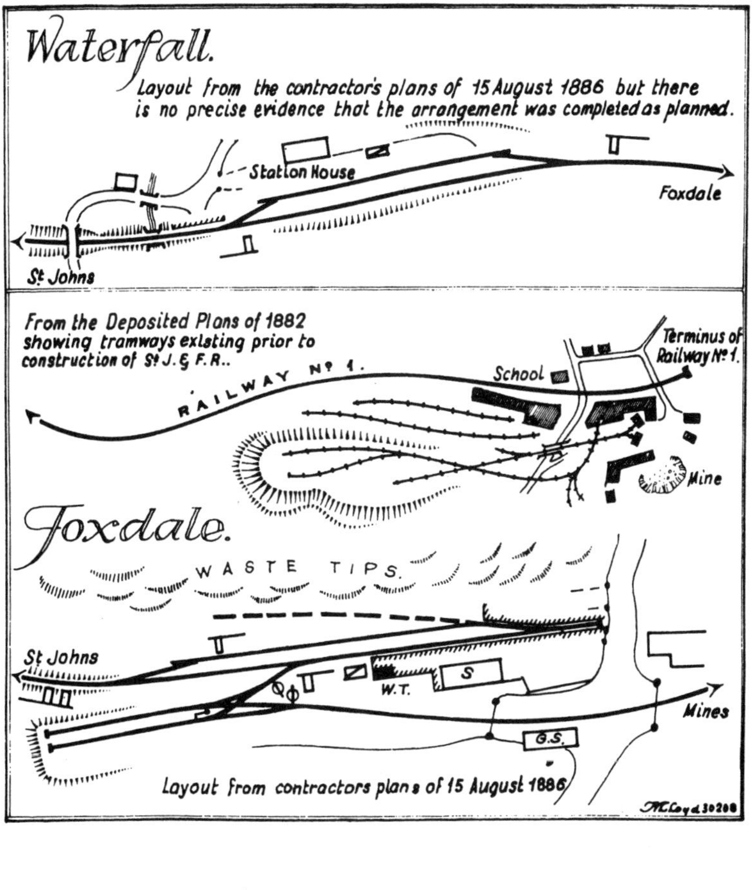
Waterfall.
Layout from the contractor's plans of 15 August 1886 but there is no precise evidence that the arrangement was completed as planned.
Station House
Foxdale
St Johns
From the Deposited Plans of 1882 showing tramways existing prior to construction of St J. & F. R..
RAILWAY No 1.
School
Terminus of Railway No 1.
Mine
Foxdale.
WASTE TIPS.
St Johns
W.T.
S
G.S.
Mines
Layout from contractors plans of 15 August 1886

Level Crossings - Notices to Gate Keepers - IOMR

Special Trains 'not mentioned in the regular Time Tables' were notified to Gatemen, Platelayers, Station Employees etc. by use of a form for the purpose, with running times shown thereon. This might be 'thrown to them from passing trains by the Engineer or Guard, or handed to them by the nearest Station Agent'.

Special Trains could be run without such Notice, warning being given by 'Lamp and Tail Board Signals, as explained in the Rule Book'. After being given warning of their approach, Gatemen were required to be at their posts while Special Trains passed them, 'whether out of their working hours or not'.

The Notices were to be 'preserved and kept clean'.

The Rule Book for 1922 (p.48 Rules 187-201) states, *inter alia,* that each 'Gate-keeper' should have day, night and detonating signals. Gates must be kept closed across road or railway and when gates are opened for the road, he must 'exhibit Red Signals until the gates are closed'. Signalling Gate-keepers must stand so as to be seen by enginemen and guard of an approaching train. Notice must be taken of a passing train, to see if anything is wrong. Gates must be closed 'to the horse road' five minutes before the passing of regular trains, whether they receive the telegraph signal or not; in the case of a Special Train, gates should be closed to the horse road ten minutes after the ordinary train has passed, and kept closed until it has passed. In cases of Special Trains coming from the opposite direction, no time can be predicted; gate-keepers etc. to be on the alert and trains must approach all crossings very cautiously and give warning of approach by a long whistle. (This applied to *every* Special.)

The Permanent Way Inspector checks the clocks at crossings to agree with that at Douglas station, 'every time he passes'. Gate-keepers were of course, supplied with Time Tables.

****

'Gate-posts' are comprised of three rails held together by a 'Spider Clip'.

Level Crossings (Mileage & alternative names 1873)

Key

S Single Gates 12 ft wide (Occupation Crossings except Pulrose)
D Double Gates 25 ft wide & Wicket Gates
H Hut (Wooden) accommodation for Keeper
L Lodge (Stone) accommodation for Keeper
C See page 45.
PR 'Private Road'
PFP Public Footpath
MR 'Mail Road'
PH Public Highway

Peel Line

m	*c*						
0	51	S	Pulrose		H	PR	PFP
1	0	D	Quarter Bridge		L	MR	
4	13	D	Closemooar	Closemoar	L	PH	
4	71	D	Crosby	Crosby Rd	L	PH	
5	57	S	Cooilingle		H		
6	24	S	Northop	Rhenny	H		
6	70	S	Ballacurry		H		
7	19	S	Kerrowgarrow		H		
7	77	D	Curragh Road	Ballacraine*	L		
8	31	D	St John's		L		
9	21	S	Shenvalley	Abbey Clay Works	H†		
9	54	S	Ballawyllin		H†		
11	36	D	Mill Road	Peel	H#		

* also known as Bell's; † 'Little used'; # 'Road to river, Rope Walk, etc."
Pulrose was single gated; other single gates were Occupation Crossings.
Gate locks fitted to Quarter Bridge and Curragh Road only.
Road crossings made at Braddan & Union Mills were overbridges due to proximity of river. (Style known as 'Jack Arches').

*Port Erin Line**

m	*c*				
6	20	S	Ballalona	H	
6	40	S	Ballastrang	H†	
7	40	S	Ballawoods	H#	
8	10	S	Ballahick	H	
8	30	S	Ballasalla	L§	PH
10	10	S	Mill Road	L§	PH
13	20	S	Kentraugh	H§	
13	40	D	Level	L	PH
14	0	S	Ballagawne	L≠	
14	30	D	Four Roads	L*f*	PH
14	60	D	Port St Mary	C§¶	PH
15	30	D	Port Erin	H	
15	40	-	Port Erin Platform	-	PFP

*Comparison with the Peel Line statistics for 1873 is impossible as Port Erin Line records are missing. Single gates surviving in 1995 are Occupation/Private Crossings. There were no 'Mail Road' crossings in 1874, nor that at White Hoe.
† Cottage built 1885; # Replaced by 'private cottage'; § Double Gates in 1874 assumed; ≠ Lodge rebuilt and extended; *f* Lodge replaced by cottage; ¶ Assumed use of adjacent cottage for Keeper 1874.

Level Crossings (mileages from St John's)

Ramsey Line

m	*c*				
2	70	D	St Germain's	-	PH
6	20	D	West Berk	GH	PH
7	20	D	Kirk Michael*	-	PH
8	70	D	Orrisdale No. 1	GH	PH
9	5	S	Orrisdale No. 2	GH	PH
10	10	D	Ballaugh	-	PH
10	75	D	Ballacrye (Teare's Crossing)	GH	PH3
11	25	S	Ballavolley	GH	PH2
12	0	S	Cooilbane	-	Occ
12	20	D	Sulby Glen	-	PH
12	60	S	Kella	†	PH3
13	0	D	Sulby Bridge	-	PH
14	13	S	Ellenbane	GH	PH2
14	60	D	Lezayre	GH	PH2
15	70	S	Milntown	GH	Occ

GH Gatehouse (MNR terminology)
Occ Occupation Crossing
*Gates folded when closed
†Company house substituted for GH

PH Public Highway
PH2 Public Highway (2nd class)
PH3 Public Highway (3rd class)

Gatehouses were not provided by the MNR where there was an adjacent station (contrary to IOMR practice to have a Lodge for Gatekeepers at most stations). Some Gatehouses could be used as stopping places for passenger trains - see text in this volume.

Records of the exact situation as regards accommodation in 1879 are missing from surviving documents. IOMR records dated 10.1925 used above.

Structure Gauges

	IOMR *ft*	IOMR *in.*	MNR *ft*	MNR *in.*
Maximum height from rails to crown of overbridge arch	11	0	11	6
Height of vertical walling to carry arch	8	0	8	6
Width between vertical walling	12	3	12	0
Distance between inside rails on passing loops	6	0	6	0

Miscellaneous Systems

There were numerous projects to link either with the IOMR or MNR, and these have received mention in the first two volumes. Some of such proposals created much discussion, much paperwork and much concern as to their effects, but only a few came to reality. Others were short-lived, temporary lines which 'had their day and ceased to be' and evidence of their former existence is not always to be found on the ground today.

Another group, unlike the aforementioned which made physical link with existing lines, did not necessarily use 3 ft gauge but in one way or another, had affiliations with them. Again, not all proceeded beyond the planning stage.

A collective title for the above is difficult, and the one chosen is not ideal: however, the two groups are listed each in alphabetical order, the previous reference year is quoted to allow search in Vol. I & II and a map/diagram appears where sources permit.

(It is emphasised that only linked/affiliated systems are listed, and not all such on the Island.)

Castletown Harbour Extension*	1872	1884
Dalby Extension*		1899
Douglas; Pulrose & Belle Vue	1934	1935
Douglas; North & South Quays Extension		Various
Foxdale Branch*		1882
Glenfaba Brickworks Siding		1922
Knockaloe Branch†		1914
Peel Harbour (West Quay)		1884
Peel Harbour (East Quay)†		1914
Peel Railway*		1886
St John's Gravel & Sand Pits Sidings		*c.* 1873 & by 1884
Ballavolley Quarry#		1882
Corrin's Hill & Peel West Quay Tramway (1) (2)		*c.* 1864 & *c.* 1880
Glenfaba Brickworks Plateway#		?
Glen Helen projects* (Gauge 3 ft?) §pre-1879	1884-85	1888
Castletown District Quarries	1878	1885
Poortown Quarry Tramway#		1884

*Proposal - not carried out
†Owner: British Government
#Gauge less than 3 ft
§Documentary evidence not found; verbal information only
(1) Peel West Quay - Quarry
(2) Extension of (1) northwards along West Quay

Of the afore-mentioned, Glenfaba Brickworks Siding, the Glenfaba Brickworks Plateway, the Knockaloe Branch, and Corrin's Hill with the Peel Quay West Tramway deserve extended coverage.

Glenfaba Brickworks Siding, 1922

The official plans for this work provide for one (only) siding but Catchpole's sketch of 1938 shows a second longer siding branching off the first. The Works obtained its material from a pit (known locally as a 'quarry') some way south of the town, upstream of the River Neb on the west bank. Burnt shale bricks are claimed to have been made here since 1866 but no connection with the railway appears to exist before the early 1920s when plans for a siding were made in 1922 and Agreement with the IOMR in 1923. Rent of the siding, built by the IOMR, was 1*s*. per annum, and fencing and gates were supplied by the Glenfaba Brick Co. Ltd. Three month's notice were to be given to terminate, the IOMR would be required to lift the works on cessation.

The finished bricks were hand-loaded into IOMR wagons here. The brickworks itself was subject to several titles and changes of ownership, business tending to rise and fall according to local demand and the increase in trade due to the building of new schools, housing estates etc., and the decline thereafter, has been covered earlier. However, there was always a strong inclination to use Manx bricks in preference to imported (often from Deeside, North Wales) and a new quarry was opened in 1946. Concrete bricks were made latterly, using materials from Poortown, Turkeyland etc.

The sidings saw only occasional use up to the late 1940s, the Brick Company having gone over to road transport, but the exact date of removal has not been noticed.

Glenfaba Brickworks Plateway (date uncertain)

Leading from the quarry, along the east bank of the river to the Works was a plateway, occasionally described as being a 'last survivor' (but this is not true) but certainly unique in the Island. The cast-iron plates were 6 ft long and 1 in. thick of traditional angle section; the upturn was inside so that the flangeless wheels ran on the outer face of it upon a 6 inch horizontal flange. There were two holes each end with one central. The gauge was roughly 3 ft, precise determination being impossible; the plates were end-abutted on sleepers but not physically joined in any way. Iron spikes held the plates to wooden sleepers at 3 ft intervals. The line was roughly level throughout except for the southernmost section which fell steeply into the quarry after crossing the Neb; in 1935 the fall was *c.* 20 ft. The plates on this incline had a 10 inch horizontal flange.

At the northern end of the track there was an upward and sharp bend and bricks were laid on the crossing with the IOMR to assist the horse pulling the wagons. Here derailments were frequent and more than one

Glenfaba Brickworks Plate Tramway

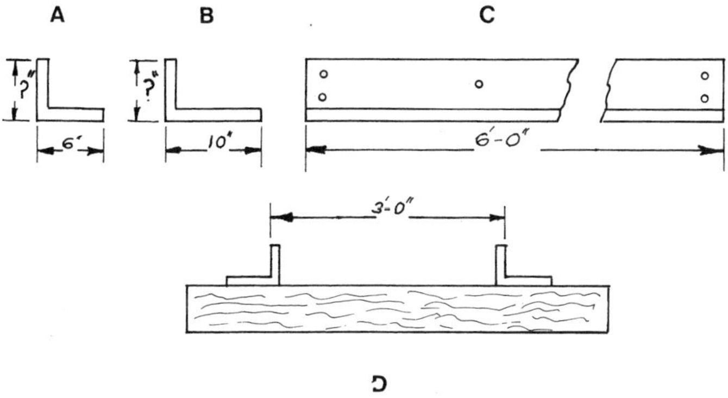

(Diagram only)

A Section of straight plate
B Section of curved plate
C Plan of plate
D Section of plateway (timber sleeper dimensions not known)

Thickness of plates not recorded

Wagon Wheels

Large diameter (at hinged-door end)	20½ in.
Smaller diameter (at fixed body end)	19½ in.
Thickness of wheel on tread	2½ in.
Wheelbase	24 in.

Source: notes by I. Macnab and L.T. Catchpole *c.* 1936

27-1-95

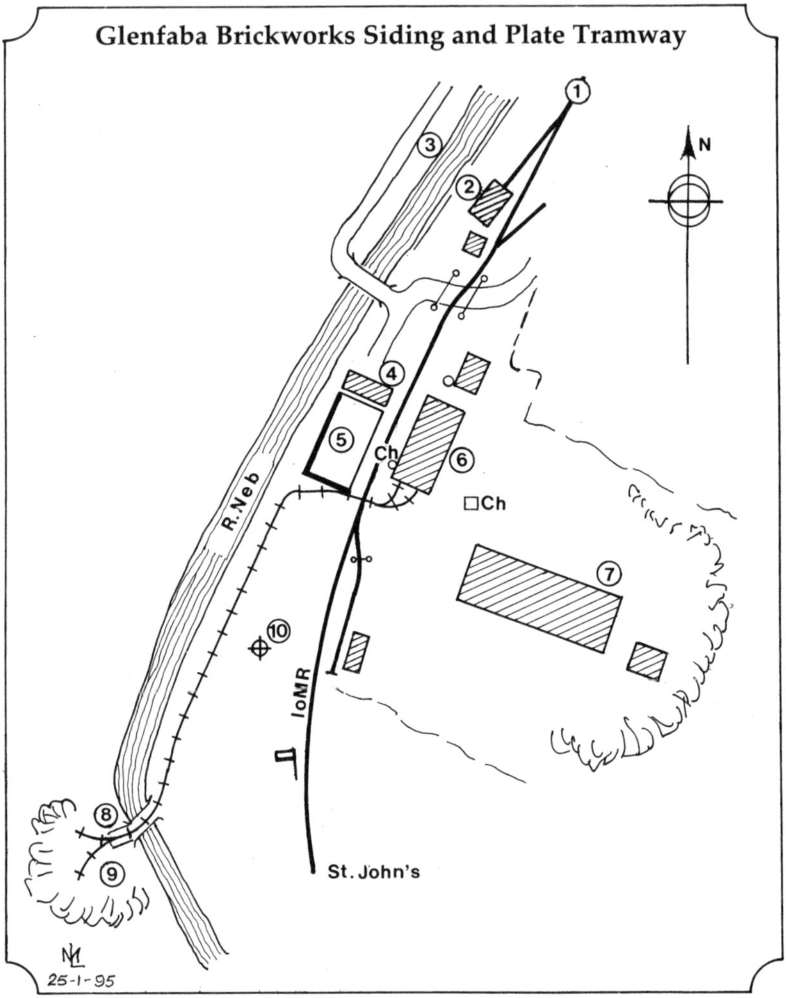

Glenfaba Brickwork Siding & Plate Tramway (Diagram only)

Key

1 Peel station IOMR
2 Locomotive Shed
3 West Quay
4 Engineering Works (formerly Flour Mill)
5 Reservoir
6 Brickworks kilns
7 Brickworks
8 Plate tramway bridge over River Neb and incline
9 'Clay' pit
10 Site of later Generating Station

horse fatality occurred. There was then another sharp turn and the plateway bifurcated to enter a shed. Elsewhere the track was inset in a bed of bricks made up to the level of the road. Total length was ⅜ mile, the quarry section being of temporary track which was moved as required. The inclined section here is not positively recorded though steam power was said to assist it; the bottom of the quarry was flooded and these features were drowned.

There were latterly three sheet-iron open wagons and one horse; the wagons had end doors, the wheels at the door end being 20 in. diameter and the others 19½ in., on a wheelbase of 24 in.: the wheeltreads were 2½ in. wide. The wheels revolved loosely upon fixed axles and the wagons are known to have survived until the mid-1950s.

There is reason for believing the plateway did not exist before July 1885 when the now-demolished brickworks was built; an Agreement permitted the laying of a tramway along a 'road' beside the Neb on condition it was horse-drawn and did not impede road traffic. The choice and source of materials for its construction remains an intriguing mystery.

Knockaloe Branch, 1914

Knockaloe, south of Peel and in Patrick, was already an established seasonal Army Camp sited to the west of the road junction at Patrick Church. After the onset of the World War I on 4th August, the Camp was chosen for one of a number of 'Concentration Camps' (an official designation though other terms were used), and the Camp was opened on 17th November, 1914.* Its proximity to Peel allowed the Harbour there to be used without interference to those at Douglas or Ramsey but it was immediately obvious that a rail link must be built to convey a considerable tonnage of stores etc. The carriage of personnel was not envisaged.

On 1st September, 1915 the Branch was opened together with an extension from Peel terminus in the form of two sidings along the East Quay; their combined total mileage was 1 m. 6 ch. The Branch diverged from the Peel Line 200 yards east of Glenfaba Mill, swung south, crossed the Neb by wooden bridge and climbed steeply towards Patrick and the Camp. Construction of both systems was by Baldry, Yerburgh & Hutchinson Ltd. on behalf of the British Government, and throughout their life the IOMR acted solely as agents of the Westminster Government. (For complete detail see Vol. II pp.45-50/53/55-56/58-59.)

During 1915 it became clear that the Camp - now entitled The Alien Detention Camp - would ultimately hold 20-25,000 persons; closure came on 14th October, 1920 (other sources give September 1919) when the Camp still contained 1,400 men, and spasmodic working of the Branch is claimed until 1923.

*The Manx Museum exhibits features of Camp Life.

COLLAR THE LOT (P. & L. Gillman: 1980) has:

> The Home Office and the Isle of Man squabbled over . . . who was to pay for removing the railway lines that had been laid on the Douglas quayside . . .*

A telephone link between the Camp and Peel station booking office was installed in July 1915 - at first the IOMR Directors were expected to pay for it but a curt memo put the matter into perspective. Furthermore, the Branch Line was maintained by 'Government-appointed surfacemen' and when in 1919 the IOMR was asked if their P.W. Inspector would examine the line, searching questions as to liability, cost etc. came from the IOMR Co.

Ultimately it was agreed J. Clague should inspect and the IOMR Report on the Branch contained the familiar pithy comment; '. . . the surface men employed on this line have not much experience' . . . and Clague found the curves were half to one inch overgauge, trap points at the Junction out of setting and three points at Knockaloe farmyard out of gauge. In October 1919 Clague re-inspected, found that no one was in charge, and recommended that both here and on the quay the points and checkrails be cleaned out before *running re-commenced.*

Records (undated) survive:

Knockaloe Junction

Cost of restoring IOMR line (points, crossing, interlocking apparatus)

	£	*s.*	*d.*
Labour	6	13	8
Materials*	36	17	11
	43	11	7

*four steel rails, fencing etc.

Peel Harbour Tramway

Cost of restoring permanent way interfered with by Tramway at Peel station

	£	*s.*	*d.*
Labour	5	13	4
Materials*	2	2	9
	7	16	1

*(2) 7 ft rails & fishplates etc.

The estimates for the above were 'provided by Messrs Cowles'.

An arrangement for the IOMR to inspect the Branch once a week for a fee of 10*s*. 6*d*. was soon terminated, for on 30th October the IOMR was advised 'the Knockaloe Camp has now been closed and is being dismantled . . . no longer necessary to send stores over this line break-up will be facilitated by

*Peel, not Douglas, would be correct: Douglas never had railway tracks on the quay.

its continued use . . . IOMR may wish to use it at own expense and so secure ensuing traffic which otherwise might be conducted by road . . . under circumstances will IOMR take over maintenance, accepting that material comprised in the Branch shall belong to the Government . . . IOMR would have right to run their rolling stock over it'. On 6th November, 1919 the IOMR obtained all right to the haulage of traffic over the Branch, and their weekly inspections were terminated both here and on Peel Quay.

In conclusion, the IOMR purchased and transported huts from the Camp (see references in Vol. II) for their own use and 2,000 sleepers 9 ft x 10 in. x 4 in. @ 1*s*. 3*d*. each., some 'flat and some half-round . . . (they) have been in use on one of the Irish Railways (5 ft 3 in. gauge) and would last a long time in our . . . sidings' (so wrote Bradshaw).

On 13th May, 1920 an estimate of labour costs - without the use of a locomotive - in recovering the Branch Line was made, totalling £226 4*s*. 0*d*. The IOMR had offered to buy the steel Branch Line 75 lbs rails and Quay Tramway 60 lbs rails, plus points and crossings @ £9 ton and £17 10*s*. 0*d*. per set, respectively. These prices would include transport of both systems' track materials to Peel station but the IOMR would not undertake the restoration of the land etc. on the Branch or of Peel Quay. The Insular Trading Co. Ltd., of Athol Street was now handling the business on behalf of the Government. An offer to use an IOMR locomotive and wagons 'as was done for the construction of the Branch' on the dismantling was accompanied by Bradshaw's estimate of 9th June, 1920 for 'Working Camp Line for one day of 9 hours', £3 0*s*. 2*d*.'. A locomotive (plus driver, fireman and cleaner incl. coal, oil etc.) @ £8 a day of nine hours, and wagons @ 7*s*. 6*d*. similarly were offered. Unfortunately the correspondence with the ITCL concludes here, but they were intending to dismantle themselves and sell the materials to the highest bidder. No subsequent correspondence survives, but in the ultimate the IOMR bought the rails and used them elsewhere.

Some figures have been assembled from remaining records:

Traffic between Knockaloe Camp & Peel Station
From 15th September, 1915 to 14th October, 1920

	1915	*1916*	*1917*	*1918*	*1919*	*1920*
No. of wagons	2208	6872	5767	3688	942	117
Amount paid by IOM Govt.	£1104	3436	2041	1107	440	71
Receipts on carriage; parcels & goods; Camp-Peel & St John's*	†£2712	*5698	*4231	*3676	1520	211

*Including Aliens' Luggage Douglas-Peel, paid for by IOM Government
†Including Douglas & Peel, Peel-Knockaloe Junc., and Hire of Wagons: Account Baldry, Yerburgh & Hutchinson Ltd.

Receipts (line three) after closure in 1920, are given as: 1921, £77; 1922, £24; 1923, £31; 1924 nil.

Corrin's Hill Tramway: Peel West Quay Tramway (*c.* 1864 & *c.* 1880)

St Patrick's Isle, on which the Castle and Cathedral stands, was connected to the mainland by a narrow causeway in the late 1790s. This formed an inlet between the mainland and the south shore of the Isle, and due to the effect of the causeway, a beach was created at its eastern end, known as Fenella Beach. On the south-east side of the inlet a timber structure arose, named the Fenella Hotel; it had a seaward-facing balcony, corrugated sheet-iron roof and towers at each end.

Harbour improvements to improve the protection of the anchorage and Manx fishing fleet which was based here, and to provide a west coast port for the Island, began in the mid-1860s; they took the form of a stone quay on the west bank of the River Neb. To bring stone for this work an inclined tramway was built from the quay; this lifted a 3 ft gauge line to about 250 ft, whence a more level course carried on for about ½ mile southwards on a spectacular ledge above the sea on the western flank of Corrin's Hill. At this point the tramway descended an incline to reach a quarry about 100 ft above the sea on the north face of Contrary Head. This tramway was possibly the first rail system on Man and was worked by horses between the inclines. On the evidence of maps it was complete by the late 1860s and terminated at the foot of the northern incline where presumably the stone could be loaded into carts on the quayside.

Further harbour improvements took place in the early 1880s when the Harbour Commissioners' project culminated in the building of a stone breakwater which was completed by 1886 but meanwhile the mouth of the river harbourage was protected in some fashion by the existence of an 'Abernethy Breakwater'.* To assist in the furtherage of this second phase, the Corrin's Hill tramway system was extended from the foot of the incline and led along the quay northwards: at this point the line doubled, curved sharply west and ended on a wooden trestle in front of the Fenella Hotel and above Fenella Beach. A back-shunt siding led to a quarry behind the Hotel, which now had tramways on three sides!

The trestle carrying the two arms of the tramway formed a high-level tipping stage. Material carried in at least a dozen wooden side-tip wagons was discharged on and beneath the trestle, completely burying it. Later, another line laid along the linking causeway brought about improvement using a similar method; the causeway, once of bridle-way width and submerged at low tide, became a roadway and dry in normal weather conditions. In this way the eastern end of the Fenella Beach was raised still further and apart from some subsequent strengthening of sea-walls etc., remains much the same today as in the late 1880s.

Steam motive power was essential along the quay for this work and took

*James Abernethy, nineteenth-century Civil Engineer, designed the 'Abernethy Breakwater' or 'Pier' which, by means of massive wooden 'A' frames sunk into the bed of the sea, could comprise a structure which might be filled with rocks etc, and its consolidation assisted by the tides. His expertise could be seen at such harbours as Heysham and Silloth.

the form of a four-coupled vertical-boiler locomotive, nick-named MODDEY DHOO or 'Black Dog' which is said to haunt Peel Castle. (For details of the acquisition of this machine and its subsequent use on the building of the Foxdale Railway, see Vol. I.) The origins of it are not known but an earlier suggestion that it might have come from de Winton & Co. of Carnarvon (as then dubbed), is erroneous. The only illustration traced (*Plate 21*) shows but limited features which might suggest Alexander Chaplin of Anderson, Glasgow as the maker - but this too is speculation.* The same illustration shows a marine-type vertical boiler and winch assembly mounted on a gantry and used to raise and lower materials between ship and quayside; it would not be beyond belief that the locomotive had been created by mounting similar components onto a wagon frame as had been done elsewhere. The locomotive appears to have been stabled in the open.

Whilst the rail gauge of the Corrin's Hill line was 3 ft as measured by fieldwork in 1984, the gauge of the *c.* 1880 development is not known; it is presumed to be 3 ft also. The track materials have not been determined on either system.

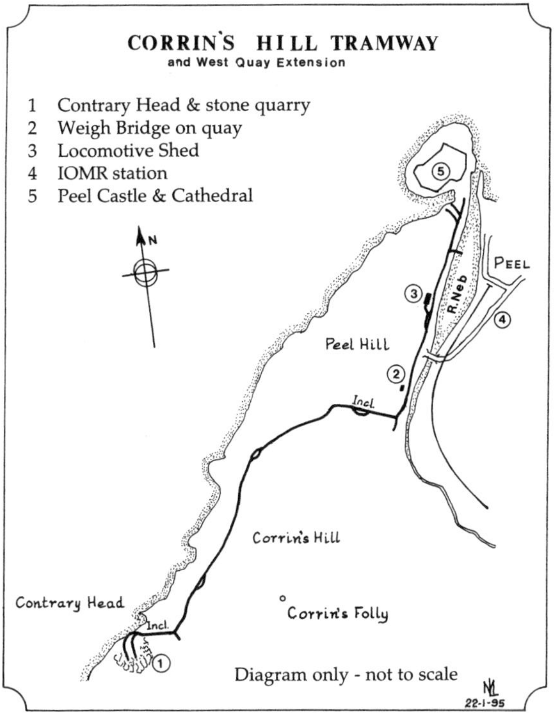

*see VERTICAL BOILER LOCOMOTIVES (R.A.S. Abbott), Oakwood Press, 1989, p.34 on.

IOMR Proposal for West and East Quays Tramways PEEL.
Greenbank. 10 April 1884

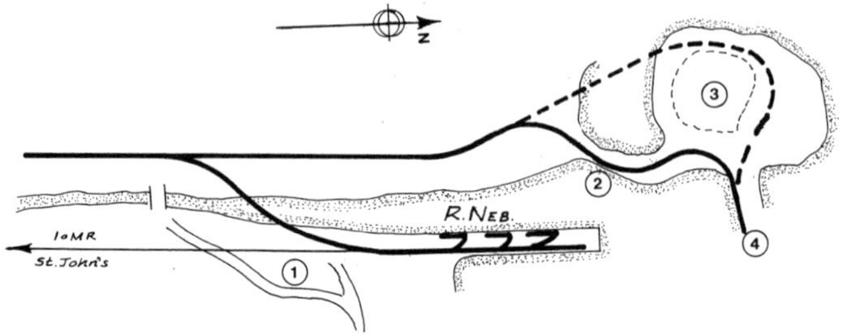

Diagram only - not to scale

'If locomotives are used beyond Y junction on west side of river, the line must tunnel under Peel Castle.'

ML
23-1-95

1 Site of IOMR terminus 1873 with proposed extension northward onto fish quay.
2 Proposals on west bank of river by means of a reversing neck across River Neb, and proceeding northwards.
3 Peel Castle with projected tramway encircling (broken line) by first crossing Fenella Beach and continuing clockwise on to breakwater.
4 Breakwater tramway proposal running along narrow cause way in front of erstwhile corrugated-iron-built Fenella Hotel, and foot of Castle walls.

PEEL DALBY BRANCH
Proposed 1899

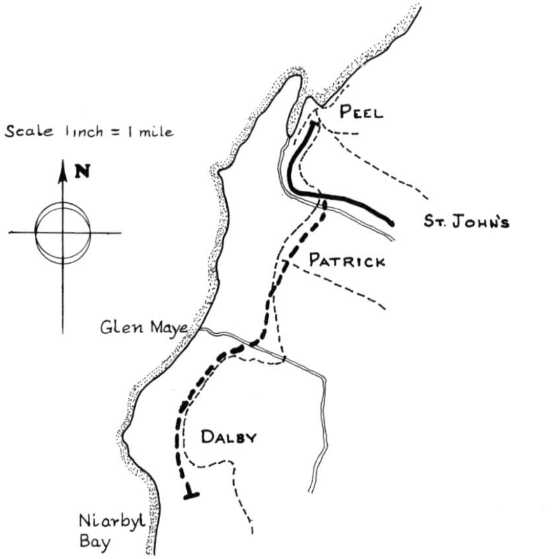

Source: Manx Museum R/168/1-2

ML
11-3-95

Glen Helen Railway Proposals

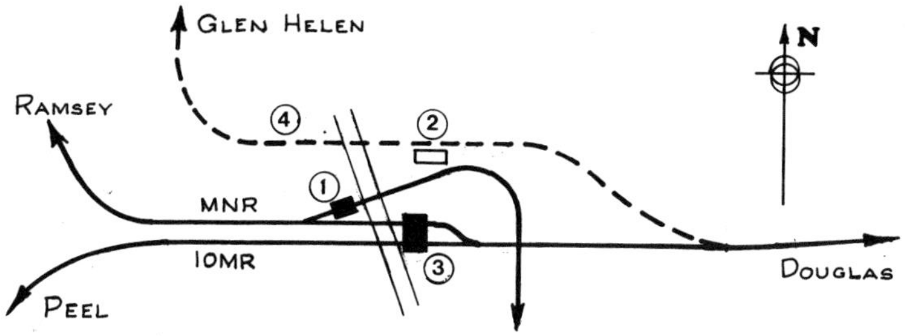

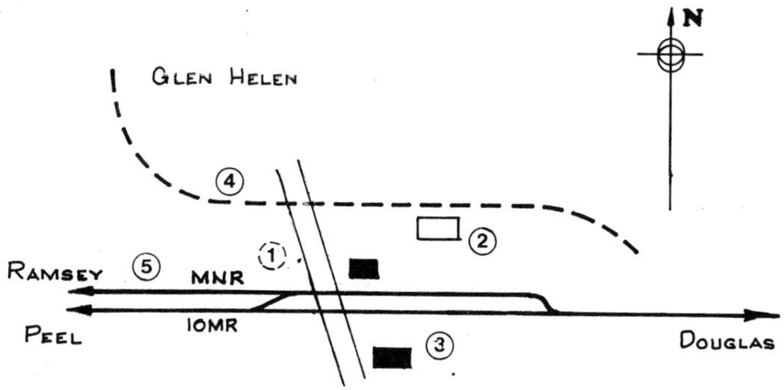

Upper: Undated sketch from Plans & Sections of 'Glen Helen Railway' showing junction with IOMR east of St John's (prob. *c.* 1885)

[This may be a development of the Manx Brick & Tramway scheme to link with the IOMR, but not prosecuted.]

1 Foxdale line station (only shown on Upper).
2 Glen Helen Railway; station proposed site.
3 IOMR station.
4 Glen Helen Railway; proposed route.
5 'MNR proposed' route (only shown on Lower).

Lower: Sketch from undated (but pre-1879) Plans & Sections entitled 'MNR proposals' at St John's. Glen Helen Railway site is further north than that shown on Upper.
There are similarities in these schemes with the earliest by William Lewis. In view of the absence of titles, dates etc. these footnotes must be treated with reserve.

Sketches not to scale.

NL
11-3-95

Permanent Way

The Island railway track is described as follows:

Isle of Man Railway	1873-1904
Manx Northern Railway	1879-1904
Foxdale Railway	1886-1904
Isle of Man Railway & Knockaloe Branch	1905-1994

Isle of Man Railway 1873-1904

The initial materials laid down reflected lightness of construction allied to the necessity to keep down costs. It soon proved to be an unhappy alliance. Rails of Vignoles (flat-bottomed) type were of iron, 21 ft long, dog-spiked to either full rectangular or half-round section sleepers of pitch-pine, larch or Scotch fir; rails were of two weights, 40 and 45 lbs per yard. Owing to the weakness of the dog-spikes, these were supplemented by fang-bolts on the South Line curves which were found to be 'spreading' after a few months of traffic, but the Peel Line with its absence of many curves, was not so treated. Ballast was of shingle or gravel obtained from the pit at St John's or the ballast hole at School Hill, Castletown. For many years it was the practice to ballast up to the railheads and the method lingered on in stations and yards where an uninterrupted surface was desirable. But the practice hid defects in sleepers and corrosion in railfoot and fishplates and was gradually abandoned between the Wars with ballast lowered to sleeper-top level.

Rails were joined by four-bolt fishplates both of plate and right-angle section (the latter introduced about 1914), the original practice being to fasten them with bolts having the nut on the *inside* of the rails.

Timber sleepers were 7 ft long, 9 in. wide and 5 in. thick; though these dimensions varied down the years, partly because suppliers trimmed down the size and were able to offer a 'trimmed price' in consequence and partly due to a continual hunt for suitable bargain purchases; the Management seldom sought tenders for sleepers, rather supply firms would keep the IOMR informed constantly of their latest 'offer'. Conservative as was IOMR policy, suppliers were few and trustworthy.

The half-round sleeper has been used world-wide, mainly because it is usually cheaper. In the Island it required additional attention after delivery because the surface was twice cut to give two sloping notches canted inwards to receive the foot of each rail, prepared with an adze. This tool resembled a small pick-axe; it was 2 ft 8½ in. long from head to handle end and the IOMR type had a notch cut in the handle 1 ft 7½ in. from its end. Laying the adze on top of a sleeper with the handle end and sleeper end in line, the notch marked where the first incision should be made; incision was approximately 4 in. wide and ½ in. deep. After completing the first, the adze was laid in line with its inner face and the inner face of the second flat begun at a point where the full length of the tool rested; the quoted measurements suited the 6 ft long sleepers which became the standard. Some men avowed that the half-round timber sleeper was superior to any other.

In an official costing made in 1895 the Company quoted the price of 'some rails at £12 ton whilst the same rails today could now be bought for £5 ton', adding that in 1872-3 all kinds of materials and labour were at their highest cost.

Heavier *steel* rails 56 lbs per yard but 28 ft long, were introduced in 1877 @ £7 5*s*. 0*d*. ton and a minimum quantity of 2,000 sleepers at the same period cost 2s. 7½d. each. The inferior quality of some first-supplied sleepers was revealed in 1878 when a policy of replacing about a mile of rotten specimens each year was begun. The inferiority of the iron rails is first noticed in Trevithick's Report of 28th May, 1875 . . . 'Continual shunting in Douglas yard has found out weak iron rails'. He blamed the contractors Watson & Smith; he had inspected twelve sets of switches which they had ordered and 'found them very unsatisfactory . . . being made from old and damaged rails, some twisted, others with battered ends and broken flanges . . . 25% worn away'. They had not been made to the drawing supplied by Rixon, the Secretary - some blades were not seating on the stock rails 'and the smith's work would disgrace a country blacksmith's apprentice'. The switches were invoiced at £208 but Trevithick considered they were not worth £100 even if altered to the drawing, and he had given up hope of using them; he recommended further purchases from Watson & Smith be stopped, either in the form of old rail or switches. As to the immediate need of the latter he suggested they be made from 60 tons of new steel rails lying at Liverpool awaiting shipment.

In March 1879 shareholders were advised that steel rails would replace iron, and that better sleepers would be used; the following year curves on the South Line were relaid in steel.

By 1895 the IOMR costing for a mile of track was:

				£	*s.*	*d.*	£	*s.*	*d.*
378	56 lbs	rails	@	5	12	1	494	5	9
756	5 lbs	fishplates	@	10	0	0	21	18	9
1512	11 lbs	bolts/nuts	@	10	15	0	7	5	12½
9,072		spikes	@	12	0	0	26	8	0
2,268		sleepers (6ft x 9 in. x 4½ in.) @ 2*s*. each					226	16	0
							776	13	7½

which was exclusive of ballast and labour.

A drawing for wrought-iron fishplates suitable for steel rails dated September 1882 is in the Manx Museum, Ref. R/39.

A delivery of steel rails in 1883 probably marked the end of precise rail lengths; this batch was 28 ft 4 in. long and for laying on curves (Vol. I p.159 gives costs and suppliers). The extra length might suit the outer rail, but the inner one would have to be cropped; random replacement even for a generous length of curved track always involved cutting to length.

By 1890 all the track except that within station limits had been relaid in 56 lbs steel rails. Even then some sidings were still in 45 lbs iron, or even the initial batch of 40 lbs, said to have been delivered in error. By 1894, the stations had been converted.

There are a few items which are outside the foregoing.

A 'Three-way Switch' drawing in the Manx Museum (Ref.R/170) dated October 1875 shows the switch end of the turnouts only with blades at 12 in. distance following each other and toggled stock rails. Was this ever installed? The sleepers shown are 6 ft x 9 in. and at 2 ft 6 in. centre intervals for plain track and 2 ft and 3 ft at the turnout. The rail gauge is 2 ft 11 in. Is this deliberate?

At a much later date (1936) cast steel crossings were embodied in pointwork at St John's and Peel stations.

When Greenbank inspected in 1886 he was concerned that 68,000 sleepers of the W&S period were *in situ*. He recommended the placing of a ⅜ in. thick steel plate under the rail of the notched sleepers but this was ignored; he felt it would keep the track in gauge on curves.

Chairs were used on flat-bottomed rails laid on baulk timbers e.g. on bridges and viaducts, and on pit roads in the Works, etc. although in some cases steel angles bolted through the rail web had been substituted.

Manx Northern Railway 1879-1904

The initial materials shipped into Ramsey on the RELIANCE in April 1878 comprised steel flat-bottomed rails from Landore Siemens Steel Co., 22 ft. long and weighing 56 lbs per yard and timber sleepers from Goldsmith & Cowley @ 2*s*. 0½*d*. each: other prices were 1*s*. 11½*d*. and 2s. 0½*d*. each. The rails were marked 'LSSR MNR Co.' A Company letter of 1894 states that 'Fastenings were originally fang-bolts but when relaid with new sleepers these were replaced with ordinary dog-spikes except at some of the quickest curves where four chairs are put upon each 22 ft rail'. Sleepers, laid eight per rail, were of larch, 7 ft x 8 in. x 4 in., uncreosoted. (A contemporary account given by the IOMR to describe MNR track said the sleepers were 6 ft long, half-round and uncreosoted.) In the same document the MNR's use of chairs is dismissed thus: 'On the IOMR intermediate chairs are omitted, and certainly appear un-necessary'. MNR records of 1894 continue: 'Ballast is excellent and of first-class gravel having a depth of 12 in. under the sleeper,

Plate 29: No. 10, the Port Erin-based engine, stands outside its home on 4th June, 1958. The nearby IOMSPCL poster offers a Day Excursion to Belfast for 19/- (95p). *R.F. Gee*

Plate 30: Port Erin as seen from the buffer stop in March 1962. Not surprisingly, few people are travelling and the train in the right-hand platform comprises but a single coach. *J.I.C. Boyd*

Plate 35: A wet, miserable day after the old 'Basket Bridge' on the Sulby River had been moved laterally out of place and the new bridge slid into position, was not ideal weather for load-testing. Locomotives are THORNHILL, CALEDONIA and MAITLAND, and the men presumed to include James Bradshaw (on bridge, wearing bowler hat) and Henry Allott (near corner of bridge). November 1914. *Manx Museum*

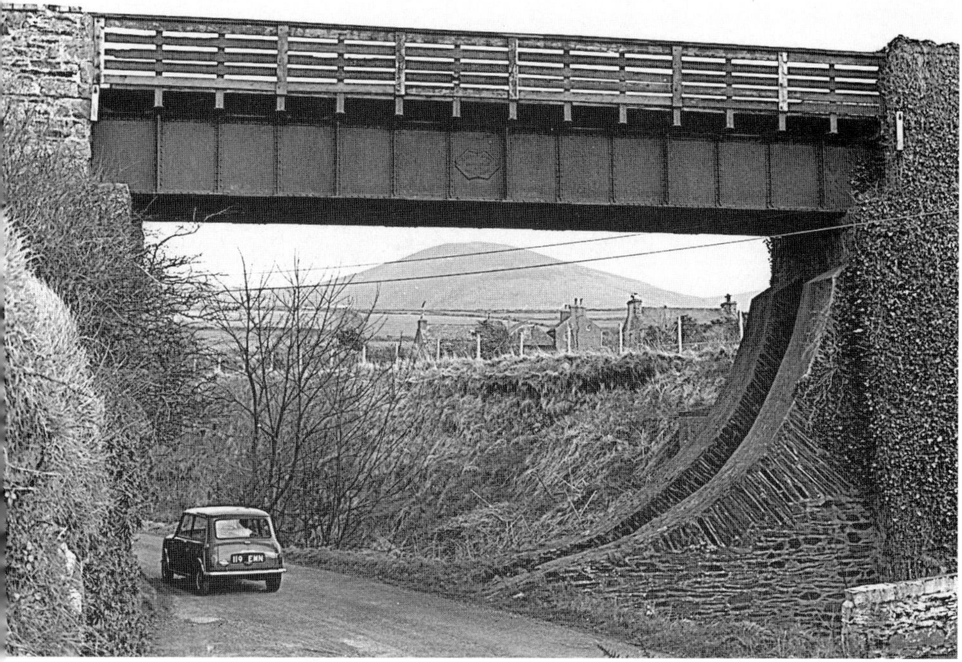

Plate 33: The strange-looking bridge over Glen Ballyre north of Kirk Michael is due to the strengthened abutment on the south side, added by the IOMR which viewed the original structure with suspicion. April 1966. *J.I.C. Boyd*

Plate 34: The rebuilt Sulby Glen station looking east to Ramsey had the luxury of a platform and canopy. The small wooden building is the goods shed provided by the MNR in 1885. April 1960. *J.I.C. Boyd*

Plate 35: A wet, miserable day after the old 'Basket Bridge' on the Sulby River had been moved laterally out of place and the new bridge slid into position, was not ideal weather for load-testing. Locomotives are THORNHILL, CALEDONIA and MAITLAND, and the men presumed to include James Bradshaw (on bridge, wearing bowler hat) and Henry Allott (near corner of bridge). November 1914. *Manx Museum*

Plate 31: Back in the 1890s, a solitary figure makes her way up from the shore beside Glen Wyllin with the MNR viaduct in the distance. *Frank Quayle Collection*

Plate 32: It is 4.12 pm as passengers await among the milk churns at Kirk Michael. The young Darby family has been visiting relatives. 26th July, 1954. *W.S. Darby*

Plate 29: No. 10, the Port Erin-based engine, stands outside its home on 4th June, 1958. The nearby IOMSPCL poster offers a Day Excursion to Belfast for 19/- (95p). *R.F. Gee*

Plate 30: Port Erin as seen from the buffer stop in March 1962. Not surprisingly, few people are travelling and the train in the right-hand platform comprises but a single coach. *J.I.C. Boyd*

Plate 36:(Left to right) Ramsey station lies in the centre of the scene, bounded by the Sulby River on the north side. The Harbour Extension has been lifted but it followed the quayside road along the south bank of the river and off right of the picture. *Manx Technical Publications*

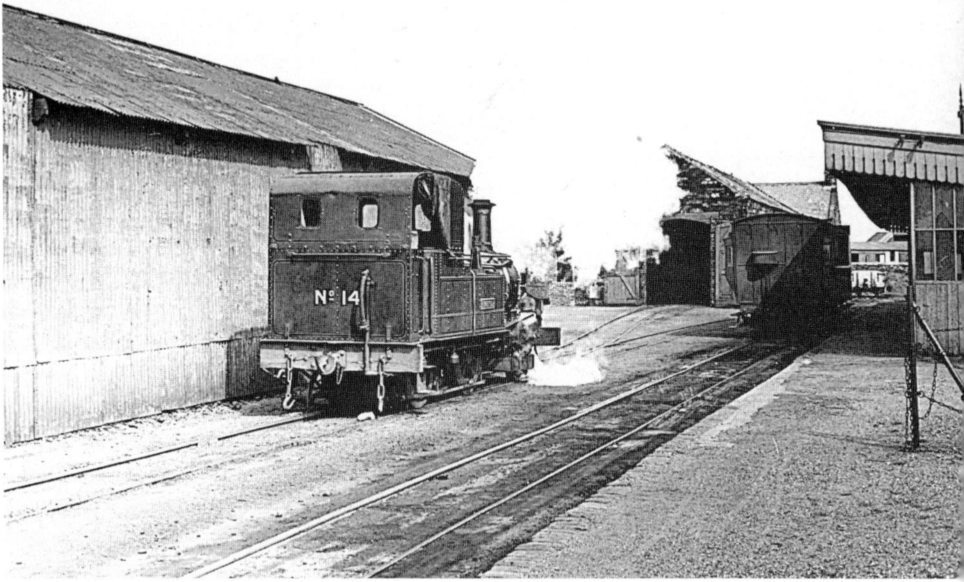

Plate 37: Even on a bright day the platform side of Ramsey station was a gloomy place which seldom saw the sun. Pictures of this side are almost non-existent. Here, No. 14 the resident engine, runs past its single coach, alongside the decaying carriage shed. April 1960. *J.I.C. Boyd*

Plate 38: How different was the south frontage on a sunny day, with its Italianate features. The availability of local Peel stone from which the other MNR stations were built, meant that Ramsey was alone of its kind. May 1961. *J.I.C. Boyd*

Plate 39: On the north sides of Ramsey's carriage shed was the locomotive water supply and coaling point. Beyond is the ore shed. The left-hand line leads through the gate, across the road and onto the quay. Note the point lever and box. March 1962. *J.I.C. Boyd*

Plate 40: The extent of the quay line at Ramsey as in the mid-1930s is alongside the ship's mast. The tall chimneys behind the swing bridge are in the Salt Works' premises. Today, there are many more craft in the Sulby River. *c.* 1936 *C.E. Box*

Plate 41: Foxdale station: in the late 1930s a train service of sorts still survives, and The Foxdale Coach still fulfils its intended role. *Ian Macnab*

Plate 42: On 8th August, 1950, Foxdale appears as unloved as in *Plate 41*. Even some mine buildings remain. But the mercurial existence of the train service is over and the next official visit will be made by the demolition gang . . . who spare the station building. *J.D. Darby*

Plate 43: The Knockaloe Branch featured a stout timber bridge over the River Neb; here the track leads off left, climbing extremely steeply towards the Camp. 1915. *Manx Museum*

Plate 44: Further along, the line curved sharply across the Peel-Dalby road, and passed through the Camp gate. Here, CALEDONIA forms the official inspection train with Henry Allott, and soldiery look on outside the Guard Room. 1915. *Manx Museum*

Plate 45: With the intention of giving the track more rigidity along the unstable cliff section at Gob-y-Deigan, chairs were added - with some benefit. April 1960. *J.I.C. Boyd*

Plate 46: IOMR signals were operated by windlass supplied by Linley & Co. To hold the signal in, the 'clear' position, the wheel was restrained by a short chain but if this feature was missing, a spade handle would suffice. March 1962. *J.I.C. Boyd*

Plate 47: The Stevens & Son patent lever was used to operate the Stevens-supplied signals on the MNR. Latterly, some interchange of signal fittings took place. April 1960. *J.I.C. Boyd*

Plate 48: In contrast to *Plates 46/47*, Douglas signalling was sophisticated and worked from a cabin giving a broad view of the whole station layout. *Peter Dobson*

Plate 49: The entrance to Douglas was controlled by a bracket signal mounted on the water tanks' plinth. As the service was run down, the signals were a target for vandals. *Peter Dobson*

Plate 50: The signal cabin at St John's was a very modest affair compared with Douglas; it was built by the MNR under its Agreement with the IOMR and most noteworthy for the house plants which formerly stood on the window-bottoms. August 1968. *J.I.C. Boyd*

Plate 51: The Kirk Michael-Ballaugh Staff is exchanged for the Ballaugh-Ramsey one; shape, colour and labels identified Staffs from each other. May 1961. *J.I.C. Boyd*

Plate 52: The Staff system was used in conjunction with Tickets (*see text for explanation*). The Tickets were stored in lock-up boxes painted in the same colour as the Staff applicable; only the correct Staff could unlock a box. *J.I.C. Boyd*

Plate 53: Orrisdale No. 1 level crossing on 9th April, 1950, looking west towards Bishop's Court. Despite appearances, the signal protected the gates from ex-Ramsey trains and was used in the informal arrangements with the Bishop to stop Douglas-bound trains at the Court! *J.D. Darby*

Plate 54: The IOMR provided minimal accommodation for gatekeepers, but that at Ballagawne (South Line) has been extended to make living quarters. 10th April, 1991. *J.I.C. Boyd*

Plate 55: At Four Roads (South Line) the original gatekeeper's building survives, but is no longer used as such. 10th April, 1991. *J.I.C. Boyd*

Plate 56: The unique action of the catch-handle is shown in action in Douglas signal cabin; the signalman's right hand has to pull the handle towards him before the lever will operate. His left-hand has pushed the handle forward so locking the lever. July 1962. *J.I.C. Boyd*

Plate 57: The Stevens & Son-supplied frame at St John's (Foxdale Line) station was more conventional and unauthorised movement was prevented by a simple bar and padlock. August 1947. *J.I.C. Boyd*

and boxed up well up on the outside of the rail. Col. Rich the Board of Trade Inspector, gives this Company great credit for the ballasting of their road'.

In anticipation of heavier wear and tear from the engine CALEDONIA, chairs were put on every sleeper at Gob-y-Deigan and Orrisdale in 1885, with keys outside the rail - though the internal position was also to be found. When later the IOMR relaid Gob-y-Deigan, they had a small lot of chairs cast by Gellings Foundry, Douglas but the original MNR rails were re-used; during the life of the MNR (until 1904 that is) the original rails were never replaced. Other parts of the MNR which received MNR chairs, continued to use such chairs until the North Line was closed and lifted. By 1886 a worrying number of the original sleepers - young as they were - had rotted.

It could be that this was due to problems of delivery with the Douglas suppliers for at first the intention was to order Baltic redwood sleepers 7 ft x 9 in. x 4½ in. but shortage of supplies caused other timbers to be acceptable. The redwood sleepers were replaced in the period 1885-88 with Scottish larch (and replacements of these continued into the IOMR regime). Whereas the MNR section continued to be plagued by sleeper deterioration, the same could not said of the rails which were of non-standard section with a generous surface to the head; in consequence over four miles of the North Line - though not in one consecutive length - still had the original rails in 1945.

After Col. Rich's inspection in the summer of 1881, Cameron, Manager of the MNR, failed to convince the Directors that it would be advantageous to relay the whole Gob-y-Deigan length with a chaired and heavier rail; instead they preferred Rich's scheme of using tie rods to keep the track in gauge and bringing up the ballast level to the same degree as was currently the practice on the IOMR.

Cameron placed an order in March 1885 for 21 lbs cast-iron chairs to be used at Orrisdale and Gob-y-Deigan; A.S. Nelson & Co. of Glasgow were the favoured supplier for one thousand and a trial length was put down at the former place. For reasons unknown, the chairs were placed with keys inside but a combination of rain-swollen keys, a low profile rail section and worn wheel treads caused the wheel flanges to hit the keys (and probably also the high cheek of the chair). So within the year, the chairs were reversed. Another trial length near St Germain's was laid with alternate sleepers having fang-bolts and chairs; it was soon altered to chairs only. The chairs themselves were partially based on the type already delivered by A.S. Nelson & Co. for the Foxdale Railway, but with lower cheeks.

Four-hole fishplates were at first of short pattern, later longer; both were of flat section. The weakness of the MNR track with its unusually substantial rail web thickness, lay in dropped joints due to the poor fit of fishplates. The Landore rails were prone to crack in very cold weather; these cracks were given first aid treatment by 'splinting' them between two fishplates.

On the viaducts and large bridges special chairs to sit on the timber baulks were used (or the angle plates mentioned previously).

In 1888 some rails of 56 lbs were supplied marked 'BARROW STEEL 3197 SEC449 MNRC' which eventually found their way to Cumberland and were removed from the 1 ft 3 in. gauge Ravenglass & Eskdale Railway during the winter 1977-78. If they could speak, they would tell us an interesting tale. (Similar rails marked 'BARROW STEEL 5 Mo 1888 56 IMR' were consigned to the IOMR: they failed in time due to corrosion in the webs.) Barrow also rolled a small number of rails to MNR section probably to construct new pointwork when the stock of Landore rail was finished.

On the Ramsey Harbour section, Bowring Road was crossed in trough section and the remainder in street tramway material.

Ballasting. There were two sources for this; at the Ramsey end where construction began it was won from the bed of the Sulby River - this obtained to a point westwards of Ellenbane: the remainder came from a borrow pit on the west side of the line in the cutting immediately north of West Berk crossing.

Foxdale Railway 1886-1904

Materials for this concern were ordered through the Manx Northern Railway and rails, flat-bottomed and of steel, 60 lbs per yard in 24, 30 and 33 ft lengths came through A.S. Nelson & Co., Glasgow: they were never replaced during the life of the railway. Makers were The West Cumberland Steel Co. and rolling date, 1883. Though the intention was to use fang-bolt fastenings, second thoughts prevailed and Cameron ordered 22 lbs chairs, again through Nelson. Whilst the shape was similar to those on the MNR the cheeks were higher and had stiffening ribs. Keys latterly could be found both inside and outside the rails but this is unlikely to have obtained at first.

Delivery: these materials were shipped from Workington into Ramsey in mid-April 1884 by the CLOFFOCK. Payment was to give some anxiety (Vol. I p.167), and in consequence of the money already owing to them, the intention to order fishplates, bolts and spikes through Nelson also was dropped (Vol. I p.174 & 183). Larch sleepers 7 ft x 8 in. x 4in. came through P. McGregor & Co., Kirkintilloch @ 1*s*. 3½*d*. each - which seems cheap in comparison with contemporary deliveries.

Ballast was partly arisings from the mines and partly St John's gravel; later 'blue' gravel from the mines, heavily charged with lead content was so successful in keeping down weed that it was used here and elsewhere.

Latterly a feature of the line in IOMR days was then-existing track in St

John's (Foxdale Line). Presumably because it had been pillaged for good materials, in 1936 the rails were of various non-standard lengths and the keys were inserted haphazardly.

Isle of Man Railway & Knockaloe Branch 1905-94

After the amalgamation of railways in 1905 there began an expensive time of improvement. The former MNR line saw a programme of renewal in 60 lbs steel rails, 30 ft long which began in 1910 and continued to 1956, but was uncompleted. The chairs were taken up on some sections and those requiring them and receiving the heavier rail, had a heavier IOMR-period chair fitted to them. Compound fishplates (to join two different sections of rail) were necessary where differing sections met. North of St Germain's, on the 'Ballanure straight' previously mentioned, a section of 'Baldwin' rails was laid. (These had been bought and stacked at Douglas in March 1905.)

The viaducts at Glen Mooar and Wyllin were fitted with check rails (to limit the effects of derailment) of exceptionally high flat-bottomed rails, 'RHYMNEY STEEL 6.77': they were probably an odd acquisition.

For the long-extended relaying programme which began in 1910 (see previously) a standard for future work was set, using short angled fishplates; rails were marked (e.g.) 'BS 60 lbs WORKINGTON 8.35'. Only approximately 3¾m. of North Line and approximately ¾ m. of Peel Line remained undisturbed by this measure. The initial purchases of 60 lbs rail were due themselves for renewal by the 1930s and, with hindsight, it can be seen that political circumstances caught the railway unprepared so that the wear and tear of the Second War was added to rail which had already given of its best, while at the same time war-time supply of 60 lbs rail was out of the question. Evidence of desperation comes in the considerable post-war correspondence; approach to Barrow Haematite Steel Co. Ltd. in 1947, reminding them of their good pre-war relationship, was fruitless as they had sold their rolling plant to the Ministry of Supply during the war and were no longer in that business - 150 tons of 30 ft length (29 ft 8 in. for curves) 60 lbs rails was the immediate need. The Workington Iron & Steel Co. could supply but the vital Manx Government licence was not forthcoming as the total allocation for the Island was already authorised.

In the customary manner of such matters, the IOMR Co. was referred to some half dozen addressees but eventually they were permitted to buy 100 tons in two 50 tons lots in 1948. To make a shipload the first consignment was to be grouped to rails and sleepers ordered by the Manx Electric Railway. There was a further problem. Rail was now produced at Workington to the new British Standard revised section and it would be

October 1948 before the original section was rolled again. The IOMR preferred to wait and the Ramsey Steamship Co. brought 100 tons into Ramsey in October.

In 1905 Douglas Corporation Water Works offered equipment which had been used on the contractor's railway in connection with the West Baldwin Reservoir construction (Vol. II p.18), and at the year end the IOMR bought 56 and 62½ lbs flat-bottomed rails mainly in 33 ft lengths; the details of the transaction are not known. Their first use was for contractor's lines in the improvements at Gob-y-Deigan (q.v.), and later use was found for them in the tracks in the then-new Carriage Shed at St John's. True to IOMR tradition, the rails have been relaid yet again, through Colby station: one drawback of mixing rail sections comes in the adequate fishplating of same. Close inspection of the rails shows them to be 32 ft 10 in. long complete with exceptionally long fishplates, giving a supported rail joint superior to any other on the Island, and virtually maintenance-free.

The Knockaloe Branch track was mixed: the flat-bottom rails were of steel 60 and 75 lbs, mainly of second-hand from an Irish source. Sleepers were both rectangular and half-round, the former 9 ft x 10 in. x 4 in., from an Irish standard gauge (5 ft 3 in.) line. When the Branch closed, the track was bought by the Insular Trading Co. Ltd. of 60, Athol St., Douglas, and much of it re-sold to the IOMR.

This material conveniently matched a quantity of ex-Great Northern of Ireland Railway 5 ft 3 in. gauge material bought in 1920; rails were steel, flat-bottomed, 27 ft, 28 ft and 30 ft long and when new weighed 79 lbs/yard. The marking is 'WEST CUMBERLAND STEEL G.N.R.I. 1875' (or 1878, 1882, 1887, & 1890). Special fishplates were bought and the Company was lucky to obtain further second-hand plates from T.W. Ward Ltd., Sheffield in 1948. The rails were at once put into the Ballasalla-Castletown section where they remain (Vol. II p.58,93,131).

In recent years materials have come from various sources: second-hand sleepers from British Rail, Douglas Southern Electric Tramways rails from the former Marine Drive Tramway, Channel Tunnel (Pilot Tunnel) rails etc. Thermit welding of joints was tried on a short section near Pulrose Bridge in 1968.

Douglas S.E.Tramways' rail was laid on the Marine Drive with 65 lbs flat-bottomed rails, 30 ft long fastened to steel sleepers. When laid on the IOMR it is satisfactory but requires additional time in matching rail-ends. Baldwin rail angle fishplates too, are in short supply; some cropping of rail-ends has to be done. For the investigative, the siding at Santon was still in Baldwin rails recently.

Those who seek evidence of recent relaying should visit the crossing loop at Colby, where the south side contains Southern Electric and Baldwin rails

- and a little South African Railways' 60 lbs material of 1928 for good measure - but the seldom-used north side still displays dropped joints, surely the very ones which caused so much mirth to us when small boys as our carriage sagged suddenly into them? Then there is the south loop at Ballasalla, now in good fettle in Channel Tunnel 75 lbs rails marked British Steel 1989-91.

For the future a quantity of 75 lbs rails of differing lengths and of War Department origin, is stacked in Douglas yard and will be laid with base-plates onto Scottish-supplied sleepers. Further relaying in this substantial material will, if followed up by regular track maintenance, improve the vehicle ride and reduce wear and tear on locomotive and carriage alike.

Track Maintenance

Permanent Way sections were as follows:

1.	Douglas-Union Mills	
2.	Union Mills-Crosby	Peel Line
3.	Crosby-St John's	
4.	St John's-Peel	
5.	Douglas-Port Soderick	
6.	Port Soderick-Santon	
7.	Santon-Ballasalla	South Line
8.	Ballasalla-Castletown	
9.	Castletown-Port Erin	
10.	St John's-St Germain's	
11.	St Germain's-Kirk Michael	
12.	Kirk Michael-Ballaugh	North Line
13.	Ballaugh-Sulby Glen	
14.	Sulby Glen-Ramsey	
15.	St John's-Foxdale	Foxdale Branch

Buffer Stops, Gradient Posts, Mileposts

The steam railways did not always use the type of conventional buffer stop familiar on the mainland. In early days of the IOMR a pile of sleepers laid across the rails was considered sufficient to prevent over-running (Vol. I Plate 1). A stockade-type was later substituted (Vol. I Plates 2, 8) and later still this was replaced by an all-timber construction having an iron face-plate to take the impact of the central vehicle buffer. (Both types are seen: Vol. I Plate 7, and the last-mentioned Vol. I Plate 25.)

Another fitting which prevented a vehicle from moving - but was hardly suitable for heavier impact - was a metal chock or scotch which would be bolted and padlocked to the rail; it had two projecting jaws which clamped on the railhead (Vol. II Plate 88).

Gradient Posts. These were white, plain horizontal boards with slope indicated by a line and figures painted in black on them. By the end of World War II, most had disappeared.

Mileposts were found on all linesides; flat-topped posts were used for full miles and pointed tops for half miles; quarter miles had the post top cut obliquely from top right to lower left, and three-quarter from top left down to lower right. Only full mileposts were numbered.

A further investigation will always repay the observant; for instance, a start could be made by an examination of the construction of level-crossing gate-posts - some, in 45 lbs iron rails, are marked 'Crawshaw'.

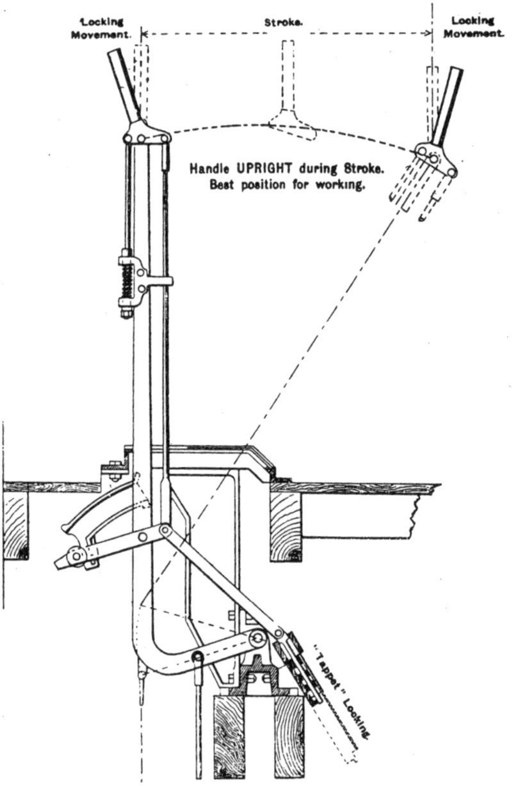

Details of Dutton & Co. frame as fitted in Douglas terminus signal box. *Ian Macnab*

Signalling

The year 1965 is a convenient date for the description of signalling and before winter closures and complete abandonment of certain sections of the Railway took place.

When the three Railway Companies came together under the IOMR in 1905, some transfer of signalling equipment from one original system to another took place, so there was no longer consistency in the appearance of it other than it reflected an economical attitude of using anything suitable. A plausible policy no doubt, but puzzling to the uninformed.

In general and until recent years, signals were of semaphore type. The MNR and FR were provided with a more sophisticated system at their opening than was the IOMR, whose earlier-age methods, though replaced in part, lasted in places until the present day. As a result, the signalling covered almost a century of history, all extant at one time and as attractive as any other feature on the IOMR. Throughout the length of the railway, signals and pointwork were operated by local levers with four exceptions; at Douglas the original installation was replaced by the IOMR in 1892 including a signal cabin which controlled most of the station. At St John's the arrival of the MNR in 1879 caused that Company to provide a small cabin to control the east end of the station where junction was made with the IOMR. Finally, at each end of the Foxdale Railway control of the yard was from an open lever frame.

Earliest evidence of the first signal on the Island is shown on the Deposited Plans (amended) by Vignoles dated August 1873*. At the entrance to the station is shown a 'Station Signal' (later 'Semaphore Signal') which is believed to have been a slotted type with double arms controlling every movement. There is no other signal anywhere on the Plans which extend to Peel (shown as a 'through' station).

In view of the lack of care in signalling matters concerned with the Union Mills smash of July 1873 (Vol. I p.65-7), the first Rule Book at least, gave no cause for doubt:

> Trains cannot pass signals without seeking permission to do so. The normal position of each signal is at danger and no signal is lowered for a train a train to pass until the driver gives warning of his approach by whistle. The driver will then see that the signal is lowered and will know that the signalman is attending to his train and that the signal has not inadvertently been left at clear and forgotten after the passage of a previous train. The Station Master is to give the sign to lower the signal, after everything is ready and clear for the train.
>
> An interval of five minutes must elapse between trains going in the same direction (there is no reference as to how the Single Line Staff was to be handled in such cases - *Author*).
>
> At 'out-stations' the signalman is to stand at the facing point whilst the train passes over. Where trains pass, they must use the left-hand running line. If two trains are to pass, one must be drawn to a dead stand before the other is allowed into the station.

---

*Plans discovered in the Board Room in October 1992 after the Author was invited to search for archive material.

As to the semaphores, the following is given:

> Red is the signal to stop: signal arm at horizontal. Green is for caution - proceed with care and slowly.* White is all clear. Signal lowered.

The rules infer that adjoining level crossings might have a mutual signalpost with arms arranged back to back, and that no train must pass it unless both arms were lowered.

Later Rule Books have additional matter to cover the 1892 Douglas

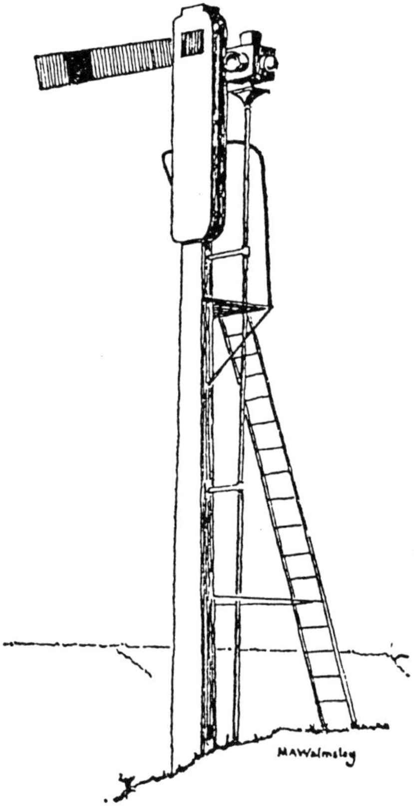

Signal at Castletown. *Maurice Walmsley*

*No indication of the arm position is given.

signalling and stressing that green is the colour for clear and red or white are danger aspects.

It is not known if there was a complete installation of signal types mentioned in the Rule Book but the IOMR 'standard layout' comprised a Home (stop) signal in the centre of the station with Distance [*sic*] (caution) signals at either side. In 1874 the Inspector wished to have Distance signals moved to a more distant position: some *were* moved and others locked with the points. Modernisation of this primitive IOMR basis came when Home signals were placed to control entry from either end of a station, and exit was in the authority of the train guard. Distance signals (Douglas excepted) were, in time, removed.

Douglas excepted, IOMR semaphores were often archaic and seldom of uniform appearance. One variety showed the arm at 45° for clear whilst on another the arm dropped entirely within the post. Lamps might be on top of the post aligned with the arm and having a red spectacle in front and a coloured backlight; when the arm was lowered both indications were white: occasionally the same fitments served but they were placed below the arm and nearer the ground. A lamp might also be placed on top of the post to revolve and display a coloured aspect, thus avoiding the requirement of a spectacle on the arm; the lamp was rotated by a vertical rod beside the post.

Operation of IOMR signals was by windlass, wire and chain, a windlass for each signal placed at each end of the layout. Later it was found expedient to place them in proximity. The windlass was held firmly when wound up by a ratchet and pawl; many of these broke and a spade handle (or) sufficed. Messrs A. Linley & Co. of Birmingham were the suppliers of most of the IOMR signal fittings (a firm notable especially for marine lamps) and also the windlasses - early references use the term winches.

A simple system of protection was recommended by Vignoles as early as 1873 whereby facing points were linked to the signal. Douglas, Crosby, St John's and Peel were had in mind. This was done by a slide in the point-blade mechanism through which a bar on the signal wire could pass if the slide was in the correct position Thus points which were incorrectly set for an approaching train would not allow the Home signal to be pulled clear.

A Report of 1874 states that all stations had Distance signals but, as yet, no others. By June that year the four facing points in the Douglas layout were recommended by Trevithick to be connected by rodding to a central place 'to save the yardman walking round'. The next year the Inspector insisted that the crossings at Closemooar, Ballagawne and Crogga be fitted with signals, in the last case Distance type; the IOMR Co. avoided expense at Crogga by Agreement with the landowner that following financial compensation, no signals would be required and it would treated as an occupational crossing.

Other than on the later installation at Douglas, the IOMR used local hand-levers for points which were weighted in favour of the favoured direction but had to be held up otherwise. Such points were trailed over, the lever making violent movements as the vehicle's wheels forced over the point blades.

On the Manx Northern the semaphore signalling had a more modern appearance save that at first all Home signals had fish-tail ends to the arm. (Signalling at St John's differed, and is described separately.) Some fish-tails were sawn off before the closure, whether it was haphazardly or to a system was not evident. Semaphores were more economically used, there being no Distant signals; the Home signals were operated by Stevens Patent Compensating Lever (the subject of an 1859 Patent by J.J. Stevens) whereby the operating wire is connected to a short chain which passes over a large pulley set in the base casting. By means of another pulley this chain then drags upward a weight which passes up the lever itself as it is pulled. The system found considerable favour on overseas railways. All the original MNR apparatus was supplied by Stevens & Sons of London.

The pointwork on the North Line had been much altered before notes were made of the original apparatus. Many turnouts had the standard IOMR hand-lever, and a few supplied by the Isca Foundry, Newport. At Ramsey (for instance) there survived a system which involved cast-iron 'boxes' sunk into the ground; a hand lever was pivoted at the top of the box with a weight suspended from it which rose in the box below when the lever was pulled. This caused the lever to resume a 'normal' position when the lever was released. A loose cast-iron lid covered the top of the box, and the lever projected through a slotted opening. Some lids were marked 'EASTWOOD, SWINGLER & CO.'*

In June 1881, the MNR having been directed by the mainland Inspector Col. Rich, to staff each station which had a passing loop with *two* men, by-passed the instruction by fitting padlocks to the facing point (trains trailed over the second point); at the same initiative, the signal levers were re-positioned near the station building allowing one man to manage operations alone.

This simple ploy was not adopted at Kirk Michael and Ballaugh where slightly more sophisticated measures were taken; however, as on the IOMR the method of weighting facing points to the preferred direction and detecting the signal operation to prevent a false signal indication being given, ultimately took the place of padlocks.

(In careful notes made in the 1930s by L.T. Catchpole, he mentions another supplier of cast-iron point-box levers as 'J. COWDY, LONDON' and equipment (not specified) by The Railway Signal Co. Ltd., although when the Author was searching in the 1940s these were not evident.)

*Eastwood, Swingler & Co., Victoria & Railway Ironworks, Derby; originally James Eastwood & Sons who amalgamated with Messrs Thomas Swingler & Son in 1867. Also bridge and roof builders, turntables, points and crossings manufacture. The firm closed in 1925. (See also drawing of similar equipment on the Talyllyn Railway. TALYLLYN RAILWAY (James I.C. Boyd) p.306.)

Douglas Signalling

The principal installation here dates from 1892 when Dutton & Co. Ltd., Vulcan Iron Ironworks, Worcester provided a signal cabin, approach and starting signals together with ground signals worked from the point blades*. (The whole establishment was dismantled when the station site was partially abandoned (detail see Vol. II) but the disused cabin still remains, separated from the running lines by road-access to bus accommodation.) The cabin formerly carried no identification but only a large enamel advertisement for soft drinks on the front; during the Ailsa regime it was given a name-board.

The 36-lever frame incorporated the maker's 'Spring Handle' Patent whereby the catch-handle and attendant locking-rod is eliminated; instead the lever handle itself is pivoted so that when the lever is pulled the handle comes back on its pivot. In full and mid-positions it is vertical and when a pull is completed the handle is pushed forwards to complete the locking movement. The quadrant plate is flat and does not hold the levers at all. The weakness of the system is that when a lever is pulled to bring a signal to the 'clear' position, an accidental knock on the lever handle causes it to fly back to vertical and the appropriate signal will return to the 'danger' position by action of its counter-weight. This could have disquieting consequences if a train was passing the signal at the same time. Aware of this weakness, the makers provided Douglas with a locking catch which might be pushed up under the handle.

The levers are coloured as follows:

Distant signals	Green
Stop signals	Red
Point levers	Black
Locking bars	Blue
Spares	White

The brass identification plates on the levers read PEEL or CASLTN where distinction is necessary and lever arrangement in the frame is not as mainland practice.

A common lever is used to connect outer and inner Home signals; there is an outer Home for each running line, carried on a bracket post which due to the curve in the track here, prevents clear sighting of the inner Home signals. The latter are carried on a bracket also, affixed to the side of the tank house; there are three arms applying to the Peel Line and two to the South Line - lowering of any of these will also lower the appropriate outer Home.

Levers 34, 35, 36 were originally spares but later connected to points.

Distant signals are 919 yards from the terminal buffers and 675 yards from the cabin; their aspect is electrically repeated therein by Siemens'

*Ref: Manx Museum R/103 (Douglas signals) n.d.

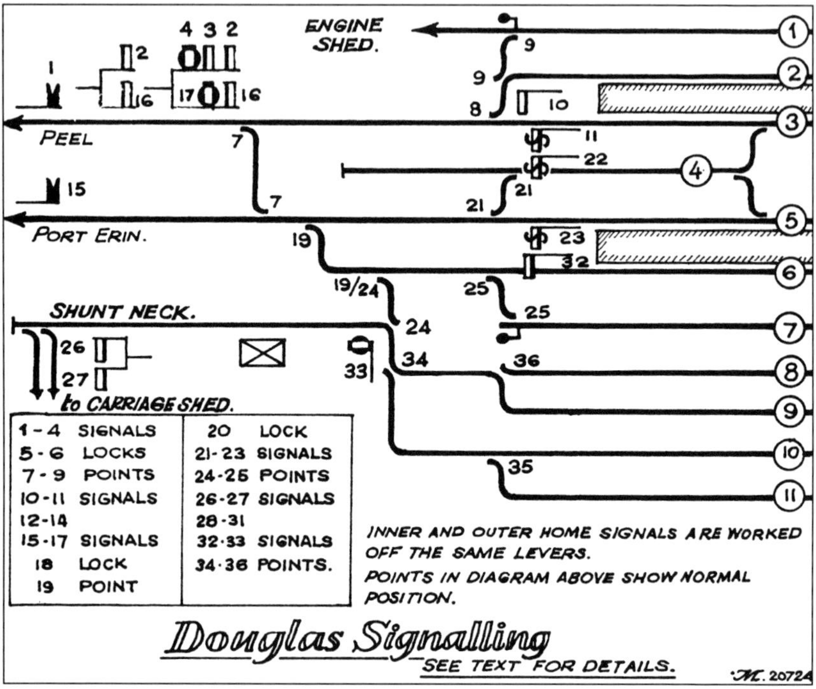

instruments. They have slack-wire adjusters.

The lever movements applying to Douglas were:

		Lever Movements							
From	*To*	*Points*			*Locking*			*Signals*	
Port Erin	Road 5				20	18		16	15
Port Erin	Goods	19	24			18		17	15
Road 6	Port Erin	19				18		32	27
Road 5	Port Erin				20	18		23	27
Peel	Road 3				6	5		2	1
Peel	Road 5		7		20	18	5	3	1
Peel	Goods	7	19	24		18	5	4	
No. 2 Road	Peel	8						10	
No. 3 Road	Peel							11	
Engine to and from Engine Shed		8	9						
To Goods Lines 8, 9, 10, 11		19	24						

From *To*	*Lever Movements* *Points*			*Locking*	*Signals*	
To Road No. 7	19	25				
Shunt to Road 8		36				
Shunt to Road 9	Normal					
Shunt to Road 10		34				
Shunt to Road 11	34	35				
From Road 4		21			22	
From Road 5					23	
From Road 6		19		18	32	
Depart from Goods Roads 8, 9, 10, 11	7	19	24	18	33	26
From Goods Roads for Peel Main	7	19	24	18	33	26

The semaphore signals are distinctive and historic; the spectacle plates are arranged one above the other and on the centre of the arm (similar to those used by the former Cheshire Lines Committee); the spectacles are red or green glass. The observant will note the arms are of two types, the position of the maker's name varying. Arms controlling subsidiary movements have a large white 'S' or 'O' affixed to the face; all are painted red on face and white on rear - this includes the spectacle plate. Earlier, the arms had a white spot on the face and a black on rear; the latter sometimes appeared as a black diamond. A signal post height did not reflect its importance, as was done on the mainland.

The arrangement of levers with the track diagram up to the time of alterations is shown below.

St John's Signalling

The simple signalling of the IOMR station in pre-MNR days has already received mention and by-and-large this system survived on the Douglas-Peel (south side) lines throughout the life of the station.

On the ex-MNR and Foxdale lines more sophisticated schemes pertained, a signal cabin being established at the east end of the station to operate the 'MNR portion' of the layout. A third system of signals controlled the Foxdale Branch station and its train movements onto the ex-MNR line: there was no *direct* connection between the Foxdale Branch and the IOMR line.

The signal cabin was formerly the sole property of the MNR and controlled the junction at the east (Douglas) end where the MNR line met IOMR metals. At the Peel end of the station there was no IOMR connection

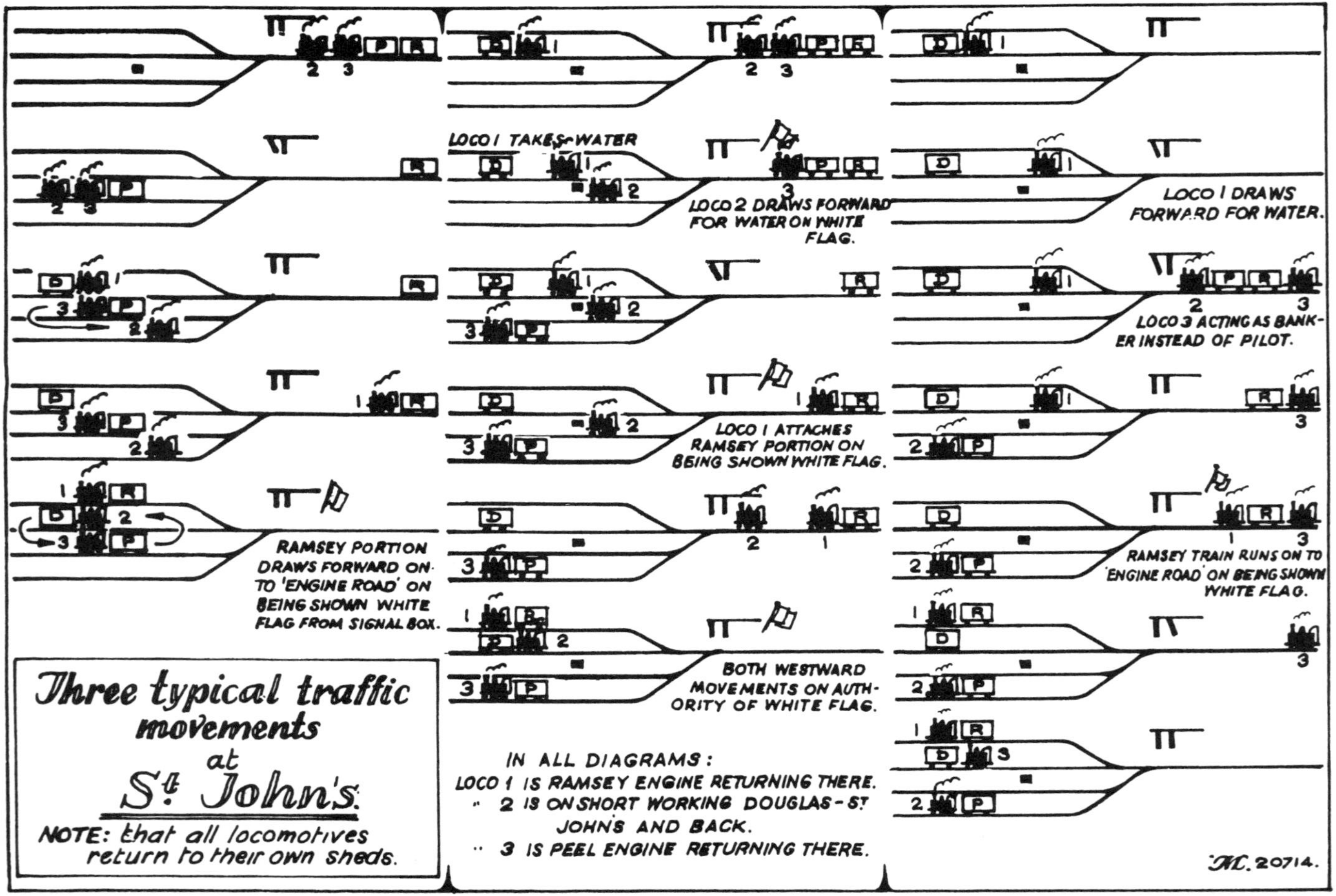

Three typical traffic movements at St John's
NOTE: that all locomotives return to their own sheds.
RAMSEY PORTION DRAWS FORWARD ON TO 'ENGINE ROAD' ON BEING SHOWN WHITE FLAG FROM SIGNAL BOX.
LOCO 1 TAKES WATER
LOCO 2 DRAWS FORWARD FOR WATER ON WHITE FLAG.
LOCO 1 ATTACHES RAMSEY PORTION ON BEING SHOWN WHITE FLAG.
BOTH WESTWARD MOVEMENTS ON AUTHORITY OF WHITE FLAG.
IN ALL DIAGRAMS:
LOCO 1 IS RAMSEY ENGINE RETURNING THERE.
" 2 IS ON SHORT WORKING DOUGLAS-ST JOHN'S AND BACK.
" 3 IS PEEL ENGINE RETURNING THERE.
LOCO 1 DRAWS FORWARD FOR WATER.
LOCO 3 ACTING AS BANKER INSTEAD OF PILOT.
RAMSEY TRAIN RUNS ON TO 'ENGINE ROAD' ON BEING SHOWN WHITE FLAG.
M. 20714.

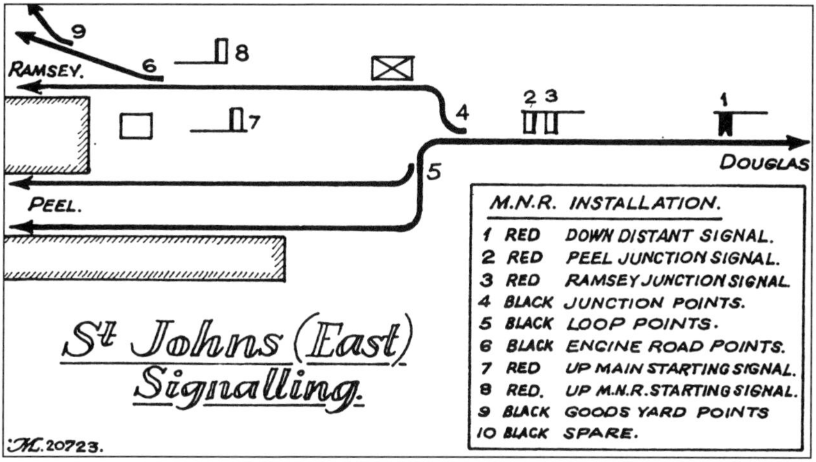

with the MNR and the points were controlled by a myriad miscellany of ground point levers! Here too was the one MNR turnout not worked from the cabin possibly on account of the distance involved - the facing point for trains entering from Ramsey. There are no Starting signals at the west end.

The cabin's frame is by Stevens, having ten levers with tappet locking. The building itself is wooden on a stone base and reached by a small flight of steps; it was also notable as most suitable for hot-house plants. The frame arrangement is:

Lever	1	Red	Down Distant signal
	2	Red	Peel Junction signal
	3	Red	Ramsey Junction signal
	4	Black	Junction points
	5	Black	Loop points
	6	Black	Engine Road points
	7	Red	Up Main Starting signal
	8	Red	Up MNR Starting signal
	9	Black	Goods Yard Points
	10	Black	(not connected)

The definitions are taken taken verbatim from the plates on the levers.

The thinking behind the arrangement was to protect IOMR trains and movements from any risk of MNR operations, so that, Douglas apart, Lever 7 worked the only other IOMR Starting signal. The system was somewhat lavish by Island standards, but the MNR was funding it all and there is the legend that the IOMR took advice - as usual - from its friends at Crewe whose standards were mainline and not insular.

At the extreme west end of the location are four signals applicable to trains travelling eastwards and of puzzling aspect to those unfamiliar with Manx railways. In the matter of the foregoing description, only two of these four signals are relevant - the third on the north side of the train entering from Ramsey and that on the south side of the incoming train from Peel, both Home signals operated from the west end of the station. The remainder is concerned with the Foxdale Branch.

Other movements in St John's combined MNR/IOMR station in which it was necessary to pass the cabin, or draw forward against a danger aspect, were given permission by a white flag waved from the cabin window.

Foxdale Branch Signalling

The Branch is considered to commence by the junction off the ex-MNR line at the west end of St John's (see mention previously). There were formerly three platform-located lever frames on the platforms, viz. at St John's (Branch station), Waterfall and Foxdale, again supplied by Stevens & Sons under the authority of an order per the Manx Northern. The nine-lever frame at Waterfall was removed in 1898.

The nine-lever frame on the Branch station worked the junction and Home signals; there were no Starting signals. More recently the frame had been reduced to six levers by the removal of three, and some of those remaining were not connected. The plates on the levers read:

1 (not connected)
2 (not connected)
3 Up Distant signal*
4 Up Home signal†
5 Up Line points#
6 Siding point§
7 Down Home signal¶
8 Down Distant signal*
9 (not connected)

An iron strap across the quadrant plate, secured by a padlock, prevented illegal movement of the levers.

Reviewing the complete St John's signalling emphasises the unusual background and the need for the rationalisation of the whole station which was contemplated in the 1920s but deferred for financial reasons. The lever locking in the cabin suggests the original intention was to use the platform lines for *all* trains whereas the most northerly loop without a platform was commonly used for Ramsey-bound trains, requiring a flag signal from the cabin as there was no suitable semaphore.

Waterfall was equipped with passing loop and signals but there is no

* removed before 1948
†removed 1955
#i.e. Junction points
§i.e. Passing Loop points later worked by ground lever
¶removed about 1950

record and the number of levers in the frame is not known.

At Foxdale the nine-lever frame was removed in 1930:

1	Spare
2	Signal from siding
3	Siding catch points
4	Siding Home signal
5	Platform Home signal
6	Main Line far points
7	Main Line near points
8	Platform Starting signal
9	Spare

The definitions given are noteworthy, as is the provision of a Starting signal due to Foxdale being a terminus.

Such ground point levers as existed on the Branch were marked 'A.S. NELSON & CO. LONDON & GLASGOW'.

Finally: over the entire IOMR system there were local exceptions to the generalisations previously made, usually because of gradients, or the lack of clear sighting of signals, crossing gates and stations. Some gates had 'targets' on them to make them more distinguishable and others locked with the signals which protected them. Generally speaking it was the moderate speeds of trains, the familiarity of all with the method of working and what, to mainland ears, appears excessive use of the engine whistle, which compensated for lack of sophistication.

Single Line Working

The single lines of the steam railways were protected from danger by the use of the simple Single Line Staff system which did not differ in practice from the mainland. Authority for any vehicle, be it platelayers' trolley or complete train, to occupy any length of single track (termed a Staff Section) was in the form of a Staff - in the Manx case originally a wooden baton recognised by shape, colour or wording thereon - there being but one Staff for each Staff Section, and carried by the driver on the engine when travelling. At each end of a Staff Section it was to be retained by the Station Master who would hand it to, or receive it from the driver as the case may be. Usually there was a passing loop at each end of the Staff Section. As the IOMR grew from infancy, more Staff Sections were necessary and from 1882 new Staffs were given sophisticated profiles on a wood lathe, though the plain outline type also persisted.

In the event of two or more trains travelling in the same direction and following one another along a Staff Section, the last train to travel the Section carries the Staff but all preceding trains carry a Ticket authorising passage along the Staff Section, and made out by the Station Master uniquely for that purpose and journey. When the driver is handed the Ticket he is also shown the Staff for the Section by the Station Master, who retains it until the last

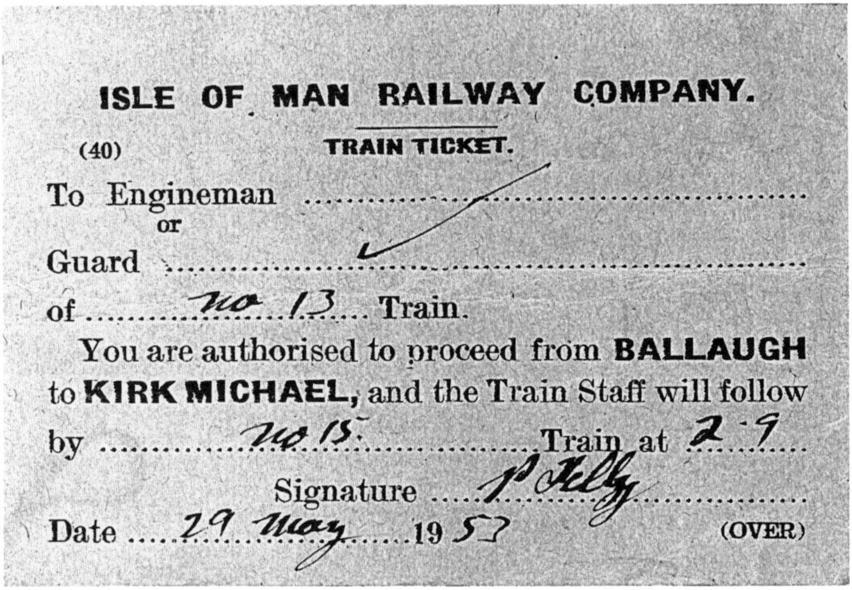

ISLE OF MAN RAILWAY COMPANY.

(40) **TRAIN TICKET.**

To Engineman ....
or
Guard ....

of ......no 13...... Train.

You are authorised to proceed from **BALLAUGH** to **KIRK MICHAEL,** and the Train Staff will follow by ......no 15...... Train at 2·9

Signature ......P Kelly......

Date ......29 May......1953 (OVER)

An example of an IOMR train ticket.

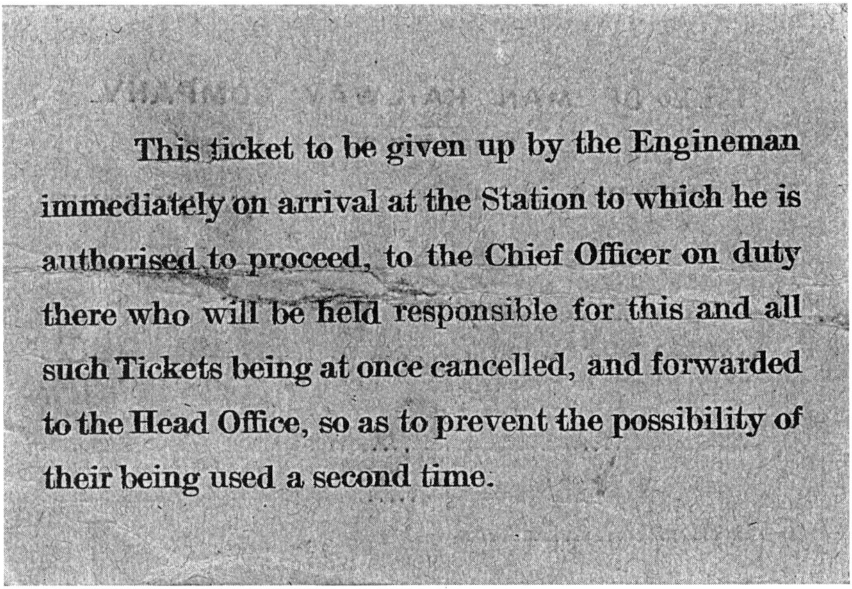

This ticket to be given up by the Engineman immediately on arrival at the Station to which he is authorised to proceed, to the Chief Officer on duty there who will be held responsible for this and all such Tickets being at once cancelled, and forwarded to the Head Office, so as to prevent the possibility of their being used a second time.

following train. This procedure ensures the Staff is always available but, in emergency, a Staff might be sent to the other end of a Section by any possible means except by rail. Ideally, the colour background of the Tickets agrees with that of the Staff.

The near-latter-day Staff Sections of the full Railway were;

Peel Line:	Douglas-Union Mills-Crosby-St John's-Peel
South Line:	Douglas-Port Soderick-Santon-Ballasalla-Castletown-Colby-Port Erin
North Line:	St John's-St Germain's-Kirk Michael-Ballaugh-Sulby Bridge-Ramsey
Foxdale:	St John's-Foxdale

The above was not the final list, as subsequent closures of stations meant that they were closed also for Staff purposes. Ticket and Staff was exchanged manually; there was no apparatus.

It was necessary that the Tickets be stored in a stout wooden box in the Station Master's office and to prevent unauthorised issue this was locked by a key attached to the Staff itself. A through station had two boxes, each coloured as the Staff for the Sections either side of it and underlining the importance of regular eyesight tests for station staff as well as trains crews. A typical box, painted Yellow Ochre, was lettered in black 'BETWEEN UNION MILLS & DOUGLAS'.

The recently-present Sections were:

Short section:	Colby-Castletown	Blue
	Port Soderick-Douglas	White: 2 Red bands
	Castletown-Ballasalla	Brick Red
	Port Soderick-Santon	Brick Red
Long section:	Santon-Port Erin	Pink
	Douglas-Santon	Green

There were a considerable number of Rules concerning Staff and Ticket Working but two are sufficient here:

95 The Guard with a Train must not give the signal to start from a station until the Engine Driver has shown him the proper Staff or Ticket.

108 When trains are assisted by a Pilot Engine, the Pilot or front Engine will carry the Staff.

Today, the Staff Sections for the South Line are still those which were described previously as 'near-latter-day',though the Staffs themselves have been subject to 'modernisation'. The men who use the modernised Staffs hold them in contempt; further, it is confusing to find the modern version is used alongside certain old Staffs.

The modern (or more accurately, the 'revised') Staff is formed by a metal rod having a turned wooden handle at each end into which the rod is inserted by a threaded portion, this in turn being secured in the handle by a locking nut. On the intermediate rod between the handles may be be placed a coloured plastic collar each denoting the Staff Section for which it is marked and colour-coded. [When the Douglas-Ballasalla section is operative for instance, the Staff will comprise the collars for Douglas-Port Soderick (Yellow), Port Soderick-Santon (Tan),Santon-Ballasalla (Brown).] Each collar is a substitute for what on the old system, would have been a wooden Staff.

If the operative Sections are changed, amendment must be made to the Staff by unscrewing the locking nut and removing the handle at one end, with adjustment to the collars as demanded; some practical difficulty may be met when the heat on the footplate has seized the locking nut and so the collars cannot be changed!

Telegraph & Telephone

Two fundamental Rules have always existed:

106 The departure of every train or engine is to announced by telegraph or telephone to the station in advance.

107 No train is to leave the station in the rear until the arrival of the previous train has been announced by the station in advance.

A Telegraph Book was kept at each station to record all such messages.

It follows that from the first the single needle telegraph instrument communication between stations was the lifeblood of the railway, for every movement of a vehicle was prefaced by its use. The telegraph had many years of use before the telephone was deemed an acceptable alternative.

The provision of the telegraph involved the most complicated correspondence between the mainland and Manx Governments, due to the need for adequate powers in the Bill for formation of the Railway Company and the Postmaster General. Correspondence involving the Governor and the various parties began in January 1872 when the right to allow the Postmaster General to enter railway property 'to construct such lines of telegraphs' and the right of the Railway Company 'to use such telegraphic wire' was considered. The Company also claimed the right to add additional wires to poles for an agreed rent.

It is pertinent to mention that this same correspondence resulted in an Agreement to carry mail, but not regarding the telegraph. The Postmaster General (PMG) would not agree to the Bill containing any rights over himself and, to summarise the considerable documentation, the Railway was obliged to provide poles and a single wire along the Douglas-Peel Line (in time for the opening?) except between Douglas and Union Mills where an additional wire gave electric bell communication with Quarter Bridge level crossing.

By March 1874 Trevithick wrote to the Directors about a proposed Agreement with the PMG, he recommended:

1 The existing telegraph line and instruments on the Peel line be made over to the PMG.
2 The PMG to provide,maintain and allow for railway use for railway messages only, one line of wire and one instrument at each station over the existing railway, and that to be constructed, free of charge.
3 Beyond the above, further instruments and maintenance must be paid for by the railway.
4 All postal telegraph officials and stores to be conveyed free of charge, whether on railway business or not.
5 The railway to provide a Government Telegraph Office at any or all of its stations, 'with fire and gas'.

Trevithick thought the PMG should be provide two wires throughout, one for the instruments and the other for electric bells which all stations and lodges should possess. He thought a single instrument would suffice at stations but two would be needed at junctions. He warned that if the PMG required to establish 'Telegraph Stations' on the line, separate buildings might be needed 'as the present stations are not large enough to accommodate a telegraph official in addition to the Station Master'. He thought that Station Masters should not be allowed to transmit Government Telegrams as 'railway duties will require their undivided attention'. In every comment Trevithick had the construction of the Ramsey line in mind.

A contract (the Railway's copy is missing) was duly made, for on 29th June Trevithick reports that the Government Telegraph Engineer is about to erect the poles and wires on the Castletown Line 'and appropriate all of that existing on the Peel Line except the single wire which the Government is bound to maintain for the use of the railway'. (At this period there was a *third* line for the prior-mentioned Quarter Bridge crossing bell but Trevithick complains that the Board have ignored his plea for every crossing to be given bells.)

It was the Postal Telegraph Engineer's duty to maintain the instruments; the 1874 Report continues;

> . . . he has not succeeded in making our instruments work . . . the railway is still as it has been from the beginning, practically without a telegraph. We have never yet been able to communicate from station to station; sometimes we can get one or two . . . never been complete or reliable.

The type of alphabetical instrument installed had already been abandoned as useless elsewhere (although Trevithick insisted that there were other alphabetical instruments which *did* work) and the Post Office had offered to put in single needle type alongside the others. 'The Engineer has worked assidiously at the instruments but the result has been nil . . . so much screwing up and regulation is required every time a message is sent . . .'

Eventually the single needle instrument prevailed though the mode of working (Code or Morse) has proved difficult to establish. The telephone took its place in 1898 (see many references under 'Telegraph' in Vol. I) and in this age of sophisticated communication, even the telephone which did duty for almost a century, has been replaced by wireless.

The troubles with the telegraph - previously ignored by historians and yet so vital to safety - were an additional worry to Board and Management in the accident-prone months of the early IOMR, and to reduce it Trevithick wisely staffed all the stations on the nascent South Line with experienced railwaymen from the mainland.

Douglas Station etc: Whistle Codes

Before reduction of the layout the tracks were given numbers and the enginemen could give the signalman request for movements by means of a code on the whistle.

Train approaching Distant signal, Peel Line - one long whistle
Train approaching Distant signal, South Line -two long whistles
Leaving engine shed for No. 1 line - four short whistles
Leaving No. 1 line - two short and one long whistle
Leaving No. 2 line for shunting purposes only - one short whistle
Leaving No. 2 line for 'right-away' for Peel - one long and one short whistle.
Leaving No. 3 line for shunting purposes only - one short whistle and one crow
Leaving No. 3 line for 'right-away' for Peel - one long whistle
Leaving No. 4 line, engine release line - whistle long-short-long.
Leaving No. 5 line for shunting purposes only - three short whistles.
Leaving No. 5 line for 'right-away' for Port Erin - two long whistles.
Leaving No. 6 line for shunting purposes only - one crow and one long whistle
Leaving No. 6 line for 'right-away' for Port Erin - two long and one short whistle
Leaving No. 7 line - one crow between two short whistles
Leaving No. 8 line - two crows
Leaving No. 9 line - whistle short-long-short
Leaving No. 10 line - two short and two long whistles
Leaving No. 11 line - two short whistles
Leaving Nos. 4, 5, 6, 7, 8, 9, 10, 11 lines for Peel - three long whistles. To be given after whistling off the correct signal for the line from which the engine or train is leaving.

The whistle code used elsewhere is summarised below:

Approaching a Home signal at danger (Douglas excluded) the whistle is sounded continuously until the signal clears; clearance is acknowledged by a sharp turn downwards of the whistle valve.

A prolonged whistle is sounded on approaching all level crossings, whether manned or not.

To call for handbrakes application, three or more short sharp whistles, according to urgency.

To call for the release of brakes, one long whistle between two short ones.

Lamps

Engines - it is not essential for engines to carry lamps during daylight and there is no head code. A lamp is carried on the front after dusk or in fog. Light engines carry a red tail lamp in the latter circumstances.

Trains - in foggy weather or after sunset every train carries a red lamp on each side of the rear end. If a wagon is attached to a passenger train, it must display a red light hung from one side of it. During daytime, a red board or flag (or an extra tail light at night or during fog) denotes Special Train Following.

All trains to have side or tail light attached to last vehicle at all times, during daytime it need not be lit but furnishes information that train is complete (rule does not actually say this lamp must be red).

Clocks & Fencing

These two features were also concerned with safety.

A signal was sent by telephone from Douglas station each day at 10 am to synchronise all clocks; the practice featured on a circular of 25th August, 1919 when it was discovered that some stations were 4-6 minutes different.

The inadequate IOMR fencing of the line was a continual complaint in the early years but the official intention - though not carried through completely - was to carry seven wires on 7 ft wooden posts at 3 yd centres. Brick intermediate posts were to be added later. Materials costs were estimated @ £170 per mile. There is no evidence that bricks were introduced but many miles of good wire still exist.

The MNR used wooden posts also, but the iron type additionally of proprietary manufacture popular with mainland systems.

Rules

An IOMR Rule Book was issued for the opening of the Peel Line in 1873, and subsequent Books have appeared:

9th May, 1878	
27th October, 1882	(with supplement on shunting)
17th July, 1890	(with supplement re 'Signal arrangements at Douglas station' to come into operation 10th May, 1892)
5th April, 1922	
3rd June, 1967	(Ailsa period), later copies from Wombwell to A.M.B. Crookall, signed
3rd June, 1974	(issued by Lambden)
May 1981	(issued by Jackson), May 1985 (issued by Jackson).*

There appear to have been two MNR Rule Books; one was issued for the opening in 1879, and a second was issued using the IOMR's Rule Book of 1890, using its printing plates with amendments and simplification where necessary. It was dated 17th September, 1890 ; there were 280 and 272 rules for IOMR and MNR respectively.

IOMR Rule Book
(5th April, 1922)

From the Company's Rule Book are given the following abbreviated extracts from, or synopsis of, the Rules, selected as being either unusual or unique (in all cases night conditions apply also to foggy weather).

Station Masters

137. Carriages and wagons in sidings are to be secured . . . 'so as to prevent them being blown by strong winds on to the main line.'

141. Station Masters are to affix additional tail lamps (where a special passenger train runs unannounced) to the end of the *preceding* train. The Guard of that train is to warn stations of what is following.

146. Station Master to see that rails are sanded for engines in slippery weather.

151, 152. One train is to come into a loop and be brought to a stand before an oncoming train may enter the other side; the signals to be held at danger for both trains and clearances to be checked before the signal is lowered for the second train.

161. Station Master to see that trains contain an adequate number of braked vehicles and that there are men for them.

162. Station Master to give Guard signal to start the train.

Gatemen

88. Gates to be kept closed, except to allow traffic to pass (a legacy of the days when road traffic was light - *Author*).

193. Gates to be closed to the horse-road five minutes before a train is due.

195. Special Trains must give prolonged whistles for crossings.

*1994. There are now new regulations for working the truncated steam railway system operated by Isle of Man Railways.

200. A red board by day and three red lights at night denotes that Special Train follows. Two red lights denote light engine follows. These to be displayed at rear of train or engine; Special (or engine) will pass within fifteen minutes.
201. A red board by day or a red light at night, hung on the front of the engine, denotes that a Special Train will shortly arrive in the opposite direction.

Enginemen

207. At the end of a loop line or through sidings entering upon a main line at a station, a white post is placed beyond which no engine may advance without instructions from the person in charge. At night a white light will be shown on this post.
213. Driver in the front engine of a train assisted in the rear, on receipt of Guard's signal to start, to give two crows to rear driver which must be repeated by the rear engine. Neither engine to move forward until that time.
242. Guard to wave green flag by day or green lamp by night to start train and (245) immediately train has left station to show white flag by day or white light by night from van, whereupon brakesmen must show a similar signal to the enginemen who will give a short acknowledging whistle. This is to show that each trainman is at his post and that neither Guard nor Brakesman [*sic*] has been left behind.

Guards and Brakesmen

251. Where there are two guards with a train, the under guard rides in the van next to the engine to note any irregularity in running, oscillation of carriage or wagon; (252). The senior guard will be at the rear of the train.
262. Guards must be careful not to put ladies in the compartments reserved for smoking.
263. To secure the attention of the enginemen, in addition to using the Cord Communication, if there be one, Guard to apply his brake sharply and then release it . . .
270. Guards and Brakesmen are not to enter into conversation with passengers . . .
274. Brakes are always to be applied at the following places:
    1. From Oakhill Cutting down to Douglas station.
    2. Approaching Ballasalla from Douglas, for the last 1½ miles into Ballasalla.
    3. Approaching Peel from Douglas, for the last ½ mile into Peel.
    4. Leaving St John's for Peel, for the first mile after leaving St John's.
    5. From Peel Road station bridge, down into St John's.
    6. From Ballaugh Distant signal to Ballavolley Crossing.
    7. From Foxdale to St John's.
275. Speed between White Hoe Hospital and Douglas not to exceed 8 mph.

Platelayers and Others

285. . . . where a broken rail is discovered platelayers must at once slur [*sic*] nearest sleepers under broken part of rail.
295. Whole line to be inspected by platelayers every morning before 7 am in summer and 8 am in winter and in the evening before they cease off work. (Platelayers' trollies are referred to as 'lorries'.)

Examples of Rates for exceptional articles - period 1907

	s.	d.			s.	d.
Barrel Organs		8	Boats requiring more than one			
Coffin, leaden, empty	2	0	truck (per mile per truck)			4
Coffin, wooden, empty	1	6	Harmonium or Harp in case		1	6
Corpse in Guard's Van with			Piano at owner risk in			
exclusive use:			Guard's Van		2	6
Adult	15	0	Gravestones	(each)	2	6
Child	11	0	Tricycles		1	0
Corpse in plain Luggage Van			Bicycles			6
without exclusive use:			Wheelbarrows			4
Adult	10	0				
Child	7	6				

(A selection from a considerable list.)

The IOMR management sent frequent circulars to remind staff that rules were being infringed, and to emphasise discipline. Some examples follow:

First Class passengers complained that holders of Market Tickets sometimes travelled in their compartments. Management pointed that 'spot checks' were to be made on occupants of First Class carriages - Port Erin-bound checks were to be made at Port St Mary,Douglas-bound at Santon or Port Soderick; on the Peel line at St John's or Union Mills; on Ramsey trains all tickets were to be checked St John's. On the North Line, examination was to be made at Kirk Michael or Sulby Bridge. Suspicion arose when passengers were heard boasting about their achievements . . .

Two old ladies were found walking along the line because it was a short-cut to home; their excuse was that everybody did it. A Special Train came along which they did not expect; fortunately the engine crew spotted them.

Saturday nights saw much sky-larking with drunken characters riding on roofs, steps and footboards. Upholstery would be cut, windows 'snatched' and broken; Service men in both wars were held to be responsible. Staff were alerted to the 1873 bye-laws.

Frequent complaints arose from passengers in a train running late, that further delay was incurred by shunting. It transpired that Station Masters had not marshalled wagons beforehand . . . 'glaring cases of thoughtlessness . . .'

A flag-man was on duty to protect Post Office Linesmen working on the line at Kirby; work continued into darkness by the light of a powerful acetylene lamp. This was flashed into the eyes of a train driver with near-disastrous results. There was a failure for the look-out to have flags by day and lamps by night. The Post Office had not made arrangements to work by night and trainmen had not been informed.

Gatemen were warned to ensure their gates were fastened securely before giving the all-clear signal. A train passing through a crossing was struck by one of the gates which was loose; it caught and smashed off the guard's ducket. By good fortune, the guard was not sitting in the ducket but was thrown to the floor violently. The gate was thought to have been blown by the wind, or the air eddying round the passing train.

Trains were being passed between certain stations without signals being given by telegraph or telephone. A Special was not permitted to leave a station in the rear of a regular train until the arrival signal for the preceding train had been given.

In hot, dry summers Station Masters were to deal with any fires 'in the vicinity of the line near their stations'.

A Circular, the effect of which was to avoid anyone being given a reply to the most innocent enquiry and to give the IOMR a reputation for secretiveness, read: 'Employees are strictly forbidden to discuss or give any information or statement concerning any accident . . . or any expression as to the cause, or any other point be made'.

Some stations were not lighting the signal lamps on Sundays. 'This is an amazing position. . .', wrote the Manager. This was in 1930 when a considerable service obtained. But the Circular was sent in September when signal lamps would hardly be needed. That same month a reminder about having a signal lamp on the Crossing Gates, 'and the use of a Hand Signal Lamp in addition' went out.

Fly-shunting had been practiced for years, but in 1930, 'Slipping of Wagons' was judged to be counter to Rule 21, and 'the practice must cease forthwith'. The instruction was honoured in the breach, especially by Down trains at Castletown, where the dexterity of the staff in detaching Brewery wagons was long admired by onlookers.

There was considerable difficulty following the installation of point detectors in the late 1920s and staff had to reminded of their function and weakness. Ramsey's two facing points were fitted in May 1929; the staff were told the signal could only be lowered when the points were correct, and that when pulled, the points were then locked; consequently the signal had to be returned to danger if an outgoing train or engine wished to use the points in the 'trailing' direction. (The outgoing movements would be a light engine running round its train or a train leaving the 'bay platform' (or 'New Road' as the Circular still names it).) By the end of May, Port Soderick (Santon end), Ballaugh (Ramsey end), St Germain's (Ramsey end), and Colby (Douglas end) were fitted. But station staff continually omitted to return the signals to danger, and trains trailed through the locked points with disastrous results; the casual way in which signals had been operated for years - in extreme cases the arm was left permanently in a lowered position - created a habit which a mere Circular could not break.

Finally, in October, the loop points at Kirk Michael (Ramsey end), Sulby Bridge (St John's end) and Crosby (St John's end) were done.

For a decade the points were operated almost without incident - or the Station Master 'forgot' to report the incident - until a derailment occurred at Port Soderick in October 1929 when an engine burst the points there (this was the scene of a more spectacular derailment the year before). This was ill-timed as the crossing gates at Quarter Bridge had been demolished shortly before entirely due of neglect of obeying a signal: in this case the driver saw the gate signal at danger and thought it would be lowered before he reached the gates. He carried on, saw the gates across the line . . . and was lucky that no vehicle was on the crossing when he struck them.

A long, vitriolic Circular ensued.

Quarter Bridge crossing was the scene of a 'photo-copy' incident on 18th October, 1944 - again without personal injury. It was stressed the crossing was on an 'S' bend and sighting was limited, therefore signals for both directions were provided.

Again, a driver optimistic of the signal being lowered, passed it at danger . . .

The locking of points and their respective signals (a mandatory state of affairs on the mainland since an enactment of 1889) was responsible for greater safety at the before-named stations but easygoing ways continued elsewhere. After the last train of the day had gone, an employee would leave the crossing signal at 'clear' and, after over-sleeping the next morning would be suddenly awakened by the sound of splintering timber as a train rammed the gates. It was a common sight to see a pile of twisted gates leaning against the outer wall of Douglas Works.

In January 1944 employees were again reminded 'that they were not permitted to give any information about the Company's business . . .'

A reversal of the practice recommended by the Company's Engineer was that from July 1940, banking at the rear of trains would cease, and a second engine was to be run in front as pilot. However, banking of 'heavy trains' up to Port Soderick would continue. (The change may be due to wartime blackout conditions: *Author*).

The Second War brought instructions to screen all carriage lights, stations and glare from locomotive cabs, the latter by pulling down the canvas 'dodger'. Recalling the passage through the countryside of a night-time train, one observer remarked that locomotive blackout was almost impossible and that he could always judge the length of a train because the guard's portion was a blaze of light!

Traffic & Operation

One of the most interesting features of the Island railways was the immensely different types of business which the building of a railway attracted. No such estimate of potential business exists for the IOMR but six years later it was possible to assess the benefits a proposed northern line might bring (Vol. I p.100). There is no end to a study of each type of traffic so created, even at the risk a repetition. A generalisation might be:

The principal source of the Island's household *coal* came from Cumberland, with Lancashire, the Midlands and South Wales also featuring. The foremost arrived at Ramsey, the remainder largely at Douglas, with a little at other ports i.e. Castletown. Steam coal for the railways continued through Ramsey until after World War II. Coal for power stations, gas works etc. came to nearest port if available, and was not an important commodity on rail. The Foxdale district mines which imported via Ramsey, formed the most important customer; depots at Ramsey and Foxdale were linked to the MNR and at Douglas and St John's with the IOMR; the last two failed to entice the mines away from the MNR. Of the Foxdale Branch, the MNR official statement of 1894 had 'MNR run two mixed trains daily in each direction, used almost solely by the miners and for the lead company's private wagons'.

It required about two days to unload a ship at Ramsey. To speed the work a few empty wagons would be pushed to the ship-side, and loaded wagons pushed into one of the shorter sidings on the quay until a goodly rake was formed. The tram-bladed points were hazardous for the engine's pony trucks but re-railing was expertly done.

IOMSPCL ships did not feature predominantly at Ramsey. Timber-carrying sailing vessels from the Baltic mixed with top-sail schooners registered in Irish, Welsh and Scottish ports. At a later date steam-ships would be found hidden among the bulky wooden sailers - 'Puffers' from the Clyde for instance. The first Ramsey Steam Ship Co. failed in 1861 but a second undertaking of that name was formed by seven enterprising Ramsey business-men and registered on 17th April, 1913. Initially it was to be called The Manx Steam Carriage Co. Ltd., and the main cargo was coal. Their first vessel was built in Larne, delivered in 1914 and named BEN VEG. The forename BEN was retained for later ships; this private concern is still in business.

Early photographs of Ramsey Harbour often show two or three MNR coal wagons standing on the quay; close inspection shows they were not loaded haphazardly, but that the lumps were carefully locked together to form a tall roof-like ridge on top so ensuring a maximum load and preventing fall-out in transit.

Ramsey was one of three harbours (the others being Douglas and Peel) to be improved under Governor Loch by Act of Tynwald, 1861. Work involved

Isle of Man Railway Company

FOR A DELIGHTFUL

DAY, AFTERNOON or EVENING

Visit THE NEW

GLEN WYLLIN

PLEASURE RESORT

Situated on the Western Shore, adjoining Kirk Michael Station.

BRIGHT AND ENTERTAINING

THE GLEN WITH THE LONGEST HOURS OF SUNSHINE!

GAMES : Tennis, Bowls, Putting, etc.
AMUSEMENT PARK : Swings, Roundabouts, etc.
MAGNIFICENT MOTOR BOATING LAKE!
REFRESHMENT PAVILION.

Music, Singing and Dancing

Delightful Ramblage in Sunshine or Shade
Meandering Stream :: Miniature Waterfalls

Miles of Even Sandy Shore. Sun and Sea Bathing

☞ DAY EXCURSIONS ☜

from **Douglas Station** (Athol St. and North Quay)
Special Afternoon and Evening Excursions

NOTE: Your Tickets on the Trains and Buses enable you to reach Glen Wyllin.

1938. A. M. SHEARD, Secretary and Manager.

EXAMINER

SUNDAY MORNING!

Kirk Braddan

OPEN-AIR SERVICE.

ENJOY A LEISURELY STROLL TO THE—

RAILWAY STATION

(ISLE OF MAN RAILWAY)

or

CENTRAL BUS STATION

(ISLE OF MAN ROAD SERVICES, LTD.)

Both adjoin the North Quay,

AND TRAVEL BY

Train or Bus

Cheapest and Best Way!

Return Fare:

Trains at 10-0 10-10 10-20 — **6d.**

Buses from 10-0 — **7d.**

NOTE.—Isle of Man Road Services **RED BUSES** are the only Buses which take you **ALL THE WAY** to **Kirk Braddan**. The **TRAINS** also take you **right to the Open-Air Service.**

1937. A. M. SHEARD, Secretary & Manager.

Printed at "Herald" Office, Douglas.

building Abernethy Breakwaters at each place in the early 1860s, but the incomplete 'Abernethy Birdcage', as it was known, at Douglas was destroyed by storm in 1865 and not replaced. (James Walker's plan for a stone breakwater at Douglas had been shelved in favour of the cheaper Abernethy timber and rubble type. Shortage of London-source funds made for inadequate harbours; the railway was to be similarly hampered a decade later.)

Horse manure formed a useful traffic from the streets of both Douglas and Ramsey. In 1886 and 1890 the IOMR was involved; the pioneer method involved a dump at St John's for the use of farmers, from which a larger scheme evolved in special sidings being provided at Crosby and Santon, and smaller dumps elsewhere, for the convenience of farmers (see Vol. I).

Wood's diary gives insight on IOMR enterprise on catering for provincial resorts which were inclined to complain if Douglas kept all the *tourist traffic* to itself. Wood organised evening excursions if it appeared they would show profit but, if risky, were underwritten by the promoters. Before the turn of the century, excursionists could enter Douglas in the early evening and return late; there were no such Boarding House restrictions as 5 pm High Tea, or 'Front Door locked at 10 pm' which killed evening traffic in more recent times. Attractions included Miss Wood's concerts, the circus, the Bishop preaching on Douglas Head, theatre, variety (after the First War the IOMR had seasonal kiosks at some places of entertainment), sports gatherings, church events, shows (Dog, Poultry etc.), horse racing on the beach, regattas, football etc. matches, and more. Of course, many of these were day-time events as well, and every one was advertised by the then common-place handbill, a brightly coloured paper leaflet hanging on a suitable board at every station which proclaimed in large heavy type 'Strawberry Teas', 'Swings and roundabouts', the fare . . . a diverse collection may be seen in the Railway Museum.

Not to be outdone, other resorts imitated Douglas to prevent it becoming the centre of entertainment; sports days, regattas, Sunday School outings could as easily take place provincially and the Railway was ready to give them financial support to the exclusion of Douglas events, the latter providing less income when the participants were Douglas-based and did not use the train. Two examples of railway-linked attractions were Glen Wyllin at Kirk Michael (Vol. I p.209 etc.) and the evening excursions to Port Soderick. The former's demise was caused by World War II, and the latter hit by the coming of the Douglas Southern Electric Tramways. More recent, shorter lived destinations were Lough Neb and Ballavolley Wild Life Park (the latter still operates without railway connection).

Military and wartime traffic affected the Island in various ways, not least its suitable position for accommodating prisoners/aliens in both major wars.

Earlier references have been made to Volunteers Camps before World War I; Territorial Army Camps; Knockaloe Camp in particular; the internment of aliens at Port St Mary and Port Erin; naval and airforce bases at Castletown, Jurby and Andreas and the *Workmen's Trains* in connection with the building of aerodromes and its affect on Sulby Bridge station; the removal of Foxdale Mines' spoil dumps for the building of runways; Ballacostain Halt (Rifle Range platform or Pistol Castle Halt) for the use of King William's College and the Army, and Poortown Quarry for instruction in the use of explosives. The list could be continued, suffice to show that this small Island made a useful contribution to the war effort in relation to its small land area. The strain upon the IOMR's limited stock and staff, and the unprecedented wear and tear which could not be fully remedied because of a lack of materials, was a battle the Company also had to fight. Against this, wartime conditions, (after producing an initial financial crisis) led to some outstanding profit figures and the failure of management to foresee what would be the post-war cost of capital expenditure and renewal. Hindsight suggests that a more prudent limitation of dividends etc. might have left the Company in a better position, but hindsight also shows that few could have anticipated how post-World War II events would effect the Island's holiday traffic.

In former times the *Church* (in a collective sense) created much extra passenger traffic. At a period when Conformity and Non-conformity was thriving, church-building and anniversaries were marked by excursions. Church premises were used for concerts, well attended Sunday Schools held imaginative picnics . . . church-related occasions helped to fill the calendar when the holiday business died down. During the Season the Sundays-only service to Kirk Braddan was unique and thousands would sit out on the grassland in confidence that the weather might hold. The Railway was adept in carrying passengers back to Douglas in the event of a downpour, and there was even an element of rivalry between staff as to who could do it in the shortest time.

*Bishop's Court Halt** follows on naturally: the original somewhat hazy operating arrangements are not among surviving records and the first mention comes in the Minute Book for 1910 complaining of the *ad hoc* system there. Persons, connected with the Court or otherwise, were taking advantage of it so the Diocesan Office was told that unless the Bishop made special arrangement, no train would stop for less than three persons. Stowell had a rooted objection to the place; why should they stop trains at the whim of the Bishop? What was the definition of 'considerable numbers' for whom

*Bishop's Court (frequently Bishopscourt). The one time home of the Bishop of Sodor & Man, sandwiched between the route of the MNR and the Peel-Ramsey road, about 1½ m. north of Kirk Michael. Consists of three sections of differing date viz: house, tower and chapel, the site being a moated stronghold. Under its original name of Ballachurrey (Latin: Balicure) it is first noted as being the domicile of Bishops in 1231. The tower is the oldest part of the existing buildings, dating from 1350-1400. The Bishop was the Chief Baron of the Island. [Extended description in ISLE OF MAN, (E.H. Stenning), pp.208-210.]

the train was bound to stop? He clearly expected back-up from the Board when he pointed out that the railway had no control over the matter. But the Board was not going to engage itself in affairs which might lead to personal embarrassment; the Island was too small to risk a dénouement. In 1902 a firmer hand decreed that trains would only stop to pick up passengers; presumably for the return they could be met at a station.

From July 1934, when visitors were invited to the Court on Tuesday afternoons, a 2*s*. return fare and a special stop was agreed; later that season the stopping of two trains in each direction for a Garden Party was arranged. Next year saw this scheme continued, but additionally the Bishop intended to make personal announcement that the gardens would be open on the following Tuesday when he took the Open Air Service on Douglas Head the previous Sunday. There is evidence that these openings and 'Garden Fetes' were held until 1936 at least.

Trouble arose in December 1943 when on two occasions trains from Ramsey failed to stop after passengers informed the guard at Ballaugh; he recommended they alight *there* as he had no authority to accede to the request. On another occasion the difficulty was met by keeping the Orrisdale signal at danger and bringing the train to a stand. If a lone passenger was to be picked up the Court would telephone either Douglas or Ramsey - oft times the train would stop to find the Halt deserted. Bishop Ralph agreed that should any of his family wish to alight, a request to the guard would suffice; the minimum of three persons to be set down or picked up applied otherwise but, in the case of a relative or 'personal friend of your Lordship's, we would be pleased to stop the train if the request is one which is made personally by your Lordship'.

Actually the Bishop said it was more reliable 'to send my signed card to Mrs Cubbon at Orrisdale crossing to ask her to set her signal at danger, but sometimes she has failed'. An informal way of stopping the train at the Halt had operated as long as anyone could remember: when an oncoming train's whistle was heard as it approached Orrisdale, the crossing signal would be held at danger and then bounced up and down until an acknowledging whistle was made.

An embarrassing situation arose when a guard at Ramsey was told to stop his train at the Halt, but forgot to inform the driver. They reached Kirk Michael and the guard 'went across the road to Mr Crowe's house . . . to use the phone . . . I got in touch with his Lordship and he said he would send his car if I would hold the train . . . I readily agreed . . . the car arrived with the stranded passenger who had been left at Bishopscourt . . .' We may hope that Sheard would have been as ready to pardon the sin as the Bishop would have been.

Other categories of passenger included visiting dignitaries, royalty, the

Governor, fishermen, school children; for important persons a train of saloons would be used, carriages filled with floral decorations, while the operating staff would be clad in new uniforms and boiler suits and stations received a coat of paint, pathways a layer of tarmacadam and whitewash freely applied to platform copings. The Governor was treated hardly less lavishly, for he was the monarch's representative. Fishermen had to use service trains and were involved only when the fishing fleet was in a Manx port, away from Island homes.

Catering for *school children, fishermen, workmen,* and *Post Office mail* involved the common denominator of carriage stock with a difference. School traffic was intermittent and the stock could be stabled out in the weather during the holidays: it was adequate but mainly of ex-four-wheelers which were added to a service train. As a train passed, the school carriages were distinguishable by the clamour within, doors being opened and shut *en route,* and exercise books being held threateningly from open windows. As for *fishermen,* they left behind in the empty carriage a pungent evidence of their passage, and the Company's inter-departmental correspondence confirms that it boded ill when the fleet was based on Douglas. *Workmen* were more acceptable and a number travelled on a daily basis, a majority when Government-backed schemes to relieve unemployment were in hand. Foxdale *miners* were locally housed and appear to have used the railway on Saturdays when Peel was the most popular source of 'entertainment': some honoured Douglas too, and the newspapers contain letters complaining about late night scenes on station and in train. These occasions paled beside the junketings following the monthly Foxdale Pay Day; there survive anguished memos between railway staff complaining that miners refused to pay the fare, climbed on to the roof, preferred to travel in open wagons and put themselves at risk by returning to Foxdale along the railway, some so drunk they would lie across the rails.

The carriage of *mail* touches upon the key to the Island's existence, the Steam Packet service; founded in 1830 the Company provided the essential link with the mainland. Though there was an amount of internal mail traffic on the IOMR, the lifeblood of IOMSPCL business was the holiday-maker from the mainland. The sailing times of the packet ships determined the frame of the railway timetable; it was common for ship arrivals to be delayed into Douglas and there was an arrangement with the Post Office regarding the amount of time trains might be held for late steamers. Basically this involved the appearance of the delayed vessel's smoke on the horizon, and a message conveyed to the station. In extreme weather when Douglas was storm-bound and Peel or Ramsey were used instead, special trains were run for the benefit of the mail . . . passengers were less important than honouring the mail contract.

Special passenger timetables co-incided with extra sailings and insular holidays; peculiar to the Island were the public holidays on *Tynwald Day* and *Hollantide*. Great pressures were put on the railway system during traditional Lancashire Wakes Weeks, Whitsuntide, Stockport Trinity etc., for they lay in the Manx 'catchment area'. The island was popular in south-west Scotland, with 'Glasgow Fair' memorable. Tynwald Day brought extra-ordinary pressures on the staff for the timetable was intense to convey the morning rush, followed by a period of waiting whilst the ceremony took place. Initial methods involved outward-bound trains every half hour using three locomotives until noon, but there were angry scenes at Douglas when due to an inexperienced booking clerk, people missed the train and arrived too late. Every piece of passenger stock would be needed; the Empress Vans were fitted out with seats taken from station platforms.

Shortage of inexperienced staff in the booking office caused timid men to lock themselves into the room to escape the wrath of angry, impatient crowds on Tynwald Days. But the problems were not confined inside Douglas station; the provision of adequate trains was a headache for the Traffic Department. In 1967 the inexperienced staff of Ailsa's regime made frantic efforts to assemble an extra working to cater for a restive multitude. Coaches, though in poor condition, were not a problem, but a locomotive with enginemen to work it, certainly was. No. 16, which seldom saw St John's except on Tynwald Day, was on standby but hardly fit to be in steam; there were holes around the firebox door whose frailty was emphasised by the large lumps of coal heaped around it on the cab floor to protect it from mishap but did little to prevent a rush of cold air ingressing over the top of the fire. As usual on such occasions, the Workshop staff had to turn out for the emergency in the persons of Bobby Corlett, (Foreman Fitter) and Tom Kinvig (Fitter), as driver and fireman respectively. The result was the unlikely scene of No. 16 at the head of a train waiting at the *Peel Arrival Platform* for the 'Right-away'. On the platform beside the engine's cab was a small group of railway men and overheard was, 'Don't kick one of those b**** lumps of coal Tom, or it'll be in the firebox without you opening the door'.

Mixed trains were run for the *markets* at Ramsey, Ballasalla and St John's (Monday, Tuesday, Wednesday respectively) with the same rake of stock . . . cattle vans and open wagons for sheep and pigs. It would be attached to the first Down train, loaded after the beasts had been bought, and returned to Douglas. Once there, often unloading on the passenger platforms, the beasts went on hoof or by lorry to the abattoir, or for shipment. Butchers, market traders and drovers had a coach allocated to them.

The *Tourist Trophy Races* had little additional impact on passenger travel; an Ambulance Train was stationed at St John's from earliest times, and was provided as a courtesy gesture (see Vol. II p.94 etc.).

The limited interference which TT races had upon the railway can be traced back to 1906. Before that year the race circuit necessitated the closing of five level crossings, but opening *was* permitted for 30 seconds when a car came into sight (motor cycle racing did not begin until 1907). As a precaution, every car driver had a copy of the railway timetable given to him before the race started, with times of arrivals at level crossings; he was instructed to fit it to the dashboard. Complaints came from farmers whose day's harvesting was postponed. The combined efforts of police and coastguards were needed to monitor the safety of spectators; doctors, ambulances and first aid staff were available every 1 -1½ miles. The event totally disordered the Island and largely because it was agreed the railway system should not be disrupted, the course was altered so that, at length, only one level crossing was affected. (The eliminated sections were mostly in the south of the Island.)

Fishing and *farming* were the historic occupations of the Manx - while the men were out in the boats it was commonplace for the women to do the farmwork. Farming methods were backward until guidance came from Scotland and later still, the formation of an Agricultural Society. Notwithstanding other special days which created special trains - even recalling the hiatus which Tynwald Day brought - it was the Island's annual Agricultural Society's Show which often led to supreme chaos. Show trains had to be sandwiched between the normal passenger timetable. and whilst a certain degree of control could be exercised over passengers, no such reliance could be placed on livestock which, in matters of numbers and time required, could not be foreseen before the Show Day itself. If a loaded incoming train of (say) 45 wagons needed to unload animals at Douglas, lines 4, 5, 7 were utilised and stock driven out onto the platforms.

Wood's diary reveals a 'Cattle Show' was held each year, at Ramsey and Castletown alternately - the diary states an 'Agricultural Show' took place in Castletown in late July and in both Douglas and Ramsey in early August. These were separate from the Flower Shows in Glen Helen, Peel and Douglas. It must have been a relief that Kirk Michael Show was out of high season, and Douglas Dog & Poultry Show at Christmas.

A condensed account* of the special traffic for Douglas Show held at Quarter Bridge on 10th August, 1939 (all other trains as timetable) shows:

Port Erin Line			
Douglas	*dep.*	6.40 am	No. 10 + F25
Ballasalla	*arr.*	7.04	
Ballasalla	*dep.*	7.10	No. 10 + K13, 17, 21, 22, 23, 25, F25
Douglas	*arr.*	7.35	

*From the observations and personal collection of the late M. Walmsley.

Peel & Ramsey Lines

Douglas	dep.	8.20	No. 5 + K8, 6, G1, K17, 13, 23, 25, 21, 22
Union Mills	arr.	8.28	
Ramsey	dep.	7.00	No. 8 + F17, K2, 26, 11, 18, G5
Sulby Bridge	arr.	7.09	
	dep.	7.13	pick up G9, K19, 15, 20, 5
Sulby Glen	dep.	7.16	
Ballaugh	dep.	7.23	
Kirk Michael	arr.	7.30	
	dep.	7.35	pick up K12, H25, G2
St Germain's	arr.	7.47	
	dep.	7.50	pick up G11, K6, G12 (note duplication of K6)
Peel Road	arr.	7.53	
	dep.	7.57	load bull into G12
St John's	arr.	8.01	
	dep.	8.10	pick up G10, K14a, 14
Crosby	arr.	8.20	Cross train No. 2. Detach No. 8.
	dep.	8.35	attach No. 12*. Pick up H13, 23
(Depart 10 min. late)			
Union Mills	arr.	8.43	
	dep.	8.46	attach No. 5 + Special from Douglas
(Depart 13 min. late)			
Quarter Bridge	arr.	8.53	unloading livestock from train now consisting of: Nos. 12 & 5 + G2, 5, 9, 10, 12, H13, 23, 25, K2, 5, 6, 8, 11, 12, 13, 14, 14a, 15, 17, 19, 21, 22, 23, 25, 26, F17. (This train was put down as 32 vehicles)
(Depart 17 min. late)			
Douglas	arr.	10.06	

*No. 12 had worked out on Train No. 2 from Douglas; No. 8 worked it forward from Crosby.
H wagons were carrying sheep and pigs.
[Note activity of railway before Show had opened.]

There was also the traffic which was conveyed under the heading of *minerals* and *goods;* this included stone chippings and tar in barrels for the *Highway Board* who had a depot adjacent to Crosby station to which coal was delivered for the Board's steam rollers. Poortown Quarry supplied much of the stone and a much smaller quarry at Ballyvolley had its own siding off the MNR and sent stone to Ramsey for domestic building. There were occasional loads of difficult proportions for the *Harbour Board,* an example being the conveyance of some massive piles for Peel Harbour; in this a number of idle four-wheeled coach underframes were coupled together and fittings added to frames to adapt them suitably.

Previous references to *sand* and *gravel* used for building and for the construction of sea-front promenades at Douglas, reveal that St Germain's, Peel and St John's area were the exploited sources, the IOMR having its own pit at St John's. Bricks were made at Glenfaba (Peel), St John's (Abbey Works), and West Craig, etc. Only Glenfaba had direct railway access, and in the last instance they were loaded at Sulby Bridge. Though closed down after World War II, *Castletown Brewery* sent its produce over the whole Island by rail; the station's siding was the usual haunt of several 'G' vans carrying barrels to and fro. The Brewery used a steam wagon for local delivery.* Another railway customer in the 'Thirst Trade' was *Downward's* (appropriately enough), makers of aerated waters. Thinking that plenty of space would be found in the Guard's van at Douglas for the family luggage, how often had it been usurped by closely-stacked crates of their Ginger Beer . . .

A less visible liquid was the conveyance of *milk* in churns, also in the Guard's van, a remunerative business for the IOMR but lost to road lorries as soon as post-World War II restrictions were removed.

Lime from quarries around Ballasalla was loaded at Castletown and dumped at stations for use on the land.

Stations and gatehouses were permitted an allocation of *coal* on a monthly or annual basis. Extra fuel might be thrown from the engine 'by private arrangement', in these such instances without slowing. An informal ruse to service the section Santon-Ballasalla was to couple a wagon of coal on the end of a Port Erin train. The wagon would be detached at Santon, some coal unloaded and then, with a rope attached to the brake handle the operator jumped on and, gravitating westward, he held the brake 'off' by pulling upwards on the rope. At Ballalona a stop would be made by jumping down on the brake lever (similarly at Ballawoods and Ballahick) and so to Ballasalla where, unloaded, the wagon would be pushed into the siding for return to Douglas. Was management a party to the practice? Dare one ask if such occupation of the single line was covered in some way?

Bog ore was latterday means of keeping down weeds (see Vol. II p.117). Round *timber* was rarely seen on a train, but the 'twin' bolster wagons were used; more often their load was a signal post or telephone poles. *Oil* was not carried until Ailsa's regime and proved to be a short-lived idea.

The foregoing list is exhaustive; social and economic changes have today brought about the total eclipse of these many-sided activities; within three decades they became history.

Now to pass on to the related subject of train operation. The early days were marked by incidents caused mainly by employees' unfamiliarity with railway procedures, together with the limited resources the infant IOMR could afford. There were few sidings and a wagon would be left on the

*This was a vehicle by Charles Burrell & Sons Ltd., St Nicholas Works, Thetford, Norfolk. First supplied to Norman E. Box, Haulage Contractors, Ardwick, Manchester. It is illustrated in Burrell's catalogue: Works No. 3494, 5 ton type, 2-speed. Supplied new 9th July, 1913.

running line to load/unload - this must have meant propelling the wagon in front of the engine at times. Such tactics were more persistent on the MNR so at the take-over a horrified IOMR management took steps to tighten discipline immediately.

By 1897 the IOMR was preparing schedules to run separate goods trains in an attempt to speed-up services against the threat of a spread of electrification (see Vol. I p.224/229). Before that all trains had run mixed. Wood was aware of threatened competition and had prepared a scheme the previous year '. . . to . . . improve and increase our train service so as to popularise the Railway and make it more attractive to tourist . . .' Sproat would examine the possibility of speeding up trains 'and if drivers could do with less time at stations'. Two more Peel Line trains daily would come on in the summer; Wood said he expected Sproat to have a sufficient number of good competent and reliable drivers and firemen to work the trains'.

The Douglas Inspector received a complaint from Wood concerning the delay at stations due to wagons being attached to trains '. . . annoying to passengers to be shunted about and detained . . . especially at St John's . . . would it be practical to run separate goods trains . . . one on the South Line in the morning and one on the Peel in the afternoon. You will have to consider lime traffic, bricks from Peel, cargo from the steamer, fish, cattle and general goods . . . would you require an extra engine; shunting at Douglas must not be lost sight of . . .'

In reply the Inspector felt the scheme could be beneficial but could not be operated 1st May-30th September, 'passenger trains are too numerous'. He recommended that insular newspapers carry an advertisement that wagon working on passenger trains will be discontinued and a note added about the times of goods trains, goods to be delivered at goods sheds one hour before departure time. At the time stone was being carried from Ballasalla (see Vol. I p.110/178) and Crosby to Quarter Bridge for the Highway Board and required an extra engine twice daily.

The Inspector said a 'Heavy Goods Brake Van' would have to be built, with wide doors suitable for carrying pigs and sheep which always delayed loading into passenger vans. Lime would be carried daily from Ballasalla by a goods train, empty wagons being brought from Douglas. Loaded brick wagons on the Glenfaba siding could be pulled out by the previous passenger train engine whilst it was idle in Peel station awaiting departure time, and empty wagons pushed into the private siding by the same engine (confirming the siding existed in 1897).

Regarding the specific complaints about shunting delays at St John's; all goods traffic for the MNR 'is worked on slow passenger trains and is attached behind their passenger vehicles' i.e. no shunting on the part of the IOMR was needed.

Isle of Man Railway Company.

SPECIAL NOTICE.

CONVEYANCE OF FISH.

The Railway Regulation Act, 1878, Section 26, provides that

"THE Company shall not be bound to convey Fish or any "Goods of a perishable nature, or which might cause damage " to other goods if placed in contact therewith or near thereto, " unless reasonable notice be first given to the Company, so as "to enable them to provide waggons or trucks for the separate "conveyance of such Fish or other goods."

THE ISLE OF MAN RAILWAY COMPANY GIVE NOTICE that they will only receive Wet Fish for conveyance subject to the above section of the Railway Regulation Act, and, that they will not be responsible for any loss or damage that may arise through the Fish being delayed at any Station, waiting the arrival of a suitable Waggon in which to convey the Fish.

THOS. STOWELL, Secretary & Manager.

Douglas, 1904. B. & S., Ltd.

Finally the Inspector doubted they had sufficient wagons and siding space for Wood's plans. Notwithstanding, goods trains on the Peel Line commenced on 26th March, 1897, being one morning and one afternoon train in each direction. Fish and livestock wagons could still be attached to passenger trains, also wagons to and from MNR. Drivers were warned to 'run slowly' when descending gradients and 'to be able to stop at any moment'. Five minutes were allowed at intermediate stations.

Later that same year a similar pattern of goods trains was run on the South Line, with comprehensive instructions for train crossings and use of the Staff and/or Ticket. Certain trains travelling on a Ticket were required to carry 'a red signal' in the rear; in the case of a goods train following with the Staff, 'a red signal must be carried in front'. Precise rules were in force i.e. certain passenger trains on the Ticket bore a red signal in the rear and on the Staff, a red light in front. For the operating staff, the introduction of goods trains brought these daunting procedures which must have had their complications at first.

There must have been a change in circumstance regarding *fish traffic*. When the IOMR opened it was considered that there would be no demand as fish was landed at Peel then shipped to the mainland by steamer; possibly the number of visitors had created sufficient call to have fish wagons built on old coach chassis to carry, barrels, boxes and baskets of fresh catches by the first available passenger train into Douglas.

Trevithick had made some novel suggestions about passenger loadings and (private) sidings, a shortage of which lasted until the turn of the century. He recommended private sidings *between* stations (for instance, the brick yard at St John's), 'the iron rails of the siding to extend only as far as the boundary fence', after which wagons could run on wooden baulks . . .' of course, the engine would never go into the siding, and the points locked with bolt and padlock, out of the control of the owner of the siding'.

He commented on the weather being the greatest factor in numbers travelling, and that during his employment there were four trains daily which ran empty if wet but after an hour's warm sunshine, two of the daily trains would be filled. A train consisted of six (four-wheel) carriages.

Turning now to post-World War II days, seven bogie coaches was the limit for one engine but this was reduced to six on the South Line as maintenance became poorer - if over six, a banking engine to Port Soderick was employed, even working through to Port Erin if ten coaches were one train; in this way the train could be more easily handled at Port Erin. Up trains in this period had a banker east of Ballasalla if loaded to more than eight coaches. In summer 1961 a ploy long adopted was in being - to clear Port Erin of visitors at the day's end, the 4 pm departure was run as two trains; the first stopped only at Ballasalla having left Port Erin at 3.50 pm with seven coaches. The second left at 4 pm with eight on and was banked on days when there was a spare engine to await it at Ballasalla. This was effected by the *modus operandi* just described, the previous arrival had an engine at each end.

It had been a long-standing practice to use a banking engine, or 'helper', when necessary as an extra 'pusher' behind a train. The most common section where such expedient was used lay in assisting heavy trains up the gradient from Douglas to a point near the summit at Keristal where the driver of the banking engine could sense that the train engine had overcome the climb. As soon as this was reached the assisting engine, which was not coupled to the train, would shut off steam and drop back in a cloud of smoke from its brightly-burning fire. If the Douglas station shunting engine was thus used, it could resume that duty with the least delay.

More recently, the banker has been coupled to the train but by means of a hole drilled through the coupling 'chopper', and a rope or chain passed through it leading back to the footplate, the chopper could be jerked clear of the rearmost vehicle of the train. Even more recently, the Inspector has frowned upon such historic and simple aids to expedition and the banking engine has to be coupled and chained, then uncoupled when it is stationary!

Until recent years, the timetable was always dictated by the coming and going of the Packet Boats. The form of the 'Railway Choir's' music was, as it were, determined by the composer but interpreted by its resident conductor, whose skill lay in making last-minute changes was only matched by the Choir's competence!

The highlight of the summer's Douglas station scene was after arrival of the morning steamers from the mainland. There would be a sudden invasion of people, on foot, by bus and diligence, together with handcarts, and steamer porters each with his registered number on an enamel plate attached to his armband. The luggage would be piled into the vans whilst the anxious owner checked that his property was safely on the correct train, and porters made their way along the train to re-assure passengers they had done their task, and to collect a tip.

The Port Erin train (as just described) might be a lengthy one and the banker at the platform-end would be the first IOMR locomotive to meet the visitor's gaze; not all would spare it a second glance but each would notice how diminutive it seemed compared with those they knew at home. Was it capable of getting them there? The train would be a long one, many passengers confused, and the lifting of the safety valves on the train engine, plus the warning whistles of the railway staff, only heightened their nervous tension.

On the other side of the station, the combined Peel and Ramsey train would be drawn up, the scene of equal mayhem. Two engines would be at its head. Hung from the handrails of the guard's composite coaches were long red-painted, yellow-lettered boards proclaiming the destination of that portion, Peel in front, Ramsey at the rear. Station staff carefully monitored the loading, and at St John's they would have to do the same.

Departure time came; platform whistles blew, engines did the same, and two trains surged forward in a glorious cloud of exhaust steam from chimneys and drain cocks and, to bring up the rear and not be outdone, the Port Erin banking engine passed by with its own cacophony, to begin to blast its way up The Nunnery Bank. It was an exhilarating and final 'Amen' to a daily spectacle.

Such Douglas scenes are but memory, but their existence is undoubted. Not so at Ramsey. An imaginative plan to initiate a passenger service along the quay line from the Market Place in the early 1900s came to naught. The quay was an unpredictable place and the tracks often impassable; horse carts could finish loading if they were over half-full, otherwise they *had* to move for a train. Human nature being selfish, this was too much to expect. Implementation of the idea would involve trains of six coaches in the summer and half that number in winter, but only in daylight. The Harbour Commissioners could see problems . . . as they did about a Douglas extension along the quays.

Accidents

There is plenty of evidence that the Island had its share - and perhaps more than that - of accidents, in part due to the limited source of suitable labour, the fascination of the railway to public vandalism, the attractions of alcohol, inadequate fencing, and the vulnerability of the Island to high winds. These are only a selection of causes and human frailty could be found in most incidents; it is re-assuring that apart from fatal accidents to employees, fatalities to passengers were rare.

The number of accidents can be assessed by noting the many references given to them in the first two volumes, with possibly the Union Mills collision in 1873, that of a 'runaway train' at Douglas in 1925 and between a light engine and train at Oakhill in 1928 as coming the most prominently to mind. These have already been described. A more explanatory picture can be assessed by listing the main causes involving trains:

Animals on the line due to poor fencing.
Collisions with farm vehicles on occupational crossings.
Vandalism; mostly in the form of obstructions on the line within the vicinity of Douglas.
End-on collisions, mostly in shunting and often at St John's.
Drunks and vagrants using the railway as a footpath.
Impact with crossing gates, either full or sidelong.
Runaways, derailments or gate-opening due to gale-force winds.
Passengers struck by lineside objects when riding in open wagons.
Frequent fatalities to crossing keepers unaware of trains approaching.
Derailments due to flooding, fallen trees.
Facing points on loop lines not being properly closed/forgotten/ position not appreciated in darkness/vandalised to prevent operation.
Trains out of control due to skidding wheels making brakes ineffective (especially due to mists, for which the Island is well-known).
Locomotive derailments especially in running bunker-first, due to lack of attention to the permanent way.
Unsatisfactory state of maintenance of rolling stock; that taken over from MNR was justifiably suspect.
Staff failing to judge the position of trains correctly, and being knocked down.
Rolling stock being left on running line, or too near it, causing collision.
Knockaloe Branch had particular hazards; trains hit road vehicles on the ungated crossing and wagon derailments were frequent due to poor trackwork.
Glenfaba Brickworks' tramway crossing; a scene of several fatal accidents causing death to the horse. IOMR not responsible.
White Hoe level crossing; many collisions with medical and commercial vehicles. A notorious location.
Detached from train - runaway vehicle. The only serious instance demolished the crossing gates at Ballasalla (see Vol. II p.220).

Such was the influence the IOMR Co had over the local press that both pictures and accounts of mishaps were frequently unreported, but the

Governor received a report on each and usually made comment in due course . . . often showing his ignorance of railway working.

Although this summary of the causes of accidents does not allow individual cases much detail, such are considered more fully in the previous chronologies; a few additional instances are of interest. Information on working the Knockaloe Line is scarce and in the collision mentioned the IOMR denied their driver was responsible: the date was 16th May, 1918 when CALEDONIA with five empty opens was 'proceeding very slowly down the Knockaloe Camp Road . . . about 22 yds from the road crossing the guard at the main entrance signalled it to stop . . . to allow a cart to get clear. After sounding the whistle . . . the engine had just started . . . Guard Clarke had just stepped off it to see if the crossing was clear when a motor van belonging to Mr Faragher, Douglas rounded the corner travelling much too fast and did not sound his horn . . . the Guard narrowly escaped being caught between the engine and the motor car . . .'

Col. Rich's Report dated 9th August on the 1873 collision* at Union Mills adds details of the considerable train at this early date; it left Peel at 5 pm and consisted of an engine running bunker first, a brake composite carriage with attendant brakesman, 'nine carriages, a guard's van with a guard in it and a goods waggon with platelayers in it'. Arrival at Union Mills eight or ten minutes late; tickets were collected there and all the time the Home signal showed 'clear'. The 'Ballasting Train' which ran into the first mentioned comprised twelve or fourteen loaded wagons . . . the men on the wagons could not apply their brakes in time. Rich stressed that he had received a previous undertaking from the Company that only one engine in steam (or two coupled together) would operate, and the line would be worked by the Staff System. 'I told the Manager that trains should not be allowed to follow each other until the *block telegraph* was in operation'; it appears that the Staff System did not come into use until after the accident. 'The trains were worked on no principle at all and the ballasting train ran about the line as the ganger in charge thought fit . . . no Railway Servant was appointed to look after it . . . the ganger in charge had no experience of single line . . . the Station Master at St John's where the train started, and at Crosby and Union Mills were quite inexperienced in railway management . . . they had a book of Regulations which was not explained to them and which they did not understand'. It was a damning Report.

The steep incline from the back of Foxdale station gave runaway wagons a hearty start if the brakes were imperfectly applied; on occasion RAMSEY waiting in yard, was hit. Imitating the Foxdale miners who rode the open wagons back to St John's rather than be fare-paying passengers in the carriage, a lad jumped onto the back of the last wagon un-noticed. He clung there with his hands intending to drop clear when the train slowed but when

*The original Report is deposited with the Manx Archives.

he did release himself, his jersey was caught on the coupling and he was dragged along the track and fearfully mutilated.

Lost chimneys are not a common event, but a falling tree on The Nunnery Bank in the winter of 1937-38 dislodged the chimney on CALEDONIA: legend has it that this was the original chimney, it being preferred to that supplied when the boiler was renewed because the latter led to poor steaming.*

(Newspaper accounts available in the Manx Museum include; Union Mills, MANX SUN, 19th July, 1873; Douglas, IOM EXAMINER, 28th August, 1925.)

Report of the Inspector Appointed by his Excellency the Lieutenant-Governor To Inquire into the Accident Which Occurred at Douglas Railway Station On Saturday, 22nd August, 1925.

To His Excellency Major-General Sir William Fry, KCVO, CB,
Lieutenant Governor, Isle of Man.

Sir,

Under the Warrant given under your Excellency's hand on 24th August 1925, in pursuance of Section 6 of the Railway Regulation Act 1896, appointing me an Inspector for the purpose of inquiring into and reporting on the cause or causes which resulted in No. 7 train of the Isle of Man Railway Company colliding with the stop block at Douglas Station at about 12.50 pm on Saturday 22nd August 1925, in which collision the fireman of the train lost his life, and requiring me to report to you the result of such inquiry, I now beg to submit the following report for your Excellency's information.

I sat to take evidence on Tuesday August 25th and again yesterday on both occasions at the Douglas Court House. The lapse of time - eight days - between the two sittings was due to the fact that the engine driver of the train in question was suffering from shock, and was unable to appear at the first sitting; the enquiry was therefore adjourned *sine die* and though still weak from the effects of the shock, he was able yesterday to give his evidence quite clearly and intelligently.

Both sittings of the enquiry were held in open Court. I allowed Advocates acting for the Attorney General, the Railway Company, the engine driver and the next of kin of the deceased fireman to appear and cross examine witnesses. Representatives of the Insular press were also present and reports of the proceedings hitherto have already appeared in the Insular newspapers.

I examined the following witnesses in order given:

1. William Chas. Teare, guard of the train in question.
2. Thos. Ed. Teare, porter brakesman (on Port Erin platform).
3. Robt. Ed. Shimmin, brakesman on the train in question.
4. Thos. Sayle, relief signalman in charge of Douglas Signal Cabin at the time of the accident.
5. Jno. Thos. Quayle, foreman shunter at Douglas Station.
6. Geo. Hy. Hogg, Station Master at Union Mills Station.

*A narrow gauge locomotive on the 3 ft gauge Tralee & Dingle Railway in Co. Kerry also lost a chimney but without effect on the engine's steaming; it was not noticed until the train stopped.

7. Albert Ed. Leeming, relief man and goods clerk at Douglas Station in charge at Douglas Station at the time of the accident.
8. Robt. Alf. Kelly, parcels office clerk; received telephone message from Station Master Union Mills.
9. Wm. Stanley Clarke, porter-clerk at Union Mills (age 15½).
10. Wilfred Tranter, Carriage & Wagon Examiner at Douglas Station.
11. James Bradshaw, Locomotive Superintendent of the Railway Company.
12. Wm. Hy. Costain, engine driver of the train in question.
13. Albert Jno. Hogg, Chief Traffic Inspector of the Railway Company.
14. Mr Thos. Stowell, Secretary and Manager of the Railway Company.

On the 23rd and 24th August I viewed the scene of the accident and subsequently made a careful examination of Engine No. 3 PENDER which was drawing the train in question. I also initiated and witnessed on the 28th ult. a braking test with a train of similar composition and approximately the same weight and in similar conditions of weather with a view to ascertaining if it were possible to bring it to rest with only the steam brake on the engine in action, the engine being the same in all essential points as the damaged engine when in working order. The train to which the accident happened consisted of 10 passenger coaches followed by 8 trucks representing a total weight of 143½ tons, of which the engine represented 18½ tons.

Cause or Causes

From the evidence given before me, and from my own personal examination of the engine, it is abundantly apparent that the cause or causes of the accident are not to be found in the mechanical equipment of the engine and train at it was. Every mechanical device for use in controlling the train was in perfect working order up to the moment of impact. As to whether the accident could have been prevented or its results minimised by a mechanical equipment superior to and more up-to-date than the existing one, is another matter which I deal with later on in this Report. The cause or causes must, therefore, be sought for in the human side, and in examining the question in this direction it is much to be regretted that the one witness who could cast the most light on the question is unfortunately beyond our reach. I mean Fireman Lord Wm. Robinson.

The accident in my opinion is attributable to a series of misapprehensions combined with laxity in the observance of the Rules and Regulations laid down by the Company, as I endeavour to show in the following pages. The Isle of Man Railway Company issues and and supplies *gratis* to all its employees a book of 'Rules and Regulations for the conduct of the Traffic and for the guidance of the Servants' of the Company and in a prefatory note it is enjoined upon every officer and servant of the Company to make himself thoroughly conversant, not only with the section of rules applicable to his own immediate duties, but also to 'become acquainted with all the duties of other officers and servants of the Company and with the Rules to be observed throughout the service'. I have perused this book of Rules and Regulations; every eventuality that could be humanly foreseen appears to have been provided for, except one, which no rule or regulation can ever deal satisfactorily with, viz., an error of judgment or the liability to make a mistake which sometimes happens to even the most careful and conscientious of men.

The line at Union Mills is on a curve, the station platform and offices being on the outside of the curve; at this station, tickets are collected on all homeward bound trains. The guard of the train commences collecting at the front end of the train and the brakesman at the rear end and they work towards one another. When a train of this length draws up at Union Mills Station platform, the hinder part of it is over the points leading to the sidings. If any shunting of trucks has to be done, it is, therefore, necessary to draw the train ahead clear of the points. The position of the engine driver when the engine is in motion is on the right hand side of his engine looking towards the funnel; when the engine is travelling cab first, this causes him, in the particular case of Union Mills Station to be on the outside of the curve and owing to this he is unable to see what signals are made to him by the guard who, by the Rules, is held responsible for the starting of the train and the movement of the engine if used in shunting. Owing to this inability to have the guard in view when at Union Mills, the engine driver almost invariably steps down from his engine and stands a few feet away from it on the outside of the curve. From this position he can see any signals made by the guard standing on the platform.

This was done on Saturday August 22nd. The guard while or immediately after collecting the tickets, walked up to the driver and told him that there was one truck to come off and here it is that the first misapprehension occurred. The guard's statement was perfectly correct but the driver thought that it was the last truck on the train which had to come off, whereas it was that last but one which had to be left at Union Mills. The trucks were uncoupled by the porter/clerk at Union Mills whilst tickets were being collected. It was the intention of the Station Master and guard to hold these two last trucks by their own brakes while the rest of the train was drawn ahead clear of the points, then to drop the first truck into the siding and afterwards drop the last truck back on to the end of the train. This operation could be quite easily carried out without any assistance from the engine as the line at this station is all on a gradient falling towards Douglas and very little manual power would suffice to move the trucks. When the Station Master and guard were ready to commence shunting operation, the latter signalled the driver to move ahead by a continuous waving of the hand. Having seen the train begin to move ahead, he turned round and set off in the direction of the trucks to be shunted. At stations where the line is straight it is customary when shunting for the guard to signal for the engine to move ahead by waving the hand continuously until it had proceeded far enough for the purpose in view and then to signal for it to be stopped by either extending both arms horizontally or blowing a number of short blasts on the whistle. It appears, however, that at Union Mills, owing to the above mentioned difficulty of seeing round the curve a custom has sprung up of leaving it to the driver to judge when he has moved sufficiently far ahead to leave the rear of the train clear of the points. In this there is an evidence of laxity in observing the Rules and Regulations of the Company.

Another point which should be mentioned is that the Station Master on many occasions has plenty of help to assist in shunting the wagons and does not require to delay the departure of the train in order that he may have the assistance of the guard or brakesman for shunting operations. The Rules relating to the starting of a train are most explicit and are as follows:

The guard must wave a green flag by day . . . as a signal to start a train and the engineman must not start until this signal has been given. Immediately after a train

Plate 58: A close-up of the Douglas starting signals. The arm with 'S' affixed allows a shunting movement to draw ahead past the signal under the auspices of the signalman. April 1966.
J.I.C. Boyd

Plate 59: A train approaching Douglas would be controlled by this bracket signal: the left-hand post applies to Peel Line trains and the right-hand the South Line. The top-most arms apply to the arrival platforms and the lower to diverging movements. *J.I.C. Boyd*

Plate 60: The two main lines approached Douglas side-by-side, and outer Home signals gave early indication. August 1947. (This was not a junction splitting signal as it would be on the mainland.) *J.I.C. Boyd*

Plate 61: Another confusing trio of signals stood on the approach to St John's from the west; they were sited as by some child setting out his train set. The nearest is the ex-MNR Home signal; the next controlled the St John's & Foxdale Railway junction and in the distance on the right, stands the Home signal applying to trains from Peel. But even yet, there is a train movement for which there is no signal. 1st August, 1947. *J.I.C. Boyd*

Plate 62: The Up Distant for the Peel Line approaching Douglas had an extra Shunt Arm for Down trains during the period when spoil trains were working into Pulrose siding. 1936. *C.E. Box*

Plate 63: At the eastern entrance to St John's this splitting Home signal of MNR origin did duty; the upper arm is lowered for the Peel platform. 8th April, 1950. *J.D. Darby*

Plate 64: Starting signals at the east end of St John's; the more modern was installed by the MNR and the elderly slotted-post example is a vintage IOMR specimen. 13th May, 1951. *J.D. Darby*

Plate 65: The Peel Home signal was a curious assembly of ancient components *c.* 1935.
J.W. Sparrowe

Plate 66: The Santon Down Home signal betrayed its MNR origins. April 1960. *J.I.C. Boyd*

Plate 67: The Santon Up Home signal remained a classic IOMR type to the end.
Oakwood Collection

Plate 68: The St John's turntable was still in use in 1937. *J.I.C. Boyd*

Plate 69: The turntable that was, that was to be again, but never was. The ex-CDRJC locomotive-frame turntable, unused on the IOMR, at Ballasalla for disposal in 1974. *Peter Crane*

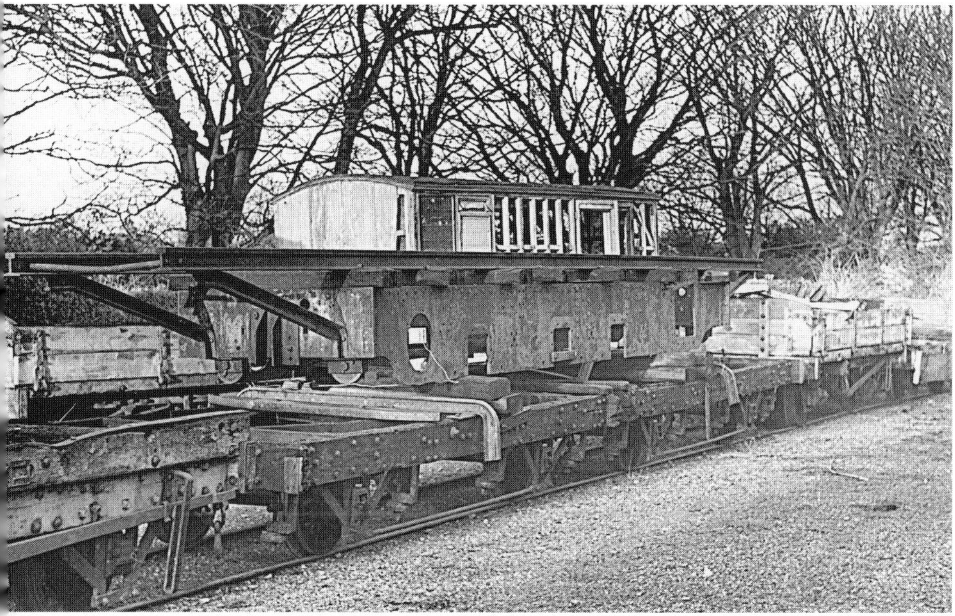

Plate 70: Traffic; potato sacks being unloaded by aliens in the Knockaloe Camp. 1916.
Manx Museum

Plate 71: A confusing notice? At Douglas it was the perennial habit to hang these notices on the separate portions of the combined Peel and Ramsey train. But in May 1961 it was not possible to reach Peel by rail. (See Vol. II p. 151). *J.I.C. Boyd*

Plate 72: On 12th November, 1909 (Hollantide) the special late train from Douglas hit a fallen tree at Ballacurry. No. 2, the pilot engine, was thrown on its side into a field.

J.I.C. Boyd Collection

Plate 73: A train too far. No. 3, engine of the runaway at Douglas on 22nd July, 1925 (the picture's caption has the wrong date), rose up over the concourse. *J.D. Darby Collection*

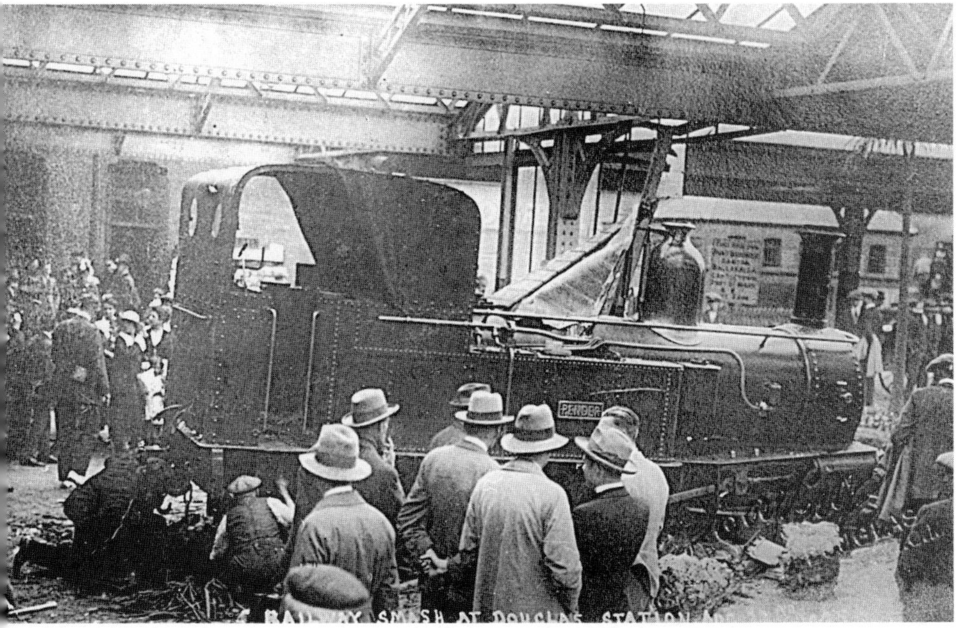

Plate 74: This was a major derailment caused by worn pointwork and a defective spring. No. 12 lies stricken at Port Soderick on 14th September, 1928; the big crane assists.

J.I.C. Boyd Collection

Plate 75: 1928 was a bad year; No. 7 & 10 had collided on 15th November and were still locked together at Douglas. No. 12 had also derailed (*see Plate 74*). All three await official Enquiry.

A.D. Lamberton Collection

Plate 76: September 1983 was a bad month for No. 13. On 15th it left the track between Santon and Port Soderick . . .

Plate 77: . . . and the next day made a more thorough job at the entrance to Douglas station.

(both) J.D. Darby

Plate 78: On the Manx Northern the blizzard at Poylldooey, on the outskirts of Ramsey in 1895, was such that train services were suspended . . . *Manx Museum*

Plate 79: . . The combined efforts of MNR Nos. 4, 1 & 2, plus the big snowplough attached to No. 4, cleared the line. *Manx Museum*

Plate 80: On 5th March, 1965, No. 15 was seen charging snowdrifts at Ellanbrook under the watchful eye of Donald Shaw, Locomotive Superintendent. *W.S . Basnett*

Plate 81: Standing at the east end of St John's, No. 8 with plough hidden by snow, and No. 2 had made an emergency run to take water. 5th March, 1942. *A.D. Lamberton Collection*

Plate 82: The inner harbour at Ramsey: a Clyde Shipping Co. steamer is about to unload coal into a MNR wagon. *c.* 1895. *J. Valentine*

Plate 83: Beyer, Peacock's graceful boiler mountings on No. 14, then doing station pilot duties Douglas, June 1957. *J.I.C. Boyd*

Plate 84: Detail of No. 5: Ross 'Pop' safety valves, high-pitched whistle, injector and re-railing traversing jack. Peel. September 1967. *J.I.C. Boyd*

Plate 85: No. 1 in the 'new' sand and gravel pit, St John's. 12th May, 1951. *J.D. Darby*

Plate 86: Snow is not anticipated in July 1962, but No. 15 with the medium-size (*front*) and small size (*rear*) ploughs attached, has been dragged from storage at the author's request. *J.I.C. Boyd*

Plate 87: Front-end details of a 'Small Series' locomotive with sloping smokebox door and domestic kettle to hold oil. Pony truck springs are prone to breakage. August 1947. *J.I.C. Boyd*

Plate 88: The front end of a 'Large Series' locomotive shows subtle differences from the previous picture. These include the smokebox, drawbeam and vacuum brake. Now the restrictions of the Second War are over, engines have been re-painted and lined. April 1966. *J.I.C. Boyd*

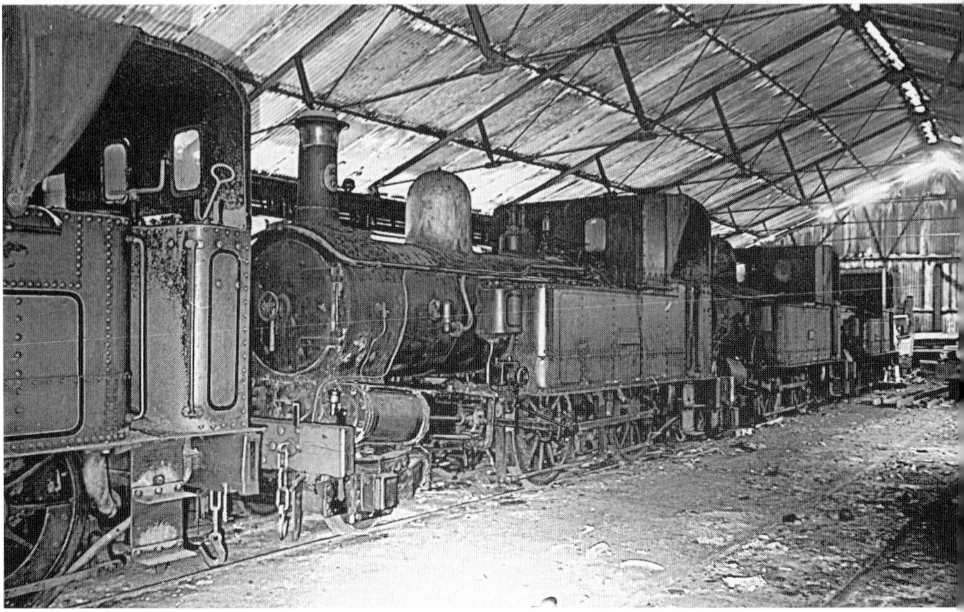

Plate 89: There was enough light penetrating the perforated corrugated-iron roof of Douglas carriage shed in February 1967 to distinguish Nos. 6, 4?, and 9. *D.A. Robinson*

Plate 90: A melancholy sight in October 1967 as No. 12 drags Nos. 6, 4, 1, 14, 3 and 16 from the Douglas carriage shed, for intended storage in the shed at St John's. *D.A. Robinson*

has left a station, the guard must show from his van a white flag by day . . . whereupon the brakesman must show a similar signal, and the engineman must give a short whistle to show that each train-man is at his post and that neither Guard nor Brakesman has been left behind.

From evidence given, it appears that this rule is not stictly observed in that very often the flags are not used, the signals being given merely by the arm and hand. It is readily seen, therefore, how easy it may become to confuse a mere shunting signal to start a train.

At Union Mills, because of the curve of the line, the signals from the guard's and brakeman's vans respectively, after the train is in motion are given from the right hand side of the train when coming towards Douglas and are received by the fireman who passes the word to the driver. It appears from his evidence that the driver of the train, when he had pulled ahead as far as he deemed necessary for the rear of the train to be clear of the points and was on the point of stopping the train, received word usually given by the fireman to indicate that the guard and brakesman had given the signals from their respective positions in the train. Instead of actually coming to a stop, therefore, he blew his whistle and started off for Douglas. He seems to have concluded that the Station Master had sufficient help to handle the wagons and that the guard and brakesman, not being required to assist, had boarded the train and all was well. He never had any suspicion that these 2 officials were not on the train until after the crash at Douglas Station.

Everything appears to have gone normally until the train reached the crossing gates at Pulrose, when it appeared to him that the brakes on the train coaches were not being applied as usual. In accordance with the usual practice, steam had been shut off at Braddan Bridge and the engine handbrake applied lightly between Quarter Bridge and Pulrose crossing. At the Home signal, a distance of 565 yards nearer Douglas, he applied the engine steam brake and put his sanding gear into operation and blew the whistle as a signal to the guard and brakesman to apply their brakes. He seems to have realised that there was very little chance of his being able to stop the train before reaching the stop-blocks in Douglas Station, and seems to have built upon the hope that the continued application of his own brakes would so reduce the speed of the train that it would be possible for any official who might be waiting at or near the end of the Station platform to jump into the brakevan immediately behind the engine and apply the brakes there, trusting that his own efforts supplemented by this fortuitous additional braking effect would so reduce the speed of the train that the stop blocks would bring it to a standstill without causing any damage.

As a matter of fact he was not disappointed in getting the additional braking effect. As the engine ran in alongside the platform at Douglas Station, the driver saw Leeming standing about the middle of the platform and shouted and signed to him to jump into the brakevan and apply the handbrakes. Fortunately, Leeming grasped the situation at once, jumped into the van and began applying the brakes. Quayle, the foreman shunter, saw Leeming jump into the train and he also, grasping the situation, instantly followed suit and jumped into the guard's brakevan and applied the brakes. There is no doubt that the prompt action on the part of these two men materially slowed the train before the impact and averted more serious consequences.

As it was, the rear buffer beam of the engine struck the stop blocks carrying them away, the cab of the engine struck two of the subsidiary channel iron stanchions supporting the verandah which covers this portion of the station; both were badly bent, and the one on the Driver's side was completely carried away, together with the woodwork and glass screen which closed in this portion of the station. The engine finally came to rest with the buffer beam about 12 feet from the wall of the Station buildings. I enclose six photographs showing the state of affairs; Nos. 1-4 were taken about an hour after the accident; Nos. 5 and 6 were taken on the 24th *ultimo.*

As soon as the Station Master at Union Mills realised that the train had definitely started for Douglas without the guard and brakesman, he sent the usual electric bell signal to the Quarter Bridge crossing gatekeeper and telephoned to Douglas Station. His call was taken by the Parcels Office clerk. The Station Master's message was to the effect that the train had gone without guard or brakesman and asking for the Assistant Inspector or the Station Master at Douglas. The clerk replied that they were both away, and he was directed to send a messenger to the Assistant Inspector who lives in Railway Terrace. He dispatched a messenger and then went out on to the platform with the intention of telling Leeming what had happened, and suggesting to him to try and jump into the brakevan and put the brakes on. Leeming at the time appears to have been on the South side platform attending to the Port Erin train which had just come in. The clerk, not seeing him, returned to his office. Neither he nor anyone else, seems to have realised what might happen.

The train is booked as leaving Union Mills at 12.52. The clerk received the message at 12.53; the train passed the Douglas Signal Cabin at 12.57. The engine would, therefore, reach the stop blocks at 12.58 as nearly as can be estimated. The schedule time allowed on the timetable is six minutes for the journey from Union Mills to Douglas, a distance of 2⅓rd miles nearly, equal to an average speed of say 24 miles per hour. It is obvious therefore that this train was not making the journey at a speed in excess of the ordinary. Eye-witnesses state that it appeared to come along the Station platform at a speed not very much greater than usual.

There was an interval of 4 minutes between the time the message was received at Douglas Station and the time the train passed the signal cabin; had there been telephonic communication between these two points, the signalman could have been made aware of the state of affairs and been able to keep his signals against the train. This would have caused the engine driver to commence pulling up at the distant signal, a distance of 919 yards from the stop blocks and the train would have stopped in all probability about 100 yards short of the signal cabin, which is 244 yards from the stop blocks. I found, by the aforementioned braking test that a train of this weight could be stopped in a distance of about 580 yards by means of the engine steam brake only, without sanding the rails on a dry day such as Saturday, August 22nd was.

The material damage done was slight, considering all things. The engine was the only part of the train which suffered damage. The wood of the stop block was partly rotten and in these particular circumstances it is as well that it was so as it gave way under the impact and was carried along under the engine, rubbing against the ground so that it formed a substantial but pliant resistance at the first impact and afterwards helped to retard the motion of the engine. What induced the fireman to give the word 'Right away' to the driver at Union Mills will, of course, never be known. He is said to have been a careful, conscientious man; it can only be surmised therefore that he was quite certain that everything was in order before he passed the word to the driver. I think that the most probable explanation is that he saw the Station Master at the points lever but did not see the other two and thinking that it was the last truck only that was to be left at Union Mills, concluded that they were in the train and did not wait for their signals; also the train being 20 or more minutes behind time, he would naturally be anxious to save all the time possible. The shunting operation of dropping off the last truck only and leaving it for the Station Master to handle, either alone or with local help has been so frequently performed at Union Mills without any mishap, that it is not surprising that he should have come to the conclusion indicated above.

But whatever conclusion he came to, there is no getting away from the fact that had the rule relating to signals between respective Train-men which is quoted above, been observed, and the flags used as described, he could not possibly have been under any misapprehension. A strict observance of these rules connotes the waving of a green flag to start the train and the waving of white flags after the train had started - a series of operations which occupies a certain amount of time and demands a certain amount of definite attention and admits of no mistake being made as to the identity of the persons making the signals.

I find, therefore, that the causes of the accident were as follows:

The driver did not clearly comprehend the full extent of the shunting operation.

There was laxity in not giving the signal for the train to stop after it had moved ahead to clear the points.

There has been laxity in giving the starting signals and the 'all right' signals by hand instead of with flags, in accordance with the rules.

There was a misapprehension on the part of the fireman in concluding that all was in order for starting on the journey to Douglas.

A collateral cause is to be found in the fact of the line at this point being on a fairly sharp curve, but as this is a permanent unchanging condition, the giving of the signals can be adapted to suit the situation.

A similar accident to the one under notice occurred in July 1905, when a similar sized train on the same line collided with the stop blocks, damaging the engine and one carriage, and causing injury to six passengers. In this case, the train men were on the train, but did not attend to their brakes until too late.

I have the honour to be, Sir, your Excellency's most obedient Servant,

(Sgd.) W.H. Baker, Assoc.M.Inst.C.E.
Murray's House, Mount Havelock, Douglas, Isle of Man, September 3rd, 1925.

To detail the various accidents would be impossible but it is worth noting that a Ballawoods fatality in July 1875, a runaway 18th March, 1876, a Colby fatality 19th December, 1885, the same at St John's on 11th November, 1893, the train which hit a tree 17th November, 1909 and the Oakhill head-on collision of 17th November, 1928, were all more or less successfully kept from the papers, a practice at which the IOMR was quite adept. The more intriguing episodes have already received mention.

The lax operating methods and the uneducated habits of the public, especially as they were allowed to 'travel; in open cattle trucks' led to a boy knocked out of one by the bough of a tree at Union Mills, on Tynwald Day 1875. Trespassing was common, and led to a boy's death when he tried to race away ahead of a train as it crossed Glen Auldyn River bridge in August 1891.

In 1879 St John's station had been 're-modelled' for the convenience of - and at the expense of - the MNR, and there are numerous asides to suggest that MNR movements there were a trifle slap-dash. On 11th November, 1886 a locomotive and two coaches 'dashed through the level crossing gates at St John's in the dark, and demolished them'. Over six years after the alterations, the MNR gates were still without lamps.

As recently as 8th June, 1993 the 2.10 pm train from Douglas hauled by MAITLAND struck a car driven by a nurse at the notorious White Hoe occupation crossing. Fortunately she was not badly hurt. But a railway is a risky place for unwary public and employee alike and puts extra responsibilities on station staff and train crews when holiday crowds wander across tracks . . . the public today, accustomed to using roads rather than railways, can be misled by the 'miniature scale' of the Manx railways.

Yet, for all this, enquire as to the last time a member of the public met with a fatal accident.

The IOMR tried to settle with farmers, whose animals had been killed on the line, out of Court but sometimes this was impossible. There was an amusing side to a case heard in early 1951, Cringle *v.* IOMR, concerning the first train out of Port Erin on a winter's morning which killed a young horse between Colby and Ballabeg. The driver, whose vision was obviously limited by darkness, was partly to blame . . . unfairly, so it would seem.

A mare and foal were in a field beside the line and had managed to open a lineside gate; the foal was soon on the line and when the train approached, she ran in front of the train until falling through rails into the cattle creep.

It was the ganger's responsibility to check the restraining chains on lineside gates and under cross-examination, he maintained the gate was secure and the chain padlocked. Prosecution claimed the chain was faulty. The chain itself was picked up and left in the Manager's office. At the hearing, when the offending chain was to be produced, the Manager was unable to comply, saying the chain had been lost during recent decorations . . .

Snow Ploughs and Snow Clearance

In June 1972 three sets of loco-attached snow ploughs were aside in detached state in Douglas yard. There had been a number of winters since the Second War when a small plough had been left permanently attached to the leading end of an engine working out of Douglas, but there is no record that any engine working out of either Peel or Ramsey (the railway to these destinations had closed in 1968) had had a plough fitted at the cab end to work out from there should snow fall unexpectedly. Until 1968, should major snow clearance be necessary, Douglas housed the major capability for dealing with it but if the services of CALEDONIA were required at a time when this engine was housed at Ramsey, it was possible, with the aid of that engine and the MNR plough usually kept there also, to attempt clearance from Douglas and Ramsey simultaneously.

Precautions against snow do not feature in records, but the effect of snow on the railway was ever a sudden risk and the risk of snow drifting into cuttings (especially on the ex-MNR section) was greater than the depth of the fall itself. This hazard was made worse by the coastal exposure to wind.

The procedure for dealing with it appears to be a custom rather than a rule, drawn from years of variable experience so that not until a message was received (often that a train had been brought to a stand in a drift) were any emergency steps taken. Receipt of any message was by no means assured, as often the wind had brought wires down, and it was therefore transmitted from the nearest farmstead or police station. The Station Master in whose section a train was stranded would liaise with the ganger for that section, and together station staff and ganger equipped with tools from the ganger's hut, would set out to assist the train crew to dig out the train. If required, a Station Master had the power to engage extra labourers locally.

Meanwhile, the Chief Inspector at Douglas might have received messages about snowfall, drifts and stranding; he would use his judgement about a rescue, relying on his men on the ground to be their best in the circumstance. He might send an engine or engines out, with or without a plough, but he would be mindful that when final approach was made to a stranded train, that train would be carrying the Staff and if it had been freed meanwhile, might be oncoming towards his rescue train which would be moving without the protection of the Staff . . .

The ploughs available receive no mention in the mountains of statistics created at Douglas, presumably because they were but an adjunct to rolling stock and the management was not interested: in former days with an intensive timetable it is hard to imagine the three seen in 1972 comprised the full complement. Their past is only legendary; the large plough was of ex-MNR origin and attached to CALEDONIA, and the two small ones, to avoid doubt, had the engine numbers chalked upon them.

An account* of a blizzard at Christmas 1908 relates how a St John's-

*SRN No. 77 Winter 1986, p.8.

bound train, 5.50 pm from Ramsey, stuck in a drift in the cutting south of Gob-y-Deigan on 23rd December; Douglas had sent out two engines and a plough which reached Peel Road but could proceed no further and returned to Douglas. The stranded train was eventually rescued but it was 3 pm the following Saturday before a train passed the same place again. Had the rescue train gone on, it would have been obliged to reach Ramsey as the cuttings behind it were already filling with drift.

There were operational problems too. If plough-fitted engines got through to a terminal and further snow blocked their return at once, a situation was sometimes reached where the desirable ploughs were at the wrong end of the line. The big plough would only fit CALEDONIA's chimney end. Ramsey improvised a small wooden plough in order to keep a shuttle service going to Kirk Michael as this length was less prone to blockage. A second makeshift wooden plough was used to keep the Peel Line clear.

To emphasise the parlous state into which the MNR might be placed, on 5th February, 1895 and thereafter, six feet of snow fell in Ramsey and required the efforts of all the men there to release the three locos imprisoned therein. Worse, the arrival of a ship loaded with coal posed problems as no wagons could traverse the quay line; eventually the load was simply dropped on the quayside. Further clearance as far as firstly, Kirk Michael and eventually, St John's, was made without the use of engine or plough but by men with shovels, personally led and inspired by John Cameron. It was then 15th February; fifty men were employed to tackle some drifts 20 ft deep and with the swathe cut in the snow between Kirk Michael and St John's but the width of the engine, hardy travellers transferred to covered goods vans for this section, as carriage footboards would have been ripped from their brackets in the narrow clearances.

Within living memory snow hit the northern line on 27th January-7th February, 1940 and ten men were engaged in clearance. The diary reads:

28th Jan.	Standing by with engine No. 3 in steam
29th Jan.-2nd Feb.	Clearing snow between Ramsey Signal & Bow Bridge Storing manure ex SS BROOM
3rd Feb.	Snow plough clearing Ramsey Yard
3rd-5th Feb.	Clearing snow Bow Bridge, Lezayre, Ellenbane
5th Feb.	Erecting crane Ramsey Yard
6th Feb.	Clearing snow Ellenbane, Sulby Bridge Delivering goods with engine No. 5
7th Feb.	Clearing snow Ramsey Yard, Sulby Bridge, Ballaugh

The same blizzards took two men at St Germain's four days to clear and re-clear the station, crossing gates, points and signal, and walk home to Kirk Michael when finished. On the next six days they joined other men and with the help of the Ramsey plough from the north and a Douglas plough with

CALEDONIA from St John's, they had cleared Ballaugh to West Berk.

A hint of desperation is contained in a rough note left for Sheard on 23rd January, 1941 at 6.5 pm:

> Engine Driver Caine rang this office and left this message. They packed up at 6 o'clock as the men were pretty well exhausted and they are going to start very early in the morning, they are progressing as well as can be expected, the snow at West Berk is as high as the engine and is packed tight with the rain there is one foot of ice at the bottom, Driver Caine does not think that they will be finished by tomorrow.

There are painful tales of conditions from 5th March, 1942 on which day a special train from Port Erin at noon was run as the children were sent home early from school. It was stopped by a drift at Ballaquaggin and propelled back to Ballasalla. CALEDONIA was sent from Douglas, and brought the train in. Other workings were cancelled. The next day was difficult on Peel and South Lines but some trains went through. Not so on the North Line to which CALEDONIA and Driver Quinney had been sent. A double-headed Ramsey-Kirk Michael-Ramsey train battled through, snow at Rhencullen being responsible. Quinney and CALEDONIA then cut through to Ramsey.

> Engines Nos. 2 & 15 took the 1.45 pm from Ramsey but were held 42 minutes at St Germain's (as Costain was somewhere about between St Germain's and St John's). At about 4.20 pm we sent the Ramsey engines home from St John's with CALEDONIA assisting. Unfortunately CALEDONIA which was leading got a leading pair of wheels derailed at Knocksharry. The plough engine No. 8 was locked in between CALEDONIA and the coach with No. 2 engine at the rear. No. 8 with the plough should have been at the rear. No. 2 engine got back to St Germain's eventually and was sent out again to try and pull the coach and No. 8 back but they had to give up owing to shortage of water the fires were pulled out of the engines. There were five lady passengers on the train who were put up at Knocksharry and at Cowells and at St Germain's Crossing.

On Saturday 7th March the South Line was assisted by No. 11 with plough, and there were no difficulties going to Peel, but there was more drama on the North Line.

> Driver Crosby had taken No. 11 and plough with a special from Douglas at 11.5 am. Quinney had already gone to St John's to try and get through to St Germain's; he was back at St John's when we got there and the snow drift had been cleared at Peel Road. Picked up the men just before Lhergydhoo bridge and quickly through to St Germain's where men got dinner. We then got Fowler's engine and pulled it back to St Germain's, then the coach and then Costain's engine and the CALEDONIA, the leading wheels of the latter being pulled up on the ramp. A rail had broken by the CALEDONIA and we took all the rolling stock back to St John's where all the engines got water and boring tackle and fishplates obtained to rebore the rail. Left St John's at 4.30 pm and arrived Ramsey 5.45. We left three men to repair the broken

> rail and we charged through two heavy snow drifts at Ballakaighen. There was also two heavy drifts which we went through at Orrisdale No. 1 & 2. There was not much beyond Ballaugh to Ramsey. Returned from Ramsey 6.20 pm arrived 8.10 pm. No passenger services run on the Ramsey line this day.

On 17th March 1947, the Chief Inspector sent a curt letter to Sheard:

> Guard Corlett's journal for 15th instant; Train No. 17 ex Ramsey. Stopped at Cronk Ould through snow. Propelled train to Sulby Glen and derailed coach F.7 at Cooilbane. Coach was re-railed Sunday morning . . .

These glimpses of a bygone generation reflect the working of a railway when it was still a prime means of transport, and railwaymen could demonstrate their loyalty in common cause.

This account began by stating that three ploughs were visible at Douglas in June 1972; these were each of the small type and the large plough was not visible. For long periods it was attached to CALEDONIA which was kept in the running shed ready for duty. Photographs appearing in SRN No. 110 (Winter 1994/5) show CALEDONIA fitted with small plough at the rear end, on the next day, with the large front plough added. In support, No. 11 is fitted with small ploughs at each end: dated 4th-5th March, 1965.

Stormy weather could oblige sailings to terminate in Peel rather than Douglas, and a special train would be sent to collect the passengers. One bad winter this coincided with heavy snowfall, and the RUSHEN CASTLE berthed 72 hours late. To overcome the snowdrifts, a train made up of three coaches and four locomotives - two at each end - made the journey successfully. (When Greenbank was Engineer he permitted double-heading so long as the engines were coupled cab-to-smokebox: he condemned cab-to-cab working as the four driving-axle weights so close together exceeded the recommended safety limit for bridges). The same storm left the North Line snow-bound. Some unfortunate passengers off the ship, now safely back in Douglas by train from Peel, were stranded there but 'with a huge fire in the waiting room all night, they made the best of their plight . . .'

While 'The Great Storm' of 1895 which lasted four days without let-up, was the most horrific in memory as when waves broke over ships in the gale, they cascaded onto decks as ice, the snows of early 1940 brought chaos to the railway unequalled to that time. It was made more dramatic than the curtailed account (above) as the RUSHEN CASTLE had received conflicting signals as to whether the ship should make for Douglas or Peel - the confusion was due to war-time security. Anxiety was felt for the Governor and his daughter who were among the 106 passengers on board. While the ship rode out the storm in Peel Harbour unable to come alongside safely, food aboard ran short and the lifeboat was sent out to deliver bread etc. The

IOM WEEKLY TIMES had a poor picture of the rescue train loading at Peel station; the locos involved were Nos. 13 and 11 at the head, with Nos. 10 and 5 in the rear - surely the strangest train ever run? (In Macnab's IOMR book is shown a sketch of this train *en route* for Peel and approaching Glenfaba Corn Mill; the quoted date should be 1940.)

In the matter of dates, the newspaper account states that the event occurred over a month previously but that it was not permitted to publish the fact because of security.

At one time the IOMR was considering the purchase of a second large plough for which Bradshaw had obtained drawings from Beyer, Peacock dated 2nd April, 1914. Probably the onset of the First War blocked further pursuit.*

Today, one small plough survives in the Port Erin Railway Museum.

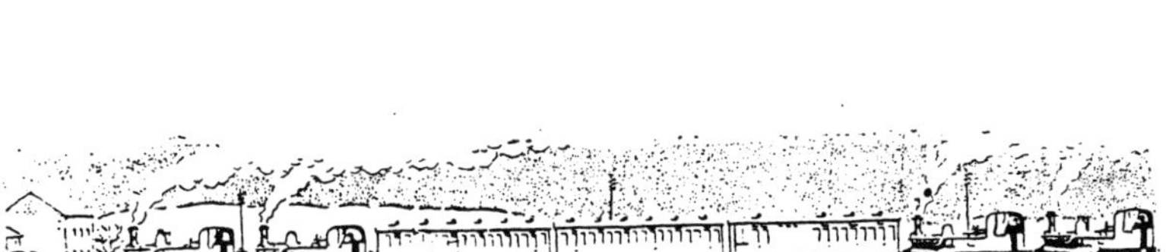

Ian Macnab

*Source: Sunnycroft Collection

School Trains

It has proved extremely difficult to investigate operation of school trains as they seldom appear in the records and were not itemised in the timetables. It appears that the carriage of school children was always subsidised by the authorities involved but there was no 'recognised' conveyance of children until progress in education meant older pupils (for whom new schools were built outside of their locality) had to be provided with transport. As the Education Authority has not retained past records only the date of payment of contract by an authority to the Railway can give a date to the start of an operation; however, as the IOMR Minutes do not regularly note the subject it cannot be covered with much confidence. Worse: the effort to recall personal memories of using the train to and from school has met with an extra-ordinary reluctance by those approached to voice their recollections. This is easily explained by the smallness of the Island; there are some who later saw 'High Office' who would prefer that their behaviour when young is not recalled by their contemporaries nor revealed to those whose esteem of them might be dented. For the antics and behaviour of unsupervised children on such trains is better remembered than any aspect of the trains themselves.

Some aspects of those days were exciting; the early attempts to roll a cigarette and light it; the challenge of jumping on the moving carriage or alighting therefrom without the notice of the staff. Overhanging branches could be pulled into the compartment through an open window and released with terrifying speed from the moving vehicle. There were frightening aspects too; the bullying of small boys who might be lifted onto the luggage rack or stuffed under the seats; or whose heads were pinned out of open windows to endure wind and rain and a shower of smuts. In truth the Manx school trains were no different to any others.

It is not necessary to emphasise that accommodation was provided in term-time only and even then no *special* trains were involved; vehicles of a 'lower order' were kept for the purpose and stabled in sidings during the holidays and day-time while children were in school. For instance, Kirk Michael had a morning school train to Ramsey which comprised two carriages stored in the siding overnight and attached to that train. In the evening the train left Ramsey at 4.15 pm and pupils from the school had to rush to catch it; the carriages were detached at Kirk Michael. Similarly there was a rake of slightly seedy-looking coaches which stood at inoperative times, in the siding nearest the river at Peel. The Schools which created such traffic included the High School at Douglas, the Ramsey Grammar School, and the last-to-be-built Castle Rushen School in Castletown, of 1960. In addition, though not acquiring subsidised status or special requirement of the IOMR, were the pupils going to King William's College and the Buchan School at Castletown. Between the Wars, travelling by train to and from school became a significant part of life for Island children on leaving their local school.

It is recalled that in Douglas up to 1929, pupils used the horse trams or cable cars; later, special buses were laid on to convey them to the High School from the railway station. In Ramsey, the station was near to the Grammar School but loitering could be disastrous in either direction . . .

The IOMR preferred to use the open carriages as the children could be more easily monitored by railway staff; boys and girls travelled in separate carriages . . . or were presumed so to do. There was a section set aside for younger children who were supervised by two older ones or prefects nominated for the purpose by the school.

The saloon carriages were considered too grand for the purpose, and coaches used by summer visitors were also taboo. In winter in the 1950s there would be buses available after wartime shortage, and spare ones could be used for school purposes: but it was back to the train in summer.

School train travel has left an amount of folklore in its wake. To save carrying his games' kit home from Kirk Michael station, there was a lad attending the Ramsey School who would drop the bag from the train as it passed over Balleira bridge; passing under the bridge on the way home, he would pick it up. One day his father, learning of the ruse, went to the bridge before his son came along . . . the result is easily deduced

There were complaints that the glass of lineside greenhouses and coldframes were broken as soon as the term resumed; the 'guillotining' of small boys whose heads were held out of open windows (as described) and arrived home with tear soot-streaked cheeks angered parents, as did a home-coming without any trousers. Then there was the boy who was found on the roof at St John's . . . There is no record as to how many complaints were made to the school authorities, but many reached the Railway Manager who fought a losing battle with generations of pupils, each learning further desecration from their elders. Two examples among many will suffice:

General Manager's Office
24th July, 1946

. . . There has been considerable amount of wilful damage, presumably by children. I noticed one brakevan in particular (F.19) on the Ramsey Line and it is about the worst case I have seen of names cut in the woodwork and holes bored through the partitions. We must tighten up on this sort of thing . . .

Or another:

Notice to Ramsey Station Masters & Train Staff
Schoolchildren Tampering with Carriage Doors

It has been reported to me that parents are viewing with apprehension the possibility of serious accident owing to children attempting to open carriage doors before the train has arrived at the station . . . on one or two occasions . . . Kirk Michael children on the 4.10 pm from Ramsey have actually had the doors open at Balleira . . .

. . . .warn children that any attempt to touch the door handle before the train comes to a stand still will be reported to the Head . . .

Fortunately one period of school travel is well remembered, being the time following World War II when buses were in short supply and extra trains left Douglas during term-time just after 7 am and made their way to Peel and Port Erin respectively to form departures thence at 8.5 and 8.10 am. Presumably the public could use the Down workings and half of one carriage was set aside on the Up trains for their use.

At this time the Peel Line special was made up to seven coaches on which 218 children age 11 upwards travelled in compartment coaches, the boys being separated from the girls. The compartments were designed to seat ten but as this was a special working, eight were allowed-for. On 27th September, 1947, one compartment held twelve sitting boys while two standing up, played conkers. In the contest, a conker flew off its string and hit a sitting boy in the eye; he lost the sight of it. A Court case ensued, the parent of the injured boy suing the Education Authority for failing to provide staff on the train to monitor behaviour. The case went in the boy's favour but on appeal, the Authority was cleared of negligence. Apparently school prefects on the train crowded into one compartment; in future there was to be a prefect in each compartment.*

The same case highlights other complaints; the Western District Education Association said there was no heat or light in the train and that the cushions were damp. A parent blamed the Authority for allowing his son to be 'guillotined' through a window. In the same period a boy was stripped of his trousers which were passed outside the train to a girls' compartment, never to be seen again. Questions were asked at school about a boy who arrived there wearing a towel . . .

School trains formally ceased in the 1961-2 school year although throughout a lengthy 'Are they provided or are they not?' period they were (for instance) still calling at Lezayre after that station was officially 'Closed'. Some individual pupils continued to use the train after officialdom decreed the bus was the recognised transport (so long as a train was suitably timetabled); such persons are notable for their active support for the railway today. In late 1994 it was still possible for pupils to use the South Line in season and they could travel without charge if they held a Resident's ticket, whereas they would pay 10p per journey if travelling westwards home from Castletown.

An enlightening account of escapades, devilment and misery appeared in

*(Documents relating to this Case, and others such as claims against livestock killed on the Railway (etc.), if the subject of Court Proceedings, are held by the Rolls Office.)

the IOM EXAMINER for 20th September, 1988. Two observations arose from this: 'many people of influence today have unpleasant memories of travelling on school trains, and this has hindered the acceptance of the Railway as an integral part of the heritage of the Island'; and, 'A-- B-- of C-- was the hooligan responsible for the closing of the school trains. He afterwards became 1st Officer' (here a well-known ship of the Cunard Line is named). He was always badly behaved on the train'.

The subject in particular made personal impact on several generations of Manx people in a way quite different from any other feature described herein; the railway was *imposed* on them in their formative years, with detrimental effect in some cases - whereas when viewed impartially, it was the railway which gave them access to higher education, and '*ad majorem gloriam*'.

(The Author is grateful to those who have not been too embarrassed to recall these escapades of youth: in a small community such disclosures are not easy.)

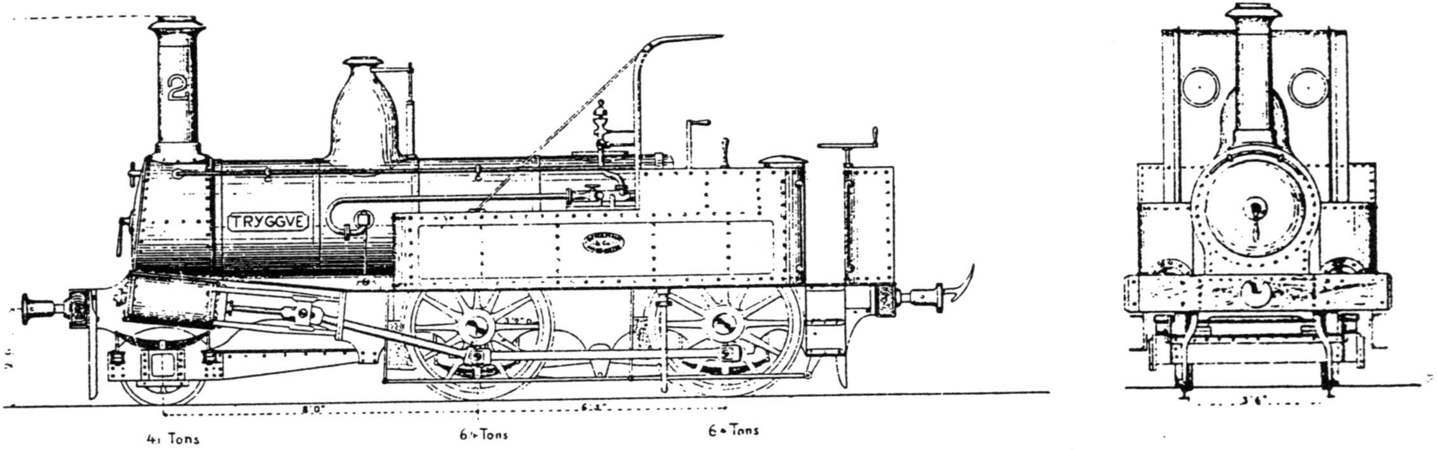

Beyer, Peacock, & Co. Ltd. derived the IOMR design for locomotives from this pioneer type which went to Norway.

Steam Locomotives

The first locomotive to be seen on the IOMR (but not the first on the Island) was that belonging to the contractor whilst building the Peel Line, and later on the South Line (Vol. I pp.43 & 46). It was said to be built by R. & W. Hawthorn of Newcastle-on-Tyne and named MONA: with construction complete, it stood on the site of the present Douglas station for some time. It may have been maker's No. 1045 of August 1858, supplied to a Mr Graham of the Neath Abbey Coal Co. Ltd. to 'about 2 ft 8 in. gauge' and named IRON DUKE. It was four-wheeled tank engine with 8 in. x 6 in. cylinders and 2 ft 4 in. diameter wheels. (This is the nearest identifiable machine in Hawthorn's records).

By October 1872 Beyer, Peacock & Co. Ltd. of Gorton Foundry, Manchester had received orders from the IOMR for three engines; it appears that no other maker had been considered but in 1871 this firm had supplied three locomotives to Norway's first constituent of the State Railways system of 3 ft 6 in. gauge, and the Manx design was a derivative. The design can be traced in this country in the numerous 4-4-0 tank engines for the Metropolitan Railway of 1864, and there were examples with family likeness in Ireland and many places overseas. Vignoles was closely associated with the Gorton Foundry which had supplied engines to overseas companies with which he was associated, and the links between Gorton and the IOMR were to become strong and satisfying to both parties.

Proof of this confidence was the evidence in fifteen similar machines owned by the IOMR from 1926, all from the same 'stable'; some of these are in operation today (1996) and though other designs have been considered and discarded, steam power remains the prime mover. The advantage of having a single supplier of motive power, some interchangability of parts between engines, a stud of locomotives of approximately the same all-round capabilities with no restriction on route-availability, proved priceless.

After some discussion as to whether the leading wheels should be on a fixed axle with radial axleboxes, or on a pony truck, the latter course was adopted making the design very close to the Norwegian engines. In the early years these pony trucks were officially designated 'bogeys' by the IOMR staff, a quite different interpretation to that used elsewhere.

The first engine, No. 1 SUTHERLAND, ordered for the opening of the Peel Line, was steam tested at Gorton on 8th March, 1873; it reached the Island on 27th March, all three being there by 19th June. The name VIKING was chosen for No. 3 but during the time of construction was changed to PENDER. Unofficially these earliest small engines were often termed, 'Our No. 1 Class'. One was leased to the contractors along with a number of wagons, and used to assist ballasting of the new lines.

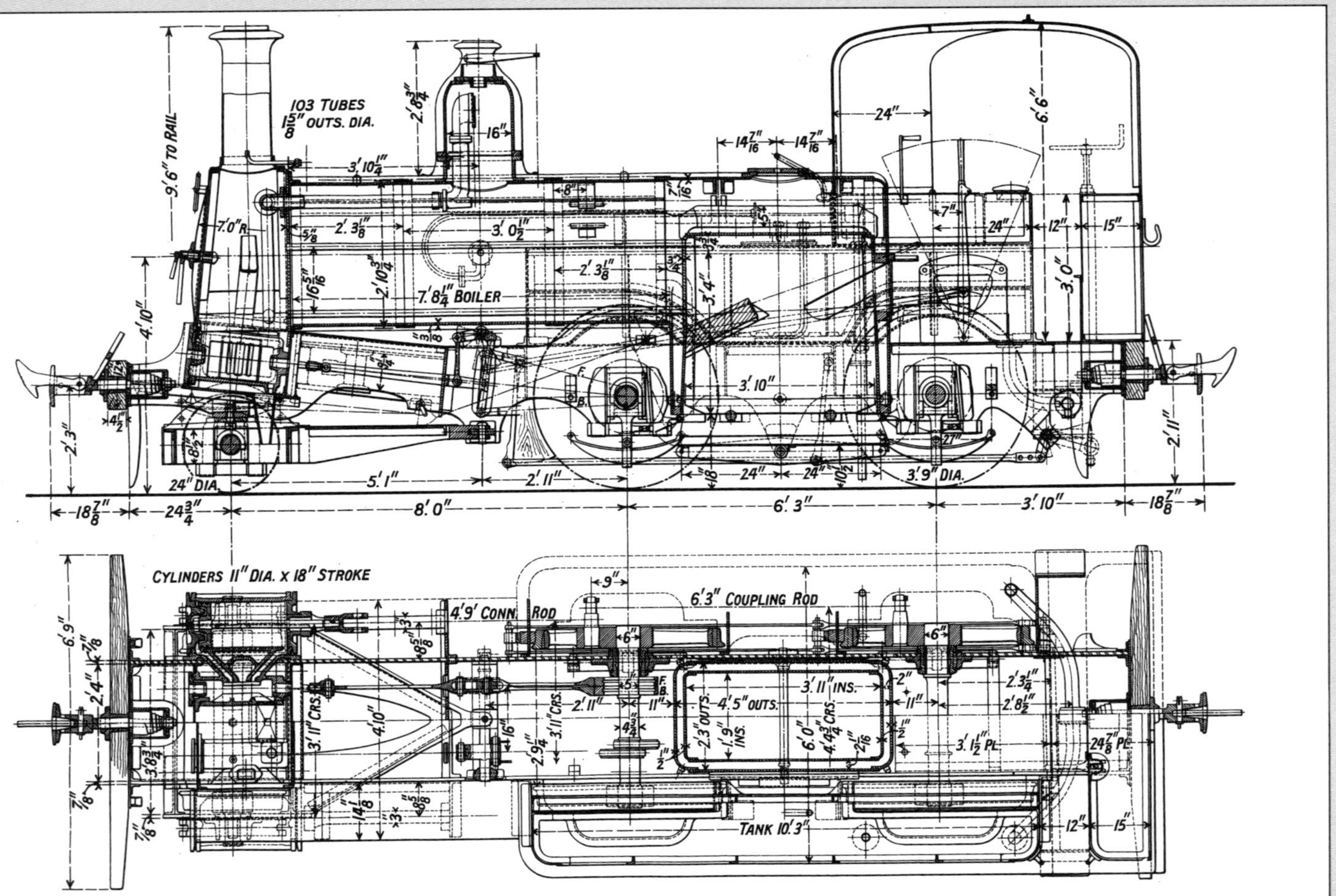

Drawing of the first three locomotives of 1873

No. 1	**SUTHERLAND**	**Works No. 1253**	**of 1873**
No. 2	**DERBY**	**1254**	**1873**
No. 3	**PENDER**	**1255**	**1873**

The leading pony wheels had outside axleboxes, but the four driving wheels had them behind the wheels. The engines were sometimes described as having 'American trucks', the first in the United Kingdom to be so fitted. The outside cylinders were inclined at 1 in 9, the footplate above them rising similarly. The somewhat narrow firebox dropped between the frames and the coupled driving axles, which were 6 ft 3 in. apart. Above the pony truck the main frames were exposed and projected forwards to carry the front buffer beam. The valve chests were integral with the box of the smokebox; to withdraw the valves the buffer beam has to be taken off. On the first engines, the smokebox front was sloped backwards.

These first engines carried small boilers only 2 ft 10¾ in. in diameter with 7 ft 8¼ in. between tube plates. The side tanks were but 2 ft high and carried a mere 320 gallons. Later, larger tanks to hold 385 gallons were fitted, 2 ft 6 in. high. Cabs were of the wrap-over Gorton pattern (the makers called them 'houses') with minimal side-sheets and round spectacle glasses front and rear; later engines had rectangular glasses but the earlier engines could always be identified by that feature. Canvas side-sheets were used to close off the side openings in bad weather. Coal was carried in a narrow bunker at the rear of the cab, any surplus being piled on the floor. Buffer beams were timber. The driving axle boxes were given leaf springs and there was a compensating lever between boxes on each side. Driving was from the right-hand side.

Slide valves were driven by Allan's Straight Link Motion. Hand brakes worked wooden blocks on the driving wheels; replacement blocks were obtained from Douglas timber merchants. There was a brass displacement lubricator on each side of the smokebox and a large clack box on the middle ring of the boiler, on each side. The injectors lay along the tank tops, so were not self-priming and could be playful at times; later, some engines had improved replacements. Keeping company on the tank top was a re-railing jack on one side, and a tool box of wood on the other. Sanding of rails was done through boxes fitted in the front corners of the cab, a most unsuitable place; the gravity feed to the rails between the driving wheels passed outside the connecting rod.

Boiler mountings were more than functional; true to the maker's tradition they were graceful embellishments which marked Beyer, Peacock's products the world over. The tall, tapering chimneys with copper cap had the engine's number in brass numerals each side. There was a large bell-mouthed brass dome enclosing the Salter safety valves and a high-toned whistle on a

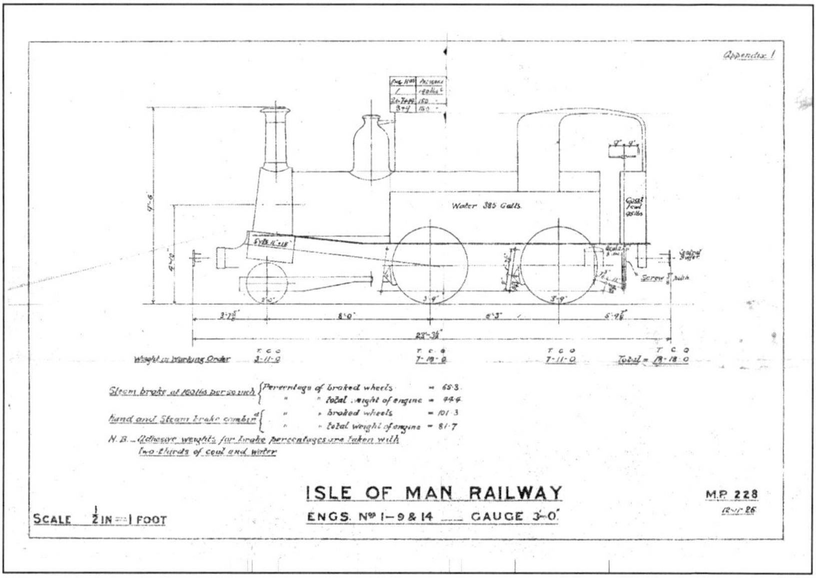

Diagrams prepared in connection with brake trials in 1925. *IOMR*

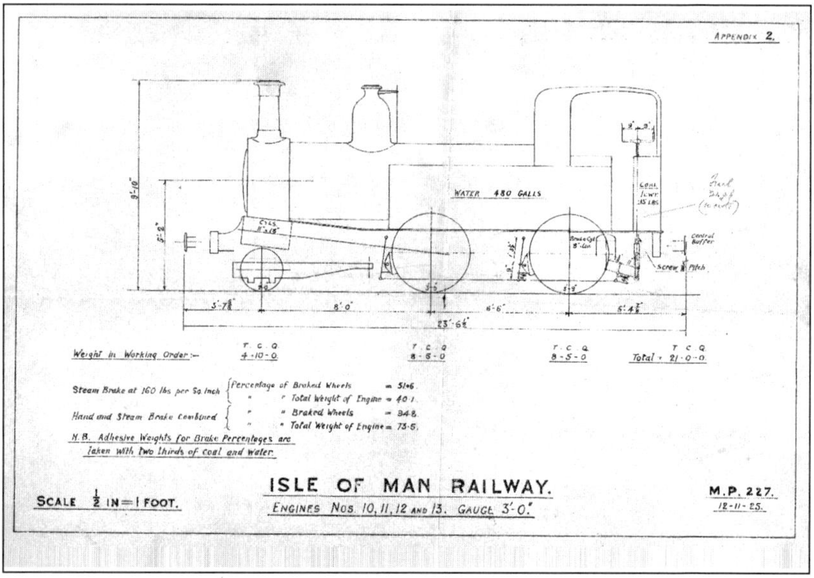

mounting before the cab front sheet.

The maker's plates appeared on the boiler barrel behind the smokebox, a position favoured by road-engine manufacturers.

Ultimately the boilers wore out and it became customary to give them a further lease of life providing steam for the Work's stationary engine; one found its way to Rushen Abbey where it was used in the Jam Factory until 1932.

The specification included the ability of these first engines to haul fifteen four-wheel coaches (load 360 passengers) up 1 in 65.

No. 4 LOCH Works No. 1416 of 1874
No. 5 MONA 1417 1874

Consideration of additional engines for the opening of the South Line was made in December 1874; Beyer, Peacock's tender was accepted. The two engines (*above*) were ordered and at Mackenzie's insistence they had larger tanks and bunkers than their predecessors; spectacles in the cab were rectangular.

No. 6 PEVERIL Works No. 1524 of 1875
No. 7 TYNWALD 2028 1880

The growth of business made it necessary to order two more engines; they were identical to Nos. 4 & 5 and though boiler pressure was nominally 120 lbs, the IOMR considered 125 lbs to be their 'standard'. A few notes on the engines bought to date show how they were behaving in service.

Until 1909 these engines remained outwardly much the same as when delivered, but when No. 2 had a mishap in that year the cab was renewed and the rear spectacles became rectangular; also that year No. 4 received a new boiler 3 ft 3 in. diameter, (by which the maker's plates disappeared), side tanks of 480 gallons capacity, and the cab roof was raised 5 in. By these, the engine now resembled Nos. 10-12 which were the most recent delivered then. In 1911 No. 6 was rebuilt as No. 4 and next year No. 2 received 385 gallon side tanks and the front circular spectacles were removed in favour of rectangular . . . careful study of the last-named assists the dating of illustrations. No. 3 was dealt with similarly in 1913 but glasses in the cab were not altered; in 1914 No. 1 also came in for the change whilst No. 5 was rebuilt as had been No. 6. So the first six engines had each changed in appearance before World War I began.

Repairs undertaken up to 1914 include considerable patching of firebox sides, turning of all four driving wheels (this being necessary on No. 2 for

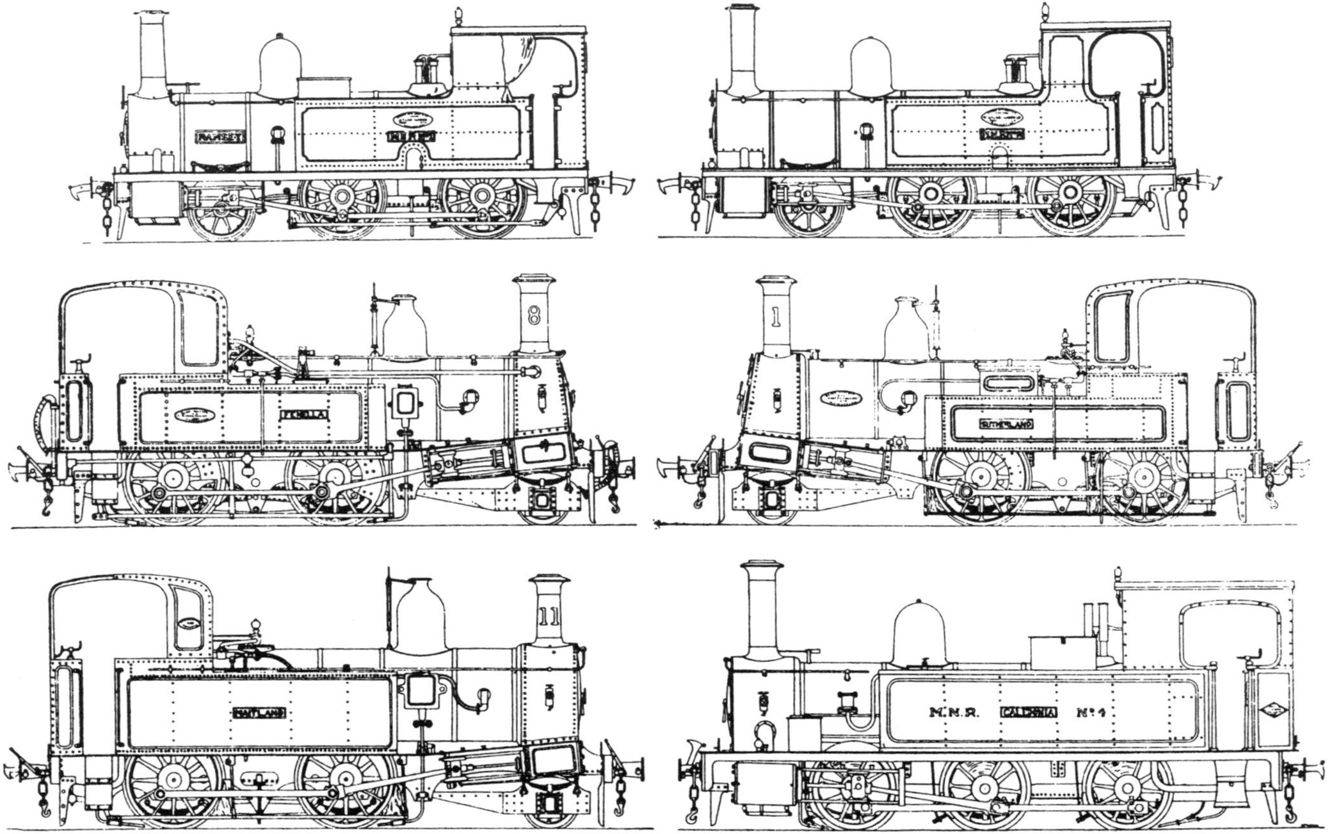

M.N.R. No. 1, *Ramsey* (now scrapped)
I.M.R. No. 8, *Fenella*
I.M.R. No. 11, *Maitland*

M.N.R. No. 2 *Northern* (now scrapped)
I.M.R. No. 1, *Sutherland*
M.N.R. No. 4, *Caledonia*

Omnibus of sketches of Manx Locomotives. *Ian Macnab*

instance, within four years of being delivered; Hunt was very pleased with tyre performance as the engine had covered 37,006 miles up to 1877. This represented approximately 500 journeys a year to Peel and back). By July 1878, the first five engines required re-tyring and Hunt sent the General Purposes Committee a profile of certain tyres, explaining that he was now changing the tyres front-to-rear and vice-versa and hoped the results would be more favourable. He was trying a new tyre section on 'bogeys' and was concerned to retain a good flange *depth* to prevent the pony wheels from riding up over the rail.

> The thin-ness of the flanges . . . not affect the steady motion . . . appear . . . not to come in contact with the rails . . . wheels would run without flanges as well as some Stephenson 6 coupled early engines which had drivers without flanges . . . the bogey wheel flanges were thinner on the left side than on the right . . . I have made a hand-turning tool to remove the sharp edges of the flange . . . without taking out the wheels . . . and putting into the lathe.

Consideration was given to ordering more locomotives with 12 in. in place of 11 in. cylinders in 1893 but BP recommended a pressure of 160 lbs be used to achieve the same result. Two more engines were delivered at this pressure: they were the last built with small boilers.

No. 8 FENELLA Works No. 3610 of 1894
No. 9 DOUGLAS 3815 1896

Reviewing the foregoing: Nos. 1-5 had nameplates mounted on the side tanks. On Nos. 1-3 the injector pipe discharged at the tank top but on Nos. 4-5 it was carried down externally to the base of the tank, passing over the name plates which were lettered accordingly so as not be obscured - LO CH and MO NA. When the first three were given longer pipes as Nos. 4 & 5, their plates were moved to the forward end of the tanks; Nos. 6-9 had the forward position from new. Many alterations of plate position, chimney numerals and minor detail make general comment tedious; the shrill whistle of these engines is perhaps their best-remembered feature, especially in summer when the first morning train threaded its way from Castletown to Port Erin with its whistle sounding imperiously for each crossing and across the cornfields . . . a careful listener could judge its progress exactly. Later engines had bigger whistles with deeper tone.

Eleven years were to pass before the stud was expanded; this was necessitated by the incorporation of the Manx Northern Railway and the need for engines to work the 26-mile section from Douglas to Ramsey. Two suitable, larger-boilered engines were delivered in 1905 and one each in 1908 and 1910.

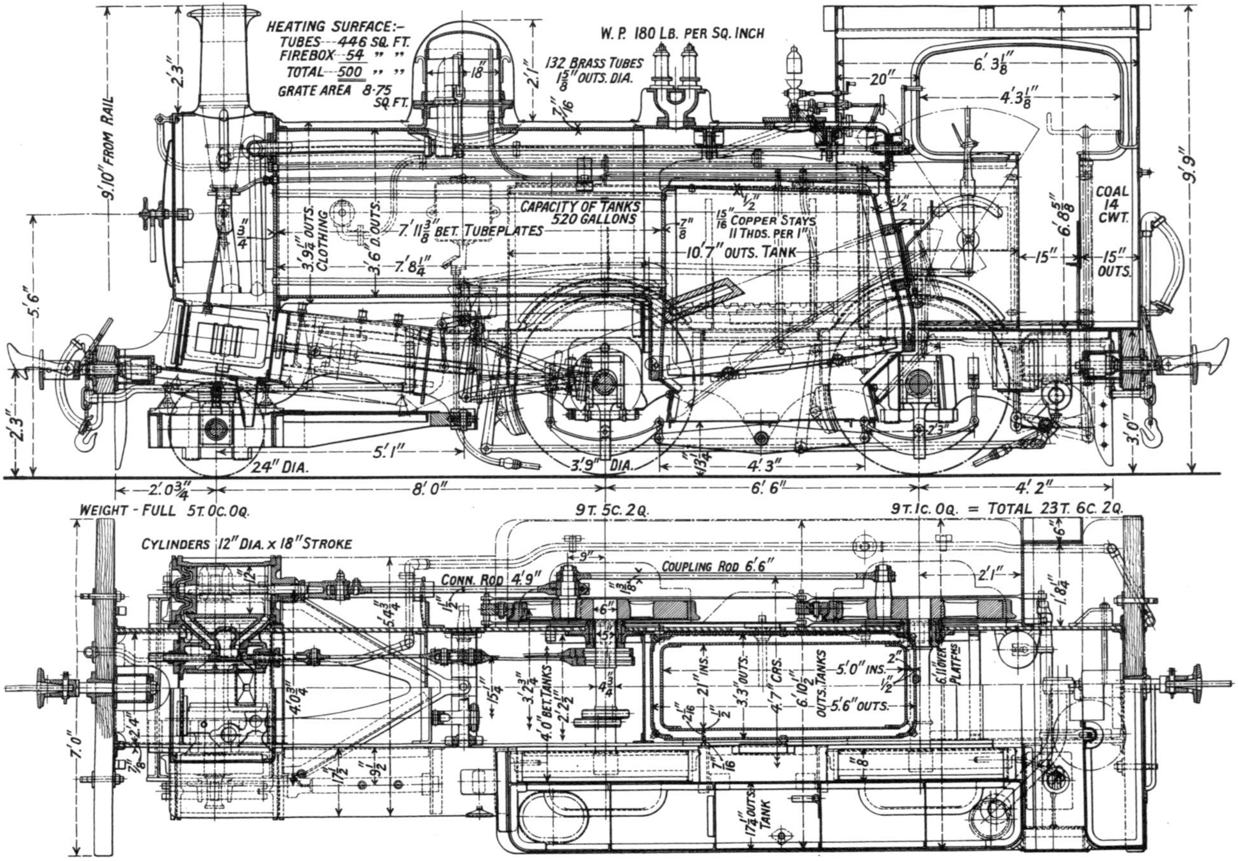

Drawing of the last IOMR steam locomotive No. 16 of 1926.

No. 10	**G.H. WOOD**	**Works No. 4662**	**of 1905**
No. 11	**MAITLAND**	**4663**	**1905**
No. 12	**HUTCHINSON**	**5126**	**1908**
No. 13	**KISSACK**	**5382**	**1910**

They were named after officials of the Company. The IOMR suggested they should have Marshall's valve gear, but the maker's, clearly unhappy to depart from a well-tried design, 'did not think any improvement would come of it'. Nos. 12-13 received spark arresters when new. Altogether bigger, the boilers were 3 ft 3 in. dia. pitched 4 ft 10 in. centreline from rail; tanks of 480 gallons capacity; driving wheelbase extended to 6 ft 6 in. and cab height from rail by 5 in.

No further motive power was considered until 1919, when heavy traffic brought the case for a more suitable engine before the Board; an engine like No. 13 was contemplated, but having 11½ in. dia. cylinders, steam brakes (with iron brake blocks in place of wood), and mechanical lubrication. However, a quotation for £3,000 - double that of No. 13 in 1910 - frightened the Board and it was decided 'to defer the matter for the present'. But by the mid-1920s Bradshaw's view that what they possessed would suffice had changed and Beyer was asked to produce a suitable specification for the South Line working with maximum axle loading of 10 tons; by reducing tank capacity from 550 to 520 gallons weight could be brought down to 23¼ tons. An order was placed and delivered in 1926 and the locomotive carried the same boiler, 3 ft 6 in. dia., throughout its working life.

No. 16 MANNIN Works No. 6296 of 1926

Boiler pressure was increased to 180 lbs; steam sanding, steam and vacuum brakes and a spark arrester were fitted. Mainly used on the South Line, it was to be found on Tynwald Day specials and occasionally on Sunday trains to Kirk Braddan.

This completes a summary of IOMR steam power; so back to 1923 when Beyer had two boilers under construction of the type so long established. Bradshaw then asked if the Salter safety valves with bell-mouthed domes could be replaced by closed domes and Ross-type 'Pop' valves which prevent staff from tampering with the valve setting. The makers could not comply with this as the boilers were far advanced, but kept the bell-mouthed dome and placed a single 'Pop' in it, with a second similar valve on the front boiler ring in front of the dome. With these two boilers unique before or since, they were at first fitted to Nos. 2 & 7 respectively in 1923.*

Four locomotives passed from the MNR to the IOMR in 1904; the first two being:

*Boiler changes are summarised on p. 215 to avoid detail which may not be of interest to the majority.

Drawing of MNR No. 2. The Sharp, Stewart & Co. Ltd. locomotives were basically the same but surviving drawings show minor differences: different chimney; pony wheels with 10 spokes; minor variations in lining out (as shown); tool box and nameplate fitted as indicated in broken line.

No. 1 RAMSEY Sharp, Stewart & Co. Ltd. Works No. 2885 of 1879
No. 2 NORTHERN 2886 1879

(Nameplates were not actually carried until 1892-3 when boilers were renewed, but names may have been applied in paint soon after delivery. Queries have also arisen about these long-accepted Work's Numbers.) *

The specification was mainly the work of W.H. Thomas, the MNR's Engineer who wished to have *three* engines, but the MNR was impoverished . . . Tenders were sought in December 1878 and the following responded:

Sharp, Stewart & Co. Ltd.	£1,100 each
The Avonside Engine Co. Ltd.	£1,137
R. & W. Hawthorn Ltd.	£1,240
Beyer, Peacock & Co. Ltd.	£1,285
Hudswell, Clark & Rodgers	£1,425

Only the first two were considered, but the former received an order in January 1879, to be delivered Ramsey by the end of May. Construction was made at the Atlas Works, off Oxford Street, Manchester and was contemporary with three smaller locomotives of similar conception and the same gauge for the Southwold Railway. Delivery was late; in July only one engine arrived; the other came on 1st September: this gave the precarious financial position a little breathing space.

In respect of cylinder size, boiler and wheel diameter and power output these engines were the same as IOMR No. 1-9 but their appearance was quite different; the Northern engines had straight footplating and the cylinder centre line was horizontal aligned with the driving wheel centres. All axle bearings were inside with the front axle in radial type but, in contrast to the IOMR engines, it was set behind the cylinders rather than in front. At speed the overall wheelbase was unable to prevent violent oscillation, whereas the Beyer engines with their leading pony truck set forward of the cylinders, rode acceptably well. There were problems in giving sufficient lubrication to valve gear and boxes too and the makers were called upon for certain modifications; when a third engine was obtained (of the IOMR design) the shortcomings of the Sharp engines behaviour was emphasised. Though these alterations to springing etc. pleased the locomotive department, the engines now hammered the curved track; a small bonus in their favour was their suitability for the Ramsey quay line and St John's sandpit, accessed from the Foxdale branch.

These engines lacked the finer points of the Beyer draughtsmen, the boiler mountings were conventional but pleasing. Springing was laminated leaf throughout, those for the leading wheels were set above the footplate. There was gravity sand feed between the driving wheels and access through

*Certain statements quoted here are given in MANX NORTHERN RLY. (Hendry): 1980. The whereabouts of supporting MNR records apparently removed from the Island, remain undisclosed.

a door in lower side of the tank to fill the reservoirs. The maker's brass plate was in the upper centre of the side tank; below was a rectangular brass plate reading 'M.N.R. No. 1' (or). The later name plates were located forward of the tanks on the front boiler cleading.

The original chimneys tapered outwards towards the top and had a polished cap. Brass domes were fitted but these were soon painted over; double whistles on the cab roof were reduced to one and conventional Ramsbottom safety valves were sited over the firebox. New fireboxes were given to both engines in 1893, while in 1901 No. 1 required another. Fireboxes were obviously troublesome for as early as 1882 the IOMR had to lend an engine while a party of Sharp's men plus their own, passed an anxious time with three engines simultaneously unreliable in service.

Driving was from the right-hand side and a screw jack for rerailing was carried forward on the running-board. A wooden tool box was mounted on the side tank and the bunker was inside the cab at rear, but the cab's large side openings had to closed by rear wooden side sheets and canvas curtains at the front in bad weather. An extra-ordinary fitment added to the engines in 1883 was a 'blower pipe' which clearly was a *replacement* for that already provided; the parts were supplied from Glasgow. By and large, these Sharp engines required much work to be done on them in the early years and there were occasions when the availability of a locomotive hung on a knife-edge; the MNR's opinion of the makers, and its men sent to Ramsey to carry out critical repairs, gave them no credit. Tyres for returning had to be sent to Glasgow and a man sent from there to Ramsey to re-fit them. As if this was not enough, troubles with the leading radial bosses plagued the engines' early years, but Sharp insisted that they had run trials on the line at 45 mph without concern. In March 1891 when new replacement radial boxes were delivered they were to the original faulty pattern!

At this stage it is opportune to consider how many of the MNR's problems might have been eliminated from the first if relations between it and the IOMR had been good; instead it appears that a policy of 'Nothing good ever ran on IOMR metals' and for the MNR to 'do its own thing' (apparently fostered at Board level) left the operating and maintenance staff with an outsize headache. A modicum of collusion on design, suppliers and experience could have gained the MNR advantage at no cost; the simple matter of driving wheel tyres and fitting could have been done in Douglas Works for a fraction of cost.

New boilers being due, RAMSEY received one made by Dübs & Co. in 1892, and NORTHERN's of 1893 came from the same maker. At this period too, both engines had trouble with brass/cast iron slide valves and wear on the valve faces which was never overcome satisfactorily.

These engines had firebox attention in 1901/2; now the dome covers were of steel and NORTHERN had a new chimney in 1899 which tapered the other way. Some 'artist' painted the Legs of Man on the smokebox door of RAMSEY, but after the amalgamation of 1905 no attempt was made to re-paint them yet the MNR number plates from the side tanks were removed. Sproat, the Locomotive Superintendent of the IOMR, kept them on their native territory as, until Ramsey's quay line had been relaid in 1909, he would not permit IOMR engines to traverse them. Even then results were dubious and Sproat's report of 1909 saying they ' were not in a safe condition to haul traffic on the main line' confirmed an uncertain future. In 1910 they were allocated Nos. 16 & 17 which they never bore. Bradshaw, replacing Sproat in 1912, condemned them, as delivery of IOMR Nos. 12-13 made them surplus. Employment was occasionally found; No. 1 became a 'hack' to the Permanent Way Department, being used as Ballast Engine at Port Erin in 1911 for a short period during extensions, whilst later that year it was still fit for spoil removal at Foxdale, afterwards being dumped in St John's goods yard out in the open.

Ultimately both engines were stored at Ramsey shed. Ward's and B.M. Renton & Co., both of Sheffield, declined to buy so when Reynolds, a scrap dealer from Douglas, was offered NORTHERN for £78 he accepted and, with the engine towed to Douglas, it was cut up there in October 1912. Its last duties were on shunting at Ramsey.

RAMSEY, still in the shed in 1917, was offered for sale the next year. Mr Knox-Gilchrist, a Director of the British Commercial Lorry & Engineering Co. Ltd. of 66/68, Bridge Street, Manchester bought it for £350 requesting that it remain in Ramsey shed. In 1919 he offered the engine for sale 'in first class condition' in THE LOCOMOTIVE magazine, but no buyer was forthcoming. By April 1922 it had been moved into Ramsey carriage shed and when the IOMR Co sought expedition of the BCL&ECL, they learned the Company was in liquidation and the owner was now Thomas Carter, 170, Trafford Road, Salford, 'a general automotive agent and consulting engineer'. Carter had attempted to sell without success and was given until 22nd June, 1922 to remove the engine. That date passed uneventfully and the IOMR Co, now the legal owners by default, sold it to J.P. Purcell of Ramsey who intended to sell it in connection with extensions to Liverpool Docks. It was now June 1923, the engine standing between engine and carriage sheds at Ramsey . . . but not for long. After several other promising enquiries, negotiations collapsed and the engine was towed to Douglas Works and dismantled . . . possibly by Reynolds.

The biography of No. 1 has claim to be the most tedious of any Manx locomotive!

No. 3 THORNHILL Beyer, Peacock & Co. Ltd. Works No. 2028 of 1880

From the opening of the MNR it was evident that two locomotives were insufficient and tenders for a third were sought from Sharp's, Beyer,Peacock and R. & W. Hawthorn of Newcastle. Sharp's were told they would have to improve the leading wheel arrangement and their tender was the cheapest. However they could not deliver within the specified four months and Beyer received the order. In their Works the construction was 'twinned' with IOMR No. 7 TYNWALD (see p. 179). The engine was named after J.T. Clucas residence and carried three nameplates, one on each tank and one on the cab rear. No number appeared on the chimney. A useful specification of the livery was set down as, 'Lake colour, lined with black and vermillion'.

A new boiler was supplied by Dübs in 1896 (boilers are listed on p. 215) and the maker's plates removed at the 1910 re-boilering.

Delivery was made to Ramsey in early July 1880; wheels were sent to Dübs in 1888 for new tyres but work on the cylinders and motion was done at the maker's. The purchase was deemed to be a splendid one, boiler-life being especially notable. The re-boilering of 1910 was done by fitting the second boiler belonging to LOCH (fitted 1893); in 1913 the engine received DERBY's 1893 boiler and in 1916 MONA's 1895 boiler. An entirely new boiler was fitted in 1921 (when numerals were fixed to the chimney) and was notable in being the last having Salter safety valves.

The engine was allocated No. 14 in 1910 but the number did not appear until 1918 and then only on the bunker back. Like other engines, steam heating apparatus was fitted in the 1930s but it was the last working engine to have vacuum brakes in the late 1940s. (The writer recalls a hectic descent into St John's from Peel Road in 1947 when running late, the steam brake was fully applied and the handbrake was assisted by the use of the Single Line Staff to gain extra leverage on the brake handle).

Along with other existing engines, whose boilers were unsafe, it was given a coat of near-suitable paint and was among the caravan of stored engines in the carriage shed at St John's which was put on daily display during Lord Ailsa's regime. The locomotive is now privately preserved on the Island.

No. 4 CALEDONIA Dübs & Co. Works No. 2178 of 1885

It was Col. Rich, the Board of Trade Inspector,who had advised the MNR that when a fourth locomotive was obtained - and there was already enough traffic to necessitate this - neither of the two existing designs would be suitable for the Foxdale traffic. The MNR faced the undesirable position of having two designs of engine already, and a fourth inevitable; with hindsight the situation might have been foreseen and avoided, but the Company's early shortage of money was really the culprit. The haulage of ore from the mines to Ramsey was secondary to the problem of carrying coal from Ramsey to Foxdale - with its final 1 in 12 incline up to mine level - for the pumping engines. Tenders were sought from Sharp, Beyer, The Hunslet Engine Co., A.S. Nelson (as agents), Neilson & Co. and The Lowca Engineering Co. Ltd. (the latter confused both rail gauge and wheel arrangement at the first two attempts). Quotations were as follows:

Lowca (for 2-4-0 tank in error)	£995
Beyer, Peacock	£1530
Dübs	£1215
Sharp	£1350
Nelson (supplier not given)	£1125
Hunslet	£1425
Lowca (corrected)	£1135

The MNR preferred to buy a engine of the six-coupled type supplied by Beyer to the Ballymena & Larne Railway in 1877-83, but a design by Dübs proving cheaper, Dübs received the order. The loading gauge was fined down to make it suitable for the IOMR's 10 ft 9 in. vertical clearance, rather than on the MNR at 11 ft as through running to Douglas was then the MNR's persistent desire and the Company was hopeful it could build on its useful links with Henry Hunt, Locomotive Superintendent of the IOMR, to that end.

The specification and price were not at first finalised, and a suitable name gave problems, but CALEDONIA was chosen.

It was intended that payment for the engine should be made by Matthew Baird whereby it was to be leased to the Company. The terms were for five years commencing 31st December, 1886 and a yearly rent of £270 in the first four years and £293 12*s*. 8*d*. in the last, payable half-yearly. However, a completed lease does not survive, nor does a photograph confirm that an owner's plate was fitted to the engine as required by the Draft Lease. On completion of the leasing period, the MNR had the option of buying the engine for One Pound.

CALEDONIA was the largest and heaviest engine on the Island. Its tractive effort was more than twice that of other engines; there was a fixed wheelbase of 11 ft and the adhesion weight was 27 tons. (For leading dimensions see Table for all locomotives p. 192.) The appearance was distinctive, with a typical Scottish touch in the wingplates to the smokebox. The copper-capped tall chimney was noteworthy and the Ramsbottom safety valves had tall brass extension pipes to keep escaping steam off the spectacle

O-6-O T. LOCOMOTIVE "CALEDONIA".

BUILT BY DUBS & C° IN 1887 FOR MANX NORTHERN RLY.

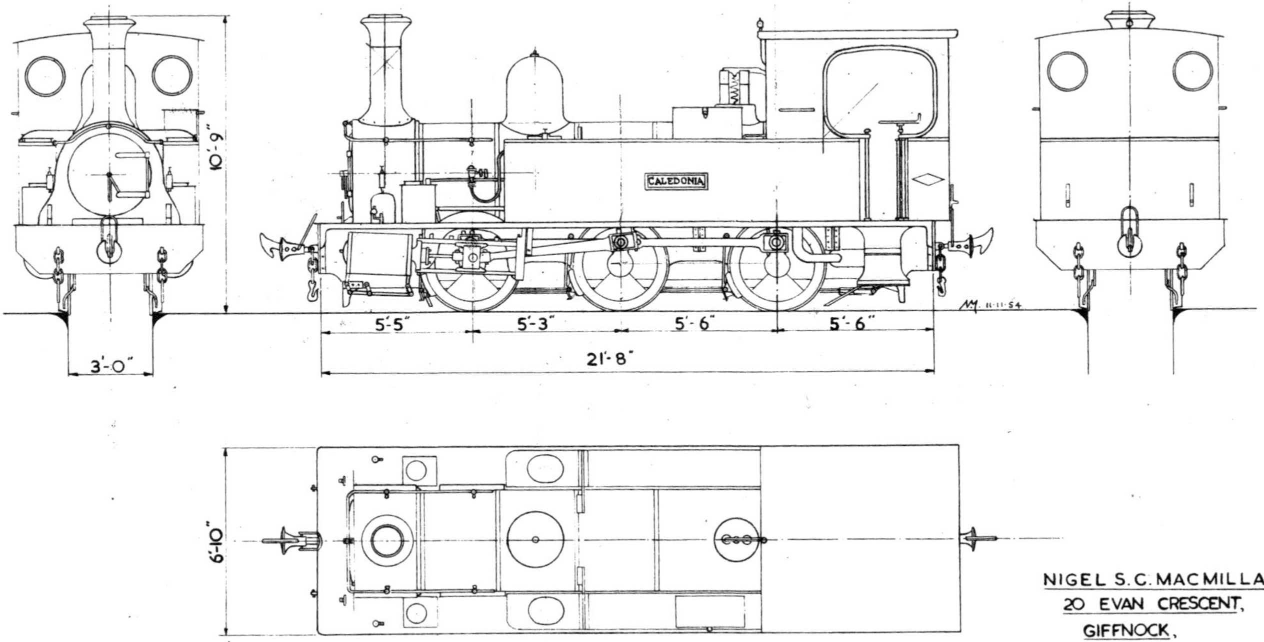

NIGEL S. C. MACMILLAN,
20 EVAN CRESCENT,
GIFFNOCK,
GLASGOW.

glasses. All wheels were sanded.

When in 1922 it received a boiler from Beyer,Peacock, 'Ross Patent safety valves' appeared; new side tanks too. The shorter chimney complete with numerals then delivered has been replaced in recent times.

On the MNR the engine was confined to Ramsey-Foxdale operation despite the optimism of through running; on the IOMR its duties included emergency work with snow-ploughs attached, hauling long and heavy agricultural show specials, Foxdale Mines' spoil clearance, or operation of the heavily-graded ertstwhile Knockaloe Branch during World War I - no regular work was available to keep it in constant use. Failures 'on the road' were often due to the uncertainty of the injectors resulting in the crew having to throw the fire from the box due to low water level. It acquired something of a reputation for being '*un enfant terrible*' in consequence. The pipework and tubes as constructed were undersize, frequently leaking. The wheelbase was long by Manx standards and it became necessary to chair some curves on the northern section to prevent the gauge from widening.

The engine was hired to the Snaefell Mountain Railway Association in 1895 to assist in the construction of the railway from Laxey to the summit (see Vol. I pp.224-25). The engine was shipped from Ramsey to Laxey and then taken through the steep streets up from the harbour on baulks and rollers. An additional rail to 3 ft gauge had to be laid pro tem to accommodate the engine and some hired ballast wagons which it pushed up the mountain following the main construction party (the gauge of the Snaefell Railway being 3 ft 6 in.).* Duty on the heavily graded Knockaloe line would appear relatively easy after this for the Snaefell route climbs at 1 in 12 for 85 per cent of its route mileage of 4.9; there is a 5-chain curve near the summit.

Though lying out of use for lengthy periods, the engine was sufficiently newsworthy for cameramen to be sent out to photograph it clearing snowdrifts or on wartime aerodrome runway construction trains to collect mines' waste from Foxdale. When Lord Ailsa began his régime it failed due to habitual injector trouble when on an inaugural run. There is no photographic record of the engine in use during the years when the King George V Playing Fields were building.

The near completion of the Foxdale spoil pillage marked the engine's withdrawal for heavy overhaul in 1943; by then its appetite for burning coal had become legendary. Repaired, No. 15 broke a ceremonial tape at Lord Ailsa's Opening Day on 3rd June, 1967 and was rostered owing to locomotive shortage, to work on the South Line on 1st September. The above mentioned débacle then took place, followed by a few uneasy trips, a repaint in 'MNR Livery' to join other useless machines in St John's carriage shed from whence a new home was found in the freshly established Port Erin Museum . . . but not for long. Such a noteworthy machine has more recently been the

*See SRN Vol. 111 pp. 8-10

centrepiece of railway celebrations in the Island and, beyond the finishing point of this volume, it has returned one hundred years later to the windswept flanks of Snaefell. Meanwhile, nature reclaims the course of the railways on which it performed its primary duties.

	IOMR *1-9* *(as built)* *small boiler* *MNR* 3[5]	*MNR* *1 and 2*	*IOMR* *1-9* *(rebuilt)* *medium boiler*	*IOMR* *10-13* *(as built)* *medium boiler*	*IOMR* *16* *large boiler*	*MNR* 4[4] *(as built)*
Driving wheels dia.	3'9"	3'9"	3'9"	3'9"	3'9"	3'3"
Leading wheels dia.	2'	2'9"	2'	2'	2'	-
Wheelbase	8'3"+6'3"	5'+6'	8'3"+6'3"	8'+6'6"	8+6'6"	5'3"+5'6"
Cylinders (in.)	11x18	11x18	11x18	11x18	12x18	13x20[2]
Boiler: Length[7]	7'8¼"	-	7'8¼"	7'8¼"	7'8¼"	8'6"
Dia.	2'10"	3'	3'3"	3'3"	3'6"	3'
Pressure (lbs)	120	120	160	160	180	140
Tubes H.S. (sq. ft)	348.07	360	417.72	390	446	486
Grate H.S. (sq. ft)	43.28	40	43.28	51	54	51
Total H.S. (sq. ft)	391.35	400	461	441	500	537
Tank capacity (gall.)	Nos. 1-3: 320[6]	-	Nos. 4-6: 480	-	-	-
	Nos. 4-9/14 385	400	Nos. 1-3, 7-9 385	480	520	450
Firebox length	5'	-	5'	5'	5'	-
Bunker capacity	14 cwt.	1¼ tons	14 cwt.	14 cwt.	1½ tons	1½ tons
Weight W.O.	17t. 12c.	19t. 0c.	20t. 10c.	20t.	23t. 6c.	22t. 9c.
Boiler C/L	4'10"	4'6"	4'10"	-	5'6"	4'10½"
Ht. Rail-top chimney	9'6"	9'6"	9'11"	9'11"	9'10"	9'3"[8]
Ht Rail-top cab	Nos. 1-9,14: 9'5"	9'	9'10"	9'10"	9'9"	9'6"
Tractive Effort (lbs)	4,930	4,930	6,580	6,580	8,810	11,120
Length over beams	21'	20'1"	21'	21'	21'9"	22'[1]
Driving wheels	11 spokes: square- ended bal. weights	12 spokes	(unchanged)	12 spokes crescent bal. weights	12 spokes crescent bal. weights	7 spokes: remainder solid bal. weight

1 Over front beam and rear sheet.
2 Variously given as 11¾x18, 13½x20, 12x20. Width overall wheels 4¾". 2'9" back to back.
3 Originally - chimneys latterly swapped about.
4 IOMR No. 15
5 IOMR No. 14
6 Later 385 gal.
7 Between tube plates.
8 Short chimney - 1922.

Steam Locomotives - Loans to other parties

According to surviving documents, steam locomotive hire occurred on the following occasions:

Year	*Company making loan*	*Company using loan*
1873-74	IOMR	Watson & Smith*
1886	MNR	H. Kennedy & Sons+
1895	MNR	Snaefell MRA
1898	IOMR	IOMT & EPCL
1898	MNR	IOMT & EPCL

* Contractor to the Isle of Man Rly. + Contractor to the Foxdale Rly.

In all cases open wagons formed part of the contract and in most the party hiring the locomotive was not adequately covered by the Agreement for damage sustained to it.

IOMR to Watson & Smith

Only one reference remains of this hiring which was done through Nixon in London; on 16th July, 1873 Watson & Smith verbally agreed with William Mackenzie to pay the IOMR 30*s*. a day for a locomotive. Later, the arrangement was put in a letter to Watson & Smith:

> . . . on wet days if the engine has only her fire lighted up, a quarter of a day to be paid for. We to find driver & fireman, coals, oil & grease. Also that we pay for the use of the Company's trucks the sum of 2s. 6d. per truck per working day . . . It is understood that for any extraordinary accident the Company are not to be held liable.

MNR to Foxdale Rly. Co. per Hugh Kennedy & Son

The MNR hired their engine No. 2 NORTHERN to H. Kennedy & Son the contractors for the Foxdale Railway between March and August 1886; the MNR had received delivery of No. 4 CALEDONIA the previous year and presumably - despite contention that four locomotives were a minimum for the traffic - No. 4 was proving so reliable that a Sharp engine could be spared . . . even including the busy months of July and August.

Apart from Accounts covering the hire, the only textual evidence of the event is an unsigned, undated, longhand draft which reads:*

> We, Hugh Kennedy & Son, make application to the Foxdale Railway Co. Ltd. for the use of a Locomotive to haul the excavated materials from the cuttings upon the lands of Dumbell's Banking Co. to the site of the Railway Embankments on the new line we paying all workmen's wages, coal and all other stores required for the working and

* Original in Tower Collection.

maintaining of such Locomotive.*

The Hire of same to be arranged between the Company and us, but allowance to be given for the Engine Power provided for under the Contract - and undertaking to make good any damage other than the ordinary wear and tear that may arise while engaged at our works - the Engine to be ready to commence work at 7 am and leave off at 6 pm daily. Such Engine to be started at Ramsey for the convenience of cleaning etc., the Company reserving the right to withdraw such Locomotive in the case of any emergency arising, or when the representative of the Company was of the opinion that due care was not being exercised for the protection of the Company's said Locomotive.

The hire of the engine was @ £2 10s. 0*d*. per day plus (per day) Engineman 5*s*. 6*d*., Fireman 3*s*., Cleaner 2*s*. 8*d*., Fitter 6*s*. 4*d*. Materials were charged: Coal 16*s*. ton., Oils 3*s*. 4*d*. and 2*s*. 8*d*. per gallon., Tallow 5*d*. lb., Waste 3½*d*. lb., Paraffin 9*d*. per gallon, Colza Oil 3*s*. 6*d*. per gallon. The Accounts reveal that work only extended by one week into August and the MNR took the opportunity of fitting new brake blocks and piston rings in that week, and charging for them. The hire of wagons @ 6*d*. per vehicle per day was charged £7 2*s*. 0*d*. at the end of the work: in no month was the engine in use every day - 15-26 days a month between March and July, and only 6 in August. The total cost was £393 17*s*. 2*d*. including a deduction of £46 5*s*. 0*d*. 'allowance for ballasting'. (The comparative rarity of this type of information is deemed worthy of detailed mention.)

MNR to Snaefell Mountain Railway Association

Under an Agreement of 23rd April, 1895, MNR No. 4 CALEDONIA was hired for £20 per week, charged ex- Ramsey to return Ramsey station. The engine was to be housed and equipment etc. used during the hire to be of quality approved by the driver and Mr Cameron. Engineman and Fireman were to be supplied by the MNR, with wages 6*s*. 6*d*. for a 10-hour day and 4*s*. 2*d*. respectively. In the event of the engine being damaged beyond repair, the lessees were to provide another and charge appropriately. Two 'timber trucks' Nos. 20 & 21 were to be hired at 3*s*. each per day.

On 4th May, 1895 the TIMES had:

Work on this line is being pushed forward . . . the threatened strike . . . being averted by promise . . . increased wages according to ability . . . A locomotive belonging to the MNR has been taken to Laxey . . . getting the engine off the steamer, and from thence along the Glen Road . . . has been a very tedious business, improvised rails having to be laid the whole way.

The TIMES again on 18th May: 'The engine from the MNR is now in full swing drawing up rails, sleepers and ballast and the service way progresses well . . .'

* i.e. to work the materials' train from the pits north-west of St John's station (now a Car Park: 1995) to form the embankment up and over the IOMR at St John's.

IOMR to Isle of Man Tramways & Electric Power Co. Ltd.

IOMR No. 2 DERBY was hired in 1898 for the extension of the electric tramway which had been built by the erstwhile Douglas & Laxey Coast Electric Tramway and which then terminated at Laxey (reached 1894). The 1899 AGM was told the IOMR Co. received £195 in hire fees. The engine ran over MNR metals to Ramsey, was shipped to Laxey and once upon a low-loader, was hauled by traction engines up to the Tramway; a photograph shows the engine, below the Ramsey road near Minorca, at work with temporary wooden buffers. It shared construction work with MNR No. 1 RAMSEY at the Ramsey end and an un-named four-coupled saddle tank built by Andrew Barclay, Sons & Co. Ltd. (Works No. 713 of 1892) for Morrison & Mason (contractors) [later sold to Douglas Corporation Water Works in connection with the West Baldwin reservoir scheme].

No trace has been found of the Agreement which covered this hiring, so exact dates cannot be quoted; some known conditions were:

1) The engine was to be worked by IOMR men.
2) Delivery from Douglas station to Laxey to be under IOMR direction.
3) The engine to be returned by 21st May.
4) The Best Steam Coal to supplied by the Tramway.
5) The charge for the engine to be £2. 10s. 0*d*. per day plus wages for driver, fireman and cleaner.

In writing to Wood in April 1898, Nixon said:

> I hope the Electric Company will not knock our engine about - did not the Snaefell Coy do a good deal of crunching to the Northern Engine . . . however, our man will be there to look after ours.

MNR to Isle of Man Tramways & Electric Power Co. Ltd.

No. 1 RAMSEY was used in construction of the Ramsey Extension, working south from the car shed at Ballure at a cost of £2 10s. 0*d*. a day under an Agreement dated 12th April, 1898. 'Low-side ballast waggons Nos. 24 & 29 and timber trucks Nos. 20 & 21' were hired at 3*s*. a day. Other charges per day were : driver 5s. 6*d*., fireman 4*s*., 3*s*. 2*d*. per night for cleaner - all to be paid by the MNR and charged up.

The Agreement is dated 12th April, 1898, hiring to commence 21st April until such date as stock is returned to Ramsey station.

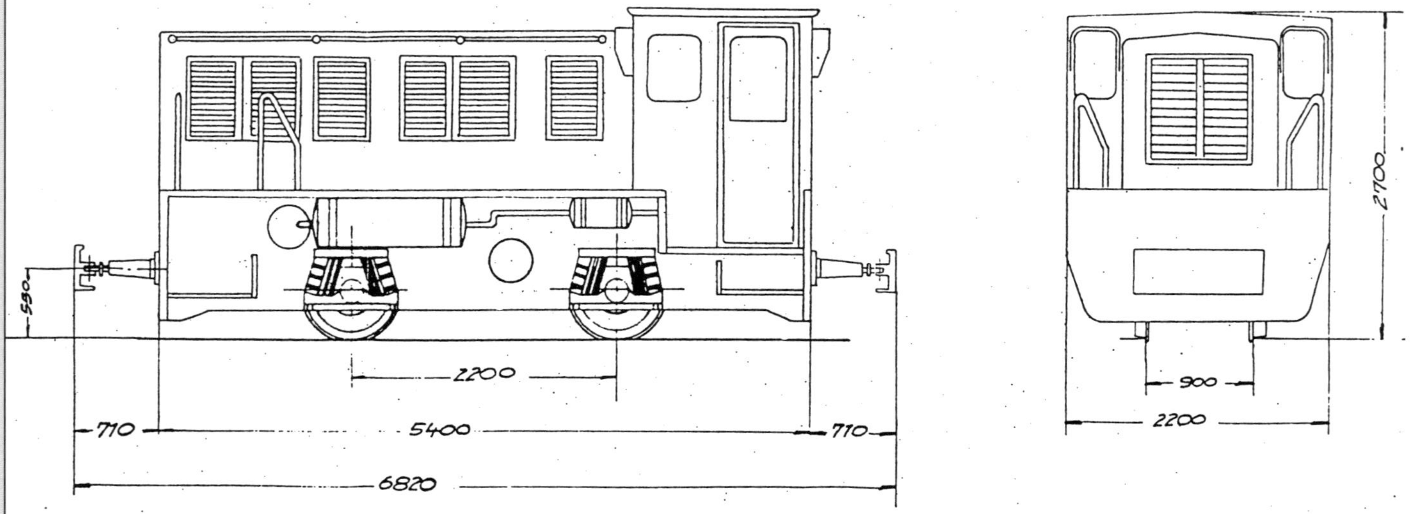

Reproduction of drawing submitted by the makers to the IOMR inspection party of No. 17.

Diesel Locomotive & Diesel Railcars

No. 17 VIKING

Brief reference has already been given to the inspection and subsequent purchase of this unit (Vol. II p.240-on). It had been the practice for some years to use the ex-CDRJC railcars - long unfit for passenger duties - as hacks for the PW Department but by 1991 their parlous condition brought crisis to a head. A chance advertisement suggested a suitable 900 mm gauge four-wheeled diesel-hydraulic locomotive was for sale at a railway works in Dortmund in Germany. It had previously found employment on a mining railway at Helmstedt. Inspection in spring 1992 appeared satisfactory except that where the locomotive stood, there were no tracks to test it in operation. It was agreed that the engine be brought to the Island and, subsequent to a series of tests in summer 1992, full purchase @ £21,000 was made (Vol. II pp. 241-42). It received the name VIKING at Easter 1993.

The locomotive has been used on various duties including the rescue of passenger trains detained by steam engine mishaps,and more recently (and outside the period of this chronology) has been given a replacement engine unit.

The loading gauge is suitable for the IOMR and the rail-gauge but $\frac{9}{16}$ in. less than 3 ft - no problem due to this. Carried on four driven wheels, and weighing 24 tonnes, it was powered by a Deutz V12 air-cooled turbo-charged engine delivering 200 hp. Drive is via a Voight 3-speed automatic gearbox through a torque converter.*

The name 'Schoema' appears on the radiator and a plate in cab states;

CHRISTOPH SCHOTTLER
GMBH
MASCHINEWFABRIK

DIEPHOLZ	BAS BREMEN
(HP) PS 200	MASH No. 2066
25T	BAJAHR 1958

Railcars. (Ex-County Donegal Railways Joint Committee Nos. 19 & 20)

Although the purchase of these railcars was not made until 1961 (see Vol. II pp.152-53) the Company had made enquiries of their builders in August 1939, Messrs. Walker Bros. (Wigan) Ltd., Pagefield Ironworks. They were sent details of the railcars supplied to Donegal. Mr E. Barton Walker called on Sheard and Vaughan in August and the firm sent exhaustive details in October of what they could supply. But the onset of war closed the enquiry. A glimmer of peace sent a man from Walker to call on 26th June, 1944 and IOMR interest was revived when Walker supplied railcars and locomotives

*For additional detail see SRN summer 1992 pp.6-8 and Christmas 1992 pp.14-17.

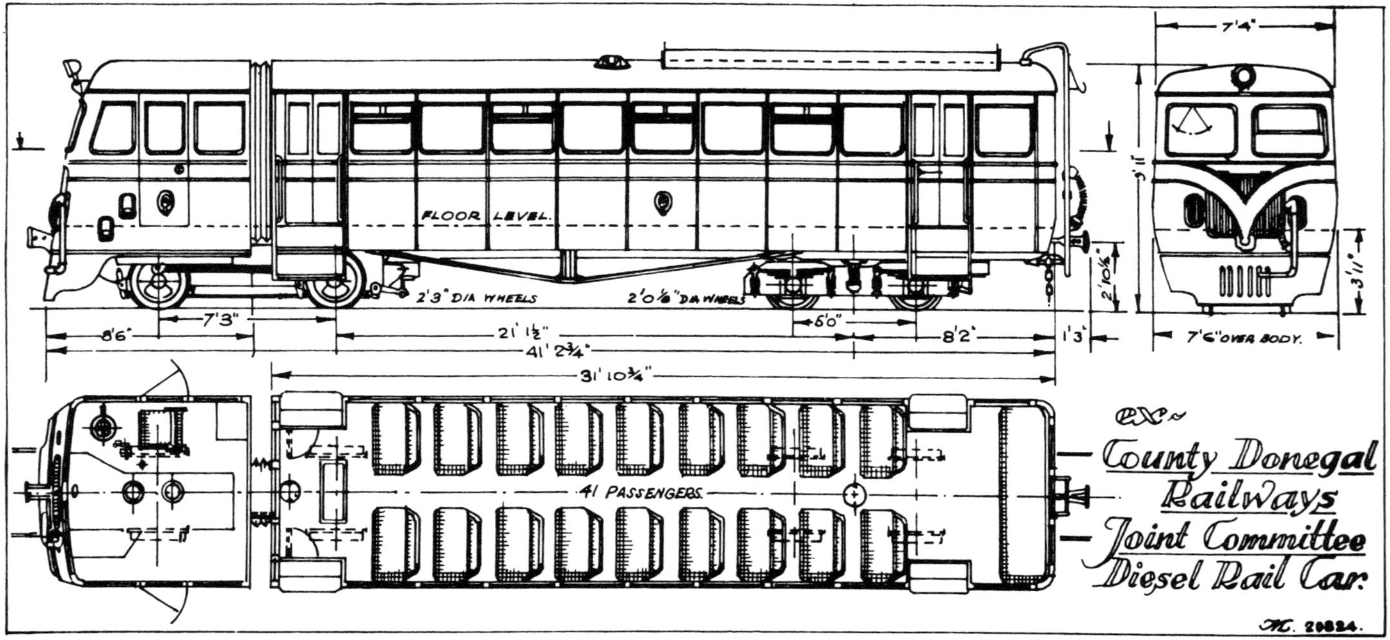
7'4"
3'11"
3'1"
2'10⅛"
FLOOR LEVEL.
2'3" DIA WHEELS
2'0⅛" DIA WHEELS
8'6"
7'3"
21' 1½"
5'0"
8'2"
1'3"
41' 2¾"
31' 10¾"
7'6" OVER BODY.
41 PASSENGERS.
ex~
County Donegal
Railways
Joint Committee
Diesel Rail Car.
20824.

to the 3 ft gauge West Clare section of CIE in 1955. In February 1957 Walker quoted for West Clare types: Locomotive £19,000 and Railcar £23,000 on the basis that a minimum of four of each type was ordered. Needless to add, the IOMR took no action.

On 1st September, 1961 the IOMR informed Walker that they had bought two CDRJC railcars at public auction and could they provide certain spare parts? Ultimately, correspondence ceased.

The General Manager's Report for the IOMR Co in 1961 contained reference to the acquisition; there were 4 forward speeds giving 7, 12, 18 and 30 mph, with a reverse speed of 7 mph. The engine was a Gardner 6-cylinder of 107 hp; the power bogie weighed about 5½ tons and the coach and rear bogie about 6 tons. The Report agrees that working back-to-back would only make the cars suitable for the Peel Line. Sheard complained to Shaw about 'the poor noise emitted by the horns' of these vehicles. 'Give up trying those you already have'; the solution was to acquire two-tone horns 'of the highest possible output' from the Road Department (managed by J.M. Sheard!).

These were the last units built for Donegal; the driver's cab is of full-rounded type enclosing the engine; there are doors each side for the driver. There was a Meadows' gearbox driving through Hardy-Spicer propellor shaft to the rear bogie axle; the driving wheels were coupled by outside rods.

Dimensions include:

	ft	*in.*
Length whole body unit	41	2¾
Height from rail	9	11
Height over roofrack from rail	10	8
Body width	7	6
Power bogie wheelbase	7	3
Power bogie wheel diam.	2	3
Rear bogie wheelbase	5	0
Rear bogie wheel diam.	2	0

These cars cost the CDRJC £6,000 for the bogie unit and £2,176 for the body, each. In the year this volume was concluded (1995/6) the cars were only fit for shunting in Douglas yard.

Other Motive Power Considered

It was the far-sighted G.H. Wood who conceived the importation of omnibuses as feeders to the railway or extensions to reach districts not so served. His first enquiries were made of the Daimler Motor Co. Ltd. in 1898, and were followed in 1905-6 when various bus-operating railway companies were approached for a summary of their experience, and the North Eastern Railway as regards their rail-borne 'Steam Auto Cars'. At a later date Stowell contacted:

April 1927	Clayton Wagons Ltd. For a light steam locomotive and separate coach.
April 1927	Metropolitan Carriage Wagon & Finance Co. Ltd. For a petrol locomotive.
April 1927	Sentinel Waggon Works Ltd. For a 'Sentinel-Cammell' Steam Rail Coach.
April 1927	The Drewry Car Co. Ltd. For a Rail Motor Coach: (internal- combustion).

All the above were planned to forestall the Island road transport undertakings which were to open a Douglas-Port Erin service in the summer; from the tone of the correspondence accompanying the four enquiries, the move from the road operators had caught the IOMR unawares, and created panic in the Boardroom.

The last pre-World War II enquiry was made by Sheard in August 1939 regarding internal-combustion railcars by Leyland.

The idea of acquiring a diesel-engined locomotive or railcar lingered on; this took the form:

April 1942	Clogher Valley Railway (in liquidation). Enquiries concerning items sold/for sale.*
February 1961	CIE. Enquiry re availability of West Clare section diesel locomotives.
March 1961	CDRJC. Attendance at auction of equipment.

Reference has already been made in Volume II to the negotiations surrounding the last two events and the ultimate purchase of railcars of CDRJC origin, but earlier proposals require a further comment. The several enquiries all put out in April 1927 underline the concern of the Directors that road competition would threaten the IOMR's future.

Clayton Wagons Ltd.

On 2nd April, 1927 Sheard wrote explaining 'we are faced with Motor Bus transport between Douglas and Peel and Douglas and Port Erin . . . we could utilise some of our present bogie coaches by having attached a Motor . . .' and asked for details of a 3 ft gauge 'Rail Motor Coach' with running costs etc. and was told they could supply a 'Clayton' Light Steam Locomotive for one man operation with controls on each side for about £1,350 delivered to an English port.

*The mystery surrounding Vaughan's visit is clarified!(Vol. II p.117)

Metropolitan C.W. & F. Co. Ltd.

Also on the same day, a similar letter but adding, 'I may add that Petrol Motors would I think be preferable to Steam Motors'. Replying with 'We have been in communication with some friends who could confidently be relied upon to supply a satisfactory article', Metropolitan listed:

Motor Rail & Transport Co. Ltd. for a 105/165 bhp 'Simplex' Petrol Locomotive @ £1,975.
Drewry Car Co.Ltd. for 100 hp Standard IC Locomotive, 0-4-0 type @ £2,445.

Metropolitan stated they preferred the Drewry and in either case would be responsible for the work being done to IOMR Co. satisfaction; both prices were ex-Works.

Sentinel Waggon Works Ltd.

This firm was approached on 8th April and the IOMR was especially interested in the catalogue illustration of the Patent Steam Locomotives working in Egypt; this was a 'CE' type, 100 hp to draw 100 tons at 23 mph on the level or 15 tons on 1 in 65 (the gradient of the two-mile climb from Douglas on the South Line) working economically, or 40 tons at 12 mph on that gradient etc. Alternative gearing was available. The 'CE' type ran at 30 mph on the level and weighed 15 tons in working order; FOB price at Liverpool was £1,395 but vacuum brake and 'finish painting' was extra.

On 13th May Sheard approached the Derwent Valley Light Railway to see a 'Sentinel' at work; Bradshaw inspected on 19th May but thought that no advantage would accrue. But Sheard pressed on and now wanted a reduction in price if two or more units were purchased, he was offered 2½% discount. Sheard and Stowell were sufficiently keen to visit the makers at Shrewsbury but on 10th June Sheard wrote that 'the locomotives we have at present are economically sufficient for all our requirements'.*

Drewry Car Co. Ltd.

While Metropolitan's suggestion of using a Motor Rail locomotive was not pursued, a direct approach to Drewry was made on 8th April who confirmed that only a driver and conductor were needed. They mentioned a suitable coach, the first of which had been 'supplied to the Weston, Clevedon & Portishead Railway in Somerset some five years ago . . .', and the four similar coaches then on order for the Great Southern Railways of Ireland

*See also Vol. II p.76.

(two of which were for 3 ft gauge, 40-45 hp petrol-engined, to climb 1 in 75 at 23-25 mph.)

No interest having been shown by the IOMR, Drewry wrote to Henry Allott in Manchester enclosing details of the GSR coaches which had appeared in MODERN TRANSPORT for 25th August, 1928.

Leyland Motors Ltd.

Leyland had supplied engine and hydraulic transmission for a number of two-axle single-engined railcars supplied to the London Midland & Scottish Railway which claimed Sheard's attention; he wrote on 5th August, 1939 but was told that Leyland would have to 'co-operate with a bogie manufacturer' and recommended the type supplied to New Zealand Railways. The opening of World War II then put an end to further schemes.

Clogher Valley Railway

On 22nd April, 1942 the IOMR tried to track down the disposal of Clogher Valley locomotives, diesel railcars, wagons and wheelsets etc. through John Ross & Co. of Belfast, the auctioneers. These had gone to five principal purchasers at Aughnacloy on 14th April. Vaughan was to be dispatched to Ireland to view and assess what was still available, but was delayed in obtaining the necessary documentation (Exit Permit etc.) introduced as a wartime measure; meanwhile the IOMR made further enquiries which were not encouraging. A railcar was sold; two steam engines (one 0-4-2T and one 2-6-2T) were on hand but in need of repairs; the Beyer, Peacock 2-4-0T ex-Castlederg & Victoria Bridge Tramway, of the same type as on the Island, had driving wheels which were beyond expense; the Eire Government had bought the 18 open wagons lying at Tynan for use on the Cavan & Leitrim section (where they were used to carry Arigna coal). It is not clear if Vaughan actually saw *all* the above but he visited the Bessbrook & Newry Tramway Co. in late May. His notes state:

> . . . I went to Bessbrook on 27th. The tramway does not run very frequently so I got a lift on a cart. (It is about 4 miles). It is a very tumble-down affair run mostly for the workers at the Spinning Mill. I met Mr. Morris who seemed very decent. He told me they had bought 20 pairs of wheels and only needed 10 pair so this 10 pair was for re-sale . . .

While the purchase price was attractive, the cost of transport and shipment to Douglas was ridiculous.

A further eight CVR 'Ballast Wagons' lying at Tynan for which Vaughan enquired at Derriaghy, had been sold by the time he reached there 'to a small railway near Portrush' (for ultimate use on a turf bog?). The price had been £26 each.

(Word had reached Vaughan by the usual 'railway grape-vine' channels that the Clogher Valley steam locomotive boilers 'were no good and would not steam' but clearly he was too professional to accept this on hear-say.)

CIE ex-West Clare Section

In August 1961 Sheard and Donald Shaw went to Ennis, Co. Clare to inspect the 0-4-4-0 diesel-mechanical locomotives which Coras Iompair Eireann were selling after the closure of the West Clare section on 1st February, previously. There were three of them, and CIE also offered four diesel railcars and some trailers. The IOMR told CIE it had already purchased ex-CDRJC railcars at the sale (see Vol. II pp.152-53) so CIE submitted full mechanical details of the locomotives, saying their sale would be advertised in due course; ultimately notices appeared in THE RAILWAY GAZETTE and MODERN TRANSPORT and on 22nd August the IOMR inspected one 1955-built 0-4-4-0 locomotive, four 1952-built Walker railcars and three light-weight 2nd class coaches. The two remaining locomotives would be offered in the following December; as stated (Vol. II p.153) the IOMR's offer of £1,200 for the one, free on rail at Dublin, was unacceptable.

In October 1962 the IOMR re-opened the matter on the basis they required tyres for their Walker railcars. Yes, tyres were available, also three power bogies removed from the West Clare railcars. As to the three double-bogie locomotives, these were still on hand and were being considered for conversion to 5 ft 3 in. gauge; meanwhile they could be bought for £7,500 each.

Sheard wrote again to CIE in May 1965, but was informed the locomotives were not for sale.

County Donegal Railways Joint Committee

The purchase of two railcars in 1961 has received adequate coverage in the previous volume; as regards the cost to the IOMR of £2,500 plus transport for the pair, in a private letter to the Author the CDRJC Manager said the cars were sold for £160 each (and the turntable for £22). In addition, dismantling and Port Charges were £165, and Burns & Laird shipping costs £250 . . . in the latter case the IOMR was fortunate as the ANTRIM COAST was larger than the regular vessel, and the cars *just* fitted into the hold with the buffing gear removed and, for good measure, it was calling at Douglas on other business. A figure of £2,500 still seems excessive, even with Auctioneer's commission, Customs' charges, etc.

The railcars were given as 16 ft long (driver's section) and coach section 33 ft long. Weight 7½+3+2 (coach bogie) tons = approximately 12½ tons. These figures differed slightly as to source!

A further saving of expense came in the form of low loaders from Quiggin & Co. Ltd. to take the railcar bodies from the Battery Pier to the station on Sunday 7th May, free of charge. The power and non-power bogies were shipped separately.

(The turntable was also shipped and a site proposed for it adjacent to Quiggin's wall, Douglas. It was never installed. A second turntable which the IOMR wished to buy was sold by the CDRJC by mistake with the general scrap. The option of buying the turntable at Killybegs - made from a steam locomotive mainframe - proved too expensive for the IOMR to consider.)

Additional Notes on 'Sentinel' Enquiries

The close interest in the purchase of a locomotive(s) of this make is confirmed by the considerable correspondence as well as the visit to the Derwent Valley Light Railway. Bradshaw had written to Anderson, Chief Superintendent of Motive Power, LMSR who had reservations about the chain drive, small diameter of boiler, ability to gain or lose steam pressure very quickly, and the short rigid wheelbase which he confirmed might cause the wheels to ride up the rail on the IOMR's sharper curves. The IOMR coal consumption was 13 lbs per mile for a light train, whereas the Sentinel might require 25-30 lbs per mile.

Bradshaw was given a footplate ride on a 100 hp engine with 7 ft wheelbase on the Shropshire & Montgomery Railway, 'with two coaches'. Running into Shrewsbury the speed was about 15 mph 'which was very rough riding. I spoke to the driver on one or two occasions and had to shout to make him hear owing to the noise of the engine and chain gear underneath. I am not satisfied with the behaviour of this engine when taking the curves . . . at one time the driver had to reduce speed to 8 mph and the curves at this place were not nearly so severe as on our lines. One of our small engines would be more advantageous for the winter traffic.'

Projected new design of steam locomotive; Beyer, Peacock & Co. Ltd.

The year 1944 was a time when Sheard was envisaging the future without close knowledge of high costs and long deliveries which would bring such dreams to a sudden end. His Report to the 1945 AGM revealed optimistic plans to include a review of the locomotive position (see Vol II p.123-on). On 7th May, 1945 it might have been noticed that there was a third man on the footplate of No. 10 between Douglas and Port Erin, and back. He was D. Patrick, a representative from Beyer, Peacock who had seen Vaughan and Sheard and handed them drawings for two projects, 1) a 'modified proposal for a new engine' and 2) proposed modifications to Nos. 3 & 5 and Nos. 10-13.

Further correspondence is missing, but commences again with Patrick's Report to his employer of 6th December, 1945 from which it is clear that Sheard had misled Patrick in May and second thoughts had taken place; furthermore Sheard had not taken the precaution of contacting Allott. On 10th December Patrick wrote to Manchester stating details of Sheard's views of the new locomotive design, asking for quotations and delivery date.

The drawing for a modified Nos.10-13 showed an enlarged rear bunker, additional tank of 300 gallons and modernised cab. Sheard approved the concept (which did nothing to improve the outlines of the original design).

As for the new design of 2-6-2 tank, the maximum length was determined by the 30 ft headshunt at Douglas, a width of a maximum of 6 in. more than MANNIN and accommodation of the sharpest turnouts (at Crosby and Port Soderick) 'which were traversed at running speed'. All the foregoing was fruitless (see Vol. II p. 126).

The narrative having gone ahead somewhat, return must be made to correspondence with Allott, which did not begin until 19th December, 1945, i.e. following Patrick's letters of 6th and 10th December and before Beyer, Peacock produced their modified 2-6-2 tank design in January 1946; it refers to Beyer's original 2-6-2 as 'out of the question as it is much too powerful for us and much too big'. The blame is put on Beyer, Peacock. Allott was asked to comment on a smaller 2-6-2 design, liaise with the builder and give an opinion on bridge strengths as they did for the proposed locomotive in 1925.

Replying on 28th December, 1945, Allott gave approval for a modified 2-6-2, and on bridge loading; they recommended the centre driving wheels should be flangeless. Two informative asides were: the sharpest curve was then one of 8½ chains radius at The Nunnery and the sharpest turnout of 5.8 chains radius on the loop at St John's end of Crosby station.

So died an adventurous concept.

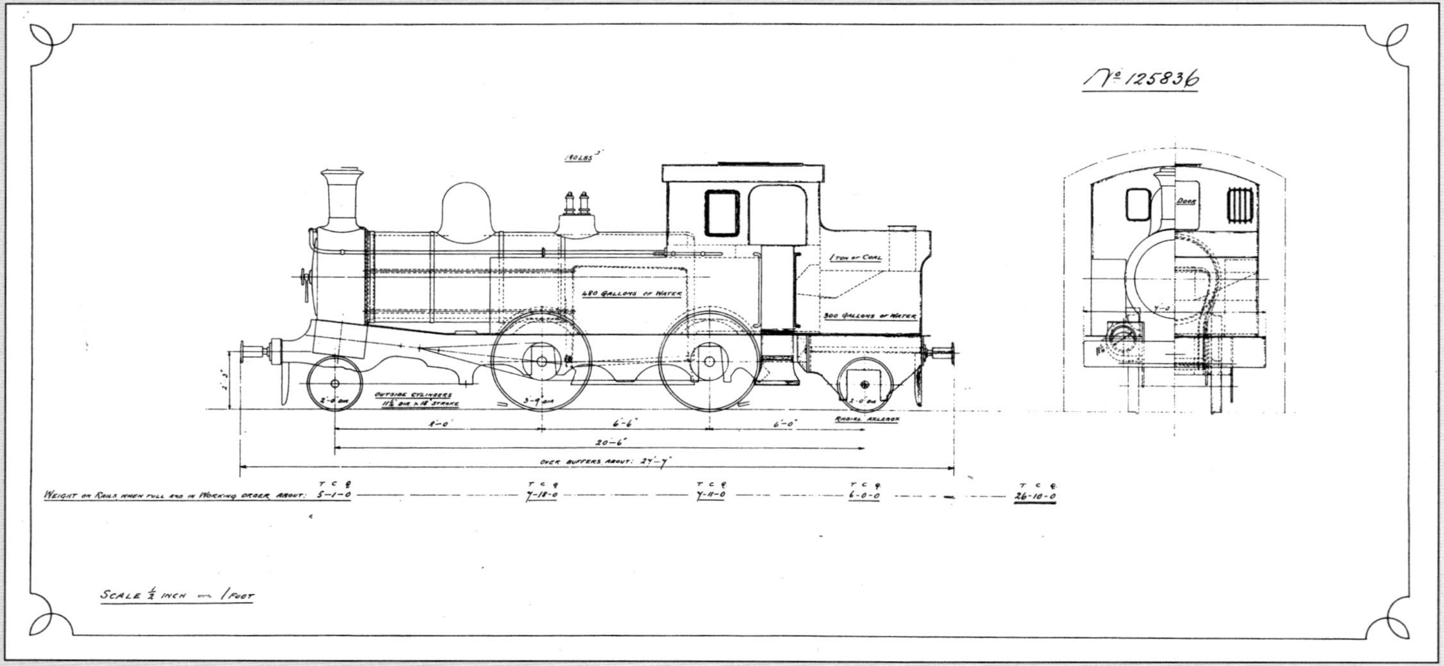

Projected design for a rebuilding of Nos. 10-13, 1945. *IOMR*

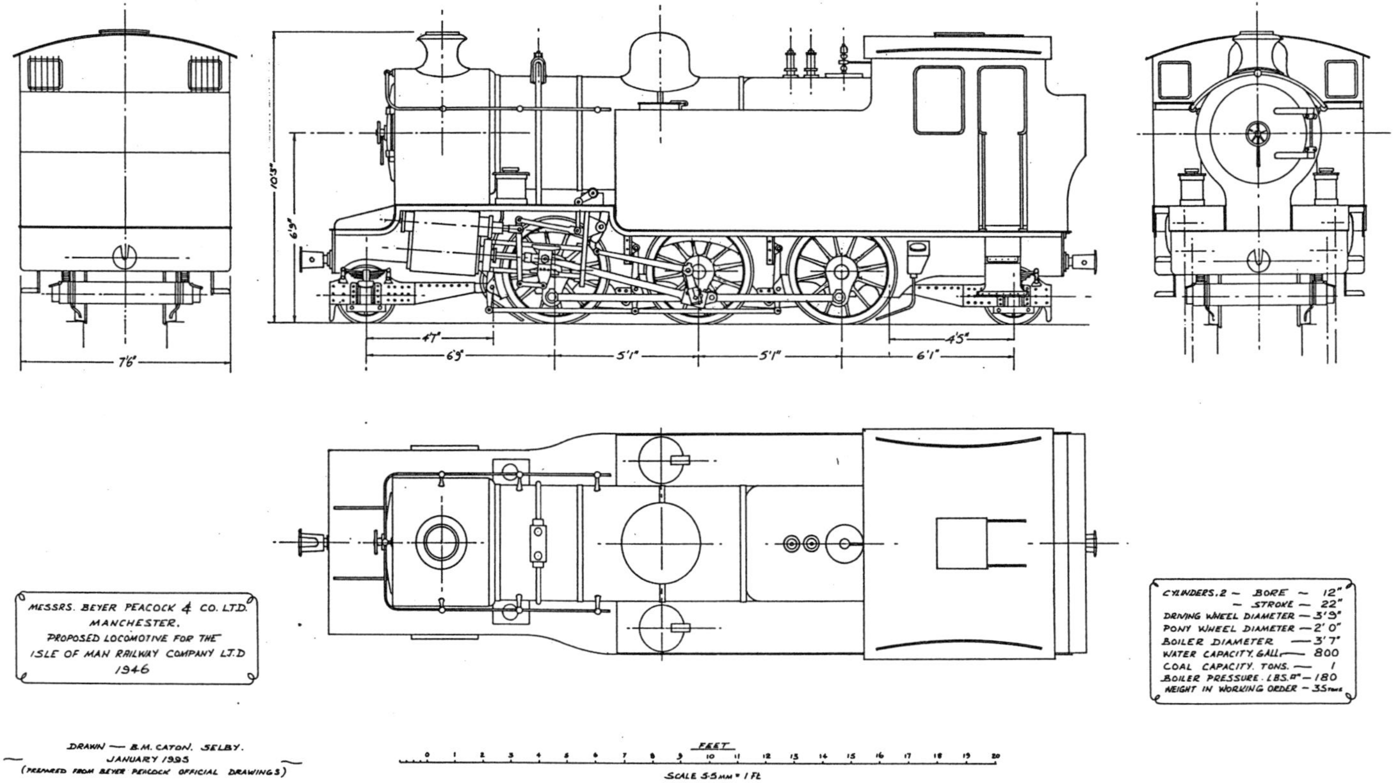

Projected new design of 1946.

B.M. Caton, per Beyer, Peacock & Co. Ltd.

Locomotive Appendix

[Extracted from official records, courtesy of the Engineer].

The official dimensions of MNR Nos. 1 & 2 (supplied by the North British Locomotive Co. Ltd. in 1939) were;

Cylinders	11 in. dia. x 18 in. stroke.
Leading wheel dia.	2 ft 9 in.
Coupled wheel dia.	3 ft 9 in.
Height	9 ft 2¾ in. rail to top cab roof.
Height	10 ft 0 in. rail to top chimney. Length over beams 20 ft 1 in.

Douglas Works records show:

No. 1 RAMSEY
Sold in 1917; had done only 212 miles that year, working in July and November.
Mileage to 1905: 399,777½.
Mileage since new when 1893 boiler fitted: 94,500.
Average annual mileage since takeover by IOMR 1905 - 700 monthly.
Boiler work done July 1912; trial run to Peel 10th August, 1912.

No. 2 NORTHERN
Sold November 1912; last used September 1912.
Mileage to takeover by IOMR 1905 388,121½.
Mileage since takeover 19,285½.
New boiler fitted 1893 @ 74,000 miles.
'Had many months out of use after takeover'.

No. 3 THORNHILL
New Dübs boiler 1896 @ 176,000 miles.
Taken out March 1910: replaced by 'duplicate boiler'. Worn-out tanks replaced by those on IOMR No. 4. 'Duplicate boiler' scrapped 1913.
Boiler off IOMR No. 2 put in March 1912.
Boiler off IOMR No. 8 put in July 1916.
New boiler 1920.

No. 4 CALEDONIA*
Mileage to takeover by IOMR 1905 258,293¾
1908 'Monthly mileage app. same as all other locos'.
1911/12 'Very little used'.
1913 'Out of use'.
1914 200 miles.
1915 3,100 miles.

*FOXDALE, ATLAS or SOUTHERN (the last-named in view of the projected Ballasalla Extension) were names also considered.

Plate 91: A contrast in power; No. 6 of the 'Small Series', but now fitted with larger boiler and side tanks, as seen in Douglas yard with the largest engine in the fleet, No. 16. *c.* 1936.C.E. Box

Plate 92: The new arrival from East Germany is about to leave Douglas on a test run to Santon, 29th September, 1992. Seen in the picture (*left to right*) are Paul Ogden, Graham Warhurst, Robert Smith and Dorothy Boyd. *J.I.C. Boyd*

Plate 97: In the summers of the 1930s the afternoon Boat Train from Port Erin included F75, being the four-wheeled saloons mounted as a 'Pair' in 1926. Here it is, among the hub-bub of farewells at Port St Mary, August 1936.

D.C. Boyd

Plate 98: By June 1957 F75 was painted cream and red, and kept in immaculate condition. Douglas.

J.I.C. Boyd

Plate 97: In the summers of the 1930s the afternoon Boat Train from Port Erin included F75, being the four-wheeled saloons mounted as a 'Pair' in 1926. Here it is, among the hub-bub of farewells at Port St Mary, August 1936. *D.C. Boyd*

Plate 98: By June 1957 F75 was painted cream and red, and kept in immaculate condition. Douglas. *J.I.C. Boyd*

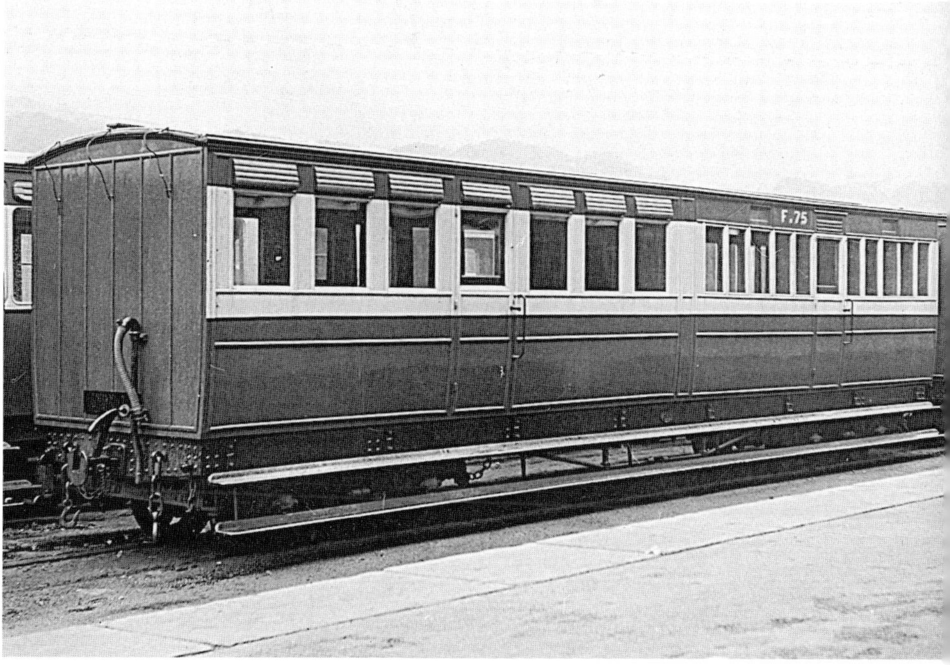

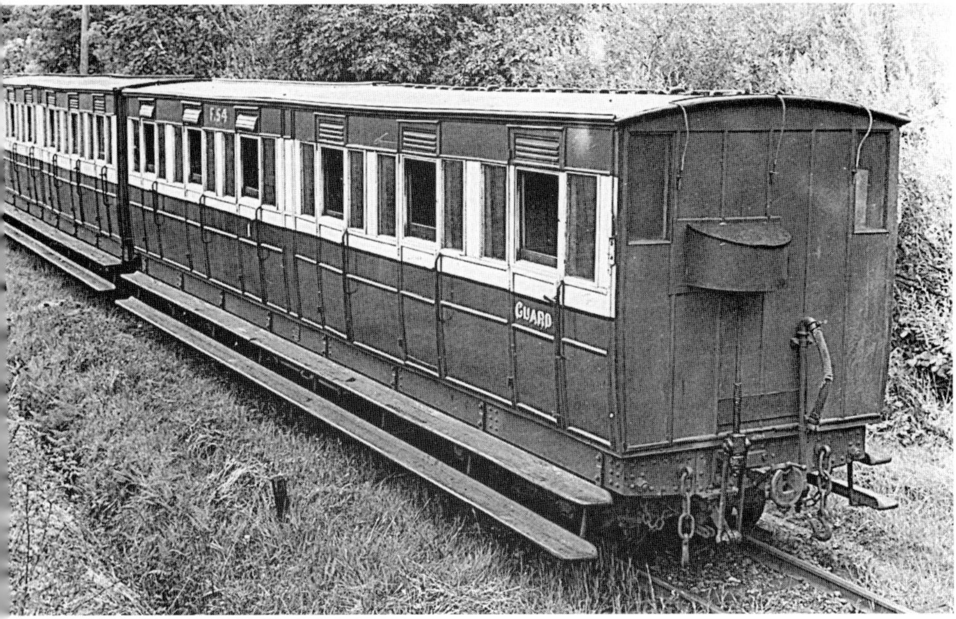

Plate 95: A modified 'pair' carries No. 54 and several 'extras' such as electric lighting. It was the only pair fitted with a brake end. August 1961. *J.I.C. Boyd*

Plate 96: The axlebox covers on the four-wheeled carriages were embellished with the Legs of Man. *J.I.C. Boyd*

Plate 93: A smart turnout for an old pair of coaches; F74 comprising an all 1st and an all 3rd, now in all-brown livery, at St John's on 8th May, 1950. *J.D. Darby*

Plate 94: F62 betrays its origins as two separate bodies: in two shades of brown livery. Douglas. 1936. *C.E. Box*

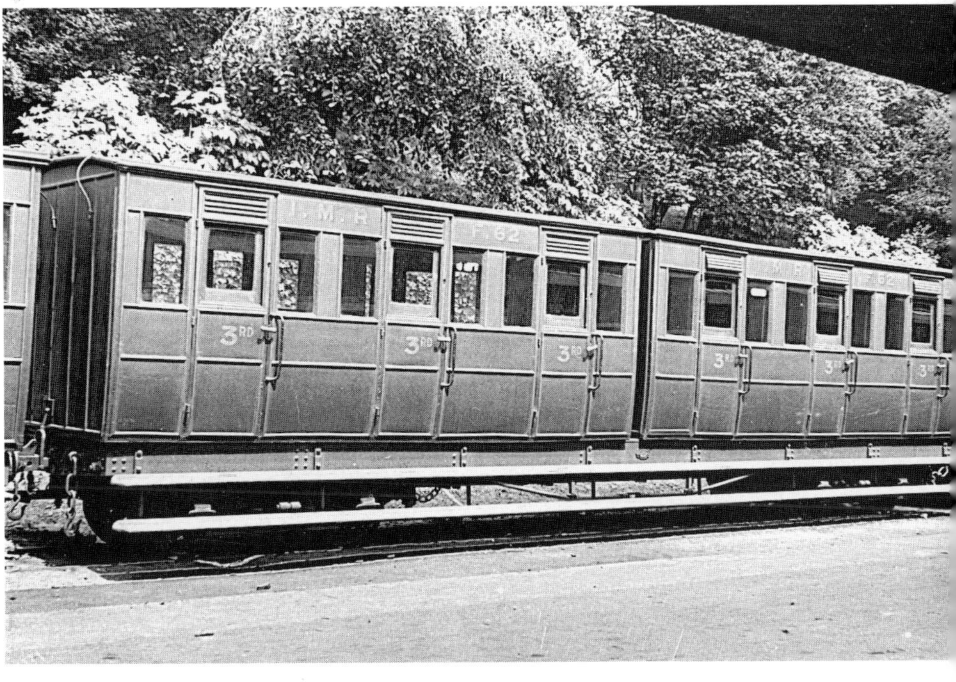

Plate 91: A contrast in power; No. 6 of the 'Small Series', but now fitted with larger boiler and side tanks, as seen in Douglas yard with the largest engine in the fleet, No. 16. *c.* 1936.C.E. Box

Plate 92: The new arrival from East Germany is about to leave Douglas on a test run to Santon, 29th September, 1992. Seen in the picture (*left to right*) are Paul Ogden, Graham Warhurst, Robert Smith and Dorothy Boyd. *J.I.C. Boyd*

Plate 99: The interior of the Duke of Sutherland's saloon (F75). May 1960. *J.I.C. Boyd*

Plate 100: F3 from the original batch of bogie coaches, in all-brown livery at Kirk Michael. May 1951. *J.D. Darby*

Plate 101: F5 was the fifth carriage of the first batch of bogie coaches supplied in 1876 by Brown, Marshalls: they lived up to the confidence of the General Superintendent. April 1966. *J.I.C. Boyd*

Plate 102: Post-Second War painting imparted a very smart appearance on the earliest bogie coaches. On F6 it appears two liveries were used. A shortage of paint? Colours are cream and brown. Peel. 6th August, 1950. *J.D. Darby*

Plate 103: F10 of the second batch of bogie coaches was in cream and red at Douglas in June 1972. *J.I.C. Boyd*

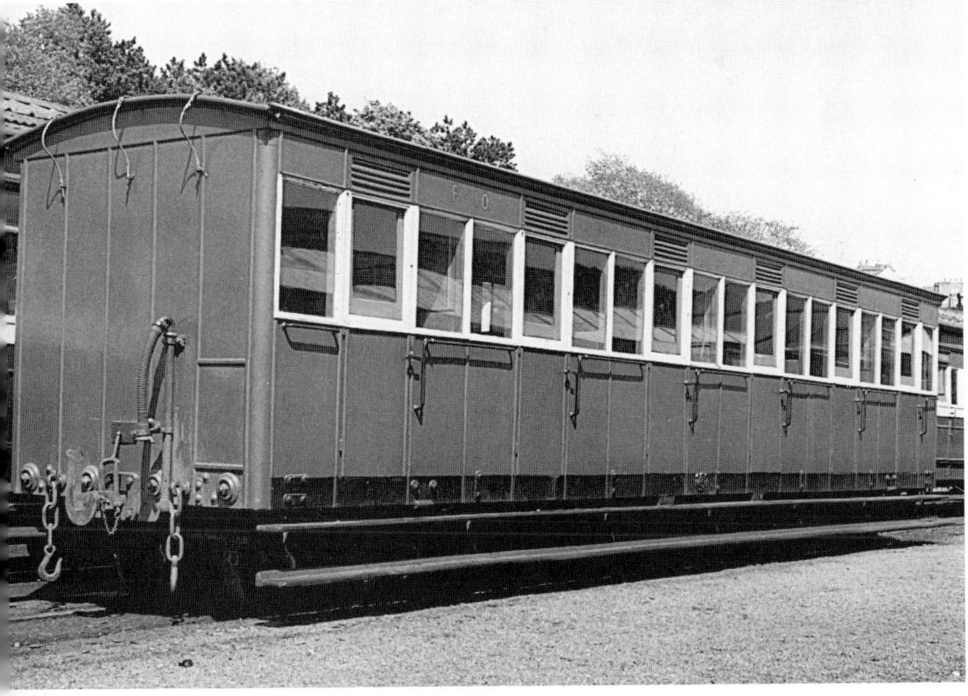

Plate 104: From 1894 carriage bodies were supplied with waisted sides, as shown in F15 about to leave Douglas for the South Line. Platforms have yet to have canopies. *J.I.C. Boyd Collection*

Plate 105: A mixed bag of all-brown coaches at Port Erin in August 1947. F16, F71 and F69. *J.I.C. Boyd*

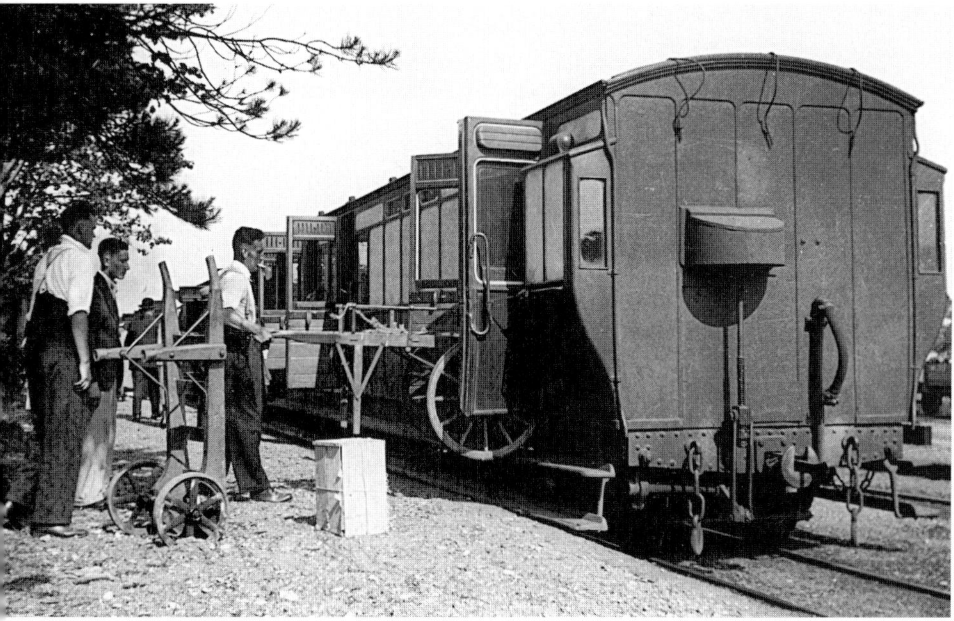

Plate 106: Traffic: traders' handcarts being loaded with boxed fruit from the guard's van, St John's. *c.* 1937. *J.I.C. Boyd Collection*

Plate 107: F19 was a rather special and different coach (*see text*). Note the passenger (*right*) entering from the non-platform side. St John's. May 1961. *J.I.C. Boyd*

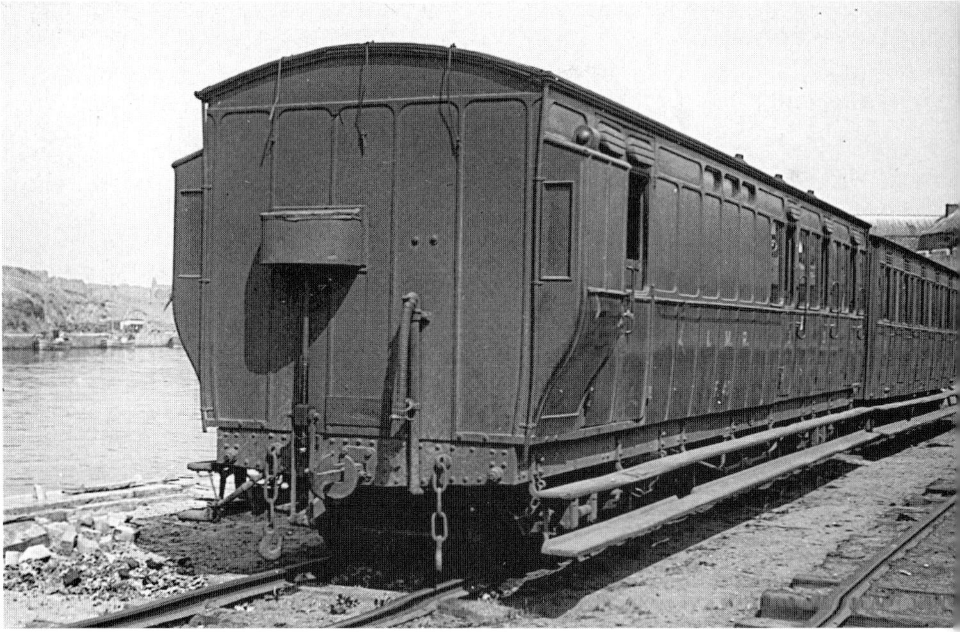

Plate 108: Stabled at Peel on the erstwhile carriage siding, are two vehicles which could be attached to a Douglas train in case of need for school children. The nearer is F40, a development of F19 shown in *Plate 107*. August 1947. *J.I.C. Boyd*

Plate 109: As F40 (*Plate 108*), F43 seen here with variation on the rear-end moulding and now painted cream and red, forms part of a spare rake at Port Erin. The large luggage capacity of these coaches was essential for the South Line. July 1960. *J.I.C. Boyd*

Plate 110: F46 was one of two coaches supplied in 1913 with a small guard's compartment. Douglas. July 1960. *J.I.C. Boyd*

Plate 111: Maker's photograph of F47 of 1923; it was the same as F46 but with a passenger compartment in place of a guard's. *Metropolitan CW&F Co. Ltd.*

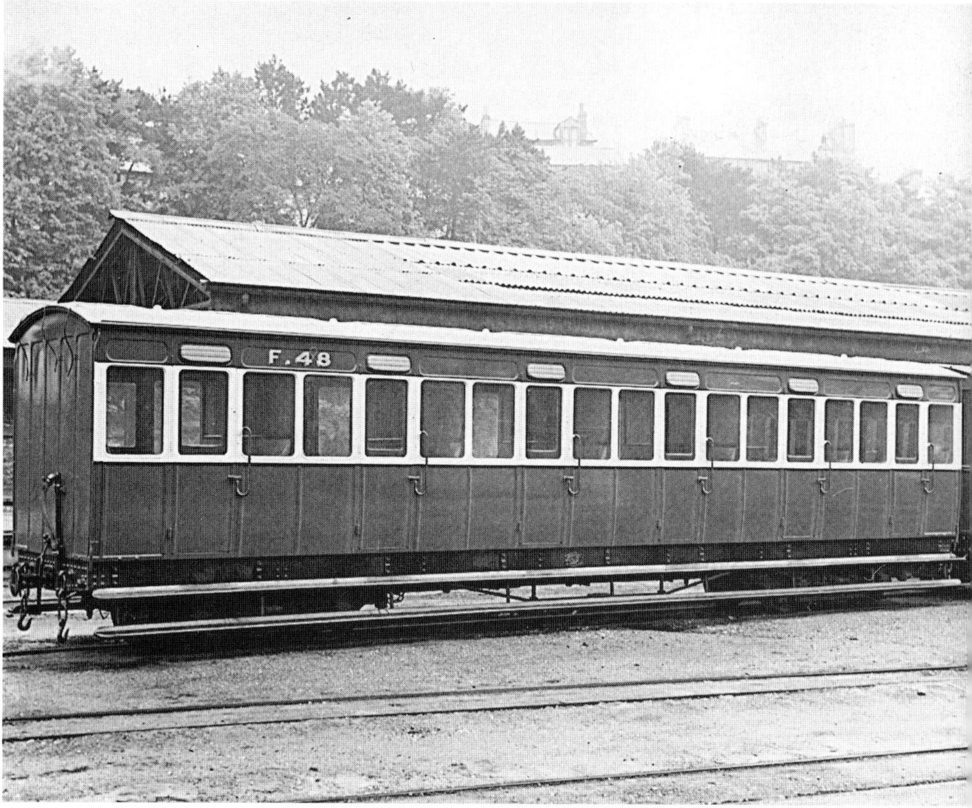

Plate 112: F48 was similar to F47 and both were usually found on the South Line. Regular passengers always chose them. Douglas. June 1957. *J.I.C. Boyd*

Plate 113: Maker's photograph of F49, the last to be supplied and fitted with vacuum brake as new. *Metropolitan CW&F Co. Ltd.*

Plates 114-115: IOMR E-series vans enjoyed an extra span of life if chosen for goods storage. Shorn of its underframe, one (114) stood at Peel Road while E5 (115) became a mobile warehouse adjacent to the South Line platform at Douglas. July 1960. *J.I.C. Boyd*

Plate 116: About 1898 some worthy from The Gloucester Wagon Co. (who never supplied stock to the Island) visited Ramsey. He was met by David McDowall (one foot on footboard) and naturally took photographs of F23, built by a competitor! The far carriage is F8. *c.* 1899.
Gloucester Wagon Co.

Plate 117: In January 1992 many coaches survived which bore the effects of standing out in all seasons without shelter. Such vehicles pose great problems for management, finance and skilled workmen - more than can be detailed in a short picture caption. *J.I.C. Boyd*

Plate 118: The Gloucester visitor was not content to record the exterior of the almost-new F23; this was the 1st Class interior in which he travelled . . .
Gloucester Wagon Co.

Plate 119: . . . with next to it, the spartan accommodation for the lower class. Note the shutter to close off the brake wheel, and the seat boxes to contain re-railing equipment.
Gloucester Wagon Co.

Plate 120: A typical coaching vehicle end, with no visible buffer beam. The chopper rests against its protective plate. Use of the side chains is mandatory. Truss rod ends, Mansell wheels, handbrake screw, double footboards, lamp bracket and bogie retaining chains are visible . . . as is also the piece of scrap timber to prevent the vehicle from moving. 1966. *J.I.C. Boyd*

Plate 121: The 'Norwegian' type couplers embodied several essential components - their working is described in the text. *J.I.C. Boyd*

Total mileage 20th April, 1905-1st January, 1916 = 22,618
1916 *c.* 10,900 miles.
1917 *c.* 11,000 miles.
1918 8,571 miles.

No. 15 (formerly No. 4)

In the period 1921-25 (exact date not recorded) the bottom lower corners of the buffer beams were cut away with hammer and chisel to accommodate the re-railing jacks, the front beam being treated first.

No. 1 RAMSEY

In January 1898 the MNR was trying to sell itself to the IOM Tramways & Electric Power Co. Ltd. in advance of its extension northwards into Ramsey, and at the same time, it was flirting with the IOMR in the hope it would also make a bid. But neither was interested in purchasing the Northern Company. However , the Tramways approached the MNR and for a period starting in March 1898, No. 1 was hired to them for construction work; the Tramways undertaking supplied track materials to enable it to run along the roadway through to Ramsey on 21st March. It was stabled in the car shed at Ballure.

Delivery of IOMR locomotives Nos. 11 & 13

Douglas Workshop records read:

No. 11
'Arrived at Shop in parts

6th July, 1905	Trial trip to Port Erin
13th July, 1905	Loco accepted
17th July, 1905	Loco to traffic'.

No. 13
'2nd July, 1910. Brought from Battery Pier on W. Knox's trolley hauled by traction engine. Stopped several times as trolley sank in asphalt. Erected by J. Barratt of Beyer, Peacock and our men. (Haulage was assisted by J. Sproat and seven men.)'

****

No. 16

In January 1925 Allott's opinion was sought in that trains were losing time as a result of increased tare weight of carriages now that all the four-wheeled type was on bogie underframes. The Board wished to consider a new locomotive of greater tractive effort but were concerned that the bridges might not stand a weight of 25-26 tons envisaged; the present locomotives were 18-20½ tons, and the CALEDONIA 24 tons. Allott replying, wished to know if the standard 2-4-0 was contemplated, or a larger version of CALEDONIA. The Board advised that a larger 2-4-0 was in their mind, but would Allott recommend 'a six-wheeled type'?

Allott maintained that it was not the load on the main girders which was important but with a heavier 'standard' engine the effect on the cross girders 'would be more marked'; on bridges 'recently dealt with' the cross girders could be ignored. He thought a six-coupled type would not be so suitable for general purposes and the following bridges on the Ramsey Line would need cross girder stiffening 'as was done in the case of the bridge over Peel Road'.

River Neb	0 m.	32 ch.
Ballaugh	9 m.	78 ch.
Auldyn River	15 m.	63 ch.

On further questioning, Allott contended that if a new design was intended simply for the South Line, a six-coupled engine would be better. He advised dealing with the three named bridges whatever course was adopted. He had not reported on certain other bridges as they were masonry structures. The Company then turned their attention to curves; Allott was reminded that the 'standard' engine could not take curves like CALEDONIA: they cited that only the last-named could traverse the 'lower curve on the Ramsey Quay Tramway and had no difficulty with the sharp curves of the Knockaloe Line'.

On 19th March, 1925 Allott learned that the IOMR had gone ahead and ordered for 27 weeks delivery , an enlarged standard class at a cost of £2,875. The weight would be 5 tons on the pony truck and 10 tons on each driving axle; surprised, Allott pointed out he would require time over weight but the existing curves were only suited to the lighter engines. Days later he reported he

> . . . could not recommend the increased load on the driving axles . . . but the bridges for which new main girders have recently been provided, the two new viaducts and Sulby River bridge . . . would safely carry it.

He considered the effect on the cross girders of 'other bridges on the Peel and Ramsey line . . . including the recent stiffening of the Peel Road bridge . . would be to stress them above the usual limit'. He would put the limit at 9 tons per axle, unless the driving wheelbase was increased from 6 ft 6 in. to 7 ft 6 in. in which case 10 tons would be acceptable.

Allott conferred with Beyer,Peacock who proposed a scheme with a 9¼ ton axle weight on the driving wheels and 9 tons on the trailing, with consequently less adhesion. Allott approved, the maker's price was slightly reduced and embarrassment all round was avoided.

It may be asked if this was a reason for only using No. 16 on the Peel Line in exceptional circumstance - and never on the Ramsey Line?

Delivery of the engine was much as before: it was landed at the Battery Pier on 17th March, 1926 and hauled to the station on a low-loader hauled by one of R. Shimmin's traction engines to be erected by S. Bradshaw, (a fitter from Beyer, Peacock and brother of the Loco. Superintendent), and nine IOMR Co. men. The engine was shipped in parts; in Douglas yard wheels were put under the frames and the boiler mounted on the frames by travelling crane. It entered the Works the next afternoon and was out on a trial run on 26th March to St John's with the Chairman, Manager and James Bradshaw in a coach attached. In those days such smart work was commonplace and the procedure from quay to Works was that adopted for as long as anyone could remember. The engine was allocated to the senior driver, David Dow. Testing on train and yard shunting completed the early April trials and on 4th April with a load of 22 coaches attached was taken to Port Erin and back, the ascent to Port Soderick being done under booked time.*

Locomotive Costs

An undated memo from Donald Shaw's office has:

June 1908 1 - 4wheel bogie Tank Engine No. 12		£1,405
July 1910 1 - 4wheel bogie Tank Engine No. 13		£1,275
March 1926 1 - 4wheel bogie Tank Engine No. 16	£2,840	
extra for vacuum brake	£98	£2,938

It will be noted that the price was £130 less for a similar locomotive in 1910 than in 1908.

Locomotive Tools

In addition to the larger tools carried on the locomotives (shovel, pricker, dart etc.) a long-handled (*c.* 4 ft) device for closing off the firebox end of a burst firetube was carried. The handle was cranked to enable it to pass through the firedoor, and there was a socket on the 'business end'. Into this socket could be inserted a 'jimmy' or 'bung'; the device, complete with 'bung' would be used to ram the bung into the firebox end of a failed tube when hopefully a bung of the correct size would close off the offending tube. To which company this can be attributed is not known, but clearly tube-failure was frequent.

*See details of trials in SRN No. 102 pp.8-10 taken from Douglas Works' records.

Locomotive boilers - Use as Workshop Boiler

Engine No. 2 1895 boiler taken off engine at 628,560 miles. Installed as Shop Boiler April 1924. Continued until September 1945.

Engine No. 5 *c.* 1917 boiler taken off engine at 580,000 miles. Installed as Shop Boiler to replace the above September 1945.

This was the last boiler on this duty.

No. 9

In September 1965 consideration was given to renovating DOUGLAS 'to such an extent that we could place it in Glen Wyllin as an attraction for visitors: I think it should add considerably to the number of people who would visit the Glen'. Minimum cost was a factor; apparently Sheard owned a road trailer which successfully carried the mechanical shovel and he thought it would carry a locomotive. A price for a low-loader was also to be obtained.

Surplus Rolling Stock

In October 1965 Sheard was active to make the annual stock returns more in keeping with the true position. He instanced to Shaw that though it was accepted that engines Nos. 2 & 7 were withdrawn, they still appeared as in running order on the certificate for 1964. He wanted Shaw to line up all the locomotives presently stored in the carriage shed 'on the centre road' (and all covered wagons unworthy of repair in the goods yard as goods services were being withdrawn: passengers' 'Luggage in advance' would be carried in vans, only if necessary).

Locomotive Boilers

The records of boilers in the last forty years, together with replacements, mileages and locomotive condition on the date in question are fairly liberal but unsuited here to the detail of the originals. Unfortunately there are errors which tend to be perpetuated down the years, and corrections cannot be verified so are not attempted.

The listing dated 31st December, 1964, (though there clearly one or two doubtful entries), and the official list given to the Author which appeared in the 1977 edition and has added material in it, give sufficient general coverage.

IOMR Locomotive Particulars for comparison between Nos. 1-11*
(Apparently supplied by Locomotive Department to inform Manager).

		Weights of Engines	
Nos.	1-3	17 tons	12 cwt.
	4-7	18 tons	4 cwt.
	8-9	18 tons	11 cwt.
	10-11	20 tons	10 cwt.

Loading Peel Line	22 vehicles: max. grade 1 in 85: sharpest curve 10 chains radius.
Loading Port Erin Line	15 vehicles: max. grade 1 in 65: sharpest curve 10 chains radius.

Cost of locomotives - £1,250-1,500

Locomotive Coal

Coal was being delivered to the Island long before there was a railway. Two principal sources existed; Cumberland coal arrived at Ramsey by the shortest sea route and Flintshire coal came into Douglas. The IOMR required good quality steam coal and at first bought it from the Wrexham area and later South Wales (see Vol. I for suppliers). The MNR used Cumberland coal and had the advantage of the quay line at Ramsey to avoid carriage by road which broke up the coal when carted and transferred. There were instances when each Company would lend coal to the other, and, when mainland coal miners were on strike, the IOMR was instructed by the Manx Government to make their stocks available to the IOM Steam Packet Co. and a reduced railway service would result. In post-World War II years, most railway coal came into Ramsey - this included domestic coal for station staff, waiting rooms and the Douglas offices.

The IOMR was very conservative about its suppliers: in by-gone days all railways were important users for private collieries and once a Locomotive Superintendent received favourable reports from footplate crews about the quality in use, the deluge of 'begging letters' offering a free consignment on trial, could be ignored. Bad coal was an anathema; it led to poor relations on the footplate and off, bad train time-keeping and complaints about soot and smoke from those living alongside the railway. Since the decline of the mainland coal industry, the Island railway has had many such difficulties and its steep rise in cost was always a signal to the management to review boiler repair policy and, at the same time, to circularise certain firms enquiring about the capital and running cost of their diesel motive power! Such excursions by letter never bore fruit, such non-steam motive power as has been bought is second-hand and caught the IOMR's eye by an advertisement in a trade periodical.

In July 1877 Hunt made complaint about a coal cargo then being

*Undated document in Tower Collection.

unloaded from the schooner 'JTS', affirming that it was not of the quality unloaded on 3rd October, 1876. His Report said:

> This morning I made a trip on one of our engines with a light train and though we started from Douglas with steam blowing off at 125 lbs, we had not gone beyond a mile before the steam was reduced to 95 lbs and it was only by continued stirring and moving about the congealed coals that we could maintain steam even up to 100 lbs . . . during this whole journey this . . . had to be resorted to . . . and the engine was working in two notches more towards full gear than was our custom . . . During combustion there is always dense black smoke it is necessary to turn on the blower jet immediately steam is shut off . . . and an unnecessary consumption of coals . . .

(Anyone familiar with locomotive practice will re-live such embarrassing journeys!)

By 1882 Hunt was in correspondence with other railway companies over coal suppliers; currently the IOMR was using Dynevor shipped from Neath or Swansea, but the Neath & Brecon Rly recommended Aberdare or Rhondda. The Great Western favoured the Aberdare, Ely and Monmouthshire pits, and had stopped using coal from the Neath district. At this point, the IOMR changed to the harder coal of the Aberdare district. The catalyst for the change was the burning-away of copper blast pipes.

Some coal consumption tests were carried out in 1917; summarised these showed:

Dates	*Loco No.*	*Pass miles*		*Coal used*		*Coal per Mile*	
24th-30th July	5	837	S	6 ton	10 cwt	17.10 lbs	*
31st July-6th August	5	837	S	10 ton	6 cwt	27.07 lbs	†
13th-19th September	5	709	S	7 ton	14 cwt	24.10 lbs	#
13th-19th August	6	552	P	6 ton	3 cwt	22.63 lbs	†
8th-15th September	6	713	P	5 ton	16 cwt	16.66 lbs	*

S = South Line
P = Peel Line
* = South Wales coal
† = Lancashire coal
# = Point of Ayr (Flints.) coal
Engine No. 5: Driver Styles
Engine No. 6: Driver Clague

Of the standard method of coaling by wicker basket, a note was kept of the number of coaling baskets consumed; in order of the five runs detailed above, this was: 260, 412, 309, 247, 233. (The lighter consumption on the near-level Peel Line is evident, as is also the use of South Wales coal.)

At the present time the Railway favours Cwm Bargoed (South Wales) supplies, with Dore Mill (Nottinghamshire) as a secondary source.

Sources as to coal supply on the MNR are not available but it is known that Ayrshire pits were favoured, though consistent quality was lacking and the Scottish coal was sometimes mixed with coking or household coal.

								Total Locomotive Mileage at 31st December, 1964
No. 1	1873 Maiden boiler	1891 Reboilered	1919 Reboilerd with No. 7 of 1903	1923 Reboilered with No. 5 of 1907	1934 Reboilered with No. 7 of 1923			1,232,899
No. 2	1873 Maiden boiler	1893 Reboilered	1910 Reboilered with No. 6 of 1892	1919 Reboilered with own of 1893	1921 Reboilered with No. 5 of 1895	1923 Reboilered	1951 Boiler removed	1,480,088
No. 3	1873 Maiden boiler	1888 Reboilered	1913 Reboilered	1951 Reboilered with No. 2 of 1893				1,247,623
No. 4	1874 Maiden boiler	1893 Reboilered	1909 Reboilered	1946 Reboilered with No. 5 of 1914				1,523, 510
No. 5	1874 Maiden boiler	1895 Reboilered	1907 Reboilered	1914 Reboilered	1926 Reboilered with with No. 6 of 1911	1946 Reboilered		1,896,370
No. 6	1875 Maiden boiler	1892 Reboilered	1911 reboilered	1932 Reboilered				1,924,038
No. 7	1880 Maiden boiler	1903 Reboilered	1919 Reboilered with No. 5 of 1907	1923 Reboilered	1937 Reboilered with with No. 5 of 1907			1,377,403
No. 8	1894 Maiden boiler	1908 Reboilered with No. 5 of 1907	1915 Reboilered with No. 7 of 1907	1919 Reboilered	1936 Reboilered			1,347,988
No. 9	1896 Maiden boiler	1909 Reboilered with No. 8 of 1894	1912 Reboilered					912,717
No. 10	1905 Maiden boiler	1926 Reboilered	1946 Reboilered					1,013,997
No. 11	1905 Maiden boiler	1934 Reboilered	1959 Reboilered					937,474
No. 12	1908 Maiden boiler	1946 Reboilered						872,129
No. 13	1910 Maiden boiler	1949 Reboilered with No. 10 of 1926						803,728
No. 14	1880 Maiden boiler	1896 Reboilered	1910 Reboilered with No. 4 of 1896	1913 Reboilered with No. 2 of 1893	1916 Reboilered with No. 5 of 1895	1921 Reboilered with No. 5 of 1914		1,478,231 (From 20th April, 1905)
No. 15	1885 Maiden boiler	1922 Reboilered						127,438 (From 20th April, 1905)
No. 16	1926 Maiden boiler							516, 197

Official Boiler Listing: 1977

No.	*Name*	*Source of Name*	*Boiler Changes#*	*Notes*
1	SUTHERLAND	Chairman of Company	1891, 1919, (7/1903), 1923 (5/1907), 1939 (7/1923)	Rebuilt as No. 3, 1913.*
2	DERBY	Lords of Man	1893, 1912 (6/1892), 1917 (2/1893), 1921 (5/1895), 1923[1]	In accident 1909; new rear cab sheet with sq. specs. fitted. 385-gallon tanks 1912; modified front cab sheet with sq. specs. Maker's plates off. Dismantled 1951.
3	PENDER	Deputy Chairman	1888, 1913, 1951 (2/1923)	385-gallon tanks 1913; modified front cab sheet with sq. specs.*[2]
4	LOCH	Island Governor	1893, 1909, 1946 (5/1914), 1968[3]	Fitted larger tanks, raised cab, larger boiler, maker's plates off 1909.†
5	MONA	Manx name	1895, 1907, 1914, 1936 (6/1911), 1946[3]	In 1914, rebuilt as No. 6 in 1911. Cast chimney 1946.*
6	PEVERIL	'Peveril of the Peak'	1892, 1911, 1932[3]	In 1911, rebuilt as No. 4 in 1909.*
7	TYNWALD	Manx name	1903, 1919 (5/1907), 1923,[1] 1939 (5/1907)	Maker's plates off 1923. Dismantled 1945.
8	FENELLA	'Peveril of the Peak'	1908 (5/1895), 1915 (5/1907), 1919, 1936[4]	Built as Nos. 1-7 but boiler pressure 160 lbs.*
9	DOUGLAS	Manx name	1909 (8/1894), 1912	*
10	G.H. WOOD	Director	1926,[3] 1948[3]	1948 fitted cast chimney.†
11	MAITLAND	Director	1934,[3] 1959[5]	1959 fitted cast chimney; no numerals, chimney or tanks.†
12	HUTCHINSON	Director	1946[3]	1946 fitted cast chimney.†
13	KISSACK	Director	1944 (11/1905), 19493 (10/1926), 1971[3]	†
16	MANNIN	Manx name	None	Numerals removed from chimney latterly.*
14	THORNHILL	Chairman's residence	1896, 1910 (4/1893), 1913 (2/1893), 1916 (5/1895), 1921	Chimney numerals added 1921; No. 14 allotted 1910, carried from 1918.*
15	CALEDONIA	-	1922	*
(16)	RAMSEY	-	See text for detail.	Name applied 1892, MNR No. 1 removed 1906. No. 16 allotted 1910, never carried. Scrap 1922.
(17)	NORTHERN	-	See text for detail.	Name applied 1893, MNR No. 2 removed 1906. No. 17 allotted 1910, never carried. Scrap 1912.

*Engine in store.
†Engine in traffic. 1973.
#Example: 1919 (7/1903) = fitted with used boiler of 1903 off No. 7, in 1919. (Otherwise dates alone = new boiler.)

1 Special boilers per Bradshaw who wanted Beyer to alter two building at Beyer 1923 to closed domes and Pop valves; compromise made, one Pop valve on first boiler ring, a second in dome. Fitted only to Nos. 2 and 7.
2 Recently repainted 1945-period red for display purposes.
3 Closed domes and Pop valve boilers; since 1968 supplied by Hunslet.
4 Special boiler of original 2 ft 10 in. diameter, closed dome and Pop valves - only one bought.
5 Last boiler built by Beyer, Peacock.

Maker's plates Nos. 1-5 originally on boiler barrels; thereafter on side tanks.
Dismantled Nos. 2 and 7 still in pre-WWII green. All other engines Ailsa-period green, except Nos. 3 (see note 2 above) and 14 and 15 (near MNR red for display purposes).

Locomotive Work - 1937

Port Erin Line - Down Trains

Distance		1		2		3		4		5	
	Date	9th July, 1937		10th July, 1937		12th July, 1937		15th July, 1937		19th July, 1937	
	Train	5.40 pm		3.20 pm		2.45 pm		2.15 pm		10.5 am E.	
	Engine	No. 12		No. 16		No. 13		No. 12		No. 10	
	Load	4 coaches		6 coaches		7 coaches		6 coaches		8 coaches	
		4 wagons		-		-		-		-	
Distance		*arr.*	*dep.*	*arr.*	*dep.*	*arr.*	*dep.*	*arr.*	*dep.*	*arr.*	*dep.*
M. Ch.		*m. s.*	*m. s.*	*m. s.*	*m. s.*	*m. s.*	*m. s.*	*m. s.*	*m. s.*	*m. s.*	*m. s.*
- -	Douglas	- -	0 0	- -	0 0	- -	0 0	- -	0 0	- -	0 0
3 10	Port Soderick	11 53	12 20	10 36	11 16	13 4	X14 10	11 52	(P)	11 11	(P)
5 50	Santon	19 34	19 42	18 7	18 40	20 47	21 22		(P)	17 43	(P)
8 30	Ballasalla	29 14	X34 55	25 40	X27 14	28 31	29 34	24 36	X27 57	24 37	(P)
9 75	Castletown	40 13	43 35	31 56	35 0	34 9	35 25	32 32	33 28	28 24	(P)
11 35	Ballabeg	- -	(P)	39 17	(P)	39 44	(P)	38 11	(P)	32 40	(P)
12 60	Colby	51 34	52 16	42 53	43 36	43 15	X43 48	41 19	(P)	35 56	(P)
14 60	Port St Mary	57 36	58 23	48 45	51 59	48 41	49 20	46 25	47 29	40 37	(P)
15 30	Port Erin	61 14		55 5		52 4		50 26		42 48	
	Running Time	50 m. 7 s. (49 m. 0s. net)		45 m. 17 s.		46 m. 52 s. (45 m. 52 s. net)		45 m. 5 s.		42 m. 48 s.	
		Check at Ballalona Crossing. Wagon detached at Castletown		20½ mph on Nunnery Bank		16½ mph on Nunnery Bank. Signal check approaching Port Soderick.				Assisted by No. 3 on Nunnery Bank; 21 mph	

Port Erin Line - Up Trains

Distance		6		7		8		9		10	
	Date	10th July, 1937		11th July, 1937		13th July, 1937		14th July, 1937		17th July, 1937	
	Train	12 noon		4.20 pm		9.15 am		9.15 am		9.15 am	
	Engine	No. 10		No. 10		No. 16		No. 16		No. 16	
	Load	4 coaches		3 coaches		3 coaches		3 coaches		4 coaches	
		-		-		3 wagons		-		-	
Distance		*arr.*	*dep.*	*arr.*	*dep.*	*arr.*	*dep.*	*arr.*	*dep.*	*arr.*	*dep.*
M. Ch.		*m. s.*	*m. s.*	*m. s.*	*m. s.*	*m. s.*	*m. s.*	*m. s.*	*m. s.*	*m. s.*	*m. s.*
- -	Port Erin	- -	0 0	- -	0 0	- -	0 0	- -	0 0	- -	0 0
50	Port St Mary	2 34	4 2	3 1	3 27	2 54	3 30	2 40	3 13	2 46	3 25
2 50	Colby	9 27	(P)	9 30	9 51	8 54	11 48	8 13	8 44	8 51	9 16
3 75	Ballabeg	12 25	(P)	13 20	(P)	15 9	(P)	12 20	12 56	12 43	(P)
5 35	Castletown	15 57	16 46	16 46	17 20	18 42	19 21	16 57	17 44	16 14	16 43
7 0	Ballasalla	22 4	22 35	22 26	24 14	24 10	24 47	22 21	23 2	21 40	23 9
9 60	Santon	31 22	X32 0	32 17	X33 8	32 39	33 0	30 19	32 11	31 20	31 49
12 20	Port Soderick	39 3	39 23	39 14	40 13	39 20	39 53	39 13	39 39	38 27	38 50
15 30	Douglas	48 3		49 30		48 18		47 39		46 59	
	Running Time	44 m. 27 s.		44 m. 31 s.		42 m. 38 s.		42 m. 13 s.		42 m. 5 s.	
						Two wagons detached at Ballasalla		One wagon attached at Santon		29 mph down Nunnery Bank	

E = Express. X = Crossed Train. W = Engine took water. P = Pass.

Ramsey Line - Down Trains

			11		12			13		14	
		Date	14th July, 1937		17th July, 1937		Max. speeds,	19th July, 1937		28th July, 1937	
		Train	10.10 am E		10.10 am E		in mph	6.40 pm		10.10 am E.	
		Engine	No. 11		No. 11		between stations	No. 7		No. 11	
		Load	9 coaches*		7 coaches*		on Run No. 12	4 coaches		15 coaches*	
			-		-		-	-		-	
Distance			*arr.*	*dep.*	*arr.*	*dep.*		*arr.*	*dep.*	*arr.*	*dep.*
M.	*Ch.*		*m. s.*	*m. s.*	*m. s.*	*m. s.*		*m. s.*	*m. s.*	*m. s.*	*m. s.*
-	-	Douglas	- -	0 0	- -	0 0		- -	0 0	- -	0 0
2	40	Union Mills	7 11	(P)	6 46	(P)	31.2	6 58	(P)	7 3	(P)
4	75	Crosby	12 15	(P)	11 58	(P)	32.5	12 41	(P)	13 5	(P)
8	30	St Johns	21 23	W25 18	19 9	W28 12	38.1	20 36	W26 0	22 27	W27 35
9	60	Peel Road	28 42	(P)	31 36	(P)	29.2	29 55	(P)	32 12	(P)
11	30	St Germains	31 33	(P)	34 23	(P)	34.7	33 14	(P)	35 47	
15	60	Kirk Michael	40 2	X41 7	43 11	X 45 9	34.3	42 45	43 45	46 0	X47 20
18	50	Ballaugh	45 36	(P)	51 3	(P)	39.2	50 7	53 12	53 33	(P)
20	60	Sulby Glen	50 36	(P)	54 50	(P)	36.9	58 53	59 21	57 35	(P)
21	40	Sulby Bridge	52 21	(P)	56 36	(P)	27.0	62 30	63 23	59 21	(P)
23	20	Lezayre	55 29	(P)	59 48	(P)	37.1	67 35	(P)	62 38	(P)
25	0	Ramsey	59 9		63 16		26.5	71 46		66 40	
		Running Time	54 m. 9 s.		52 m. 15 s.			60 m. 56 s. (60 m. 26 s. net)		60 m. 12 s.	
			*5 coaches to St Johns; 5 thence. Assisted to Union Mills		*7 coaches to St Johns; 4 thence.			Signal check approaching Ballaugh		*15 coaches to St Johns; 8 thence Assisted to 1 m. beyond Crosby	

Ramsey Line - Up Trains

			15		16		17		18		19	
		Date	14th July, 1937		17th July, 1937		19th July, 1937		22nd July, 1937		23rd July, 1937	
		Train	11.35 am		11.35 am		8.35 pm		4.10 pm		6.2 pm	
		Engine	No. 11		No. 11		No. 7		No. 14		No. 11 & 7	
		Load	2 coaches*		4 coaches*		4 coaches*		5 coaches		6 coaches	
			-		-		-		-		-	
Distance			*arr.*	*dep.*	*arr.*	*dep.*	*arr.*	*dep.*	*arr.*	*dep.*	*arr.*	*dep.*
M.	*Ch.*		*m. s.*	*m. s.*	*m. s.*	*m. s.*	*m. s.*	*m. s.*	*m. s.*	*m. s.*	*m. s.*	*m. s.*
-	-	Ramsey	- -	0 0	- -	0 0	- -	0 0	- -	0 0		
1	60	Lezayre	4 7	(P)		(P)	6 30	6 36	5 57	6 21		
3	40	Sulby Bridge	7 35	X11 24	8 0	X15 34	11 59	16 43	11 49	12 3		
4	20	Sulby Glen	14 18	14 50	18 49	18 57	20 14	20 47	15 49	16 24		
6	30	Ballaugh	20 18	20 38	24 11	24 25	27 2	27 20	22 23	X33 16		
9	20	Kirk Michael	26 33	29 13	30 22	31 22	34 16	35 17	41 20	42 12		
13	50	St Germains	38 58	(P)	41 10	(P)	47 43	(P)	55 25	55 37		
15	20	Peel Road	41 53	(P)	44 24	(P)	51 4	(P)	59 40	(P)		
16	40	St Johns	45 1	X65 41	47 28	X65 53	54 42	X59 32	62 49			0 0
20	20	Crosby	74 37	75 0	74 47	74 59	69 29	70 12			7 42	8 11
22	40	Union Mills	81 23	81 55	80 10	81 44	76 37	77 14			13 35	14 32
25	0	Douglas	88 58		84 47		85 1				21 3	
		Running Time	60 m. 2 s.		59 m. 40 s.		72 m. 9 s. (70 m. 51 s. net)		49 m. 39 s.		19 m. 37 s. (69 m. 16 s. wi Run No. 18)	
			*Two coaches to St Johns; 4 coaches and 10 wagons thence. 1 wagon attached at Sulby Bridge. Asst St. Johns to Douglas		*Four coaches to St Johns; 6 coaches and 6 wagons thence. Asst St Johns to Douglas		*Four coaches to St Johns, 7 thence. Stop outside Lezayre. Asst St Johns to Douglas					

E = Express. X = Crossed Train. W = Engine took water. P = Pass.

St Johns-Foxdale Trains

ance Ch.		20 arr. m. s.	20 dep. m. s.	21 arr. m .s.	21 dep. m. s.
	Date	14th July, 1937		22nd July, 1937	
	Train	5.10 pm		5.10 pm	
	Engine	No. 7		No. 14	
	Load	1 coach 2 wagons		1 coach 2 wagons	
-	St Johns	- -	0 0	- -	0 0
40	Waterfall	12 44	12 59	11 43	(P)
40	Foxdale	17 14		15 13	
	Running Time	16 m. 59 s. (16 m. 29 s. net)		15 m. 13 s.	

Shunt at Sand Pit; 30 secs.

Foxdale -St Johns Trains

Distance M. Ch.		22 arr. m. s.	22 dep. m. s.	23 arr. m .s.	23 dep. m. s.
	Date	14th July, 1937		24th July, 1937	
	Train	5.35 pm		5.35 pm	
	Engine	No. 7		No. 14	
	Load	1 coach 3 wagons		1 coach 3 wagons	
- -	Foxdale	- -	0 0	- -	0 0
1 0	Waterfall	3 33	3 44	4 51	5 6
2 40	St Johns	13 52		14 38	
	Running Time	13 m. 41 s.		14 m. 23 s.	

Locomotive Work - 1938

Port Erin Line - Down Train

ance Ch.		24 arr. m. s.	24 dep. m. s.	Max. speeds in mph between stations
	Date	10th Sept., 1938		
	Train	2.30 pm		
	Engine	No. 12		
	Load	5 coaches -		
-	Douglas	- -	0 0	
10	Port Soderick	10 53	11 23	18 .5
50	Santon	18 9X	22 2	31.7
30	Ballasalla	29 2	30 6	31.2
75	Castletown	34 23	35 8	32.1
35	Ballabeg	39 23	(P)	
60	Colby	42 33	43 29	25.5
60	Port St Mary	48 17	51 5	33.6
30	Port Erin	54 17		-
	Running Time	44 m. 21 s.		

Port Erin Line - Up Train

Distance M.Ch. .		25 arr. m. s.	25 dep. m .s.	Max. speeds between stations
	Date	10th Sept., 1938		
	Train	4.20 pm		
	Engine	No. 12		
	Load	5 coaches -		
- -	Port Erin	- -	0 0	
- 50	Port St Mary	2 50	3 26	-
2 50	Colby	9 21	10 2	30.5
3 75	Ballabeg	13 30	(P)	35.4
5 35	Castletown	16 50	17 42	
7 0	Ballasalla	23 26	26 30	20.5
9 60	Santon	35 50	36 32	18.0
12 20	Port Soderick	43 43	44 43	30.6
15 30	Douglas	54 31		21.8
	Running Time	47 m. 36 s.		

One wagon attached at Ballasalla

X = Crossed Up Train. P = Pass.

Ramsey Line - Down Trains

26

Distance M. Ch.		arr. m. s.	dep. m. s.	Max. speeds, in mph between stations
	Date	10th Sept., 1938		
	Train	5.35 pm		
	Engine	No. 11		
	Load	6 coaches, 1 wagon		
- -	Douglas	- -	0 0	
2 40	Union Mills	7 36	7 56	23.0
4 75	Crosby	15 26	16 8	24.9
8 30	St Johns	24 26	30 16	32.4
9 60	Peel Road	33 14	(P)	33.3
11 30	St Germains	35 37	(P)	38.1
15 60	Kirk Michael	43 33	46 57	31.5
18 50	Ballaugh	52 19	54 30	41.7
20 60	Sulby Glen	59 26	60 46	34.1
21 40	Sulby Bridge	63 17	64 11	32.1
23 20	Lezayre	67 31		38.5
25 0	Ramsey	71 3		41.7

Running Time 56 m. 22 s.

No. 11 to St Johns, Nos. 4 & 1 onwards. Three coaches and one wagon beyond St Johns

Ramsey Line - Up Trains

27

Distance M.Ch..		arr. m. s.	dep. m .s.	Max. speeds, in mph between stations
	Date	10th Sept., 1938		
	Train	7.15 pm		
	Engine	No. 1		
	Load	3 coaches, -		
- -	Ramsey	- -	0 0	
1 60	Lezayre	4 36	(P)	
3 40	Sulby Bridge	9 25	9 38	40.9
4 20	Sulby Glen	11 45	12 27	
6 30	Ballaugh	17 48	18 16	34.6
9 20	Kirk Michael	24 58	26 4	33.3
13 50	St Germains	37 30	(P)	30.2
15 20	Peel Road	41 1	41 38	29.0
16 40	St Johns	46 29	56 54	32.1
20 20	Crosby	67 11	(P)	29.0
22 40	Union Mills	73 21	(P)	30.0
25 0	Douglas	80 16		

Running Time 66 m. 45 s.

No. 1 and 3 coaches to St Johns; No. 6 and 6 coaches onwards

Peel Line - Down Trains

28

Distance M. Ch.		arr. m. s.	dep. m. s.	Max. speeds, in mph between stations
	Date	7th Sept., 1938		
	Train	2.30 pm		
	Engine	No. 6		
	Load	7 coaches, 2 wagons		
- -	Douglas	- -	0 0	
2 40	Union Mills	8 8	8 25	26.2
4 75	Crosby	17 27	18 3	-
8 30	St Johns	27 48	32 8	31.2
11 21	Peel	40 57		29.5

Running Time 35 m. 44 s.

Seven coaches to St Johns; 3 coaches and one wagon onwards

Peel Line - Up Trains

29

Distance M.Ch..		arr. m. s.	dep. m .s.	Max. speeds, in mph between stations
	Date	7th Sept., 1938		
	Train	4.50 pm		
	Engine	No. 6		
	Load	3 coaches, -		
- -	Peel	- -	0 0	
2 71	St Johns	5 3	15 30	32.3
6 26	Crosby	24 44	25 2	36.5
8 61	Union Mills	30 49	31 14	35.7
11 21	Douglas	38 5		-

Running Time 26 m. 55 s.

No. 6 and 3 coaches to St Johns; Nos. 6 and 11, 7 coaches and 1 wagon onwards

Engine Mileage - 1963

Engine	Jan.	Feb.	March	April	May	June	July	August	Sept.	Oct.	Nov.	Dec.	Total
No. 1	-	-	-	-	-	-	378	397	-	-	-	-	775
No. 5	-	-	-	-	11½	1,139	1,399½	1,591½	584	148½	-	-	4,874
No. 8	-	27	-	159	-	1,231½	1,535½	1,547½	256	19½	28½	-	4,804½
No. 10	-	-	-	836½	568½	1,499¼	1,654	1,738½	444	-	-	-	6,740¾
No. 11	-	413	1,555¾	653	-	1,816½	1,501½	1,725	449	-	40	289½	8,443¼
No. 12	1,496	916½	204	-	663¼	1,612¼	1,883	1,731½	348½	-	-	-	8,855
No. 14	-	-	-	-	-	266¼	102½	-	-	-	-	-	368¾
No. 16	-	-	-	-	-	15½	871½	994½	79½	140	-	-	2,101
Diesels	-	-	23	184	736	800½	850½	850½	1,748	2,210	2,133	1,700	11,235½
Total	1,496	1,356½	1,782¾	1,832½	1,979¼	8,380¾	10,176	10,576	3,909	2,518	2,201½	1,989½	48,197¾

Isle of Man Railway
Engine Mileage - 1964

Engine	Jan.	Feb.	March	April	May	June	July	August	Sept.	Oct.	Nov.	Dec.	Total
No. 5	-	74½	77½	-	474½	1,075	1,551½	1,516½	399½	-	11½	11½	5,192
No. 8	-	-	-	19	1,512½	1,335¼	1,455¼	1,526	297½	11	-	357	6,513½
No. 10	-	-	18	10	746½	1,508	1,721½	1,657	315	-	-	15½	5,991½
No. 11	1,212½	170	-	-	639	1,503	1,496	1,639½	1,155	-	-	-	8,015
No. 12	-	-	-	255	707	1,441	1,549	1,509½	813	-	-	-	6,274½
Diesels	918	1,955	2,009	1,955	455	60	742½	849½	751¼	1,458	1,306	1,350	13,809¼
Total	2,130½	2,199½	2,104½	2,239	4,734½	6,922¼	8,515¾	8,698	3,731¼	1,469	1,317½	1,734	45,795¾

Isle of Man Railway
Engine Mileage - 1965

Engine	Jan.	Feb.	March	April	May	June	July	August	Sept.	Oct.	Nov.	Dec.	Total
No. 5	-	-	-	-	-	1,158	1,845½	2,159	527	-	-	-	5,689½
No. 8	256½	893	108	98	-	637	1,873	1,870	573	59½	-	-	6,368
No. 10	15½	-	-	-	-	1,319½	1,705¼	1,659½	630	-	-	-	5,329¾
No. 11	383	-	99	-	-	1,560½	1,685½	1,757½	1,301	-	-	38½	6,825
No. 12	-	-	-	90½	-	1,526	1,601	1,623	521	-	-	-	5,361½
No. 13	-	-	-	-	-	-	203	295	-	-	-	-	498
Diesels	872	388	1,103	1,296	1,604	1,041	1,381	1,348½	992	2,210	1,020	-	13,255½
Total	1,527	1,281	1,310	1,484½	1,604	7,242	10,294¼	10,712½	4,544	2,269½	1,020	38½	43,327¼

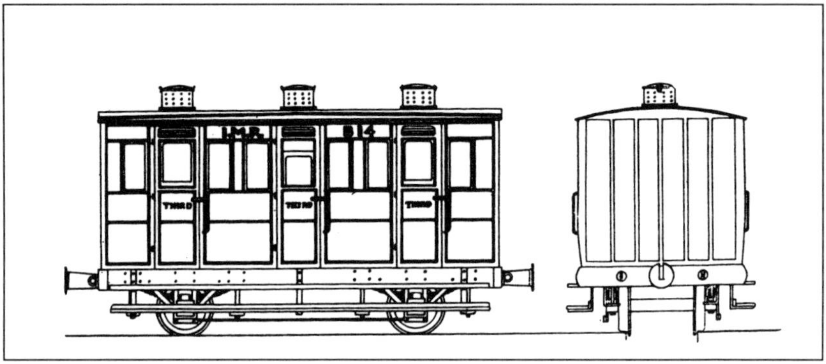

Isle of Man Railway original 4-wheeled third class coach and 4-wheeled brake van. Reproduced ⅛ inch to 1 foot. *Ian Macnab*

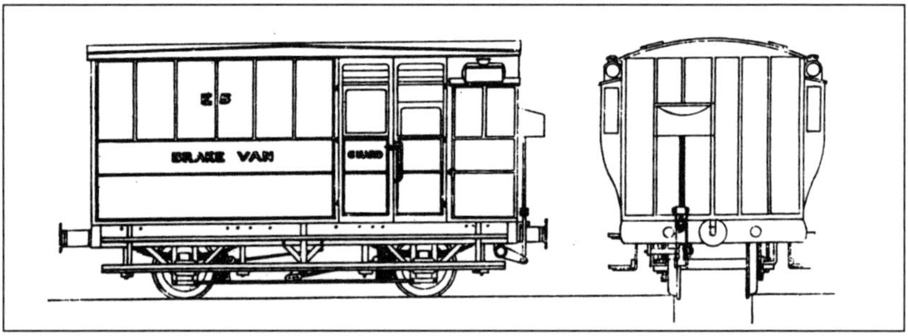

Passenger Carriages

Isle of Man Railway: *Four-wheeled Stock*

The IOMR was created for the conveyance of visitors and passenger stock has always formed the bulk of its vehicles, goods traffic taking second place. Although bogie carriages were coming into use on narrow gauge railways in the British Isles, the initial purchases for the Island were of basic four-wheeled type; Vignoles was apparently convinced of their suitability for the task and their cost would meet the slender resources available. However, their shortcomings were soon revealed and within four years bogie stock was introduced . . . far from novel, such vehicles were first introduced in America forty years earlier!

Reporting to the Board on 1st October, 1872, Vignoles said that only two classes of passenger would be carried, 'on the compartment system' as opposed to a 'saloon' type of carriage. Tenders had been invited from The Railway Carriage Co., Oldbury; The Lancaster Wagon Co., Caton, Lancaster; The Bristol Wagon Works Co., Bristol; The Metropolitan Carriage & Wagon Co., Saltley; The Gloucester Wagon Co., Gloucester. Metropolitan obtained the order being 1 Saloon, 6 First Class, 16 Third Class 'without breaks', 4 Third Class 'with breaks', and 2 Guard's Vans.

At a subsequent Board Meeting a decision to designate only First and Second Class, and carry inferior designations as required in adapted goods vehicles, was made and by 19th June, 1873 all such Thirds (none of which had yet been shipped) were reclassed as Seconds before they left Liverpool. Twenty vehicles in all, they were allocated to the Peel Line on arrival at Douglas, but their paintwork was not acceptable and the makers were obliged to send men across to re-do the work - perhaps the bodies had stood too long in the open before leaving the mainland?

For the Port Erin Line and despite the impasse over paintwork, Vignoles was told to use the same supplier; 5 First Class, 10 Second Class, 10 'breaked' Second Class and 2 Guard's Vans comprised the order. Major Taubman, the influential Douglas Director, wanted the order amending; he desired coupé ends fitted to the First Class, and some composite carriages as opposed to single class, for winter use. The first request was not acceptable but two Seconds as yet incomplete at Saltley, were delivered as composite. When the Port Erin Line opened, fifty-six carriages were available, carrying numbers 1-56.

In 1876 with delivery of bogie stock impending, numbering of the foregoing was given a letter prefix thus:

A1-A12	First Class	(A12 being a Saloon)
B1-B24	Second Class	No brakes
C1-C14	Second Class	Braked
D1-D2	Composite	
E1-E4	Guard's Brake Vans	

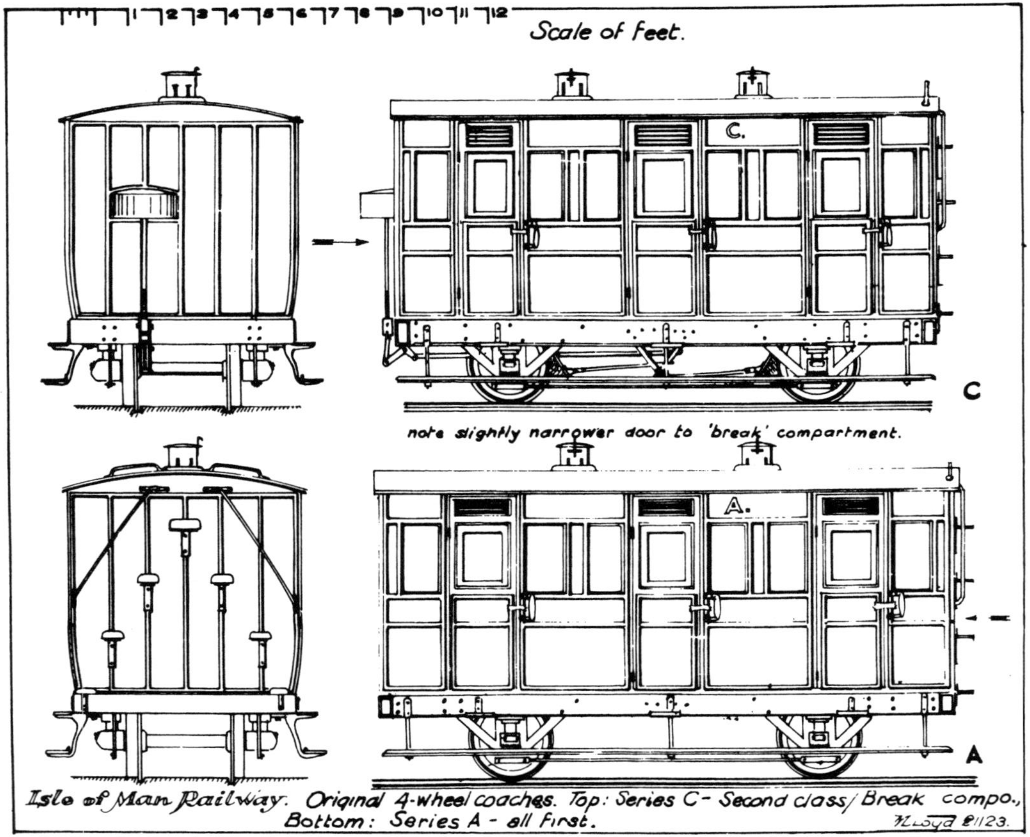
1 2 3 4 5 6 7 8 9 10 11 12
Scale of feet.
C.
C
note slightly narrower door to 'break' compartment.
A.
A
Isle of Man Railway. Original 4-wheel coaches. Top: Series C - Second class/Break compo.,
Bottom: Series A - all First.
Lloyd 8/1123.

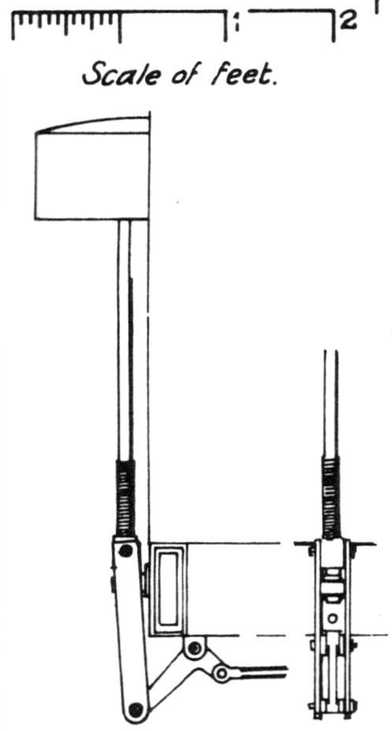

Detail of brake gear on 4-wheel stock.

M. Lloyd 21125.

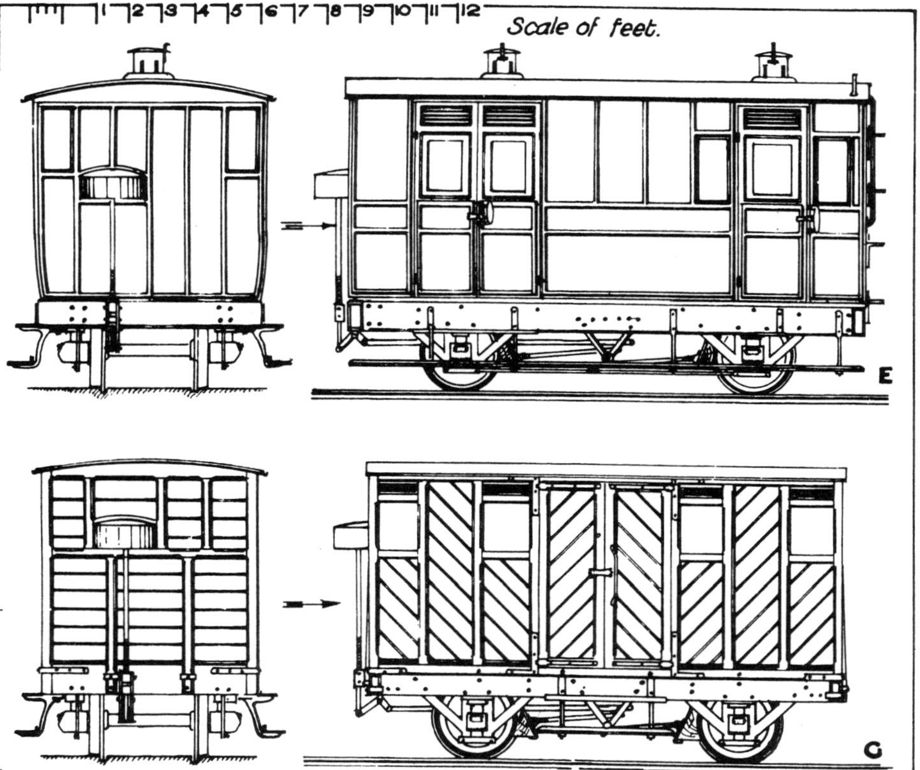

Isle of Man Railway: Original 4-wheel stock: Top: "Passenger Break Van," Series 'E'.
Bottom: "Covered Goods Wagon capable of being used as Third Class Carriage"

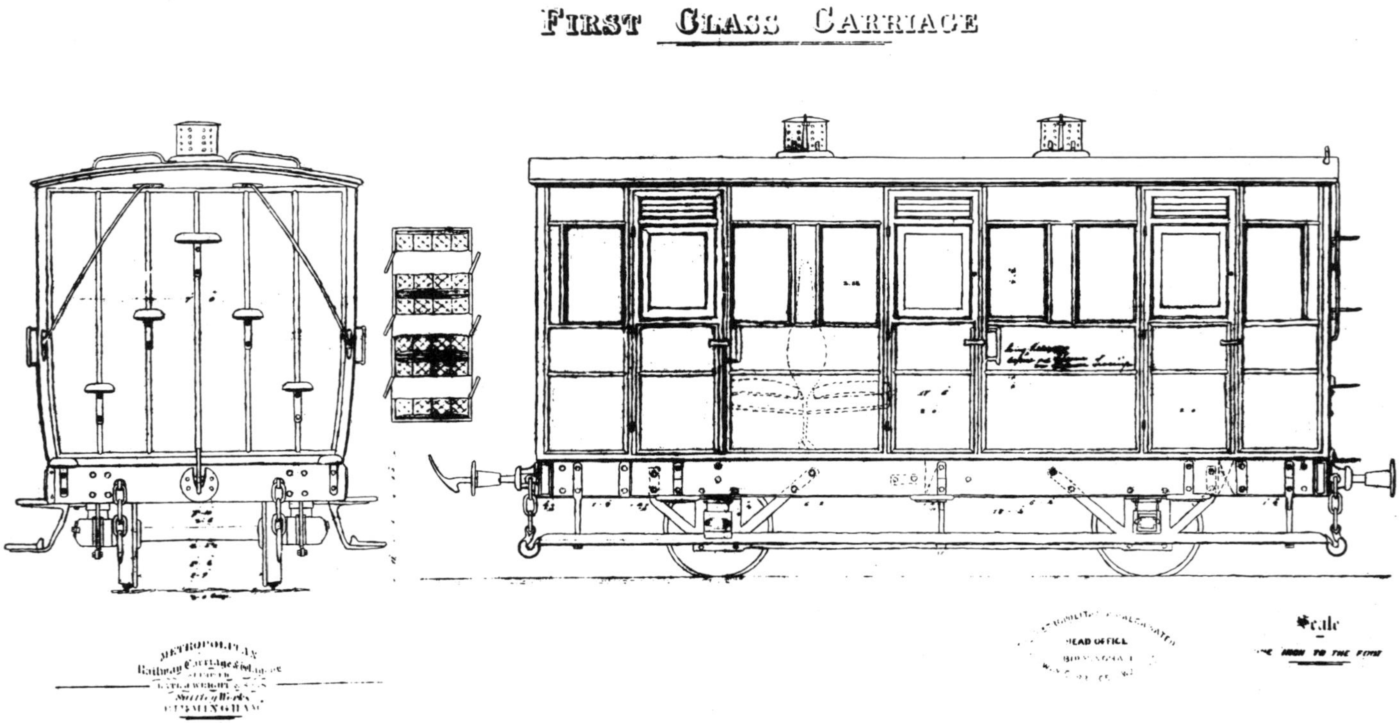

Official drawing of first class carriage of 1873.

Metropolitan Carriage & Wagon Co.

[From the same date a strategy for numbering future bogie purchases was evolved, starting with the figure '1' and the pre-fix F. This sufficed, and ultimately embodied also all four-wheeled carriages carrying the pre-fix A - D as they were converted to bogie carriages in later years. Vehicles pre-fixed E remained unaltered and four-wheeled to the end.

It is convenient to complete an explanation of number pre-fixes here - following-on the F series, letters G to M were assigned to goods stock, and the letter N to the six-wheeled passenger carriages acquired from the Manx Northern Railway at take-over.]

Now to revert to description of the original carriages.

Series A1-A11 and A12. Nos. A1-A11 were 3-compartment First Class stock, each 17 ft 6in. long holding 30 passengers. Individual seat squabs in buttoned blue cloth were provided; seat backs were upholstered up to head level, the compartment partitions being ended at this height. Later they were carried up to roof level. As the railway had no fully-raised platforms, full-length footboards were fitted; the rubber springs initially fitted gave a motion which few passengers appreciated, and subsequently they were replaced by metal laminated type. Bodies 7 ft wide with a roof-rail height of 9 ft 4 in. were carried on 2 ft 3 in. diameter wheels at 9 ft 6 in. wheelbase.

A12 had a different body; known as 'The Duke's Saloon' or 'The Governor's Saloon', it was used by the Duke of Sutherland for the railway opening ceremonies and for the Governor or visiting dignitaries thereafter. When years later it was mounted on a bogie chassis which it shared with another saloon, it was pressed into ordinary traffic and might often be found crammed full of Lancashire folk singing lustily on the Boat Train leaving Port Erin at 2.15 pm.

As built it had a central door each side, and perimeter seating round a central table at each end. There was blue upholstery and dark stained panelling with gilt beading, blue carpet, brass luggage racks and Lincrusta ceiling edged again with gilt; in common use by 1962, some of these features had disappeared. The exterior is recalled as a green vehicle with gilt lining to the panels (instead of yellow), each of two panels per side enclosing the Manx arms.

Series B1-B42; D1-D2. This series and those of C type that follow, were a foot shorter than the A type, but still had three compartments and carried 30 persons in narrower circumstance. The plain wooden seats and backs were spartan and the backs were not carried above shoulder height. Running gear etc. was as for A type.

Series C1-C14. Basically similar to B type, this series could be spotted by the handbrake fitting and that the third compartment was given over to, and labelled 'Guard'. Passengers could use it, circumstances permitting but would find its interior differed from Second Class, as there was a plain

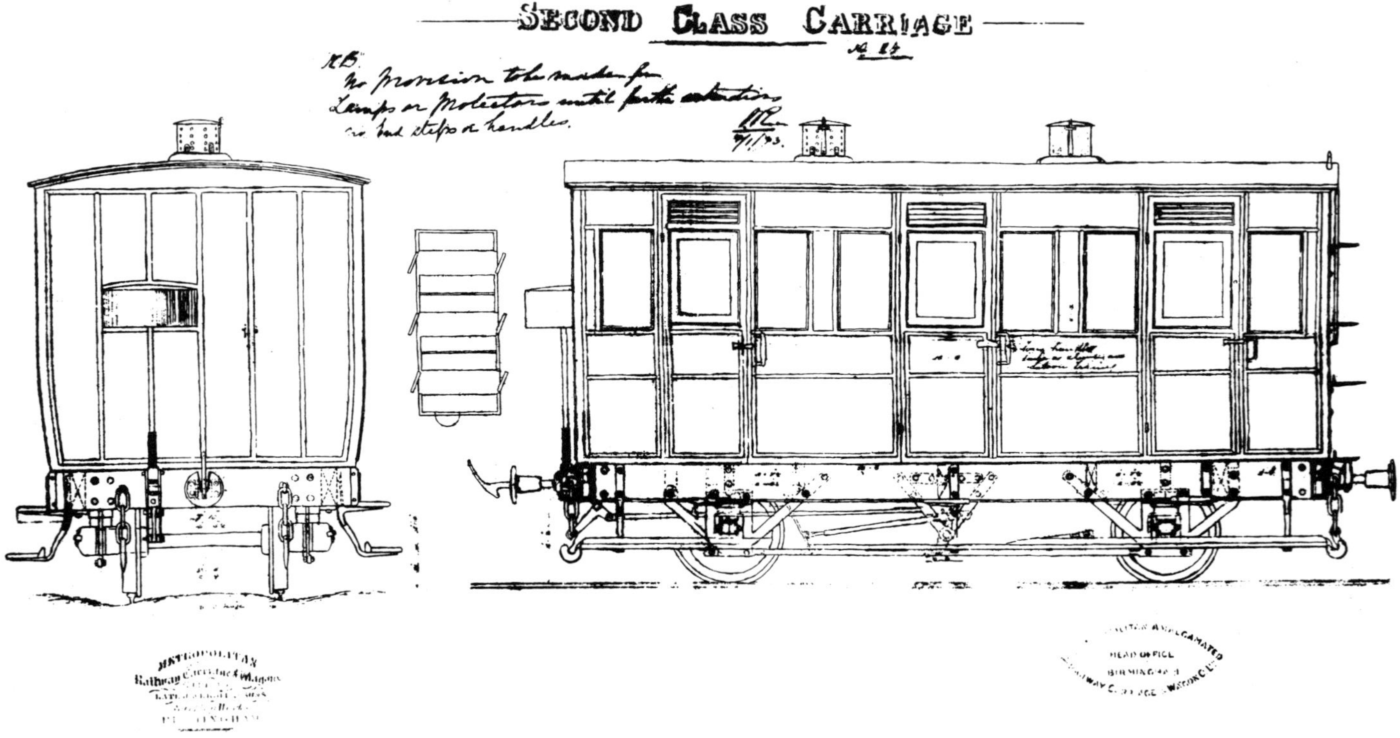

Official drawing of second class carriage of 1873.

Metropolitan Carriage & Wagon Co.

uncomfortable wooden box seat on one side; the brake handle was set in the end wall and covered by an external-projecting casing.

In 1903 C9 was re-bodied as a Saloon to accompany A12 and accommodate members of the Governor's entourage; more recently it was used to convey Railway officers on inspections etc.* It was 'paired' with A12 on a bogie chassis in 1926, the pair receiving number F75. In 1962 the seats were upholstered in brown and red jacquard design, with loose cushions, but only up to waist height; the lincrusta ceiling omitted a gilt finish. On the annual Tynwald Day the Governor and party travelled to St John's by train: C9 was nicknamed 'The Keys' (members of the House of Keys) or the Second Class or Third Class Saloon depending on the period and the name persisted after the marriage with A12.

Series E1-E7. Numbers E1-E4 were the original delivery and were the precursors of these small useful luggage, mail and guard's brake vans, numbers E5-E6 being from Metropolitan in 1876, and in the same style. They were 16 ft long with 9 ft wheelbase and with a 9 ft 6 in. rail-roof height. The original drawings show two small windows in the brake end (fittings as for C type) and at the other, a single compartment to hold 10 passengers. Before construction commenced, the end windows were replaced by side duckets and the passenger compartment dispensed with in favour of a luggage compartment having double side doors, demonstrating a change of policy to carrying passengers of inferior class (see on). The interior contained a letter rack, parcels shelf and a double locker to form a seat; double footboards ran the length of the exterior.

In 1893 E1 was demolished in collision with a Manx Northern Railway locomotive at St John's but the remains were taken to Douglas Works which managed to contrive a new goods van from them (see Series G) and numbered G7. A new E1 was supplied by Metropolitan in 1894.

Summary of IOMR E Series Vans as at 1973:

No.	*Builder*	*Date*	*Notes*
1	Metro.	1873	Destroyed in accident 1893
2	Metro.	1873	Body as Santon goods shed 1924†
3	Metro.	1874	Scrap 1921. Chassis G19
4	Metro.	1874	Body as Sulby Bridge goods shed 1909. Scrap 1923. Chassis Fish No. 3, 1910.
5	Metro.	1876	Extant†#
6	Metro.	1876	Body as Peel Rd. goods shed 1911†. Chassis scrap, 1915.
7 (later 3)	Douglas	1895	Built from parts E1. Body as Sulby Bridge goods shed (2) 1923. Scrap *c.* 1937. Chassis K5, 1924.
1 (later 4)	Metro.	1894	Extant†§

*On Saturdays in 1936 it was reserved for passengers from 'Ballaqueeny', Port St Mary, on the Up afternoon Boat Train.

†In 1973 these bodies/vans were still extant.

#Used occasionally until 1958; thereafter stored at buffer end of South Line departure platform, Douglas. Moved out 1963. Still in all-over brown livery with traces of 'Brake Van' on lower panels (1973).

§As re-numbered E4, withdrawn 1925, converted to Breakdown Van to run with Gibbins crane and two match trucks. Originally painted red oxide, but grey in 1973.

The foregoing comprised all the four-wheeled carriages and guard's brake vans owned initially by the IOMR and identified by a number prefixed between A-E.

[Series E8-E11. These were Guard's Vans of Manx Northern Railway origin and are considered separately (see p. 260).]

'Lower orders' would not be accommodated in the above-mentioned stock and special vehicles which could carry excursionists when necessary were envisaged; this was followed by a formal decision in July 1878 to cater for a Third Class. Preparations to build stock for carrying such excursionists with drawings for 'convertible' covered vans and open wagons were made at the outset, but there is good evidence that no such special vehicles were built in this form for the July 1878 policy-change not only introduced Third Class but abolished Second, Second Class hereafter being designated Third. Second Class remained unprovided-for until 2nd June, 1956 when mainland precedent was followed and all Third Class was designated Second.

When George Armstrong of the Great Western Railway made his inspection in 1886 (see Vol. I p.179) his solution to the rough riding of these coaches was to short-couple them together in pairs with convex and concave side buffers; 'they would ride almost as easily as the Bogie Carriages'. This was carried out and the coaches remained in the same pairs when ultimately they were mounted on bogie frames.

Regarding the harsh ride, Armstrong suggested two causes:

There were varying forms of existing springing; in answer to complaints, the rubber springs under the First Class had been changed to laminated which, by some mischance were not fitted centrally with consequent uneven wearing of the axle brasses. Because of this, the axle boxes tended to jam in the horn plates so affecting the vertical freedom of movement. Other coaches had Sterne's Patent spiral springs which Armstrong suggested were too elastic under the varying weights they supported. (The drawing for an amendment he suggested is missing.)

A note on the matter of couplings dated 1887 tends to throw doubt on the number of vehicles altered to Armstrong's ideas - as some had been. The 'pairing' had been successful . . .'it almost halved the time necessary to couple-up individual four-wheelers'. A modified arrangement had been evolved; the middle couplers were removed from the matching ends of a pair and spring-loaded side buffers were fitted to one of the pair. The adjoining end was given circular plates against which the buffers could rub. Linkage was by simple link and pin, drawn up tightly.

So these coaches served in the form described until 1903 when, as said, a 'double-saloon' was created. Six years later it was decreed that as the bodies would serve for many more years but the running gear was unable to give the smoother ride of the bogie coaches - even allowing that the drawgear springs had been changed to eliminate their part-rubber content in favour of all-steel and so reduce the awesome fore-and-aft jerking - it would combine good practice and economy to mount the pairs onto bogie underframes supplied from the mainland, and at the same time the redundant four-wheel chassis thus released could be used on which to build additional bodies for various traffic in the Works. This ploy was successfully followed in the periods 1909-12 and 1919-26 and later the vehicles were numbered in the F series from F50.

Isle of Man Railway: *Bogie Stock*

Vignoles had informed himself by visiting other narrow gauge railways in the spring of 1871; the tour included the Festiniog Railway where bogie carriages were already in use. As already mentioned, he did not think such were essential for an initial purchase by the IOMR. In any case, out of the £26,000 for stations and rolling stock (of which £16,000 less 7% for contractor's profit and superintendence was allocated for stock) given to Watson & Smith under the contract, there remained a net sum of £14,800 for Vignoles' purchases. His options were limited.

Series F1-F6. Although there is no evidence for the decision, Trevithick, the General Superintendent, advised the Board on 12th January, 1875 that he had received tenders from Brown, Marshalls & Co. of Birmingham, The Ashbury Carriage & Iron Co. of Manchester and Metropolitan for six new bogie carriages. He strongly recommended the foremost and his opinion was accepted; the vehicles were to be braked, and to be four Second Class and two composite carriages with delivery not before 1876. This was the last order placed for 'Second Class' coaches.

F1-F4	G/2222/2	later	G/33/33/3
F5-F6	G/2/1/1/2/2	later	G/3/1/1/3/3

The bodies were 35 ft long, 7 ft wide and 9 ft 4 in. roof-rail on spoke-wheeled diamond-frame bogies with timber bolsters set at centres 25 ft 10 in. apart, and 4 ft 6 in. wheelbase. Brakeblocks were of wood and all wheels were braked. The body sides were straight and carried down to mask the frames. The guard's compartment contained braking arrangements in the style of the four-wheeled carriages and this compartment and those in the First Class, were fully partitioned; the open Second/Third Class compartments as built, have subsequently been altered to close them off.*

The First Class was upholstered to head height and fitted with arm rests, curtains, carpets, luggage racks and leather-covered side and door panels. The bare Second Class had some shaping to the seat backs.

*A line below the figures in the content-tables denotes open construction without partitions.

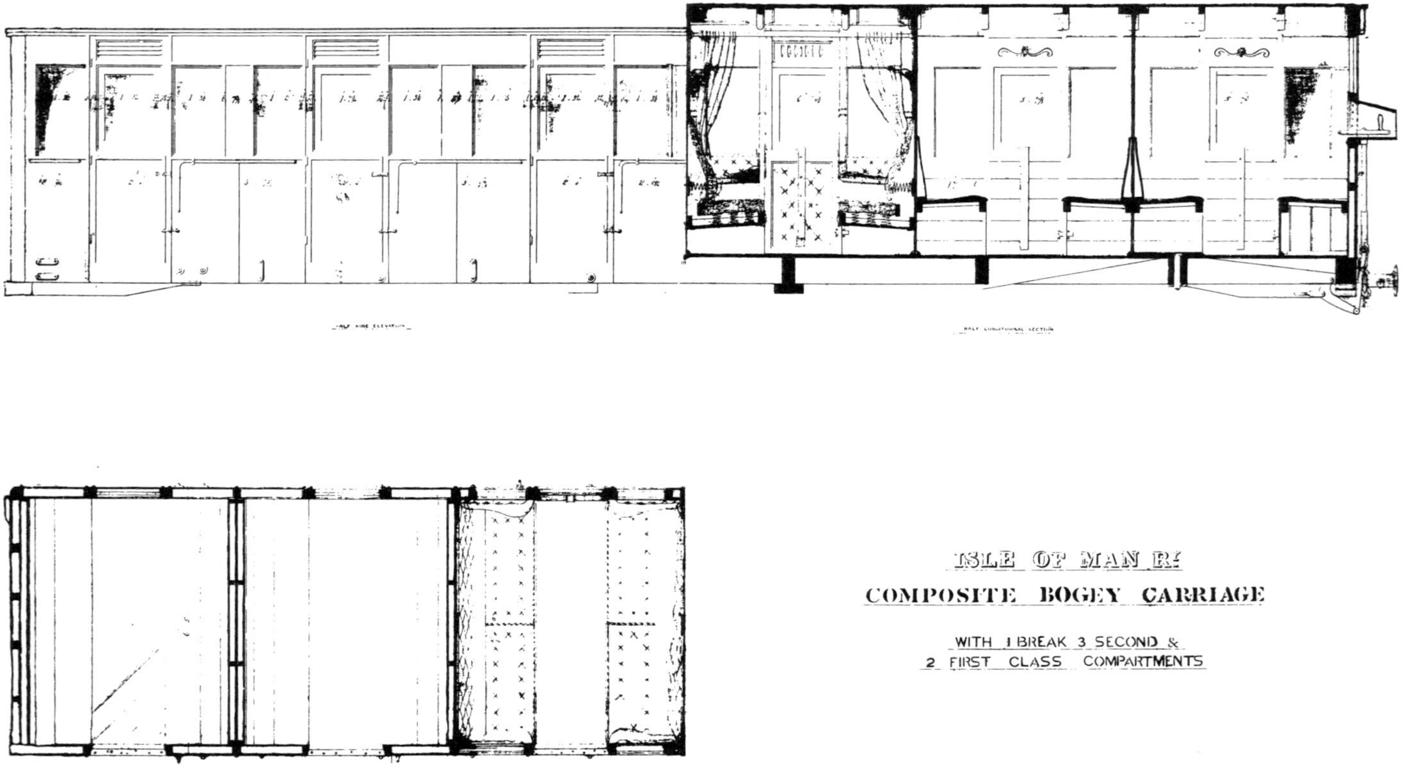

Official drawing of Ashbury composite carriages Nos. F5-F6 *c.* 1875.

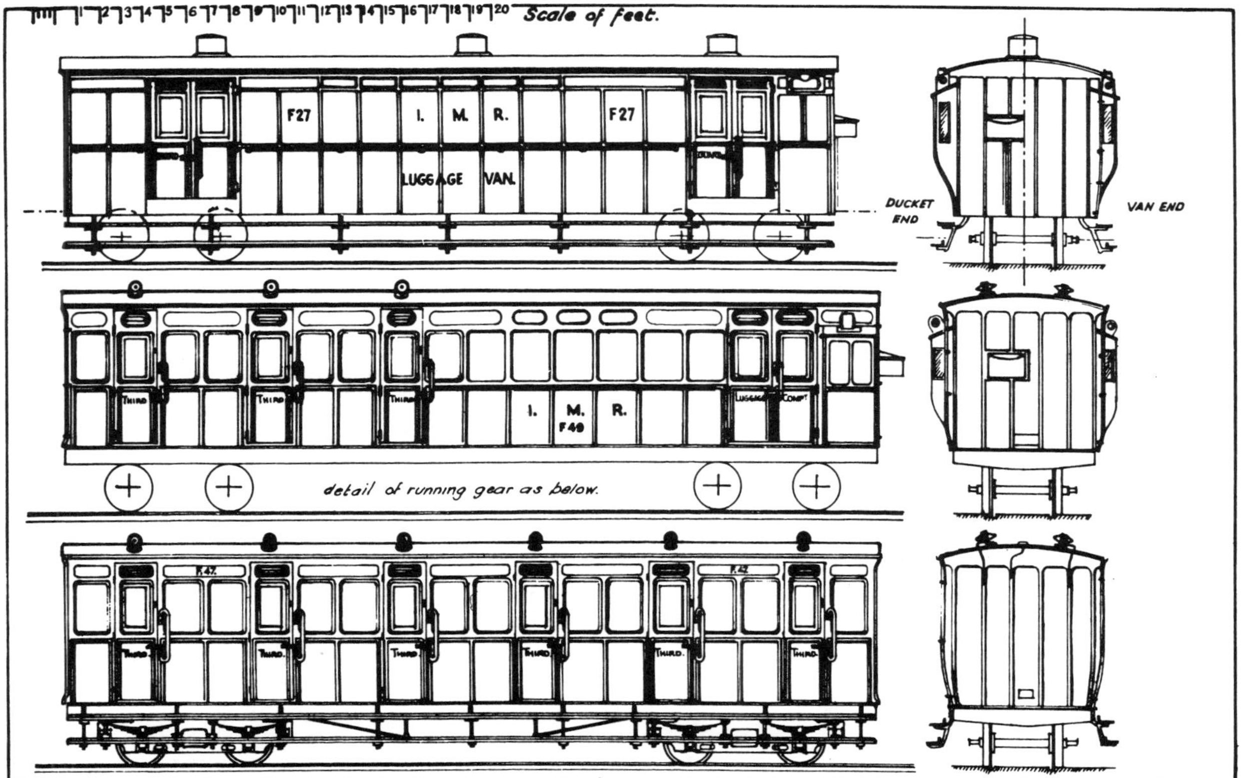

Isle of Man Railway. Bogie stock. Top: Luggage Van (Empress Van). Centre: Third/brake composite. Bottom: All third. Running gear detail for Third/brake as for All-third. All taken from Official Drawings.

JKLloyd 21104

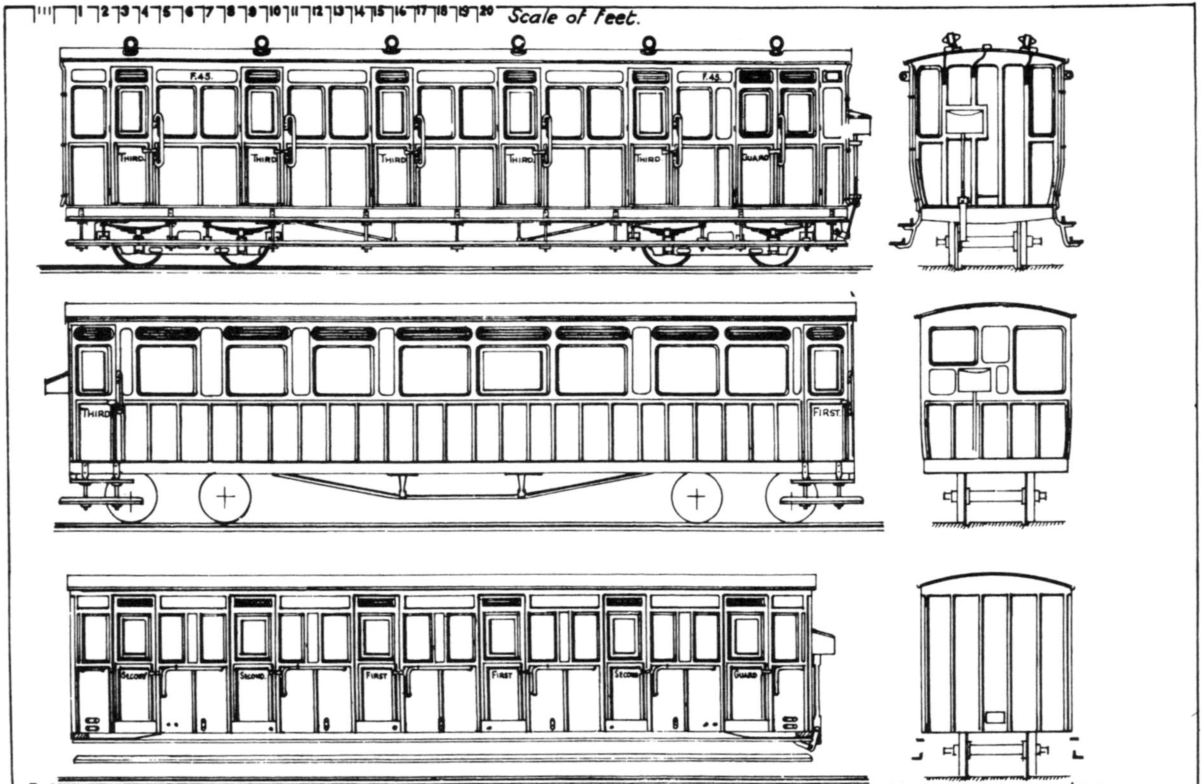

Isle of Man Railway Bogie Stock. Top: Third/Guard No. F45. Centre: 39-foot "Observation-saloon" First/third. Bottom: First/Second/Guard compo. F5-F7. All from Official drawings, note different systems of projection. G.M. Lloyd

Series F7-F12. A second batch of bogie coaches was delivered in 1881 and included the first bogie coaches to have Third Class denomination from the start; it may have a trial to have the first two carriages built by Ashbury (F7-F8). Brown, Marshalls supplied the remainder which were unbraked.

In 1884 F9 was converted to composite but was downgraded to all Third in 1909, retaining its First Class partitions. Similarly, F8 became a composite in 1885 but later its 'First Class' designations were painted out but the Stock Returns continued to list it as a composite.

F7	G/3/1/1/33		
F8	G/3333/3	G/3/1/1/3/3 (1885)	G/3/3/3/3/3 (later)
F9	3/33/33/3	3/33/1/1/3 (1884)	3/33/3/3/3 (1909)
F10-F12	3/33/33/3		

Series F13-F19. This batch was similar to Series F1-F6 except that the lower panels were waisted inwards; Brown, Marshalls was the builder in 1894. F19 has a luggage compartment with double doors; a drawing did exist proposing both single and double doors at the guard's end, but clearly not adopted. Each coach had three separate windows at the brake end, a shorter one over the brake housing. When built, open construction for the Third Class was still favoured.

F13-F15	G/3/1/1/33	F15	G/3/1/1/3/3 (later)
F16-F18	G/33/33/3		
F19	G-/3/3/3		

Series F20-F26. These were similar to Series F13-F19 and supplied 1896; F21-F24 were 11 in. longer than the remainder of the batch. A number of accommodation alterations took place.

F20	G-/3/3/3				
F21	G/1/1/1/1/3	G/3/1/1/3/3	(1928)		
F22	G/1/1/1/1/3	G/3/1/1/3/3	(1929)		
F23	G/1/1/1/1/3	G/3/1/1/3/3	(1930)	G/3/1/1/33	(later)
F24	G/1/1/1/1/3	G/3/1/1/3/3	(1929)		
F25	G/33/33/3/3	3/33/33/3	(later)	Handbrake retained	
F26	G/33/33/3/3	3/33/33/3	(later)	Handbrake retained	

Metropolitan were again the builders.

Series F27-F28. Along with F20-F26 the same source built two fine luggage vans of similar outline to these carriages, in the next year, 1897. Bodies were 37 ft long, 7 ft wide (8 ft 6 in. wide over duckets), 9 ft 4 in. roof-rail on 4 ft 6 in. wheelbase bogies at centres 25 ft 8 in. apart. The standard wheel diameter of 2 ft 3in. was maintained. The duckets and handbrake were found at one end only, but each side had two double doors and bore

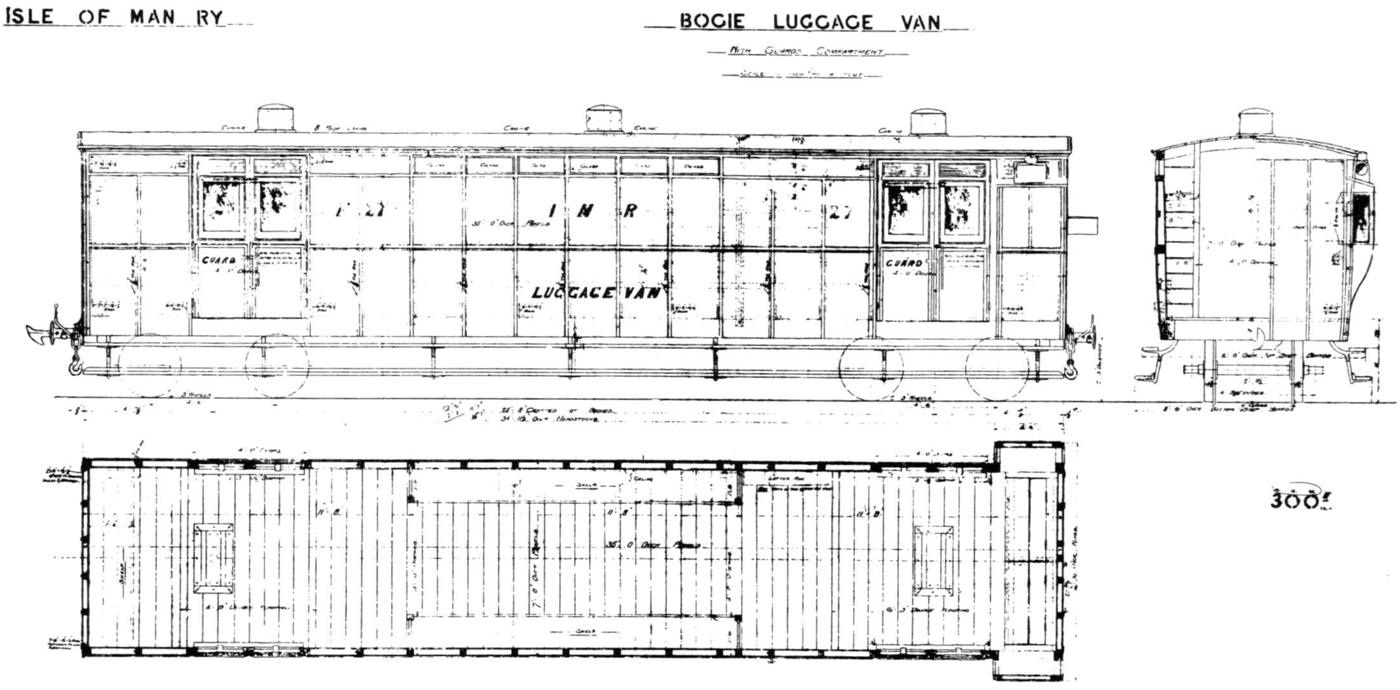

Official drawing of 'Empress Van' Nos. F27-F28 of 1897.

Metropolitan Carriage & Wagon Co.

the legend 'Luggage Van'; there were no end windows but six shallow window lights under the cant-rail either side lit the dark interior. Double footboards extended the full length; nick-named after the Empress Queen Victoria whose Diamond Jubilee was celebrated in 1897, they acquired the title 'Empress Vans'.

For reasons unknown, when the passenger stock was fitted with vacuum brake gear at a later date (see p. 262), these vans were ignored completely.

Series F29-F32, F35-F36: When the IOMR took over the Manx Northern and Foxdale Railways Stowell, the IOMR Manager,was anxious about the sufficiency of passenger stock; he was convinced that the existing stock of these two Railways was unfitted for the task, as the bulk of the MNR vehicles were forbidden to place a wheel on IOMR metals, an IOMR Board decision which had firmly stood its ground since the MNR opened. Hunt approached Greenbank to suggest a design for modern stock as used on the mainland.

Greenbank's preference was for a corridor type of coach akin to those rapidly gaining favour for all but suburban work, and so the series gained the name 'Corridor Coaches' though they were not the side corridor variety which prevailed on the mainland. The enquiry was sent to Metropolitan who went to some lengths to prepare a design; the first was a saloon version with three doors each side and vertical matchboard panels similar to that adopted by the Great Central Railway, accompanied by a matching Third Class and Guard's Brake saloon. In the end no guard's brake provision was made, and the saloons as supplied ran attached to a conventional compartment style Third with guard's end.

These vehicles were the showpiece of the line and the builders were asked to design and mount a suitable crest on them - the first to be applied since the ducal saloon. Delivery was made in 1905 and the numbers applied so as to straddle F33 and F34. They were fine pieces of coachbuilding and the handsomest yet seen for narrow gauge tourist traffic in the British Isles. Entrance was made by end vestibule having glazed ends. This led by sliding door into a central gangway running through each saloon compartment; there were seven side windows in the Thirds and eight in the First/Third composites - the entire side was glazed.

The side panels differed from previous stock and ended above the solebars, giving the coaches the appearance of riding higher than their fellows. Steel underframes were a new feature, a development which the Traffic Department were quick to notice as the trains became considerably heavier. With doors being only at the ends, the double footboards were short; again for the first time, electric lighting featured.

The Third Class interiors were divided by a solid partition to make two compartments, Smoking = 19 seats, 14 ft 6in. long and Non-smoking = 22 seats, 16 ft 11 in. long. Apart from fixed upholstered seats which were fitted

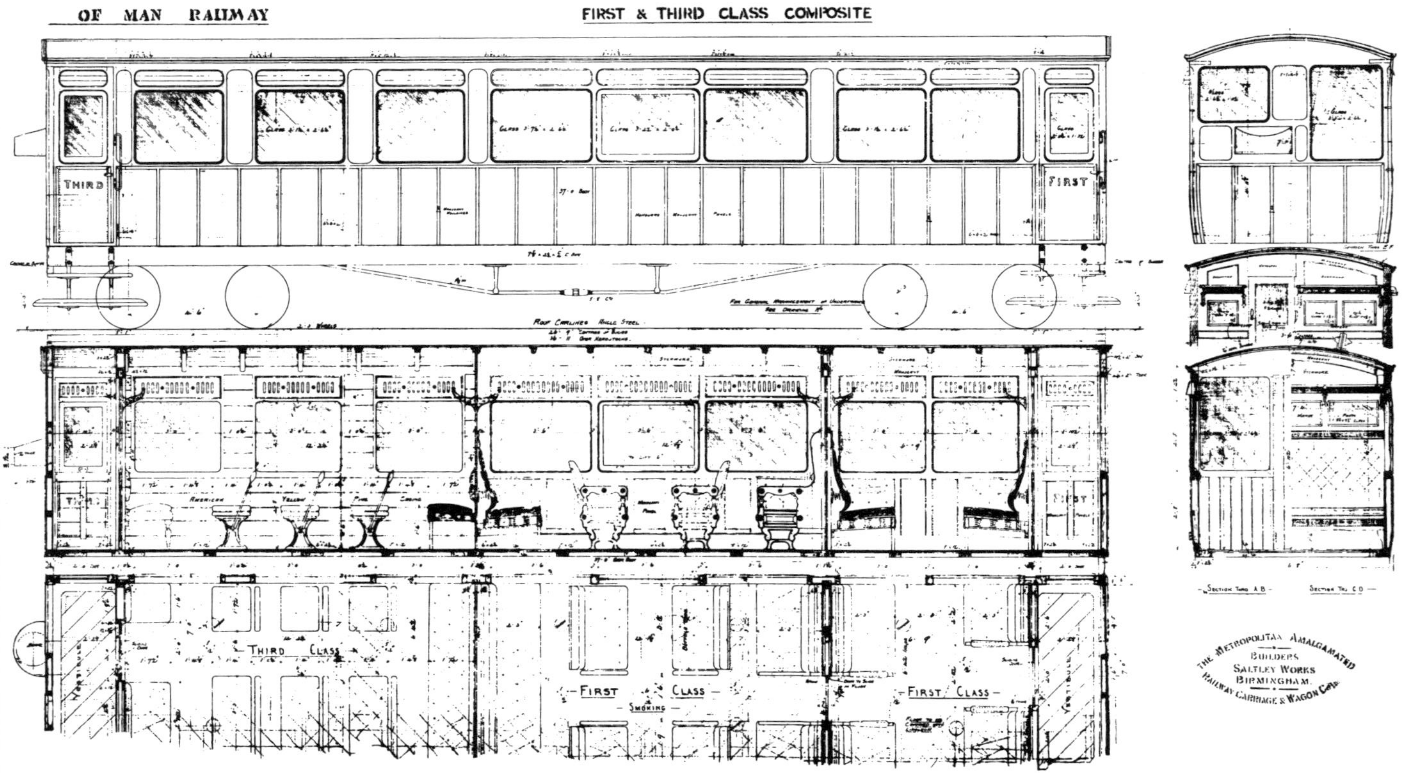

First/third saloon carriage of 1905.

Metropolitan Carriage & Wagon Co.

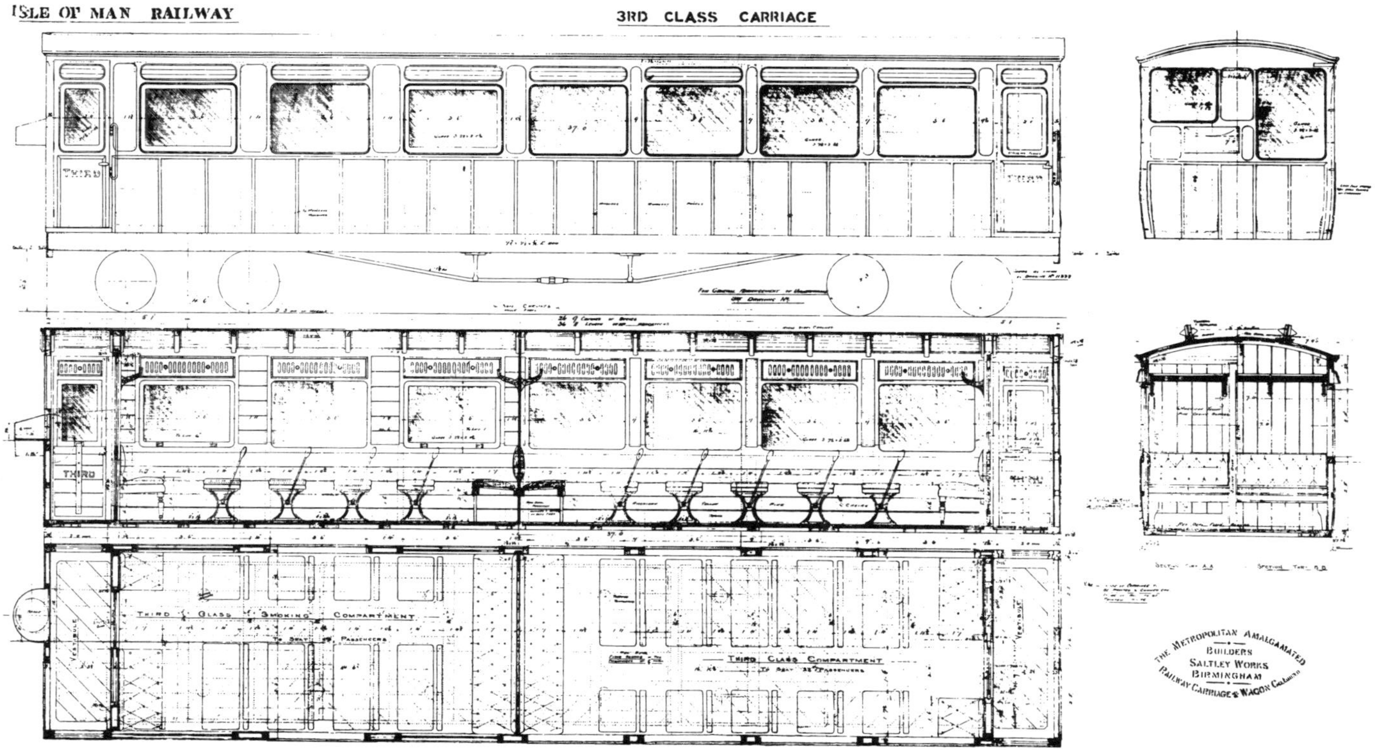

All third saloon carriage of 1905.

Metropolitan Carriage & Wagon Co.

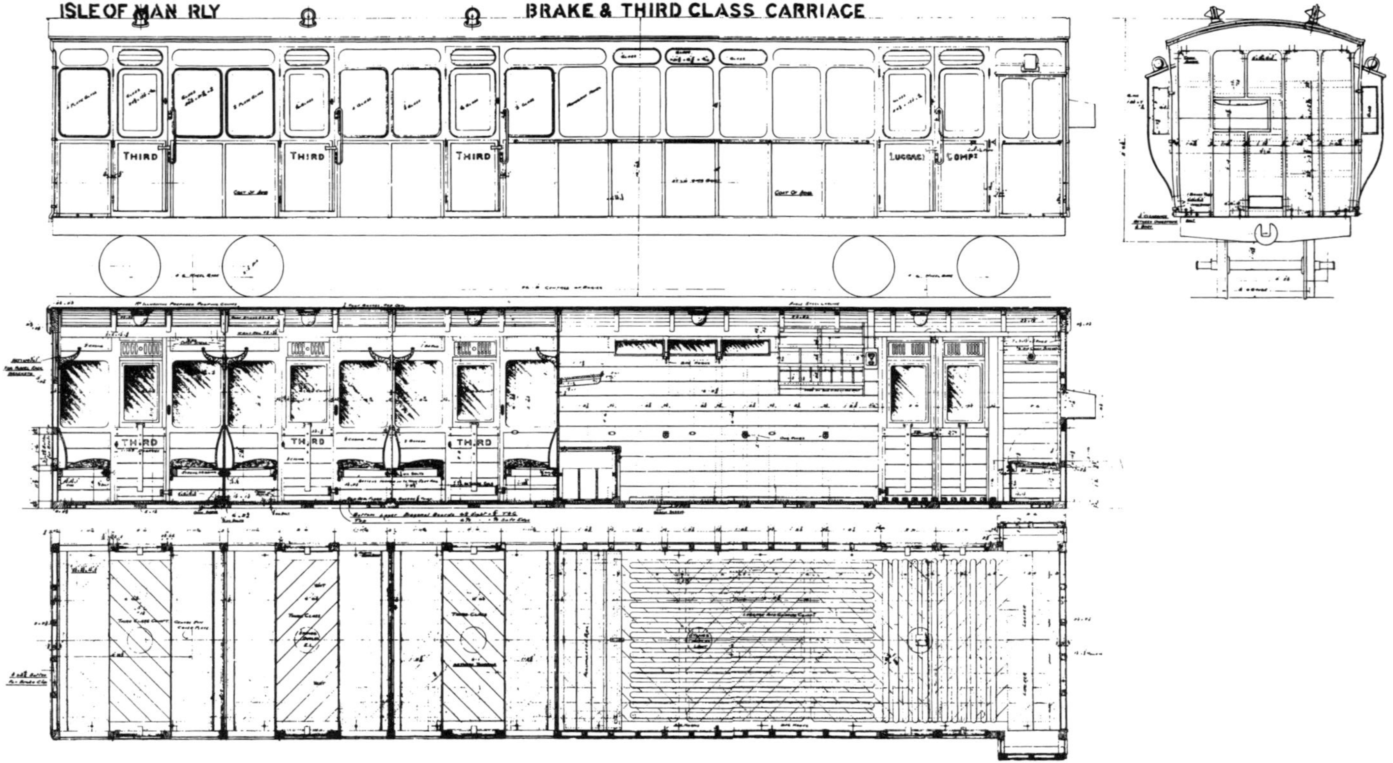

Guard's brake with three third class compartments with large luggage compartment, 1905. *Metropolitan Carriage & Wagon Co.*

up against the central and the two vestibule partitions, the seating was of the reversible tramcar type, holding a single passenger on one side of the gangway, and two on the other. Passengers did not find these seats as comfortable as in the compartments, although their use was widespread in the world. Certain of the side windows could be opened by lowering them but poor ventilation coupled with the large area of glass gave the saloons a bad reputation. In the First Class an electric fan was tried but all in all, the saloons had disadvantage to both operator and user, and they did not meet the optimism engendered or the mileage intended. Each vehicle was brake-fitted with the brakewheel in the Third Class vestibule.

Nos. F29-F32 were all Third Class having 16 seats each and a light grained-oak interior. F35-F36 were composite, with an inner partition dividing the classes; the First had a subdivision by sliding door separating Smoking and Non-smoking. The former had 5 seats for non-smokers in what was a snug little room of its own with two very large single seats against the vestibule. Thirteen smokers were accommodated adjacent; the intermediate seating along the gangway, though amply upholstered, was of the reversible type and equalled the best American Inter-urban Electric Car practice of those times. First Class interiors were panelled in sycamore and mahogany.

The coaches were 36 ft 11 in. long, 7 ft wide and somewhat higher than previously from rail to roof, 10 ft 3 in. Diamond-frame bogies having 4 ft 6 in. wheelbase on 2 ft 3 in. diameter spoked wheels, were set apart 26 ft 9 in.

In 1963 F36 was used as a Royal Saloon for the Queen Mother's visit, for which the pressed steel bogies from F61 were substituted, which meant disconnecting the handbrake. Being used for varying dignatories subsequently, including a visit of 2nd August, 1972 when it was accompanied by F35, it later became the Cardinal's Coach; it is best-known as 'The Queen's Coach'.

Further modifications followed in 1984 to F35, F31, F32 (in that sequence) to make up a 'Party Train'. (See Vol. II p.224.)

Series F33-F34. In the same year as the saloons were delivered, Metropolitan supplied two Thirds with Guard's Brake end to a design which remained a standard; they resembled the saloons with their higher bodies and visible solebars. Most noticeable, was the length of the luggage compartment, reflecting the amount of trunks, cases etc. which was now brought by visitors, much of it sent on in advance of their personal arrival. The three Third Class compartments had the luxury of upholstery for the first time. Double footboards extended the full length of the vehicle and the luggage portion had double doors, duckets, and was lit by small upper lights as with the Empress Vans. Bodies were 37 ft long, 7 ft wide but 8 ft 6 in. over the duckets; oddly the roof was lower at 10 ft exactly; running gear was identical with the saloons.

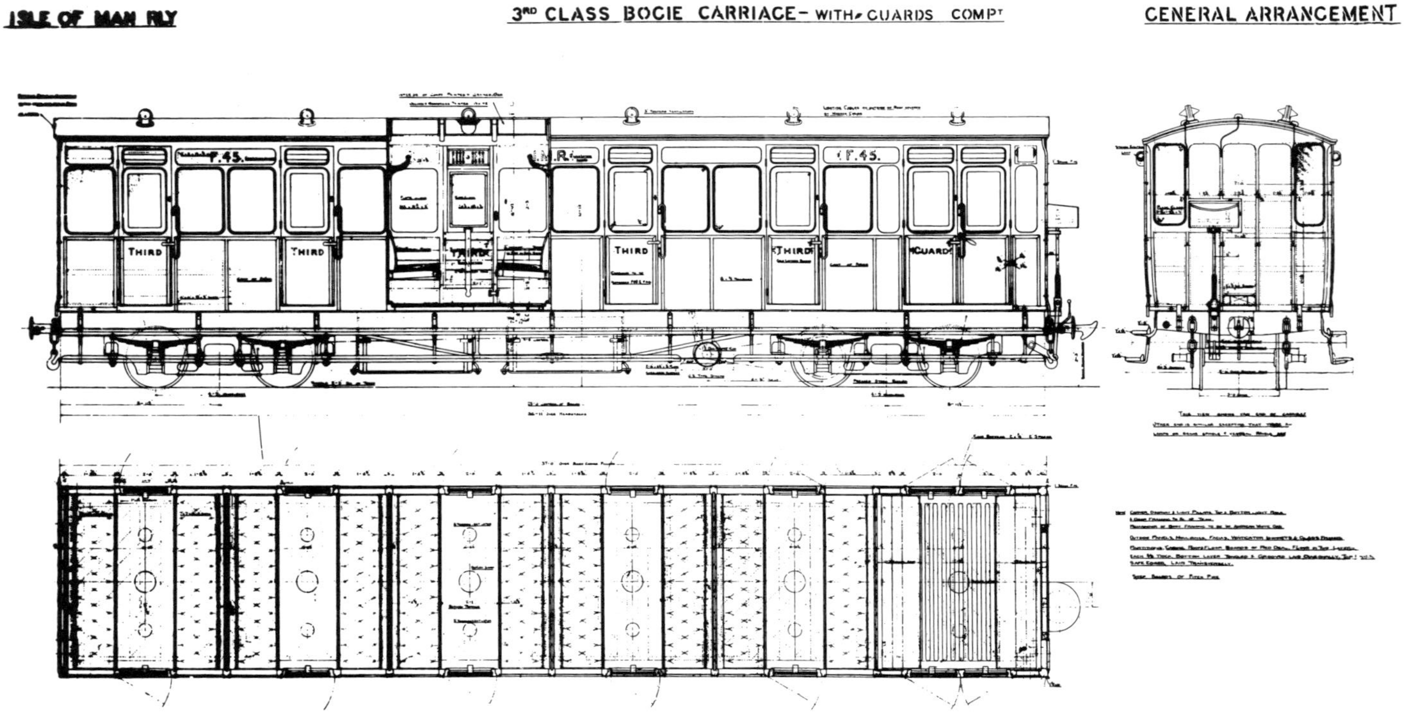

Brake/third carriage No. F45 of 1913.

Metropolitan Carriage & Wagon Co.

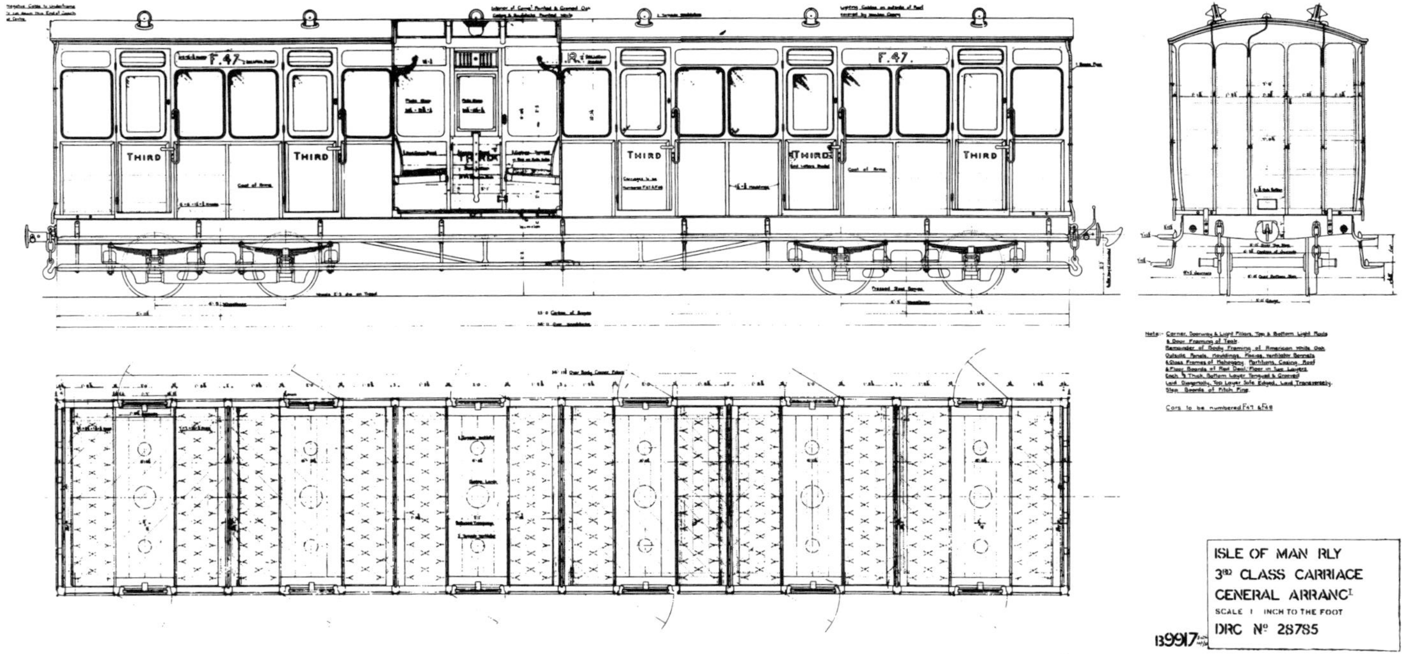

Third class carriage of 1923.

Metropolitan Carriage & Wagon Co.

Series F37-F38 and F39. These were bogie vehicles from the absorbed Manx Northern and Foxdale Railways and are described later (see p. 256).

Series F40-F44. These were a batch of five identical composite coaches from Metropolitan in 1907-8 - three in 1907 and two the year following. They were to the design of F33-4.

Series F45-F46. From the same builder as before came two Guard's composites in 1913; the body arrangements differed in that there was a short Guard's and luggage section and five fully compartmented Third Class portions; the batteries for the lights were under the floorboards at the guard's end, there being no other place for them. To squeeze in as much luggage etc. as possible, there were hinged seats in the Guard's compartment and there were design difficulties here as a drawing of January 1913 shows a different arrangement, not used. There are no look-out duckets either. In 1927 the interiors were altered from G/3/3/3/3 to G/3/1/1/3/3, and both have seen duty on Royal Trains; these, and the two of the following series, ran on pressed steel bogies of pattern first used in 1910 by the makers on the chassis designed to take the pioneer four-wheeled bodies. Dimensions are: Length 36 ft 11 in., width 7 ft, height rail to roof 10 ft 1 in.; bogies are at 25 ft centres with 4 ft 9 in. wheelbase. (Needless to add, a small difference in body height would be affected by the condition of the springs.)

Series F47-F48. After a break in supply caused by the First War, in 1923 Metropolitan delivered two six-compartment Third Class carriages in the style of the previous series, but having a passenger compartment in place of the Guard's.

Series F49. Similar to F33-4 which had proved their worth since 1905, in 1923 came the last coach to be bought. This brought an innovation to the Island, for it was fitted with vacuum brake apparatus though, at that time, no locomotive was so equipped. Further individuality followed: in 1951 Timken roller bearings in the diamond-framed bogies were fitted as an experiment.

So concluded the purchase of new bogie carriages for the IOMR, and it is now necessary to return to 1909 when the first pair of four-wheel bodies was mounted on bogie underframes.

Series F50-F75. By the time the exercise of pairing carriages with numbers prefixed by A-D was completed in 1926, twenty-six 'new' bogie vehicles had been created; they were known as 'The Pairs'. It was not the first intention to treat them all, rather those on good condition would be so involved and the remainder allowed to rot away in traffic in their existing form.

A complete list of paired coaches was compiled before deterioration set in and was published in a former edition as below:

Now	*Originally*	*Frame Date*	*1972 condition*
F50	B7 + B8	1925	333 + 333
F51	B3 + B5	1912	333 + 333
F52	A2 + C2	1912	3/3/3 + 33/3
F53	A5 + B21	1919	1/1/1 + 333
F54	A7 + C10	1923	3/3/3 + 33/G
F55	B2 + C6	1912	333 + 333
F56	A8 + C8	1924	1/1/1 + 333
F57	B16 + B20	1919	333 + 333
F58	B18 + C3	1922	333 + 333
F59	A6 + C4	1920	3/1/1 + 33/3
F60	B13 + B24	1923	333 + 33/3
F61	A10 + C12	1921	3/3/3 + 333
F62	A1 + B1	1926	3/3/3 + 333
F63	B6 + B10	1920	333 + 333
F64	B19 + C1	1912	333 + 33/3
F65	B22 + C7	1910	33/3 + 33/3
F66	B11 + B15	1920	333 + 333
P67	B23 + C14	1922	33/3 + 333
F68	A9 + C13	1909	3/3/3 + 33/3
F69	B4 + B17	1923	333 + 333
F70	B9 + B14	1922	333 + 333
F71	B12 + C5	1911	333 + 33/3
F72	A3 + D2	1926	3/1/1 + 333
F73	A4 + D1	1920	3/3/3 + 3/3/3
F74	A11 + C11	1921	3/3/3 + 333
F75	A12 + C9	1926	3 Saloon + 3 Saloon

A 9 in. space was left between the body ends for maintenance, but this was covered over in the 1930s. All frames had pressed steel bogies; the frames under the A bodies are 34 ft 2in. long, and the remainder a foot shorter. In 1973 F54 still had handbrakes but all C bodies had them removed when mounted; some brake ends retained their end windows and so revealed their origins. There were exceptions: C9 had the brakes removed while C10 retained them.

Reading the surviving correspondence with the makers, confirms that the IOMR's practice was to order an underframe to the exact length of the paired coaches and yet from the first they left this gap between the bodies, creating approximately a 4 in overhang of the body at each end. A disadvantage was immediate; the combined draw and buffing gear consisted of three parts, the drawbar with slotted buffer head, the 'chopper' or hook, and a hinged shackle which could be raised by hand to allow the hook to pass through it when coupling was intended; the shackle would then be allowed to fall and secure the hook in the buffer slot. When the shackle (which was removable - as was the hook) was lifted to the inert or vertical position, it was dropped

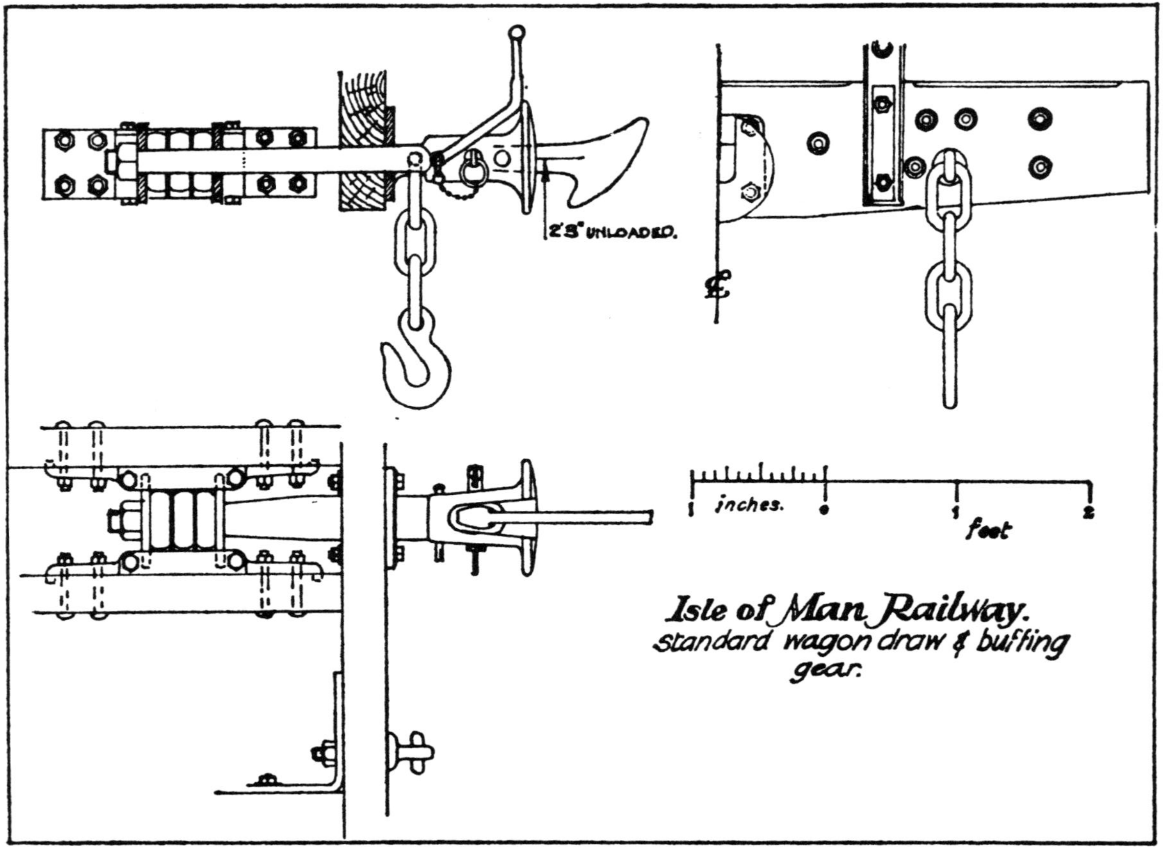
2'3" UNLOADED.
inches.
1
0
1
2
feet
Isle of Man Railway.
standard wagon draw & buffing gear.

by hand or by the concussion of buffer-impact - onto the back of the hook, thus securing the hook in the buffer head. [As a precaution against the hook jumping from the buffer slot by mischance, so dividing the train, side coupling chains were provided.] With the overhang now self-created, it was *impossible* to lift the shackle to a vertical position. In consequence it had to be lifted by hand to allow the hook to pass beneath it; the coupling of coaches by impact cannot be done with the shackle in the dropped position. (See drawing opposite.) This was a distinctive drawback when these pairs were shunted together because they would not automatically couple without human assistance. The drawing also shows the knobbed 'handle' on the free end of the shackle, standing upright ; by removing the hinge-pin of the shackle it can be turned over to the alternative dropped position, where it certain traffic situations it is sometimes preferred - in such position the handle lies horizontally and, as just described, the shackle was obliged to remain in this position on the pairs.

(Although the past tense is used in the above, these couplings are, and remain, the standard pattern on the IOMR.)

After retaining their original numbers until 1927, from then until 1934 they were renumbered into the F series but could be identified as their old numbers were painted in small figures, low on the ends . . . this was not carried out methodically, and ceased with the Second War.

In 1941 the bodies off F60 were removed and stored, open wagons M19-20 took their place only to have the position reversed in 1944. Certain of A type which still had low compartment divisions, had them built up to full height and in B22-24 one compartment was partitioned completely, probably for smokers.

During the Second War rakes of pairs were used for military, workmen and aliens; a complete rake might be stored at Peel for school use. In peacetime complete trains of pairs were uncommon except at Tynwald and other days when every available piece of stock was turned out. They were used in ones or twos to strengthen a regular rake in high season.

The Company kept a close watch on the old frames from these conversions and a regular, complete record was kept by the Locomotive Superintendent. Whether such a 'history' was essential or not, it was in the manner of those times when clerical labour was plentiful and cheap. It enabled management to check the after-life of the chassis when removed from either coaches or E vans.

Some extracts from Vaughan's 'Statement' of 8th February, 1941 are of interest:

Year	*Orig. No.*	*New No.*	*Remarks*
1909	E6	-	Frame broken; body to Sulby Bridge as Goods Shed.
1909	A9 + C13		Fish Wagons Nos. 1 & 2.
1910	E10	-	(ex-MNR) Frame broken; body to Douglas as PW Hut.
1910	E4	-	Fish Wagon No.3. Frame broken; body to Peel Rd. as Goods Shed, April 1910.
1912	B12	K13	Conv. to van for carrying sheep (only) 1924 and given No. K13a. Scrap 1927.
1912	B3 + B5	K15 & K16	K15 broken up after Foxdale accident 24 January, 1918; replaced by B16 frame, wagon H46.
1914	A2 + C2	-	Fish Wagons Nos. 4 & 5.
1919	E8	(Crane Runner)	(ex-MNR) Body to Colby as Goods Shed.
1921	E3	G19	(E3 old body scrap).
1921	B6	K2	(K2 old body scrap). Frame under wagon M55 in 1921.
1921	K2 old frame	H41	Conv. to H41 September, 1923. Running as M55 1921-24, as M61 1924-25, as M67 June-Sept. 1925.
1924	E7	K5	(ex-MNR) (K5 old wagon scrap). Body to Sulby Bridge as Goods Shed.*
1924	E2	-	Old frame scrap; body to Santon as Goods Shed.
1925	E4 (ex-E1)	-	Rebuilt as Breakdown Van (not included in Stock Returns).
1926	A12	-	Frame used for small travelling crane, 1926.

These extracts show evidence of the husbandry practiced by the IOMR: the extensive information given - and not all reproduced - gives insight into the condition of a vehicle which does not conform to a series (or) to which, by its running number, it should relate; the open wagon carrying No. H41 (*above*) is an example.

(Pre-fixes H, K, M were those applied to goods stock; see p. 265 -on)

Shipment

Shipment of carriages seems to have been at the discretion of the supplier; Brown, Marshalls erected the bodies at their Works, dismantled them for shipment and re-erected them with their own men on IOMR Douglas premises. Metropolitan appear always to ship the bodies entire on the frames, with bogies and undergear separately. Though there is evidence for transport from ship to station, it is lacking elsewhere.

F Series: Developments 1967-1973

Remarkably, the whole series was nominally intact at least as far as the Stock Returns were concerned, though this did not imply the condition was

*Note that E6 had previously gone to Sulby Bridge as Goods Shed.

good or a coach was in service. On entering his lease from the IOMR, Ailsa (or his henchmen), without legal entitlement, took it upon himself to upset the status quo.

In 1967 all bogie vehicles were painted in post-war red and cream except for fourteen carriages which still lingered on in all-brown - a set of coaches for school use being among them. A brighter shade of red had been applied to F45-F46 just prior to 1965. Taking matters into his own hands, in the same year Ailsa took the paired saloons F75 and removed the seats and luggage racks from their inner ends and cut a connection between them. (In the 1990s it might be hoped that such treatment would not be applied to items so notable in Manx history). Then, taking out the tables it was made ready to convey Ailsa and official party for the re-opening on 3rd June, 1967.

Ailsa's ill-judged container scheme (Vol. II p.167) of October 1967 required twelve bogie flat wagons which were obtained by de-mounting former four-wheeled bodies from their frames; eleven frames carried bodies which were still in all-brown paint. So discarded, the bodies were dumped on the lineside at Castletown and St John's where they did nothing to enhance the image of the new operators.

The following year F39 'The Foxdale Coach' was stripped completely and converted into a Camping Coach for Ailsa's personal use, giving it the dubious distinction of being the first coach on the Island to have toilet and cooking facilities. Some doors were blanked off and it was painted in blue and yellow, (with grey roof).*

F8 was scrapped in 1970, still painted all-brown and there survived in 1973: F1-7/9-50/54/57/62-8/70/71/73-5 of which F27 was in all-over red, F28 in brown and F45-6 had reverted to cream and red, as were all the remainder. It was noted that year that 'It is unlikely all the coaches will run again and some are part-derelict' and two decades later, this has proved to be largely the case, though underframes still find usefulness as departmental vehicles.

Of the saloons, in 1972 F35-6 were restored to superb condition for the Royal Train and other saloons were taken in hand (year-by-year developments on all stock 1974-1993 are described in Vol. II). The IOMR Supporters' Association planned to build a saloon-type body on one of the redundant underframes but the idea was not carried out; Sheard, in his phase of consideration for new stock after World War II, referred to the irony of having the oldest (four-wheeled) bodies mounted on the newest running gear, but his enquiry of Metropolitan in 1946 for designs of new bodies met with a cool reply and nothing eventuated. Metropolitan, basking in a glut of post-war orders from mainline companies, could afford the luxury of choosing their customers.

Three of the discarded 'pairs' bodies which lay at St John's in 1968 were

*These were Ailsa's family colours.

sold; A8 and B18 went to J. Walton's Steam Centre at Kirk Michael, and B24 to John Allen in Foxdale. The next year B4 and B17 were scrapped at Castletown.

Sheard was not alone in dreaming-up carriage design. In January 1880 Hunt had had drawings prepared for a convertible 'Combined 2 Class Bogey Carriage & Platform Wagon' of Brown, Marshalls outline. The body was detachable, had six compartments and was 8 ft wide over footboards; as a wagon the width was 9 ft. In either form the length was 35 ft with 4 ft 6 in. bogies at 25 ft 8 in. centres. But it was only a dream.

Manx Northern Railway: *Six-wheeled Stock*

An introduction to this subject has been made in Vol. I p.117-8 (footnote). At first the Company intended to buy thirty vehicles in all, but prudence prevailed and sixteen were ordered. Tenders were sought in December 1878 from Swansea Wagon Co. Ltd., Brown, Marshalls, Ashbury, Birmingham Railway Carriage & Wagon Co. Ltd., and Bristol Wagon & Carriage Works Co. Ltd. resulting in an order being placed with the Swansea Wagon Co. Ltd. for 14 six-wheeled carriages, viz.:

Nos. 1 & 2	First Class
Nos. 5-14	Second Class 'two with breaks and eight without breaks'
Nos. 3 & 4	First & Second Class 'to carry an iron plate stating owner. Not to be assigned or underlet'.

The yearly rent was to be £123 4*s*. 2*d*., £482. 17*s*. 0*d*. and £112 2*s*. 2*d*. respectively. A Hire-Purchase Agreement with the builders was arranged, the MNR to pay £359 1*s*. 8*d*. (included was £82 10*s*. 3*d*. interest) on a six-monthly basis, and Swansea assigned it to Isaac Jenks, Ironmaster of Wolverhampton on 10th December, 1879. The plates referred to were to carry Jenks name until the contract ended on 31st December, 1885 when they were to be removed and the MNR would then have the option to buy the stock for 20*s*. each.

The coaches were an improvement on the four-wheeled stock which had been supplied to the IOMR six years previously and there were several features in which they bore likeness to the six-wheeled vehicles of the North Wales Narrow Gauge Railways, which just pre-dated them. James Cleminson's Patent Flexible Wheelbase was adopted (as used on the NWNGR, Southwold, Donegal, and other narrow gauge systems).

It is difficult to see why the Cleminson system* was adopted as it was mainly intended for railways with sharp curvature - a feature which the MNR avoided. However, the system was extremely popular at this period

*A Patent granted to James Cleminson under Class 103, one of eight, in particular No. 3029 of 1876 relating to 'Axle Trucks and Undercarriages' and No. 370 of 1883 (similarly). [Abridged Patent in Manchester Central Reference Library; full Patent in Leeds Patent Information Unit, Leeds. LS9 8TD]

and had received considerable exposure in the technical press. Probably either the Directors or Thomas, the Engineer had been influenced. The principle involved three sets of wheels on axles and truck-gear with the centre set mounted in slides to give considerable lateral movement; the outer sets were connected to the central set by radius links and, being pivoted, the whole assembly took up a curve position when necessary. The cost of such assembly was less than the alternative of two bogies; moreover the carriage frames did not require the lateral strength of a bogie vehicle.*

The coaches were 30 ft long, economically built, square-bodied, with square-cornered windows except in the First Class where the upper corners were rounded. The axle centres were set 12 ft apart. Frames were oak, the solebars having ¼ in. iron plates to face them, flush with the sides and two tie-rods passed centrally through the length of the frame. Sagging frames, so common on IOMR bogie coaches, were non-existent. There were individual steps below each door and a full-length footboard below.

Delivery was made direct to Ramsey in summer 1879 and defects in the teak panelling due to insufficient varnishing were soon apparent. Furthermore, the couplings prescribed by Thomas were unsatisfactory and required urgent modification which was done by the IOMR in October 1879: the wheel tyre profile was blamed for a derailment of the 'through carriage' at Union Mills on 8th July 1882, the first of occasions resulting in the temporary banning of MNR six-wheeled stock from the IOMR (see Vol. I p.145). There was added trouble with wheels, separate types having to be fitted to various classes of vehicle; hot axleboxes remained a constant liability.

The Third Class were designed to hold 60 seated passengers; the ride might have been better but the IOMR provided more room! They were accommodated in six compartments, with each pair of compartments having full-height partitions. Brake gear and lighting are considered later.

On merging with the IOMR the Cleminson coaches became F40-51 but when the IOMR bought further bogie coaches in 1907-8, they were renumbered N40-51. The IOMR treated them as stand-by vehicles, of lesser calibre than the converted pairs; they would run into Douglas but appearance on the South Line is unconfirmed. From the middle 1930s with their number increasing latterly, most of them slumbered in a cocoon of boscage behind the St John's carriage shed, where they were sought out by the informed.

No. 1/N40. This all-First Class coach had three separate compartments with a door to each. In each, seating was around sides and ends surrounding an Ottoman-type central seat, so resembling a miniature saloon and holding fourteen persons (two being on the Ottoman), with but little leg-room. By 1889 the central seat had been removed, leaving a large empty space. Further

*The Author has experienced the riding of many six-wheeled carriages in general and of several having the Cleminson Patent in particular. Overall the motion is smoother and on the IOMR was superior to bogie stock.

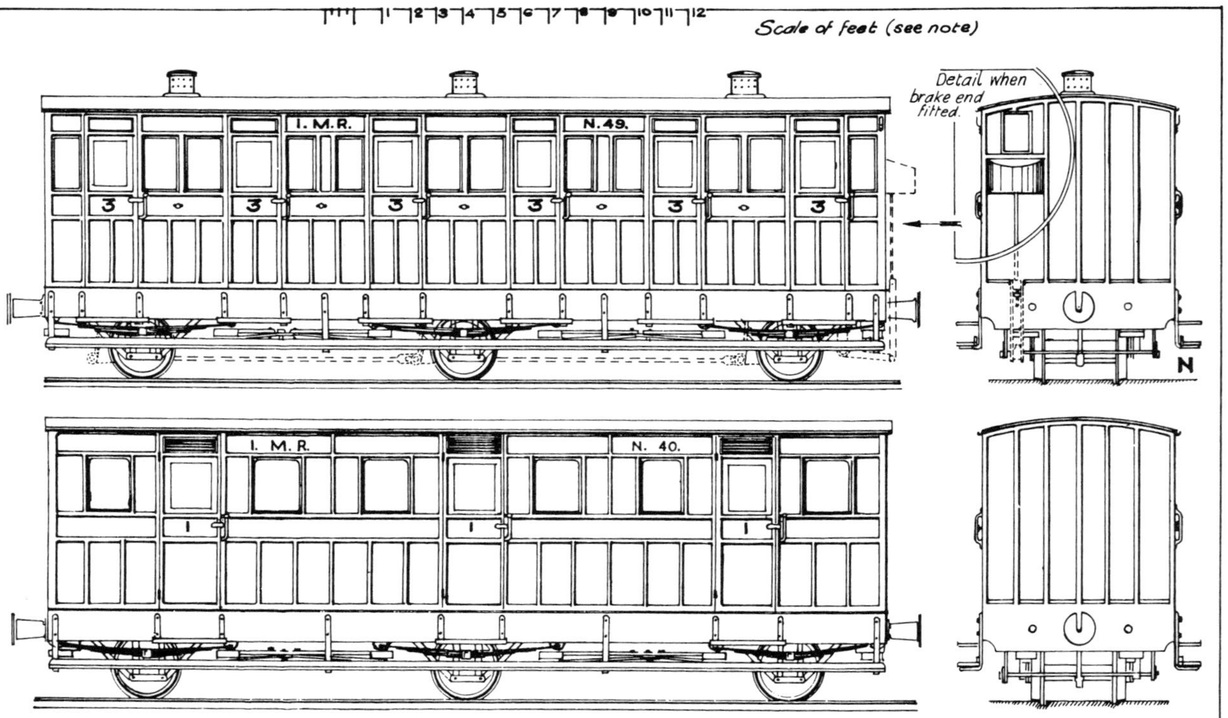

Manx Northern Railway. 6-wheel "Cleminson" coaches by Swansea Wagon Co. Ltd.. Note that the dimensions of the 'All-first' (lower) are in some degree approximate, being from sketches and photographs, not Official Drawings.

alteration in the seating reduced the total capacity to twenty-four people. Seats, upholstered to waist-level, were in brown moquette; doors were padded and the ceiling of near-compulsory Lincrusta. Interior panelling was of polished sycamore, beaded in black and gold. Beneath the luggage racks were photographs of scenes served by the MNR. Each compartment had a single oil lamp.

First class travel being much reduced, the coach was down-graded to Third in 1922 but retained its furnishings; in this guise its unusual interior did not attract much custom. It was sold to P.J. Rampton and shipped to England after the closure of the Peel and Ramsey Lines.

No. 2/N41. Identical to No. 1 , this coach was relieved of its First Class status in 1903 due to delivery in late summer 1899 of the bogie composite coaches. This time, all superior furnishing was removed, the outer doors were blanked off and with central doors only, it accommodated Third Class passengers on side seating in two unequally-sized compartments. Inside the door was a divider containing a door which led to the smaller. The 'social atmosphere' of the conversion was popular with butchers who travelled to Ramsey Mart on Mondays but after redundancy, it joined fellow stock at St John's. In 1964, with undergear removed, it became the replacement for a Cleminson body and now does duty as the Messroom outside Douglas Works.

Nos. 3 & 4/N42-3. These were composite coaches arranged 3/1/1/3 (ordered as Second Class but delivered as Third - this change applying to all passenger stock). There forty-eight seats, twenty-eight of them First; in 1880 brakes were added to both coaches, for as built, they had none; Swansea supplied the gear for £18 each. The interior arrangement was curious, being two commodious First Class and two trifling Third; to house the guard and brake gear one Third compartment was given over and the brake housed in a semi-circular projection at the rear, much as was done on the IOMR. Parcels and luggage were scarcely encouraged therein. A narrow vertical window was added in the end panels to give the guard more vision. Whilst the interior finish in the Firsts was similar to Nos. 1 & 2, the Third and Guard was puritan, (grained and scumbled), the latter being fitted with letter pigeon-hole rack.

Close inspection of the windows shows that First and Third Class compartments had their specific type.

N42 was little altered but latterly, with Ottoman and side seats stripped out, the First Class became Third almost by default, there being no attempt to keep anyone from using it. Stored *inside* St John's Carriage Shed when out of use, it was sold for scrap and then reprieved. Its fair condition was such that it became an exhibit at the Railway Museum, Port Erin in 1976 - to the credit of the IOMSRSA who financed the arrangement.

N43 became all Third in 1914 and was one of the last Cleminsons to be withdrawn. It was one of several coaches put to the torch in 1975. By 1925 it was in the regular Ramsey Mart train and acquired the nickname, 'The Butchers' Coach'.

Nos. 5-14/N44-51. This was the basic series of Third Class six-compartment vehicles; the end compartments were 4 ft 9 in. wide but the inner 4 ft 11 in. N44-5 differed from the remainder being braked and arranged G/3/33/33, there being full-height partitions for a pair of compartments and between Guard and Third. No. 5 became all-Third in 1899 when the guard's compartment reverted to Third when the brakes were removed, but No. 6 remained as supplied. (One account states that No. 5's guard's compartment was not re-designated until IOMR take-over; certainly - for reasons not revealed - the coach had full-height partitions between each compartment until 1932 , apparently the only one so treated and possibly the 1881 conversion took this form. In 1932 these partitions were taken out.) The standard arrangement of the others when delivery was taken was 33/33/33.

N46 was one of the few Cleminsons in use until the 1940s and, in case of special need, the 1950s. For instance on Tynwald Day 1950, N45, 48, 51 with N46 available, were noted. It was noted as derelict in 1968 and burned in 1975.

MNR No. 8 was not allocated a IOMR number as it was severely damaged in the accident at Douglas on 20th July, 1905 when an incoming train struck the stops; it was the body which was used as an Oil Store at Ramsey station for some years. One compartment had been converted to a guard's brake. It was formally removed from the stock records on 27th December, 1905.

N47 (No. 9) was also burned in 1975; the interior was compartmented to 3/3/3/3/3/3 in 1881 and some partitions were later removed thus creating 33/3/3/33. Evidence of these changes could be seen in the fenestration and the shared lamps in the ceiling. There is reason to believe MNR Nos. 5,6,11

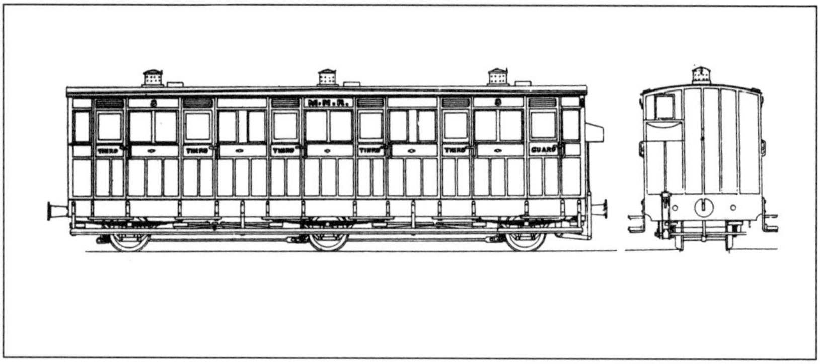

MNR original 6-wheeled carriage with guard's compartment. *Ian Macnab*

and two others also experienced this compartmenting, but were changed back again to 33/3/3/33.

N48, which was partially scrapped before 1965, retained its original interior. After standing at Douglas during Ailsa's time, what remained of the body was fired in 1975.

N49 (mentioned under N47) was among the derelicts at St John's and perished in the burning of 1975.

MNR No. 12 was not given a IOMR number. The original composite-construction wheels were often the reason for collapse, and a centre one on this coach failed on a train between Union Mills and Crosby on 4th October, 1904 to the extent of the coach being withdrawn in December following, the body being used as the Mess Room at Douglas until 1964, when it was replaced by N42 (see previously). [It was a coincidence that No. 6 also suffered a similar mishap on the same stretch of line but in the converse direction on 11th July, 1903; little wonder the IOMR distrusted these vehicles.]

N50-N51 ended their days with unchanged interiors. They too were ultimately to be found abandoned behind St John's station from which the former went to the torch in 1975 but the latter was sold to P.J. Rampton.

General Notes

Official loading for the six-wheeled stock was:

First Class 3-compartment (14 per compartment) = 42
Third Class 6-compartment (10 per compartment) = 60
Composite 4-compartment (20 First+ 40 Third) = 60

General dimensions were; Length 30 ft; width 6 ft 9 in.; rail to centre-line roof 9 ft 6 in.; wheelbase 24 ft; wheel diameter 2 ft 3 in. The 1898 Stock Returns quote two First, three Composite and only ten Third - possibly a clerical error. Three Cleminsons remain *in toto,* being the two sold to England and N45, sold to private ownership in the Island.

The fire in St John's Carriage Shed on 10th December, 1975 accounted for extensive damage to those therein awaiting scrapping, and the remains were deliberately burned afterwards.

The coaches with a guard's compartment had this feature at the Ramsey end. Axleboxes had the date of build on the lid, and lampbrackets were fixed to the end corner posts instead of the usual position, low on the carriage end. There was no heating in the Thirds, but by 1890 the Firsts had been given footwarmers which 'were not transferable'; it is recalled that this injunction was honoured in the breach. Nos. 3 & 4 were regular Through Coaches after they had brakes fitted.

MNR Nos. 15 & 16 were four-wheeled brake vans and it is more convenient to describe these later (see p. 258/260). The number 16 was also carried by one of the MNR's bogie carriages, details of which follow.

Manx Northern Railway: *Bogie Stock*

Nos. 16 & 17 were the only bogie coaches possessed by the Company, (but read on regarding the status of an earlier No. 17 used on the Foxdale Railway). They were given IOMR numbers F37 - 38 so following in sequence the Brake/Thirds and saloons delivered in 1905. They were the first in the Island to have steel frames; built by Hurst, Nelson & Co. Ltd. of Motherwell, delivery was made in early 1900. Lighted by electricity on Stone's system, they were the earliest thus fitted on the steam railways. F37 had a small guard's compartment at one end, followed by 3/1/1/3/3, each compartment being fully partitioned. F33, though outwardly the same, had a Third instead of the guard's compartment. Maker's plates were found on the solebars and on the roof member of First class compartments the builders were stated in small ivorine plaques.

Bodies were 35 ft 6 in. long, 7 ft 0¾ in. wide and 8 ft 0½ in. under buffer beams to centre-line of the roof. Like IOMR bogies, these had a 4 ft 6 in. wheelbase, spaced at 26 ft centres. Upholstery was lavish, and latterly in 'Dunlopillo', and pictures stressed the beauty of the Island's north. Their purpose was as Through Coaches and they were excellent ambassadors for the MNR when seen in Douglas alongside IOMR stock. On noting the presence of either coach in a train, travel in a First compartment was a requisite!

To denote their role in life roofboards were supplied bearing 'DOUGLAS & RAMSEY', but there is reason to believe they were not carried for long. There were end-windows to the guard's compartment and extra hinged seats if required therein, also double luggage doors. The interiors were: First - maple panels with mahogany mouldings and Lincrusta ceiling: seats dark blue with folding arms rests, and floor covering to match; Third - multi-colour seat covers with light brown panelling and white ceiling. Both classes had seat racks, pictorial embellishment and vanity mirrors. The carriages came too close to the Douglas platforms when these were given extra overhang, and the bodies had to be raised so the footboards did not strike them.

Detail alterations and differences were apparent later when the original lighting was changed/removed; problems occurred as most IOMR stock was

Plate 122: The old MNR-owned six-wheeled stock was hidden behind the St John's carriage shed in September 1962. *H.D. Bowtell*

Plate 123: As explained in Volume I, the maker's plates on the early MNR stock were misleading. The axlebox cover with '1879' is over the centre wheel set which gave lateral movement to Cleminson's Patent flexible chassis. June 1957. *J.I.C. Boyd*

Plate 124: Purple lake, gold-lined. with gold lettering (shaded scarlet) and carrying the coat of arms, was applied to early bogie carriages and continued in use until the Second War. *J.I.C. Boyd Collection*

Plate 125: N42 (ex-MNR No. 3) has survived and is now in the Railway Museum, Port Erin. St John's. April 1960. *J.I.C. Boyd*

Plate 126: N49 (ex-MNR No. 11) was one of several similar vehicles whose interior was changed twice but was always an all-Third. St John's, July 1933. *H.C. Casserley*

Plate 127: N42 (ex-MNR No. 3) and N50 (ex-MNR No. 13) [nearer camera] were well-kept and regularly in use in August 1947, most recently for the visit of a circus . . . evidence of the elephant is clearly to be seen. St John's. *J.I.C. Boyd*

Plate 128: N50 has deteriorated since the previous plate. St John's. April 1960. *J.I.C. Boyd*

Plate 129: Further use as an Enginemen's Messroom was found for ex-MNR No. 12 outside Douglas engine shed. The date is May 1961 but later, owing to its poor condition, it was replaced by ex-MNR No. 2 (F41) in 1964. *J.I.C. Boyd*

Plate 130: Not a confusing jumble of timber and metalwork, but the complete Cleminson assembly from under ex-MNR coach No. 2. April 1966. *J.I.C. Boyd*

Plate 131 & 132: Builder's photographs of the two handsome bogie carriages built for the MNR in 1899. *Hurst, Nelson & Co. Ltd., Motherwell*

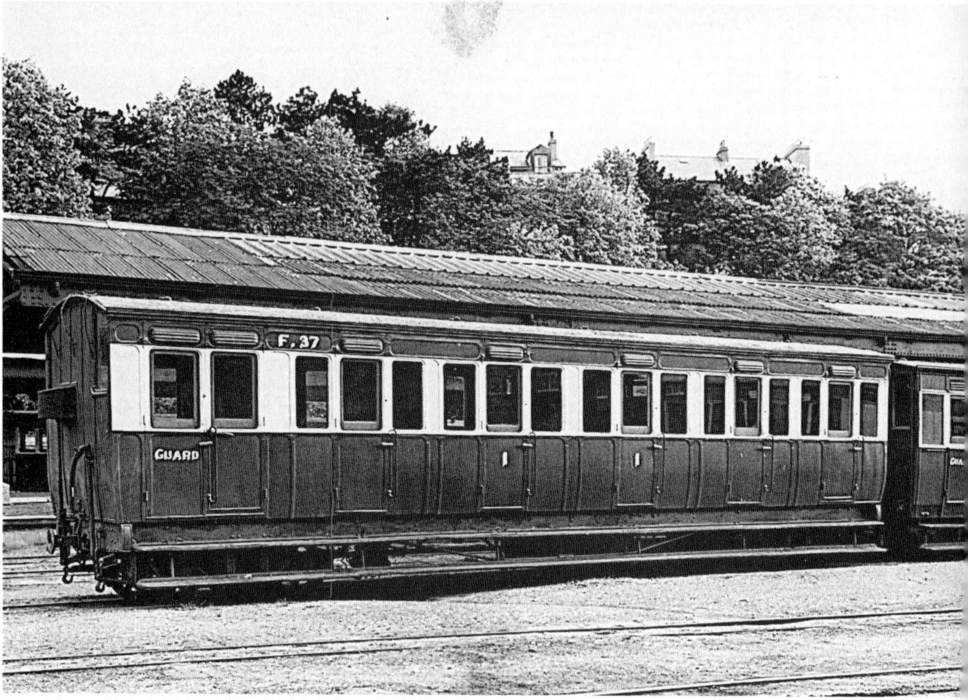

Plates 133 &134: The MNR Hurst, Nelson-built coaches became F37 and F38 on the IOMR, differing from each other only in the small guard's compartment of F37. They had steel-frames and electric lighting. Douglas. May 1961 and July 1960. *(both) J.I.C. Boyd*

Plate 135: F37 & F38 were usually to be found running on their native metals, the North Line. The comfort of the First Class compartments, and the quiet smooth ride, made them a favourite. On this occasion, J.D. Darby, Mrs Boyd and the author were travelling to Ramsey . . . and certain of us were to take lunch with the IOMR Chairman there. 9th July, 1959. *J.I.C. Boyd*

Plate 136: Until comparatively recent times, to travel in 'The Foxdale Coach' was a rare experience, as for many years it stood motionless like a waxwork's exhibit, at St John's (as here, in August 1947). Today, many find its short wheelbase gives the nicest ride on the South Line. *J.I.C. Boyd*

Plate 137: M5 is an early drop-side wagon (Ashbury 1885) carrying the spare workshop boiler. The single wheel brake with wooden brake block is evident. 1932. *C.E. Box*

Plate 138: Mr40, an ex-MNR drop-side open, fitted with a small crane for use at Peel. The jib could not be lowered for travelling. Note the loaded sacks of stones as a counterbalance. *J.I.C. Boyd Collection*

Plate 139: M45 is one of the 1911 drop-side wagons with axleboxes outside the W irons but still retaining the single brake. Decay to the edge of its floor is prominent. It was scrapped in 1971. Douglas. March 1962. *J.I.C. Boyd*

Plate 140: M55 was the first of a further batch of Improved M type wagons delivered in 1924; they had V-hanger two-wheeled brake gear on one side only. *Metropolitan CW&F Co. Ltd.*

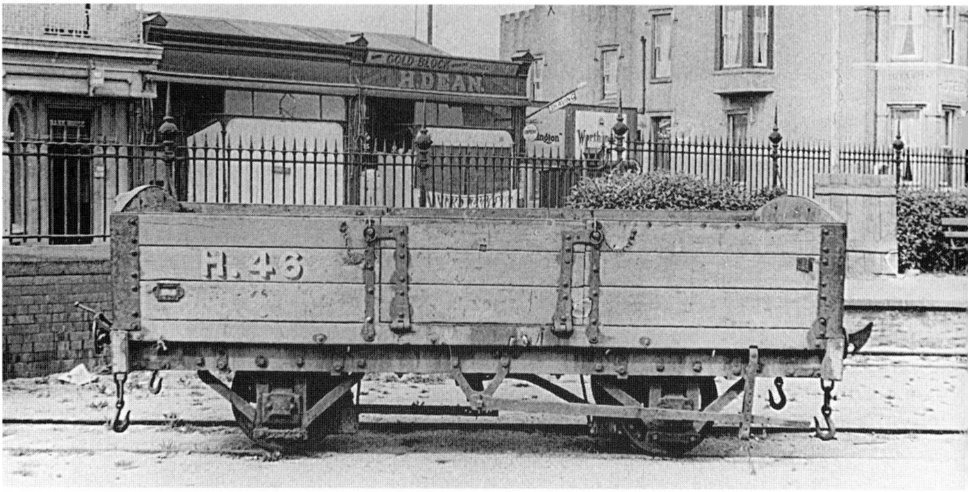

Plate 141: H46 was built in Douglas using-parts of K15 cattle van which was destroyed in an accident at Foxdale in January 1918. It is probably the only example with this brake gear. Port Erin. *c*. 1936. *C.E. Box*

Plate 142: The empty oil tank wagons built from the chassis of M61, M66 and M71 appear to be on trials as they leave St John's behind a passenger train for Douglas. August 1968. *J.I.C. Boyd*

Plate 143: Fish Wagons were built at Douglas using the underframes of four-wheel coaches; this one was due for scrapping. June 1972. *J.I.C. Boyd*

Plate 144: Stabled at the end of Douglas goods yard is the 8 ton Gibbins crane, a runner built from carriage frames at each end; some shunting will be needed if it is required in a hurry! August 1947. *J.I.C. Boyd*

Plate 145: Not all the four-wheeled carriage underframes were separated; this pair at St John's in March 1962 is still close-coupled and the nearer vehicle has had one Mansell wheel set replaced by a set with spoked wagon wheels. *J.I.C. Boyd*

Plate 146: A one-off covered van was built at Douglas in 1897 as G7, using parts from the smashed E1 van. It was seen by the author at Port St Mary in August 1935, using his first camera! *J.I.C. Boyd*

Plate 147: Vans carried on coach underframes survived the longest. The nearer is G16; the cattle van carries K13; this is 'New' K13 of 1924/1949. Douglas. March 1962. *J.I.C. Boyd*

late 148: Condemned K25 of 1923, with a amaged end; the picture clarifies the ıethod of 'mating' the old and new omponents. April 1960. *J.I.C. Boyd*

late 149: 5 ton 'Crane No. 1' as mounted n the frame of coach A12 in 1926 with ıatch truck from A3, and used as a yard :ane in Castletown. 1936. *C.E. Box*

Plate 150: David McDowall, Manager of the MNR, leans against MNR open wagon No. 12 (built Swansea Wagon Co. 1879), a brakeless vehicle constructed for the Foxdale mines' trade. Ramsey yard. *c.* 1899. See also *Plate 116*. *Gloucester Wagon Co.*

Plate 151: A 'standard covered van' of the MNR, formerly their No. 15 now IOMR G12, at Castletown. *c.* 1935. *J.I.C. Boyd Collection*

Plate 152: The landscape to the west of Foxdale once included much evidence of the mining era, notably in the form of chimneys, engine-houses, water-wheels and spoil tips. Its bleak situation is typified by the two chimneys of Beckwith's Mine seen from the north-east. August 1968.
J.I.C. Boyd

Plate 153: A closer view of Beckwith's engine-house. Since the Second War this area has lost much of its interest as an industrial site but it is as deserving a place in the history of the Island's railways as any number of visitors seeking sun, sand, and sea. *J.I.C. Boyd*

Plate 154: The location of this station is not known, but the date given is 1889. Father discards coat and umbrella to weigh himself, while Mother waits with coin in hand and daughter seeks one for herself. *Frank Quayle Collection*

Plates 155 & 156: Director's gold Pass, IOMR. *National Railway Museum*

then 24 volts whereas F37, at that time, had only the Stone 16 volts equipment. Neither was fitted with vacuum brakes but had through pipes: F37 was given the luxury of steam heating for the unusual reason that it was used throughout the year to keep its batteries fully charged.

Although in traffic up to the Ailsa Era, both were in limbo at St John's when the sale of stock took place in 1974. Providentially, these fine vehicles were among others sold to P.J. Rampton and found their way to England.

No. 17, (later No. 15, later IOMR F39). Nicknamed by the staff, 'Kitto's Coach' or subsequently 'The Foxdale Coach' when the name Kitto was no longer appropriate, this was the smallest bogie coach on the steam railways and was specially supplied through the agency of the MNR for service on the Foxdale Railway, on which it was the sole passenger vehicle. In the memory of the living, it stood alone in a siding at St John's long after Foxdale passenger services were suspended near the start of World War II, as if waiting for the re-opening. 'That is The Foxdale Coach' would be the reply of the Station Master, pointing appropriately, and pained as if such ignorance of its important origins still existed.

Late in 1885 the MNR and A.S. Nelson Co. had considered a suitable vehicle with adequate braking power for the Branch, having discarded the project of modifying the braking system of a Cleminson. Nelson could supply two composite + guard for £347 10*s.* 0*d.* Tenders were sought from Ashbury, Brown, Marshalls and Metropolitan but Nelson obtained the order for but one vehicle . . . It contained the proviso that an arrangement of spiral and laminated springs conceived by John Crawford of A.S. Nelson should be incorporated in the special bogie designed for this vehicle, apparently against Cameron's better judgement. (These bogies still survive under the coach in everyday service during 1995. It is arguably the smoothest-riding coach of all.)

A specification for what was intended to be more than one vehicle was supplied to the potential builders and contains the following:

> The carriages are to be constructed on the American Bogie system . . . underframe and crossbeams of oak . . . Centres of wheels to be Moulmein teak . . . Body to be divided into 5 compartments - 4 for second class passengers & 1 for guard & luggage . . . Lamps 2 roof & 2 side for each carriage . . . Inside to be painted and grained light oak . . . Delivery to quay, Ramsey . . . Re-erection; price includes sending out experienced man to superintend re-erection.
> Glasgow 16th June, 1886.

Building was sub-contracted to the Oldbury Railway Carriage & Wagon Co. Ltd. for delivery to Ramsey in 'late July' 1886 but they failed to meet the date; in October shipment was arranged with the Barrow Steam Navigation Co. Ltd. but consternation ensued when the Barrow ship HERALD steamed

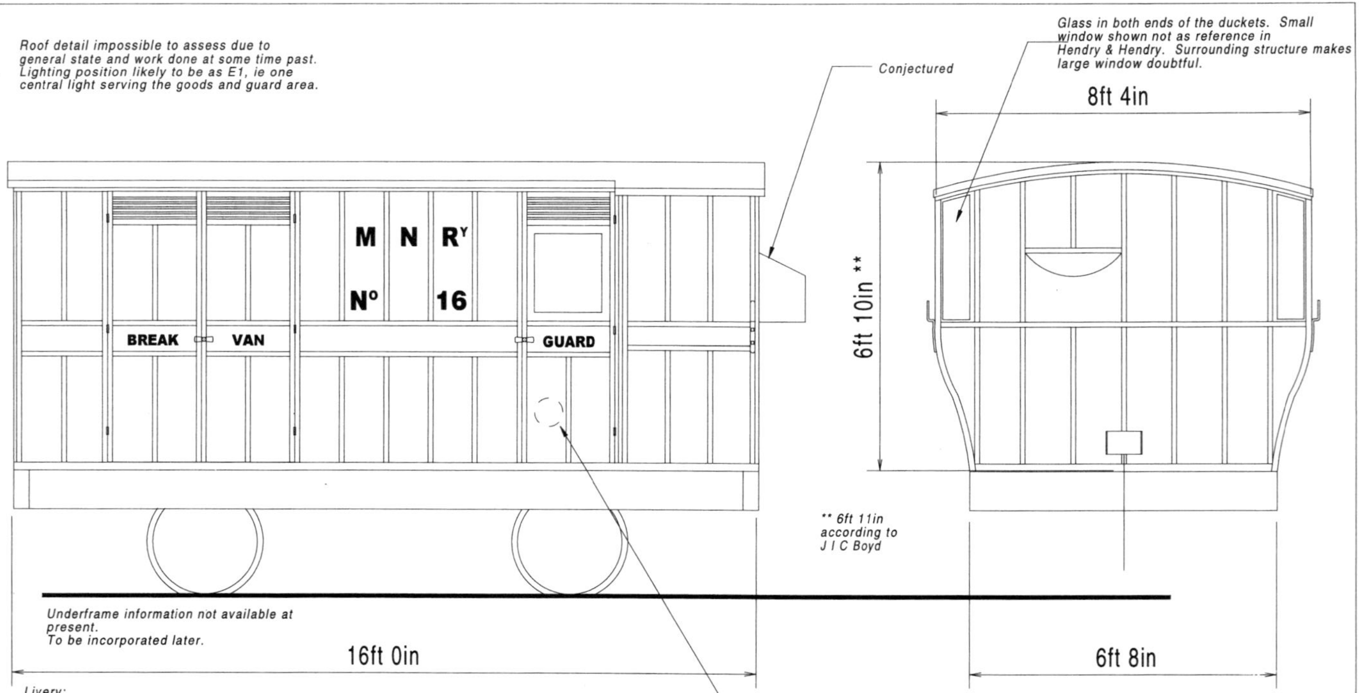

Livery:
The grounded body had obviously been covered with bitumen paint at some time past. Most of this had disappeared and the woodwork had deteriorated. Where the paint remained, when removed the underside of the flakes bore clear evidence of a creamy paint on the upper half of the body and a dark lake colour, almost black, on the lower half. The woodwork underneath was a clean varnished teak.

The lettering and numbers were clearly visible on the South side as patches of bitumen paint left on bare wood. They appear to have all been yellow, shaded red. This colouring was still visible on the South Guard's door. The word 'BREAK' is largely conjectural.

Drawing prepared from dimensions and photographs taken 1965-68.

MNR Brake Van No 16 (later 20, then IMR E10)

IMR 9501

into Douglas instead, leaving the Oldbury representative who had come with the coach, to arrange off-loading etc. and haulage to the station as best he could. Fortunately, the services of an IOMR loco were available to haul it on to St John's, where it reached 'home metals' on 6th November.

The season being well past, storage space in Ramsey carriage shed was found until early Spring. Assigned to the Branch and used most frequently by the Kitto family, Kitto made immediate complaint over the lack of superior accommodation for his family and himself*. A Third compartment was then up-graded to First.

Captain Kitto had a Free Pass over the FR/MNR system and as the provider of the intended mineral traffic, his wish was a command to the MNR.

There was insufficient ready cash so a hire-purchase Agreement dated 24th January, 1887 was arranged with the Bristol & South Wales Railway Waggon Co. Ltd. @ £130 per year for three years; the new owners had suitable plates attached to the solebars.† The internal arrangement was G/<u>33</u>/<u>33</u> but had become G/3/1/<u>33</u>, the First being upholstered in blue fabric and curtained; partitions were panelled and stained darkly above shoulder height. The two Third compartments shared a lamp by means of an opening in the partition. The guard's section had ample luggage space, a ticket rack and large duckets. Electric light was given by robbing F38 of its dynamo and each compartment then had its own lamp. A brake pillar stood inside the guard's compartment, with horizontal handscrew atop but due to indifferent performance as the rodding pushed rather than pulled the brake shoes on, the IOMR cut a hole in its floor whereby sand could be dropped onto the rail so reducing wheel skid.

MNR re-numbered it No. 15 in 1899 to make way for the two new bogie coaches Nos. 16 & 17 (see above) and it became 15R, on the IOMR F39. After the Foxdale service ceased, it found occasional use on the light St John's-Peel workings in Winter. Ailsa claimed it for his own camping coach and gave it the family colours but it became a Mess Coach in 1975, painted red and cream. For the Manx Millenium and the MNR Centenary in 1979, the Government-owned railway rebuilt it in 1978-79, and restored the interior by removing the 'camping aspect'. To emphasise the Centenary, it was given 'No. 15 ' again.

Dimensions were: Length 30 ft. Width 7 ft 2 in. Height sides including solebar 6 ft 7 in. Height to centre-line of roof from under buffer-beam 7 ft 7 in. Bogie centres 17 ft 8 in. apart and wheelbase 4 ft 10 in.

*For Kitto, see Vol. I p. 146.

†It appears there was some difficulty in finding a party who would finance the carriage. There survives a costing for borrowing a principal of £1,200 a 5% interest over five years from 31st December, 1886 with Matthew Baird of Uddingstone, Glasgow and not taken up possibly because terms were more favourable to the MNR elsewhere.

(It is regrettable that only a paucity of MNR records remains on the Island today. Their restoration to the Island in the recently-established Manx Archives would be a happy outcome.)

Manx Northern Railway: *Four-wheeled Brake Vans*

Nos. 15 & 16 (IOMR G7 & E10). As with IOMR practice, the MNR bought two four-wheeled brake vans from Swansea in 1879 which could be used variously, and could be distinguished from their predecessors by the outline of their duckets and that they were covered at cant-rail level by a projection of the roof. There were double windows at the ducket end. Dimensions were 16 ft long, 6 ft 8 in. wide, height from rail to roof 7 ft 10 in., height of side 6 ft 11 in. and with 7 ft 10 in. wheelbase. There were double luggage and single guard's doors.

It is recorded that the wheels were so badly worn in two years and being non-standard, two further wheel-sets were ordered. The rest of their condition cannot have been much better for both were withdrawn in 1895, No. 15 becoming a goods van built at Ramsey the next year: No. 16 was retained but renumbered 20 to avoid the numbers allocated to the new Hurst, Nelson vehicles in 1899. It was given the IOMR number E10 when taken into the IOMR, and a note that it was 'running on goods train' is dated 14th October, 1905. The IOMR list shows three MNR vans carrying Nos. 18, 19, 20, the two foremost having their function unstated. Though E10 was withdrawn in 1908 it was reprieved,worked with the PW train until 1911 and then the body used as a Stores Hut at Douglas, being still recognisable in 1973. The chassis was scrapped in 1915.

Nos. 18 & 19 (IOMR E8 & E9 - later E1). Two similar vans were built at Ramsey in 1895 to replace Nos. 15 & 16, and possibly the ironwork was supplied by Swansea. They differed from IOMR vans in having a brake wheel rotated vertically and required no rearward cowling to project the horizontal brake handle as did the former. E8 became a mobile goods shed at Ballasalla during World War 1 but the body was taken from the chassis in 1917 and removed to Colby for a goods shed in 1921, and where it might still be found in 1973. The chassis was purloined as a match truck for use with the Gibbins crane.

E9 was re-numbered E1 in 1921 and continued its original purpose on its native system, being found additionally on the Peel Line. It was classified as a goods van from 1940 and with duckets and single doors removed, was in continual use all over the system throughout World War II and after, only to travel to Ballasalla along with other vehicles sold for scrap in 1974.

Passenger Carriages Appendix

Carriage Lighting

Oil was used on both IOMR and MNR at first, First Class having individual lamps per compartment and Third having to 'share' a lamp in some instances, with the globe hung over the compartment divider. Electric lighting was first introduced on the MNR in 1899/1900 in the two 'Through Carriages' Nos. 16 & 17. The same Stone equipment was used by the IOMR who, undeterred by the storage out of use of many carriages in winter, converted 76 of them by 1904; by 1911 all prefix-F stock was fitted. (Much of this haste was due to competition from the MER whose stock was naturally thus lighted.) Three exceptions were the Empress Vans, fitted in 1924, and the Foxdale Coach in 1926.

Of the MNR Cleminsons, all were converted but lost it again in 1910-12 as they were stored in winter; some recovered it and ultimately N41/43/48/51 were fitted, the remainder having oil.

Of the IOMR E vans, E3/5/7 received electric light but the others used the original oil lamps until stripped of all lighting.

It became the practice for the IOMR to use rakes of coaches which included certain dynamo-fitted vehicles; owing to the size of dynamo varying, the electric output varied also, and the number of 'slave coaches' which could be accommodated fluctuated. As the train service ran down in the 1950-60 period, maintenance was a low priority and lighting fell into almost total disuse. Ailsa ran late-night trains for a short time, electricity being supplied by car batteries placed in an empty compartment.

The IOMR was slow to take up electric lighting, the usual excuse being that the cost would mar their ability to pay a dividend. Salvation came in the form of the Reserve Fund put aside for the installation of Electric Train Staff which was considered no longer necessary; implementation was carried out with all haste, beginning in 1902.

Racks of obsolete oil lamps could be found in carriage sheds, the biggest being at St John's; makers were Linley (IOMR) of Birmingham and Cowdy (MNR) of London.

Without previous experience, it was essential that the staff be informed on the procedure for electric lighting in carriages and Stowell issued a leaflet on 2nd November, 1925*.

After dark, half lights were to be switched on not more than 15 minutes before departure from a terminal and full lights 5 minutes before the train started. On arrival at the terminal, lights were to be extinguished when all passengers were out of the train.

Extensive warnings were given in the leaflet for connecting dynamo/non-dynamo carriages, with special instructions for F37. Half lights were to used where failure from any cause gave trouble in the train.

*Ref: Manx Museum B.192

Dynamo coaches were to stand no more than three weeks without a run.

Station Masters and Inspectors were given overall charge and a list of coach numbers where special attention should be given was prepared. By and large this new feature must have given the staff some additional sleepless nights.

Vacuum Brakes

Outside mainland jurisdiction, the railways on the Island were not affected by British legislation for instance, as it affected the fitting of continuous brakes on passenger trains. (Regulation of Railways Act, 1889, (52 & 53 Vict. c. 57), Para 1, Section (c).) There had been previous incidents where the fitting of an automatic brake would have been a helpful but the runaway train which hit the buffers at Douglas in July 1925 and involved a fatality, brought matters to the fore. A series of Brake Tests was begun on 25th May, 1927 with SUTHERLAND, 'supplied with Welsh coal', and saloons F29 & 31 (Tare Weight *c.* 23 tons) to Peel and back, 23 miles in all. Driver Dow and Fireman Quinney were on the footplate, together with Inspector Hogg and Bradshaw, the Locomotive Superintendent . . . not much room to swing the shovel. The test was threefold: (a) to assess the coal consumed allowing one minute at each stopping place (b) to compare coal consumed costs with the records of 'Sentinel' locomotive which Bradshaw was to observe running on the Derwent Valley Light Railway the following year, and to relate these to the costs of operating alternative road buses (c) to test the braking characteristics of the train under the control of (1) the engine only and (2) engine and coach brakes together. Of course, no automatic brake was involved and the train was deliberately light so as to simulate a winter working which would compare with road competition.

The results showed a coal consumption of 12.73 lbs. per mile. The outward journey with intermediate stops at Quarter Bridge, Union Mills, Crosby, Ballacurry and St John's took 31 minutes using engine brakes only; the inward with similar stops required 33 minutes using engine and coach brakes. The average speed, start to stop with five intermediate stops, was 21½ mph. The tests results were submitted to the General Manager, but no further documentation is available . . . perhaps the matter was quietly dropped. Certainly the Company was 'let off the hook' as the Inspector's recommendation that automatic brakes be fitted within two years was modified to an 'as soon as possible' basis, the Company having pleaded the stricture was impossible without Government finance - and none was forthcoming from that source. The last bogie coach, delivered in 1926, had vacuum brake on delivery - as did engine No. 16 delivered at the same time;

for a time they were the only fitted vehicles. A few more coaches were tackled in 1932, but then the pace quickened so that by 1940 only seventeen bogie carriages remained unfitted. Work was resumed in 1944 but ceased in 1952 after F4 was done (only to lose the fittings later). F2/27-9/31-2/35/39 were still unfitted in 1973.

All in all, the vacuum brake was not successful, especially with the small-boilered engines which could not make sufficient steam required by the ejectors, with tales of the brakes leaking on as pressure dropped. When steam heating was introduced in 1936, the trouble was compounded; it became a choice of good brakes and cold feet, or vice versa. Some coaches were given a brake cylinder but others were simply given through-piping. No four- or six-wheeled stock was involved.

Cunning was resorted to where technics fell short: in July 1941 for instance, instructions were given to guards of South Line trains that, train make-up being commonly of fitted-piped-fitted-fitted-piped-fitted (being a six-coach set), vacuum was to be created only on the first three vehicles behind the engine between Port Erin and Port Soderick but at the latter place, and for the descent into Douglas, the guard was to connect the brake hoses between the third and fourth carriages, so doubling the braking. This would require a short delay at Port Soderick where, after the hoses had been joined, the driver would have to create a vacuum along the full length of train. By this means the Company could state the train was vacuum fitted and the brake was used while at the same time saving steam (and therefore coal) for much of the journey.

Carriage Heating

Early heating by footwarmers was placed in First Class accommodation only, many a young employee having his initial experience of platform work on this task; all carriages were without any heating until the turn of the century when footwarmers were discarded by mainland companies and the Island railways bought them cheaply. Again, it was competition from the MER which forced the pace of improvement. By 1937, twenty-six F series had received steam heating, even one of these had no heaters but was simply piped, as was a second in 1944. The falling-off of services caused heating, like lighting, to fall into disrepair and there was then sufficient of converted stock to provide a 'pool' to meet reduced requirements.

Engines which were called upon additionally to make enough steam for the vacuum brakes, found yet another call on the boiler to heat the carriages as well to be the proverbial straw which broke the camel's back. Steam heating connections to the locomotive were often 'overlooked' though the carriages themselves might be connected. A nonchalant stroll down the platform to examine the locomotive at the head of the train would often reveal that, with the connivance of the guard, the engine crew had connected neither brake nor heating hoses . . .

The application of heating took the IOMR into a sphere they had not investigated, and it gave Vaughan considerable trouble to find suitable and economic suppliers. British Steam Specialties Ltd., Armstrong, Tarry Ltd., both of of Liverpool and Gelling's Foundry Ltd. of Douglas, received orders.

Locomotives fitted by 17th January, 1939 were:

Nos. 11, 16	in	1936
Nos. 2, 6, 8, 10, 12	in	1937

Carriage fitting was done in 1936-37: No. F58 'The School Coach', was only piped, it being considered that the blood of children did not require further warming.

On a historic note, in 1909 when the IOMR possessed 99 warmers filled on Ancelin's System and the remainder with hot water, they required further warmers of the former type. All mainland companies approached said they made their own water-filled type in their Works. Ultimately, another 100 water-filled warmers were bought @ 4*s*. 6*d*. each from the Maryport & Carlisle Railway which had just converted to steam heating. Another lot was purchased from Derby (London Midland & Scottish Railway) stores in January 1935 for 1*s*. 6*d*. each.

In Bradshaw's time (1925) he opposed purchase of extra warmers, saying the soft water ate into the metal and that passengers did not favour them, pushing them out of the way under the seats. (They were wont to cause chilblains.) He supported his contention with elaborate costings and extra-ordinary records of compartments per train on every day of the week; he showed that the installations to heat water at each termini would cost £40 13*s*. 2*d*. for coal if warmers for each compartment were supplied, an extra man would have to be found to handle them, and an extra boiler at the termini would be needed.*

Lastly, what of today? Santa Claus Trains were run at Christmastide, a favourite time for small railways to provide a seasonable attraction in a low point of the calendar, until 1982: suitable carriage heating was imperative, even though it meant some borrowing and scraping around the Works to find the essential 'bits'. Since that year, heating has been unnecessary.

*These records, other than items described under 'Carriages' which are from materials already in the Author's possession, are taken from the Tower Collection.

Goods Stock

The goods vehicles were divided in a manner similar to the passenger stock, by giving a prefix to the number according to the type of vehicle . . . at least, this was intention but an occasional prefix was placed in the wrong category. The last passenger letter being F, goods series began with G as follows:

G	Covered vans
H	Three-plank sided open wagons
I & J	(not used)
K	Livestock vans used indiscriminately for pigs, sheep, cattle, horses (or). Originally un-roofed.
L	Bolster wagons
M	Two-plank sided open wagons
-	Fish wagons
N, O, P, Q	(not used)
R	Bogie underframes carrying containers
-	Tank wagons (see M series)

There are/were two types of crane, a well wagon, permanent way wagons, and two varieties of four-wheeled chassis ex-original passenger stock, the latter retained for further conversions into goods vehicles.

Series G. Four-wheeled covered goods vans, load 6 tons, tare approximately 3 tons. Basic design Nos. 1-9: length 14 ft 6 in.; width 6 ft 6 in.; height from rail 8 ft 11 in.; wheelbase 8 ft; wheel diameter 2 ft 3 in.; brake fitted.

Metropolitan supplied 1-4 for the opening of the Peel line in 1873. (In fact no extra goods stock was added for the Port Erin opening.) Nos. 5 and 6 came from Ashbury in 1877, having spiral springs along with other wagons when that builder succeeded that year in bringing off an order from the IOMR. No. 7 came from Douglas works in 1897, using parts from the smashed E1 van, as already noted, and Nos. 8 and 9 culminated the series to the original design, coming from Metropolitan in 1899.

The original drawings were for a 'Covered Goods Van capable of being used as a Third Class Carriage' but in fact none was built in exactly this form, all being supplied with plain sides having ventilating 'portholes' (making them suitable to carry livestock) and not as convertibles.

Manx Northern Railway vans (ex-MNR 13-16) were allotted Nos. 10-13 having been built by Swansea in 1879, the basic design being that of the IOMR van. Body size was: length 15 ft 3 in.; width 6 ft 6 in.; and 7 ft 7 in. from under buffing beam to centre line of roof. These dimensions are likely to be approximately common to both periods of these vans' history, for in 1899 Ramsey built four new bodies to the basic style of their No. 17, a new van built by them in 1896 (and then given No. 32). Of the old bodies off 13-16, two were scrapped but two found further use, one at Sulby Bridge as a

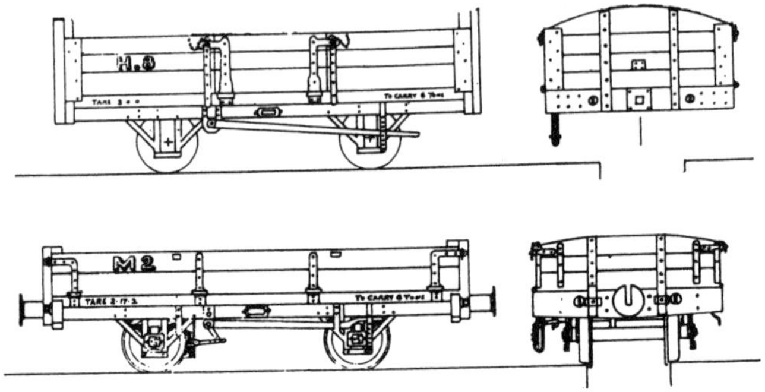

Omnibus of sketches of Manx goods rolling stock. *Ian Macnab*

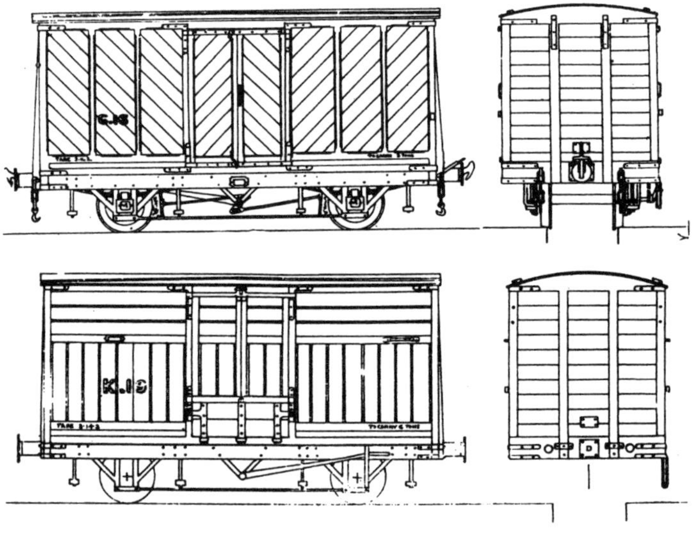

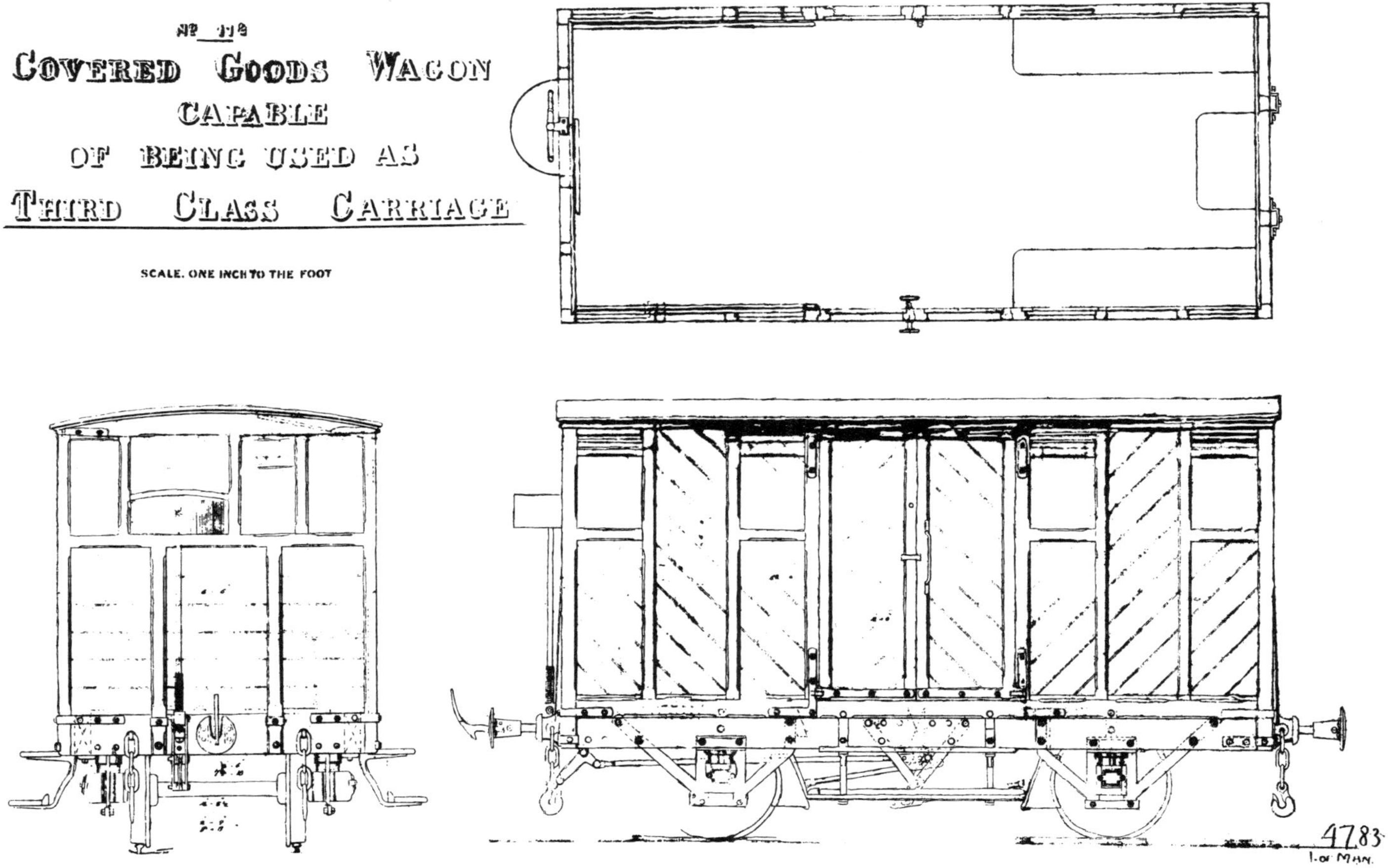

Official drawing of proposed convertible vehicle, 1873.

Metropolitan Carriage & Wagon Co.

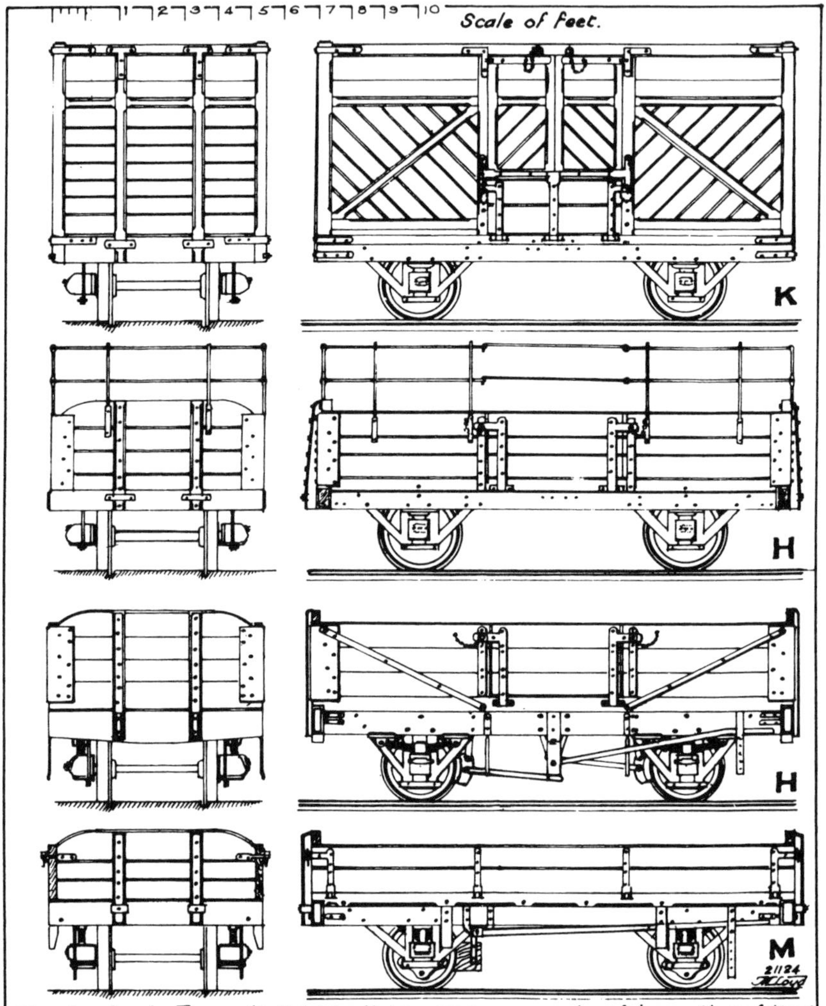

Goods stock: Types K, H & M. Note upper example of type H as fitted when used as temporary passenger vehicle.

Goods Shed until 1909 and the other similarly at Peel Road until 1910. Both sheds were then scrapped (see E Vans' summary). IOMR No. 14 was the new van built as MNR No. 32 above mentioned; it was re-numbered MNR No. 17 in 1899 and was built up on the chassis of passenger brake van MNR No. 15 in 1896.

Nos. 15-19 were built up on ex-four-wheeled coach chassis at Douglas to carry 3 tons and varied in length according to origin. A typical one would measure 16 ft 6 in. long, 6 ft 6 in. wide and be 7 ft 9 in. high. Building dates and original coach numbers were:

15 1915 chassis B19 (at first allocated No. K19).
16 1915 chassis C1 (at first allocated No. K20). Goods Shed at St John's, 1958-65.
17 1916 chassis B22 (converted from bolster L5)
18 1916 chassis C7 (converted from bolster L6)
19 1921 chassis E3

Nos. 5 and 17 were modified in coupling arrangements and piped for vacuum brakes to run between the Donegal railcars in 1964 and 1962 respectively. They were the first goods stock to be piped (or fitted).

All G vans survived but were in derelict condition in 1973.

Series H. Four-wheeled three-plank-sided open wagons, load 6 tons, tare approximately 2¾ tons. Centre dropside doors. Metropolitan's drawings (referring to the makers as 'late J. Wright & Sons') show them to be capable of carrying Third Class passengers if required, for which an iron railing on stanchions could be bolted to the upper sides of the wagon. On the Opening Day they were used for passengers, but whether they did so in ordinary service seems unlikely. The rails were probably to enable them to carry livestock. All but the original batch were delivered with handbrakes and they had rubber blocks instead of laminated springs. Typical dimensions were: length 14 ft 6 in.; width 6 ft 6 in.; height of side from rail 4 ft 10 in.; height of end from rail 5 ft 3 in.; wheelbase 8 ft; wheel diameter 2 ft 3 in. Over the years, handbrakes of varying pattern have been fitted; some have had extensions in slatted wood sides built up to carry livestock, and ultimately the springing was of laminated plates placed behind the W-irons. At an early date it was found that this type of wagon was not so useful as the M series which possessed drop sides for ballast work, and it was not perpetuated, the M series being favoured instead. Nevertheless, Metropolitan prepared a drawing dated 22nd July, 1925 at a suggestion by the IOMR, which was considering adding another twelve wagons to the stock; this is remarkable when it is noted the makers had not supplied this type since 1873.

M type was ordered instead, however.

By 1973 the type was extinct, scrapping taking place: 1925-27 four wagons, 1946-49 six wagons, 1954-58 eight wagons. The remainder went in

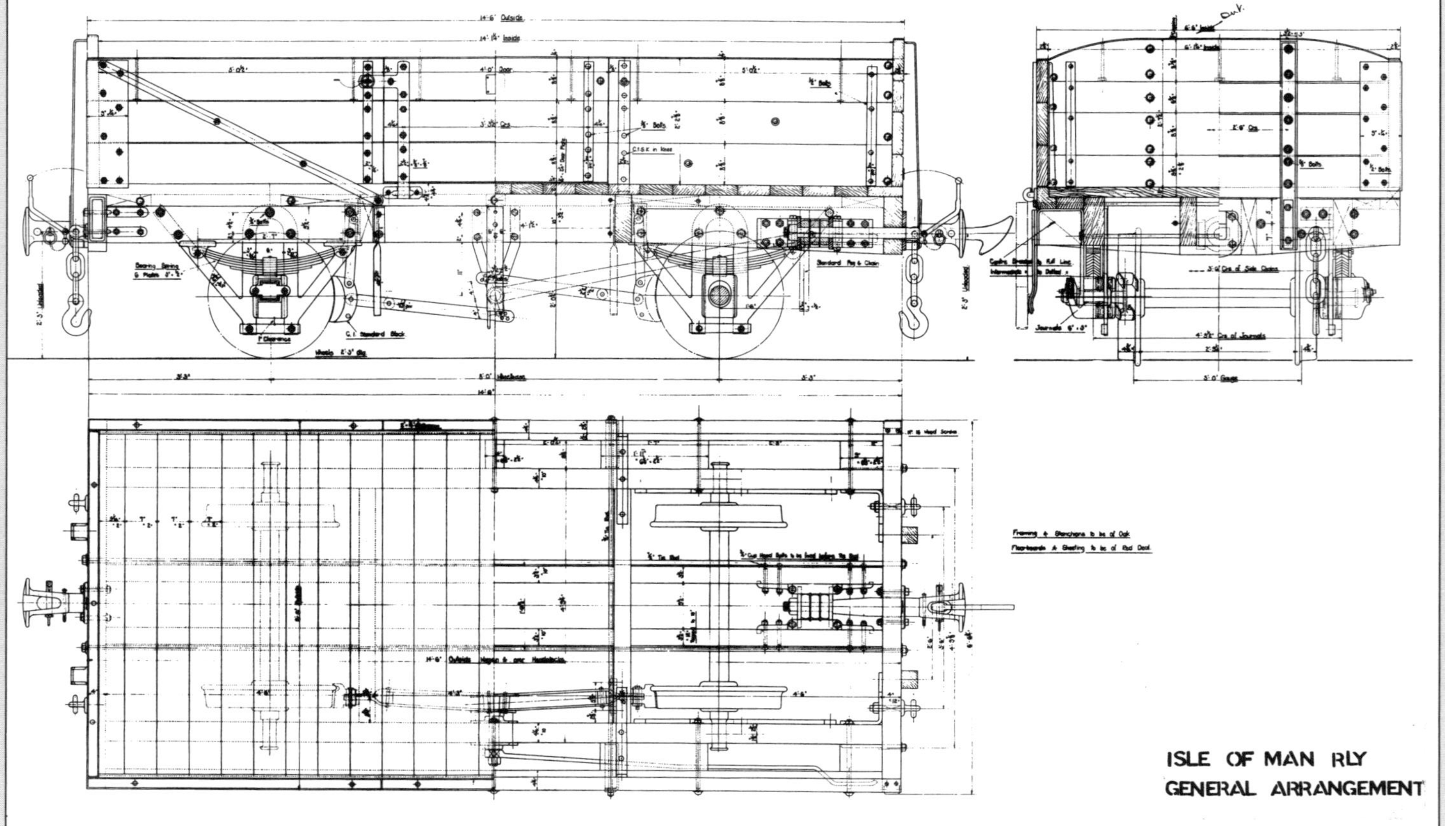

Drawing for a further batch of series H wagons in 1925. Perpetuation of the type was not approved.

Metropolitan Carriage & Wagon Co.

1960-64. Metropolitan built Nos. 1-20 in 1873 (second thoughts having prevailed about ordering only ten), No. 20 having the distinction of being the first IOMR wagon to be rebuilt (1894). Nos. 21-26 followed from Ashbury in 1877, having coil springs. There was also one IOMR oddity built at Douglas as late as 1918 and given No. 46, using parts of K15 cattle van which was mounted on chassis B3 (though H46 was not mounted on one).

The remainder was of Manx Northern origin, Nos. 27-38 being ex-MNR 1-12 supplied by Swansea in 1879, basically to the IOMR design. Ex-MNR Nos. 37-42, supplied by Hurst, Nelson of Glasgow in 1900 took IOMR numbers H40-45 (with the usual 'r' inserted as always with MNR stock). H41 was scrapped in 1925 but a replacement of the same number was provided; it was of unusual origins, coming from an M type open M55 of 1921 which had been renumbered M61 in 1924, M67 in 1925, only to be rebuilt as H41 (new) that same year!

Series K. Four-wheeled cattle vans, load 6 tons, tare approximately 3 tons. In general, similar to the G vans with diagonal outside planking at first, double side doors with drop flap, and Nos. 1-12 were supplied unroofed (there being no Island legislation making this compulsory). Rebuilt vans were given vertical planking and all rebuilds and replacements were given roofs; certain existing vans had roofs added and a few were scrapped without ever receiving a roof. Roofs first appeared in 1912. Like other stock from Metropolitan, there were rubber springs on some, but by 1905 conversion with leaf springs was well in hand. General dimensions were: length 14 ft 6 in.; width 6 ft 6 in.; height from rail to top of sides 8 ft 6 in.; wheelbase 8 ft; wheel diameter 2 ft 3 in. There were no brakes on the original batch. From 1912 many new bodies were placed on four-wheeled coach chassis carrying 3 tons, K25 measuring: 16 ft 6 in.; width 6 ft 6 in.; height from under beam to centre line of roof, 7 ft 9 in.; height from rail to top of side 7 ft 4½ in.; wheelbase 9 ft 6 in. Ex-MNR vans were slightly bigger (see on).

No.	*Maker*	*Date*	*Notes*
1	Metropolitan	1873	Scrap 1921.
2	Metropolitan	1873	Body scrap 1921. Chassis ultimately to H41
3	Ashbury	1877	Roofed 1924. Scrap 1960-5. (Fitted coil springs.)
4	Ashbury	1877	Unroofed - used for sheep traffic. Scrap 1946. (Fitted coil springs.)
5	Swansea	1879	Scrap 1924.
6	Swansea	1879	Roofed 1916. Scrap 1960-5.
7	Swansea	1879	Unroofed - used for sheep traffic. Scrap 1960-5.
8	Metropolitan	1899	Roofed 1916. Scrap 1960-5.
9	Metropolitan	1899	Roofed 1927. Scrap 1960-5.
10	IOMR	1908	Rebuilt unroofed from M45.* Roofed 1916. Scrap 1947.
11	IOMR	1908	Rebuilt unroofed from M43.* Roofed 1916. Scrap 1946.
12	IOMR	1908	Rebuilt unroofed from M44.* Roofed 1916. Scrap 1960-5.

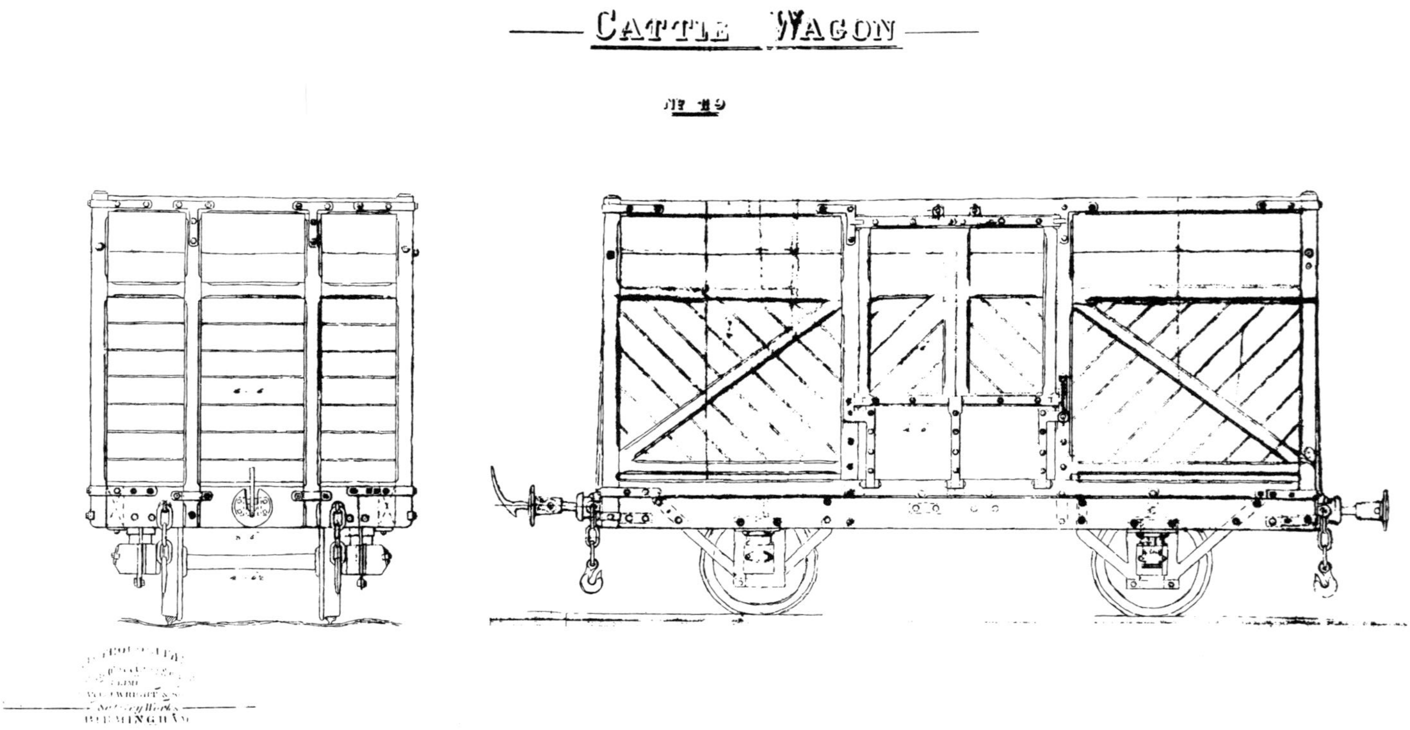

Design for roof-less and brake-less cattle wagon with rubber springs. 1973. Note the couplings. *Metropolitan Carriage & Wagon Co.*

No.	*Maker*	*Date*	*Notes*
13	IOMR	1912	Using chassis B12. Became sheep truck K13A 1924. Scrap 1927.
14	IOMR	1912	Using chassis C5. Became sheep truck K14A using B7 chassis 1924-5 respec. Scrap 1940s.
15	IOMR	1912	Using chassis B3. Cut up after Foxdale accident, January 1918.
16	IOMR	1912	Using chassis B5. Scrap 1947.
17	IOMR	1914	Using chassis B2. Scrap.
18	IOMR	1914	Using chassis C6. Scrap.
19	IOMR	1920	Using chassis B20. Scrap 1960-5.
20	IOMR	1920	Using chassis B21. Scrap 1960-5.
21	IOMR	1921	Using chassis B11. Scrap 1960-5.
22	IOMR	1921	Using chassis B15. Scrap 1960-5.
23	IOMR	1923	Using chassis B4. Scrap 1960-5.
24	IOMR	1923	Using chassis B17. Scrap 1960-5.
25	IOMR	1923	Using chassis B13. Scrap.
26	IOMR	1923	Using chassis B24. Scrap 1960-5.
New 15	IOMR	1920	Using chassis B16. Scrap 1958.
New 1	IOMR	1921	Using chassis C11. Put on chassis C14 1947. Scrap.
New 2	IOMR	1921	Using chassis B6. Scrap 1960-5.
New 5	IOMR	1924	Using chassis E7 (E3 from 1921). Scrap 1960-5.
New 13	IOMR	1924	Using chassis C3. Put on chassis B1 in 1949. Scrap.
New 14	IOMR	1924	Using chassis B18. Scrap 1960-5.

*Ex-IOM Mining Co. open wagons.
Nos. 15-19 had G bodies, 17-18 without portholes.

Series L. Four-wheeled bolster wagons for carrying timber, usually run in pairs. As built, with rubber block suspension but later altered to laminate springs behind the W-irons. Fitted with handbrake. Length 12 ft; width 6 ft 3 in.; wheelbase 6 ft 6 in.; wheel diameter 2 ft 3 in.

Nos. 1 and 2 were delivered from Metropolitan in 1874; the other two wagons of the same batch, Nos. 3 and 4, were scrapped 1959-60. In 1910 Douglas Works turned out two bolsters, Nos. 5 and 6, on chassis B22 and C7; these conversions were at first intended to be cattle vans and until 1911 ran with their intended cattle van numbers, K13 and K14. Obviously the need for them as timber bolsters must have passed with changing war conditions, and they were rebodied as goods vans G17 and G18 in 1916.

Series M. Four-wheeled open two-plank drop side, fixed-end wagons, originally termed 'ballast wagons' and the largest single series of stock on the railways. Load 6 tons, tare 3 tons. The basic design is a high-ended low-sided wagon, the upper edges of the ends being curved as in the H series. At first, it was the H series which was intended to be the standard open wagon; it was only when the first ballast wagons of series M were delivered that it

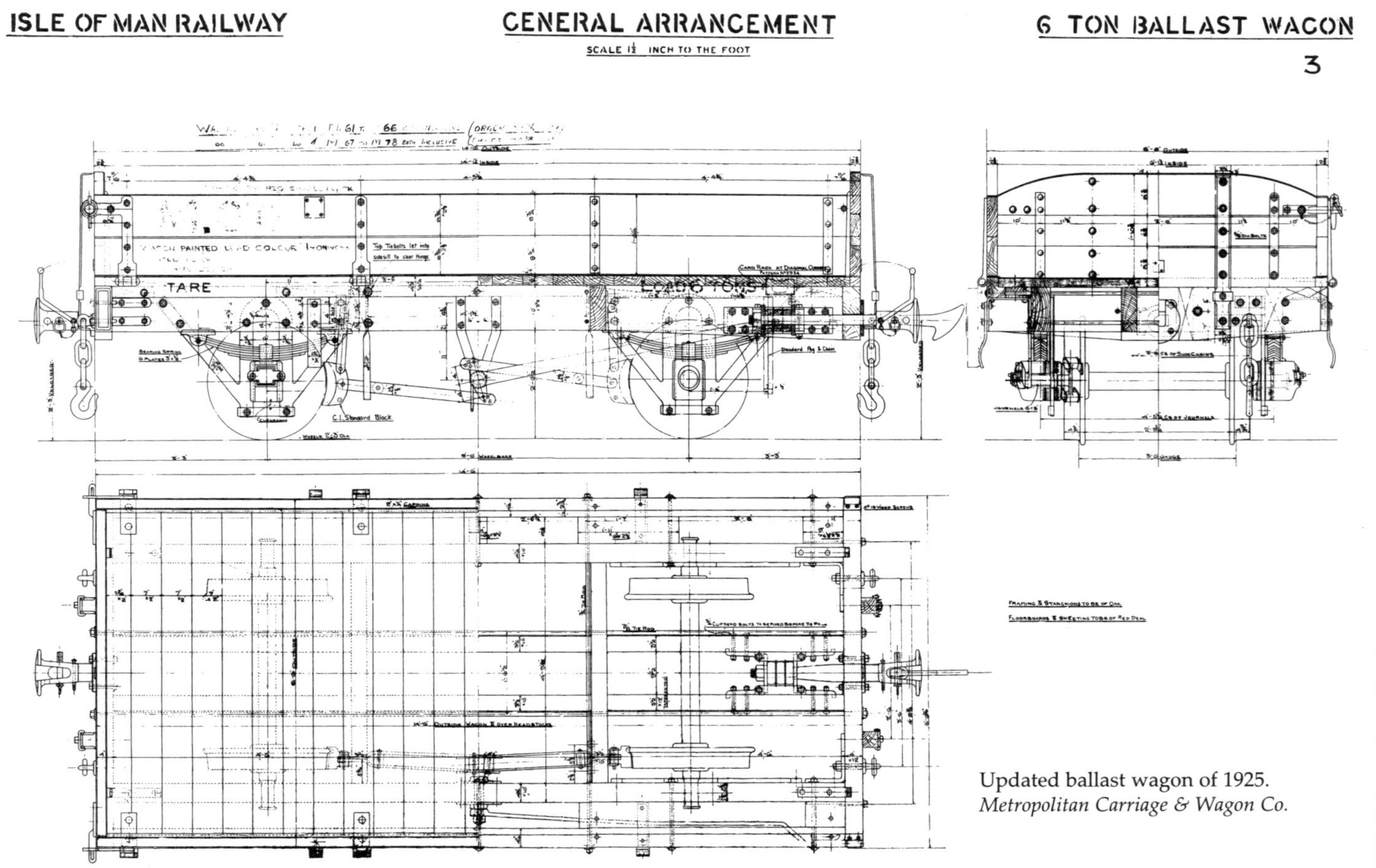

Updated ballast wagon of 1925.
Metropolitan Carriage & Wagon Co.

was found they were preferable to the H type, and no more of the latter was ordered. Ultimately the designation 'ballast wagons', though returned as such until 1906, was dropped from usage. The first batch of four came from Ashbury in 1877 and all lasted until the 1960s. At first, like other stock from this source, they had coil springs, but leaf springs fitted behind the W-irons took their place in 1907. The usual single-wheel handbrake and wooden check-stops for the drop doors were features of the original design; these were: length 14 ft 6 in.; width 6 ft 6 in.; height of side from rail 4 ft 4 in.; height of end from rail 4 ft 9 in.; wheelbase 8 ft; wheel diameter 2 ft 3½ in. (some batches having Mansell pattern). Wagons built to this design were Nos. 1-45; 55, and an improved type came out in 1911 to which Nos. 43 (new)-45 (new); 46-54; 55 (new); 56-78 were built. In the last batch the bodies are 4 ft 8 in. from rail to top of sides and 5 ft 3 in. to top of ends. Two-wheel brakes, central V hangers, steel door stops and modern springing and axle box arrangements evolved over the years. These wagons were frequently seen attached to the rear of passenger workings, carrying barrels, crates, timber and, in times of high season, passengers' luggage. Breakdown of the series was (1974):

No.	*Maker*	*Date*	*Notes*
1-4	Ashbury	1877	1, 3, 4 scrap 1960-5. 2 scrap 1967.
5-7	Ashbury	1884	5, 6 scrap 1960-5. 7 extant.
8-19	Ashbury	1888	All scrap except 9.
20-27	Metropolitan	1899	20, 23, 25 27 scrap 1960-5. 21-2 underframes scrapped 1941; bodies mounted on F60 bogie frame; removed and scrapped 1944.
28-35	Matthew Baird, Glasgow	1884	Ex-MNR Nos. 22-29 for Foxdale traffic. 30, 33, 34, 36, scrap 1960-64. 32 scrap 1951. 35 scrap 1958. 29, 31, scrap 1974.
36-37	Ramsey	1894	Ex-MNR Nos. 30-31. 37 scrap 1958. 31 scrap 1974.
38-39	Ramsey	1896	Ex-MNR Nos. 32-33. Withdrawn 1960-64.
40-42	Ramsey	1898	Ex-MNR Nos. 34-36. 40 fitted with small handcrane for temporary use at Peel: scrap 1974. Remainder scrap 1958-64.
43-54	Metropolitan	1911	'Improved' M type (purchased as alternative to buying six diamond frame bogie open 'coal' wagons from same suppliers; capacity 12 tons, 27 ft 6 in. long). 45 scrap 1971. 51 scrap 1960.

(43-5) Original wagons carrying these numbers were owned by Isle of Man Mining Co., Foxdale, possibly built by MNR at Ramsey. They were four-wheeled 9 in. side open wagons for carrying lead ore, built *c.* 1900 with single handbrake. They were sold to IOMR in 1906 and rebuilt into M series at Douglas in1906. In 1908 they were rebuilt again at Douglas as cattle vans, viz. M43 to K11, M44 to K12, M45 to K10.

(55) Original wagon of 1921 on chassis K2 carrying this number became M61 in 1924, M67 in 1925 to make way for fresh batch M series.

55-60 Second batch of 'Improved' M wagons from Metropolitan in 1924, having improved V hanger two-wheel brake gear.
61-66 Supplied by Metropolitan in 1925, exactly as 1924 batch. Bodies off 61 and 66 scrapped 1968 (*see note below*).
67-72 Exactly as for 61-6, body off 71 scrapped 1968.
Note. Bodies taken off 61, 66, 71 and second-hand roadtanker tanks placed thereon for oil traffic. Tanks removed and sold to Electricity Board 1969.
73-78 Second part of order involving one dozen wagons 67-78 inclusive. Delivered 1925, but stored St John's and paid for 1926; taken into stock 1926. 74 scrap 1959.

An oddment dated 3rd May, 1941 and scribbled on the back of a Great Western Railway Co. shareholder's Proxy Form has:

> 'M' wagons stock census. Empty wagons at Foxdale: 8, 13, 14, 18, 19, 39, 48, 53, 57, 61, 66, 70, 71, 74, 75, 76.

These wagons were the most over-employed on the system and critical to the war effort at that time. On no account was their condition to deterioriate to the stage when they had to be withdrawn from heavy repairs.

Fish Wagons evolved as a result of the need for a low-sided vehicle to carry herring and mackerel in crans, baskets, boxes or barrels; they were a lot of five four-wheeled open wagons built on coach underframes, load 3 tons. There were two (or more) planked sides and ends, outside frames, flush solebars, lift-out doors in the centre sides (sliding between grooved stanchions) with single handbrake. Dimensions: length 17 ft 6 in.; width 5 ft 10 in.; door width 4 ft 9 in.; side height only 1 ft 3 in. Painted grey, they were lettered FISH WAGON in 8 in. white lettering shaded black. They were at first intended to follow the H series without a prefix and carried numbers 46 upwards, becoming 1-3 in 1913.

1	(46)	IOMR	1909	Using chassis A9	Scrap 1974
2	(47)	IOMR	1909	Using chassis C13	Scrap 1960-5
3	(48)	IOMR	1910	Using chassis E4	Scrap 1951
4	-	IOMR	1914	Using chassis A2	Scrap 1960-5
5	-	IOMR	1914	Using chassis C2	Scrap 1960-5.

Series R. This series was introduced after eleven of the conversion bogie underframes had been stripped of their bodies in 1967 to carry containers. F series coaches Nos. F51-3, 55-6, 58-61, 69, 72 were the vehicles involved. This followed unsuccessful attempts to carry them on M wagons and the lengthening of the well wagon for the same purpose. Even the runner for the small crane was given a flat floor and tried out. In 1968 the eleven frames were numbered R1-10, the final one not receiving a number except in chalk! Stripped in late 1967, they were simply known as 'runners'. R3 was rebuilt into a well wagon in 1967 and lengthened - this conversion was to be a prototype for the remainder but the whole scheme folded up before this was carried into effect. Later, in 1968, R4 was given a wooden floor and ran as a bogie flat. Brake gear had been removed.

Tank Wagons (see under M series).

Service Vehicles - Cranes. By 1973 the oldest piece of service stock was a small travelling crane of 5 tons lifting capacity supplied by Thomas Kiss, of Birmingham. It had its own unbraked four-wheeled chassis, with wooden jib and a ballast box running out on a beam, typical of small goods yard cranes at the turn of the century. The other parts were in cast iron, activation by hand. When a second crane was delivered, it was referred to as 'Crane No.1'. In 1926 the crane portion was mounted on the underframe of A12, and the original one was scrapped. From the early 1930s it ran with a match truck made from the underframe of A3, which was left unfloored. It received a floor in 1967 to carry a container (see series R above). Neither vehicle was identified by number or lettering.

Crane No. 2 is a breakdown crane supplied in 1893 by Richard C. Gibbins & Co., Birmingham, mounted on its own four-wheeled chassis, the whole being of metal construction. Hand operated, it lifts 8 tons. The hinged sides let down to the horizontal to form a working platform, and a counterweight rolls out on small wheels along a beam. The jib has a 14 ft radius and when raised measures 16 ft 6 in. from pulley to rail level. Underframes E8 and A5 were made into match trucks for it in 1919 and 1920, forming part of a breakdown train, the whole painted red oxide and lettered LOCO DEPT at first. In 1924 brake van E4 was converted into a breakdown van to accompany the train.

Temporarily in the early 1930s, M40 carried a small handcrane for use at Peel. Sacks of stones were placed on a 'tray' to act as a counterbalance!

Well Wagon. A single four-wheeled well wagon built at Douglas about 1936, partly in H-section steel girders and partly in timber. It was at first used to carry the mechanical excavator used at the gravel pits, St John's, and at the Foxdale tips, used for spoil on railway, seabank and aerodrome work. In 1967 it was modified and lengthened to carry containers.

Permanent Way Wagons. There were four four-wheeled coach underframes converted for carrying lengths of rail. They were run in pairs, still close-coupled with small double-buffers at one end, butting against steel discs on the opposing vehicle; coupling between them was by link and pin, the original arrangements for close coupling the four-wheelers survived. At opposite ends, the conventional chopper couplings served. These conversions carried slides, mounted across them in the form of an inverted U and made up from old doubleheaded rail, the flat portion being laid side to side across the floor. A4 and D1 were converted in 1920 and A7 and C10 in 1923.

MNR Goods Stock

A separate list of MNR vehicles and the numbers allotted to them by the IOMR is appended, with notes as desirable.

No.	*Date*	*Builder*	*Specification*	*IOMR allotted No. in 1906*
1-12	1879	Swansea	Open Wagon	Hr27-38
13-16	1879	Swansea	Covered Van	Gr10-13
17-19	1879	Swansea	Cattle Wagon	Kr9-7-8
20-21	1880	Ashbury	Timber Bolster	Hr39
22-29	1884	Swansea	Ballast Wagon	Mr28-35
30-31	1894	MNR	Ballast Wagon	Mr36-37
32-33	1896	MNR	Ballast Wagon	Mr38-39
17	1896	MNR	Covered Van	Gr14
34-36	1898	MNR	Ballast Open	Mr40-42
37-42	1900	Hurst, Nelson	Open Wagon	Hr40-45

The majority of these vehicles received minor-major rebuilding during their life, many of such up to No. 21 were rebuilt twice; Nos. 22-41 were almost all rebuilt in 1914 with the exception of No. 42, rebuilt in 1927.

The MNR stock, as will be seen from the list above, was numbered by starting with No. 1 and continued therefrom without the categorisation as was done on the IOMR: when absorbed into the IOMR the stock was serialised and given a number in the series, followed by a capital 'R' of smaller size to denote origin . . . though, at more recent date, the same system was used to denote MNR springing. Confusing? Clearly the clerical staff at Douglas found it to be so, as evidenced by occasional errors in the records. Because the same staff was not aware of MNR wagons' function or the numbering system, the Counting House also erred when charging mileage of wagons when same had worked over the other's railway system. Having the longer route mileage, it was more usual to find MNR non-open goods stock on IOMR metals, than vice versa. There must have been relief at amalgamation in 1904 and more still when re-numbering took place. Heavy demands were made initially on the three MNR Cattle Wagons, open wagons used to carry sacks of lead, and, for the series H wagon, the sudden demand for labour and vehicles when a coal boat had to be unloaded at Ramsey and catch the tide. The urgencies of the last-named situations were met by running coal specials from Ramsey to Foxdale outside the times of the public timetable, breaking up the number of wagons if necessary by leaving part of the train in the St John's & Foxdale Railway station loop at St John's in order to surmount the branch gradient. The intensive usage and overloading due to traffic of Foxdale origin and destination shortened the life of the initial Swansea-supplied open stock, and gave Ramsey Works plenty of experience in wagon repair/renewal.

Nos. 1-12. These were centre drop-door open wagons which were taken into the IOMR H series in 1904. Tenders for supply came from Ashbury, Brown, Marshalls, Birmingham Carriage & Wagon Co. Ltd., Cravens Ltd. of Sheffield, and Swansea, the latter being accepted. They spent their early days in the building of the railway but their cheapness (£41 each) possibly accounted for their shortcomings, viz: faulty couplings, weak springs and the absence of handbrakes. To accept a tender for wagons without brakes seems little short of stupidity on the part of the Engineer/Board, but in 1879 a steep railway to serve Foxdale was not on the agenda; the MNR lost no time in fitting brakes.

The last MNR wagons re-numbered in the H series disappeared in 1958-63 and by the immediate post-World War II period their identity was extremely difficult; most spent their last days in the sidings around the St John's turntable.

Nos. 13-16. These were part of the Swansea delivery of 1879 and detail of their life has already been described; they were widely used over MNR/IOMR alike and survived until 1974 (one having been partially burned by hooligans in Douglas). They were immediately recognisable by their louvred sides: Gr12 is now in Port Erin Railway Museum: the other three met their end at Ballasalla 1974.

Nos. 17-19 (Later 18-20). Another much-used batch of vans for cattle traffic etc. built by Swansea in 1879; they were roofless. All were heavily repaired in 1897 and as Ramsey was building a fifth van in 1896, No. 17 was re-numbered 20 which had become vacant when a timber bolster of that number was withdrawn. The three originals became K9r-K7r-K8r under the IOMR and further rebuilding involved changing the planking in K7 and K9; K7 remained roofless to the end but the other two were ultimately covered. Though withdrawn in 1961-63, they were possibly among the unrecorded stock sent to Ballasalla in 1974.

Nos. 20-21. Two wagons supplied by Ashbury in 1880 for £60 each were described as Timber Bolster vehicles but had the capacity to be converted to low-sided opens as required. Their disadvantage was a short wheelbase which made them unsteady runners, so that when carrying 'carriages or general goods' they might discard the load. They were involved in the building of the Snaefell Tramway where they were given little respect but there was almost no timber carrying for them on their native system; the IOMR often hired them. No. 20 appears to be withdrawn in 1896 and 21 in 1901, though IOMR records state both were scrapped in 1899. As already noted, No. 20 was given to a re-numbering of cattle wagons: No. 21 was rebuilt as an open wagon, retaining its number and became IOMR Hr39, lasting until the early 1960s. There is no photograph to show them in original condition.

Nos. 22-29. A batch of eight open wagons virtually identical to, but slightly longer than, the IOM M type was bought per A.Baird & Co., 67, Robertson Street, Glasgow by order of March 1884 for the mines' traffic.

The IOMR books give Matthew Baird (a relative?) as the supplier, but clearly the notice was too short for prompt delivery, and probably why some near-half dozen enquiries including local small businesses, failed to give satisfactory terms. Baird may have regretted their offer, for when delivery date had passed by two months, they advised the MNR that shipment from Swansea would be made subject to a sailing be available - this was the first intimation that Baird had sub-contracted to Swansea Wagon . . . Worse, when the wagons arrived, they were fitted with the same unacceptable drawgear as had the Cleminson coaches fitted by Swansea.

They took their rightful place in the IOMR M series and quietly disappeared as business failed after World War II, the last going in the 1974 holocaust.

Nos. 30-31. Similar to the foregoing, two wagons were built in 1896 at Ramsey; they were IOMR Mr36-37 and withdrawn in the early sixties.

Nos. 32-33. Two open wagons of M type were built at Ramsey in 1896, becoming IOMR Mr38-39 and discarded 1960-64.

No. 17. In 1896 Ramsey converted passenger van No. 15 into a covered goods van, cattle wagon No. 17 was re-numbered 20 to take the place of a timber bolster and the now-vacant 17 bestowed on the new van. It became Gr14, and made its last journey to Ballasalla in 1974.

Nos. 34-36. Built at Ramsey in 1898, were three M type wagons which became IOMR Mr40-42. No. 40 was fitted with a small handcrane for use at Peel goods shed, and outlasted the others.

Nos. 37-42. These six opens came from Hurst, Nelson and entered traffic in 1900; the M type was abandoned in favour of H type which had been disregarded for two decades; they took IOMR numbers Hr40-45. Three had early demise in the mid-twenties, another went in 1946 and the last two in the early 1960s. The remaining three had spent their last years resting in the 'wagon graveyard' at St John's without turning a wheel.

IOMR M type wagons Nos. M5-M7. These wagons were obtained in 1881 by the Mona Chemical Co., Peel (see Vol. 1 p.158 & p.160) for their private use; the builders are given as Ashbury 1884 in IOMR records. In 1884 The Midland RC&WCL claimed they had hired the wagons and were still owed fees for three years. The IOMR agreed to pay £132 for the three in 1884.

Although the history of these vehicles is still confused, it is known each carried a plate (presumably with MRC&WCL as the owner) and they were poor runners; nevertheless they must have been put into good order and were long-lasting.

Isle of Man Mining Co. Ltd. Owners Nos. 1-3. IOMR Nos. M43-45. This concern possessed three open single-plank sided wagons, possibly built by the MNR at Ramsey in 1900, for the transport of ore in sacks. To avoid confusion with its own stock, the MNR referred them with an 'A' prefix to the number. They were bought by the IOMR in 1906 and put into M series numbers as 43-45.

The IOMMCo had discussed wagons with the MNR in 1887 but without result; they wished to carry coal from Ramsey to their own (new) coal yard at Foxdale. Cameron suggested either the Baird-built open type as used by the MNR at Foxdale, or his own design with side and end doors requiring a cradle for tipping to allow the coal to slide out.*

General note on Goods Stock

It is only possible to give the fore-going information up to the mid-1970s in such detail because the IOMR kept meticulous records until the run-down of that period. By then the staff who maintained the exact annual returns had either retired or been made redundant so that in autumn 1974 a list of vehicles 'Beyond economic repair', was not available. When such was required in September the difficult task of what there was, where it was and what number it carried was virtually impossible because the woodwork carrying the running number had vanished. Not that such a list was vital; by November all remaining goods vehicles stored at Douglas save a handful which were retained for departmental use, together with (among other things) the un-used turntable, locomotive parts etc. were assembled in Ballasalla and sold to Manx Metals. Though this depressing collection was recorded on film, no other note was kept; the contemporary Board Meeting was involved in critical decision on the future of the Railway's football Challenge Cup . . .

Delivery of new IOMR goods vehicles

It was usual for mainland builders to quote a cost price 'f.o.b. Liverpool' (or the name of their nearest port), and it was up to the IOMR to arrange and pay for shipment to Douglas. From Douglas quay to the station the Railway Company used various contractors, often owning steam traction engines or team horses hauling low-loaders.

Goods vehicles were assembled at the builders, inspected and photographed, then with their running gear removed, railed to the port; on board ship, the bodies could be stacked economically. At Douglas marriage of body and running gear was done in the Company's shops. In difficult cases, an employee from the builders accompanied the shipment until it was erected and satisfied the Wagon Superintendent. Only then did the Counting House contemplate the supplier's invoice for payment . . !

*Details from Tower Collection.

Suggested Bogie Wagons

In 1916 Metropolitan offered an alternative to further four-wheeled opens in the shape of 12 ton coal wagons carried on diamond-framed bogies. A drawing was submitted (present whereabouts unknown) showing a length of 27 ft 6 in. with two drop-doors each side (resembling the H series), and a vertical brake pillar each end having a handwheel thereon for applying the brake. (The Author suggests this may have been of War Department origin.) The IOMR advised that they preferred their standard wagon.

Gloucester Carriage & Wagon Co. Ltd.

A misleading entry amongst the records of the above concern held by the Gloucestershire County Record Office exists in the Index to photographs headed 'Isle of Man Railway'. Knowing that this manufacturer is not credited with any construction, the four photographs were checked and found to be taken at Ramsey early in this century. One is of a Swansea Wagon-built open wagon for the MNR, and the others of IOMR bogie carriage F23, built by Metropolitan.

It is suggested that a holiday visitor from the firm took the pictures, which clearly demonstrate the exterior and interior construction - an early example of industrial espionage, perhaps? The presence of the Manager David McDowell on the pictures gives a slightly 'formal' air to the occasion; perhaps the firm had sent an introductory letter to him beginning, ' . . . Mr X. from our Company will be holidaying in Ramsey during August, and would like to take the opportunity of familiarising himself with your carriages and wagons. We would be happy to reciprocate such a kind gesture should you find yourself to be in this district at some future date . . .'

Official record of MNR Goods Stock 1894

The listing below is copied verbatim:

12 High-sided Box Wagons	2 ft 9 in. high
10 Low-sided Ballast Wagons	1 ft 6 in. high
2 Timber Trucks	6 in. high
4 Covered Vans	
3 Cattle Trucks *	

All are 15 ft long x 7 ft wide, except Timber Trucks.
All carry an average of 6 tons; average tare 2 tons 19 cwt.

*These hold 5-7 beasts according to size.

Liveries 1873-1973

Livery since 1973 has been subject to fairly frequent change and in certain instances locomotives' colours vary in the interests of publicity. Occasional reference to post-1973 livery is given in the Chronology (Vols. I & II).

Dates are only approximate as changes in painting overlapped. Colours are as described in contemporary literature.

Isle of Man Railway

Locomotives:

1873. Middle green; black lining with vermilion line inside and white line outside. Wheels green.
by 1939. As for 1873 but wheels black. Red line either side of black lining.
1944. Indian Red due to accumulation of many sample drums of this colour available for use. Black lining with narrow white line each side. Black running gear and vermilion or red side rods.
(August 1947: 3/4/7 in red livery: 2/8/12/15/16 in green livery.)
(July 1950: 1/3/5/6/9/10/11/13/14 in traffic in red livery.)
1967. Ailsa period. Certain engines restored to near-1873 livery (even if in traffic or not).

Carriages:

1873-*c.* 1885. Series A. Off-white upper panels; green lower panels. Yellow lining.
A12 - Duke's Saloon. As for Series A but gilt lining.
Series B-E. Chocolate brown. Yellow lining. Bogie stock. Chocolate brown lower panels and off-white lower panels. Lettering etc. gold, shaded blue.
1886-1916. All stock in bogie carriage livery (as above) but in 1912 some carriages had cream upper and green lower panels; these were possibly F29-46 when delivered new.
1917-*c.* 1930. Off-white upper panels replaced in light brown, giving resemblance to Lancashire & Yorkshire Railway colours. Certain stock in this colour lasted until mid-1930s.
1923-26 (new stock). White upper and lake lower panels with red and yellow lining. (Lining unique to this stock).
c. 1930-1939. Majority stock off-white upper and purple lower panels similar to London & North Western Railway colours. In 1937 some coaches with 'broken white upper and maroon lower panels'.
1940-1945. Any repainting done in dark brown.
1946-1973. At first, all-over deep red as for locomotives. Later, deep red with off-white window panels, but older stock remained in all-brown where repainted. From 1968, all usable stock had off-white upper and red lower panels.

Goods stock:

Initially slate grey, later light grey woodwork. Grey or black ironwork. Lettering (large) white shaded black; (small) white. Load and Tare often painted on both ends, occasionally on sides.

Manx Northern Railway

Locomotives:

1879. Tuscan Red (Dark Claret); black lining with narrow vermilion line side.*
c. 1914. Nos. 3 & 4 into IOMR livery (but not exactly as for IOMR locomotives).
1968. No. 15 CALEDONIA in IOMR colours but Ailsa-repainted in MNR-type livery. Later, No. 14 THORNHILL treated similarly. Both locomotives used for display purposes - not in traffic.

Carriages:†

1879. 'Polished Teak'.
by 1899. 'Chocolate lower and creamy white panels'.

Goods stock:

1879. 'Dark brown', but probably creosoted. Later,light grey. Ironwork black or grey. Lettering 'M.N.R.' in white (and shaded black in the case of large characters only) on centre left of vehicle, number on centre right side.

****

A meticulous record was kept of all painting/dates and certain of these have survived in the Tower Collection; for instance,in 1954 even the lowly 'School Carriages' (i.e, F51, F55, F58) were burnt off, cleaned, painted Buff inside and Tuscan Red outside, and the roofs painted. The twelve ex-MNR coaches at St John's had their roofs painted. It was a remarkable year: 34 carriages, 11 wagons and 3 engines, (Nos. 8, 1, 13), were repainted , but no colour - except for the above-mentioned - is given. Presumably outside contractors were employed on carriages and wagons. Nevertheless, it was a year of remarkable optimism.

In recent years, locomotive painting has strayed from the practice of one uniform colour and the precise shade of green used before World War II can be found only on engines which have not been restored to traffic. To quote from an authoritative source, a blue 'similar to Caledonian Blue' (with black and white lining-out), Crimson, a dark green similar to 'the old green', Indian Red and 'Metropolitan Railway red' have been applied on the basis of one engine per colour, up to 1995 as follows:

No. 4 Crimson, No. 10 Dark Green, No. 11 Indian Red, No. 12 Blue, No. 15 Metropolitan Red. The official colour for carriages is presently Purple Lake and white.

In the Museum, locomotives are: No. 1 'Ailsa' Apple Green, No. 6 Indian Red, No. 16 Indian Red. Carriages are: Royal Maroon and Primrose (Ducal Saloon).

*Beyer, Peacock's Order Book has 'Lake colour' for THORNHILL.
†The Foxdale coach was the first to carry the MNR crest, bearing the motto 'Cocunoque Lecris Stabit' which should have been 'Quocunque Jeceris Stabit'. (The defaulting crest transfer was still available in 1950 and a copy is in the Author's possession.)

Tickets

The most complete account of tickets is that which appeared in the JOURNAL of the Transport Ticket Society No. 115 for July 1973, a copy of which is held by the Manx Museum Library Ref. B.192 1x p. 124: acknowledgement is made to the Society for the use of same. In view of the availability of such a comprehensive survey on a subject of specialised interest, the following description is limited to basic facts.

Tickets were supplied by Waterlow & Sons, London until 1955, when Williamson obtained the business. They were of the customary card type. [Some tickets were printed in Belfast in 1971/2: alias 'Irish Tickets'!] A remarkable feature was that stations were initially issued with over a hundred different ones . . . and some original bundles were never opened. First and Second Class (Third if appropriate) tickets were supplied to twenty-three stations, making journeys available from them to the twenty-two destination-stations on the Island: the Foxdale Branch had a full set of eighty-eight ordinary tickets from Foxdale alone though none can be traced from Waterfall to the Peel or South Lines.

In addition to ordinary tickets, there were Excursion, Market, Dog and Bicycle issues, and others such as Forces, Privilege and Name Tickets, some fully printed and others ex-lesser stations were blanks, completed as required.

As the MNR was worked by the IOMR until 6th November, 1880, MNR stations were supplied with tickets headed 'Isle of Man Ry. Co. Limited'. The Foxdale Railway opened in 1886 and had MNR tickets supplied from the outset. Presumably Government Passes or Travel Warrants were used on the Knockaloe Branch.

Ailsa introduced new type tickets for his Peel Line opening in June 1967, but the Ramsey and Castletown (only) routes used existing stocks. When Port Erin was reached in 1969 a further new type appeared headed 'Isle of Man Victorian Steam Railway Co. Ltd'.; by then Ailsa had closed the Peel and North Line and, when he withdrew entirely and the IOMR resumed the operation of the South Line (only), 'Victorian' tickets were widely used.

Confusingly, Ailsa-period tickets are quoted as, '. . . issues differ in almost all respects from the original Company's tickets, and from each other. . .'

The many mis-spellings in title, station names etc. are obvious; legion are the variations in title, layout, type-face, serial numbering. In respect of the last-named, ticket printing was in batches of 250 or a multiple e.g. the first batch would be 000-249 but it was unusual to issue 000, but it *was* done in the case of St Germain's . . . probably an oversight.

Enthusiasm for continued business accounted for the MNR's repeat order for St John's-Sulby Bridge 1st Cl. Single, and a further order under IOMR auspices (when under 90 of the Opening Day tickets had been sold when the line closed), meant that stocks of this ticket would have lasted 1,000 years. Similar

Issued in accordance with the Conditions and Regulations shown on Co's Time Tables, etc.

4440	Isle of Man Railway RETURN HALF THIRD CLASS **PEEL** *to* **DOUGLAS**	Isle of Man Railway OUTWARD HALF THIRD CLASS **DOUGLAS** *to* **PEEL**	4440

This Ticket is not transferable. It must be produced for authorised inspection on demand and given up at Collecting Station

DOUGLAS & PEEL

Williamson, Printer, Ashton — Williamson, Printer, Ashton

Issued in accordance with the Conditions and Regulations shown on Co's Time Tables, etc.

4440	Isle of Man Railway RETURN HALF THIRD CLASS **PORT ERIN** *to* **DOUGLAS**	Isle of Man Railway OUTWARD HALF THIRD CLASS **DOUGLAS** *to* **PORT ERIN**	4440

This Ticket is not transferable. It must be produced for authorised inspection on demand and given up at Collecting Station

DOUGLAS & PORT ERIN

Williamson, Printer, Ashton — Williamson, Printer, Ashton

Issued in accordance with the Conditions and Regulations shown on Co's Time Tables, etc.

4440	Isle of Man Railway RETURN HALF THIRD CLASS **RAMSEY** *to* **DOUGLAS**	Isle of Man Railway OUTWARD HALF THIRD CLASS **DOUGLAS** *to* **RAMSEY**	4440

This Ticket is not transferable. It must be produced for authorised inspection on demand and given up at Collecting Station

DOUGLAS & RAMSEY

Williamson, Printer, Ashton — Williamson, Printer, Ashton

Isle of Man Railway Co.—Isle of Man Road Services Ltd.

THREE DAYS 9/6 GO-AS-YOU-PLEASE

BUS AND TRAIN

Available any **THREE DAYS** (which need not be consecutive) within seven days from date hereon. Issued in accordance with the general regulations and conditions of the Companies. Not Transferable. Must be produced for authorised inspection on demand, and given up on expiry. Available 3rd class when used by Train.

Date of Issue...9 JUL 1937... *1937*

No. 1109

Sun.	Mon.	Tues.	Wed.	Thur.	Fri.	Sat.

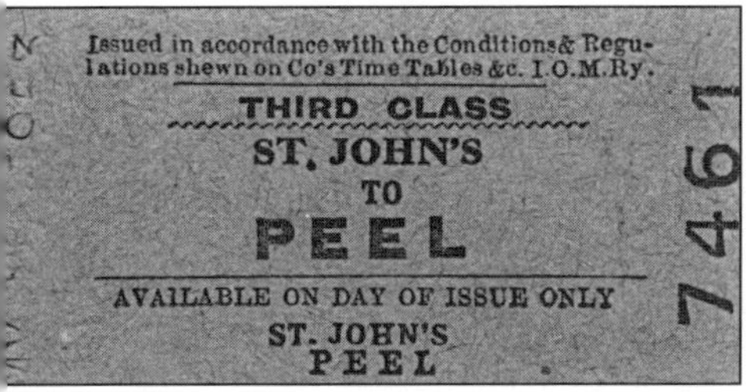
Issued in accordance with the Conditions & Regulations shewn on Co's Time Tables &c. I.O.M.Ry.
THIRD CLASS
ST. JOHN'S
TO
PEEL
AVAILABLE ON DAY OF ISSUE ONLY
ST. JOHN'S
PEEL
7461

Manx Northern Ry. Co. (Limited.)
RAMSEY
TO
ST. GERMAINS
THIRD CLASS
8479

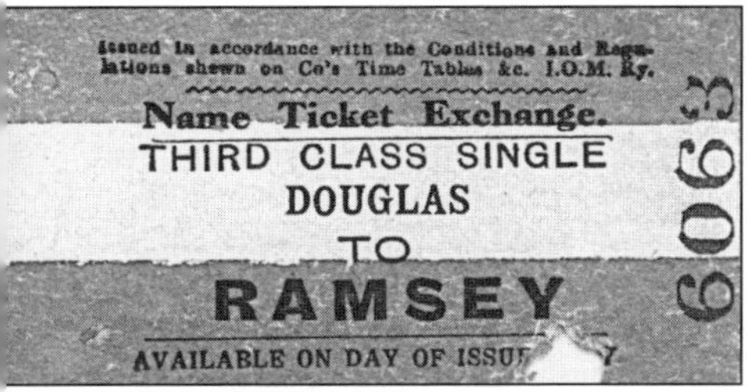
Issued in accordance with the Conditions and Regulations shewn on Co's Time Tables &c. I.O.M. Ry.
Name Ticket Exchange.
THIRD CLASS SINGLE
DOUGLAS
TO
RAMSEY
AVAILABLE ON DAY OF ISSU
6063

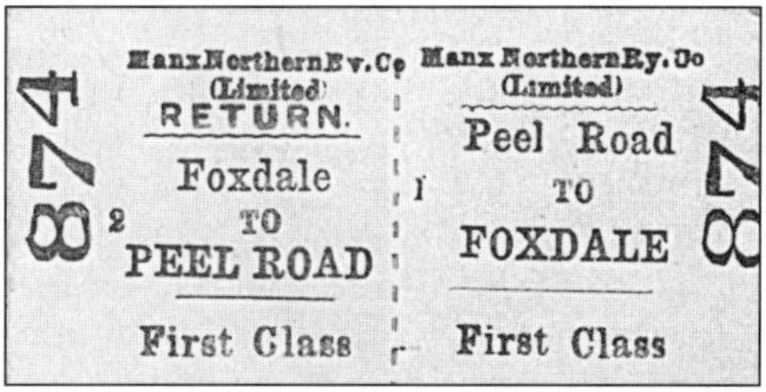
874
Manx Northern Ry. Co (Limited)
RETURN.
Foxdale
2 TO
PEEL ROAD
First Class
Manx Northern Ry. Co (Limited)
Peel Road
1 TO
FOXDALE
First Class
874

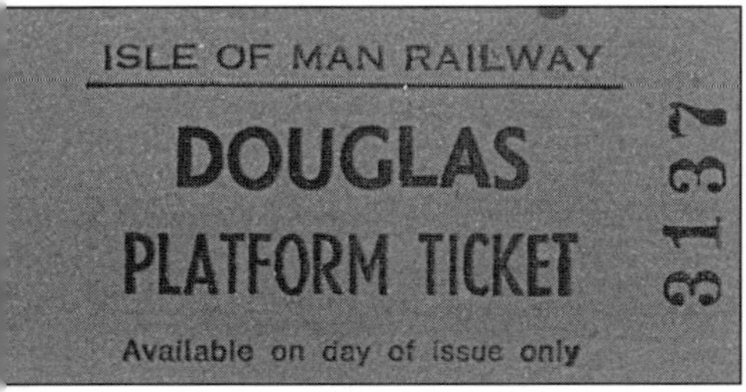
ISLE OF MAN RAILWAY
DOUGLAS
PLATFORM TICKET
Available on day of issue only
3137

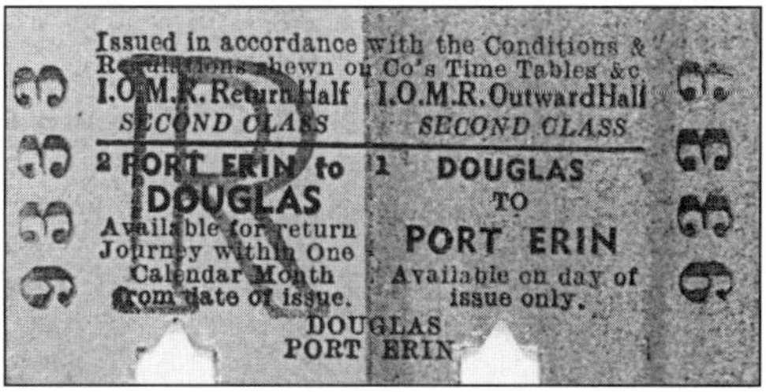
9333
Issued in accordance with the Conditions & Regulations shewn on Co's Time Tables &c
I.O.M.R. Return Half
SECOND CLASS
2 PORT ERIN to
DOUGLAS
Available for return Journey within One Calendar Month from date of issue.
I.O.M.R. Outward Half
SECOND CLASS
1 DOUGLAS
TO
PORT ERIN
Available on day of issue only.
DOUGLAS
PORT ERIN
9333

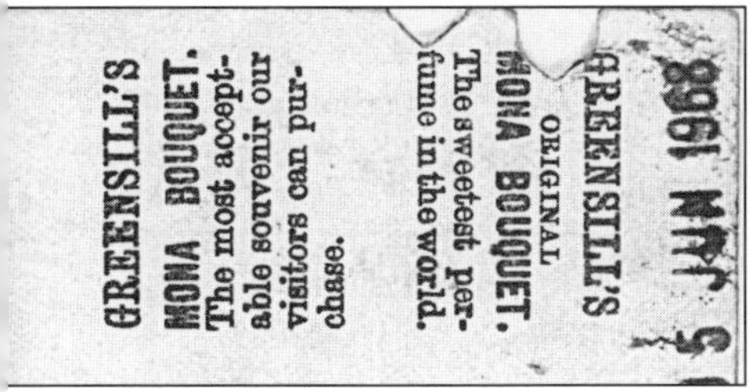
GREENSILL'S
MONA BOUQUET.
The most acceptable souvenir our visitors can purchase.
The sweetest perfume in the world.
MONA BOUQUET.
ORIGINAL
GREENSILL'S
5 JUN 1968

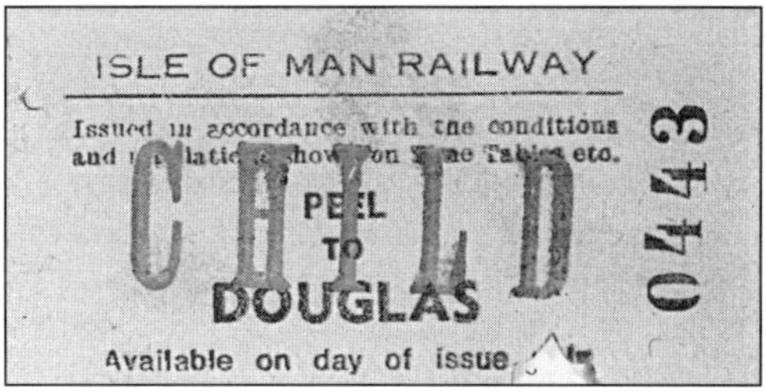
ISLE OF MAN RAILWAY
CHILD
PEEL
TO
DOUGLAS
Available on day of issue
0443

abundance was shown in St John's-St Germain's and Waterfall-Lezayre.

Advertisements appeared on the back of early tickets, the more common being for 'Greensill's original Mona Bouquet'; certain of these were available at St John's station for ex-stations on the Foxdale Branch - long after the Branch closed - until St John's itself closed . . . and thereafter through a managerial sales drive to clear stocks of items likely to be attractive to collectors. In the same category were 'IOMR/MNR Douglas-Sulby Glen Circular Tour and Sulby Glen-Douglas via Ramsey per MNR & Mona S.S. Co. Steamer FAIRY QUEEN', 1st Class on train and Saloon on ship, the return portion being on the left (therefore first quoted here) and the outward portion by steamer on the right; for short-sighted users the cramped printing was irritating.

A simple summary of types and colour codes in use up to 1973 (see the reverse of the dust-jacket for Vol. II) must be sufficient as a general guide; there may be disagreement about original colours in some instances due to age and fading. For the enthusiast requiring further visual experience, the Hendry Collection in the Railway Museum at Port Erin is extremely extensive; it includes such unusual items as a ticket divided into three portions, the third being admission to the IOMR-owned Glen Wyllin, and illustrates the overprinting of coloured stripes, bands and triangles in parallels, diagonals - in some cases to almost obliterate the availability of the ticket itself.

Platform Tickets were introduced by Ailsa in 1967 at Douglas and Peel, apparently for the first time in history.

No special 'Child' tickets of ordinary issue appeared until the Ailsa-period in 1967, though extra-ordinary types were endorsed 'Child' and had a corner snipped off. Instead, a child's ticket was an 'adult' ticket with a semi-circular or Half-Snip cut from the bottom edge. From 1967 the new issues had CHILD (or as suitable) endorsed in red; in the period this method was extended to ADULT SINGLE (or as suitable). Before 1950, 12 years was the upper qualifying age for half-fare; it was then raised to 14.

Tickets to nine named stations were available from certain major hotels and boarding houses in Douglas were advertised up to 1914, but the Minute Book (which was usually precise about such practices) has no mention of the facility; it may have commenced at the turn of the century.

Such ordinary tickets as appeared in the Ailsa-period had no class printed thereon; yellow was used for Single or Return, the latter having a green triangle overprinted for the Return half. Tickets from Douglas for the Peel Line included Braddan in its stations. The 1969 issues were colour-coded and had myriad variations; the 1971/2 printings were equally gaudy and any member of the staff who was colour-blind would have been severely disadvantaged . . .

Excursion trains were a feature of the railways from the first; their availability was announced by a bewildering array of teardown handbills available at stations, a universal railway practice which only Second War paper shortages stopped. G.H. Wood was a great exponent of this form of business, brightly coloured handbills and equally startling tickets. Some original bills are displayed within Port Erin station. Though hardly an 'excursion', Douglas Rifle Club and King William's College O.T.C. had special issues to reach Ballacostain (Rifle Range) platform, under an Agreement with the Club of 5th May, 1902. There was also a neat Angler's Ticket notable for its freedom from print-clutter.

Market Days have received mention under 'Traffic & Operation'; before the 1905 amalgamation Douglas Market tended to be emphasised by the IOMR and that at Ramsey by the MNR. Tickets apart, reduced fares for markets existed and in November 1879 the IOMR had 'all station' Market Tickets to Douglas or Ramsey available on Saturdays. It seems that the markets held in other places were not always worthy of special tickets though Peel was recognised with a ticket: at the turn of the century there were ten places holding Saturday weekly markets. Judging from correspondence from the public received by the Manager, regular users of market trains frequently abused conditions - complaints of butchers etc. using First Class compartments, soiling seats with smelly coats or dirty boots and smoking twist . . .

Finally, in this curtailed account should be mentioned the 'Go-as-You-Please' unrestricted travel tickets introduced to counter competition from the buses.

On tickets currently in use headings vary, viz. Isle of Man Railway, Isle of Man Steam Railway or Isle of Man Railways. Under the foremost are large-type Souvenir Tickets introduced for main stations by the IOMR Co. in 1975-77 which have an illustration on the face and an invitation to visit the Railway Museum on the rear. Singles are Primrose Yellow and Returns Buff or white; such tickets may be retained by the user.

Under the remaining headings are typical 'Williamson' (Ashton-under-Lyne) issues including one-colour non-divisible Single or Return tickets, and 'Golden Rail' Returns notable for their dominant colours; in the last example Douglas- Port Erin tickets are colour-paired Purple/White or Buff/Maroon it would seem, haphazardly.

Lastly, Rail Rover tickets give three days travel Sunday-Saturday. These are white, with horizontal coloured bar, green for adult, orange for children. They allow three days unlimited travel on steam or electric railways, and one trip to Snaefell summit, within seven days of issue.

Examples of the large-type Souvenir Tickets

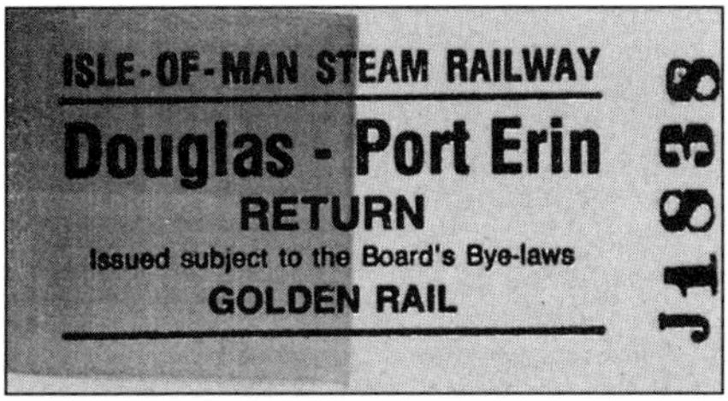
ISLE-OF-MAN STEAM RAILWAY
Douglas - Port Erin
RETURN
Issued subject to the Board's Bye-laws
GOLDEN RAIL
J1838

Sun. Mon. Tue. Wed.
ISLE OF MAN RAILWAYS
CHILD RAIL ROVER
THREE DAYS TRAVEL
SEE OTHER SIDE
Subject to Board's Bye-laws V
Thurs. Fri. Sat.
SNAEFELL
One Journey only
1027

ISLE-OF-MAN STEAM RAILWAY
Douglas - Port Erin
RETURN
Issued subject to the Board's Bye-laws
GOLDEN RAIL
Williamson, Ticket Printer, Ashton
A0326

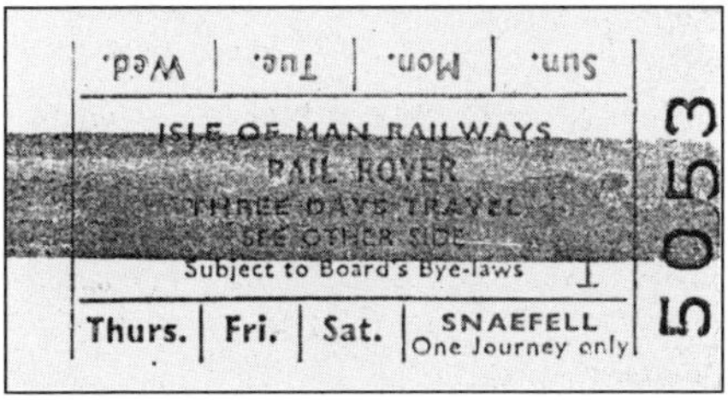
Sun. Mon. Tue. Wed.
ISLE OF MAN RAILWAYS
RAIL ROVER
THREE DAYS TRAVEL
SEE OTHER SIDE
Subject to Board's Bye-laws
Thurs. Fri. Sat.
SNAEFELL
One Journey only
5053

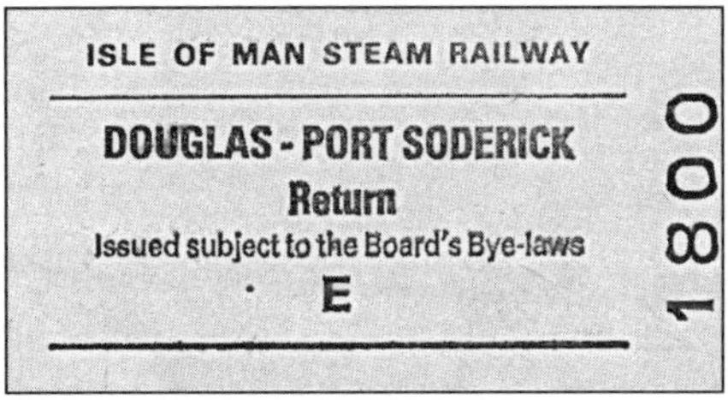
ISLE OF MAN STEAM RAILWAY
DOUGLAS - PORT SODERICK
Return
Issued subject to the Board's Bye-laws
E
1800

Tickets 1873-1973

(Isle of Man Railway and Manx Northern Railway issues used the same colours on all tickets#)

Official Title		*First Class*	*Third Class (later Second Class and original Second Class of IOMR)*
MONTHLY†	SINGLE	ALL WHITE	ALL BLUE
	RETURN	OUT: WHITE RET.: YELLOW (or BUFF). Overprint R.	OUT: BLUE RET.: PINK. Overprint R.
DAILY	SINGLE	ALL WHITE	ALL BLUE
	RETURN*	OUT: RET.:	OUT: * RET.: *
SPECIAL DAY EXCURSION	RETURN	OUT: / RET.: ? Not issued	OUT: WHITE ground: mid-vertical band of YELLOW (or) RET.: WHITE ground: mid-vertical band of contrast colour, e.g. BLUE, and overprint R.
EXCURSION (Day only)	RETURN	Complete ticket: WHITE. Broad vertical band of colour in middle covers part of both halves, e.g. SCARLET. RET.: Overprint R.	OUT: PURPLE RET.: DARK GREEN overprint R. (Another specimen) Return: BLUE with green horizontal band, each half carries initials diagonally in RED.

PRIVILEGE	SINGLE	(Third Class)	BLUE upper; PINK lower; divided by narrow WHITE line.
	RETURN		As for single: return half overprint R
MARKET TICKET		(Third Class)	OUT: RED. RET.: BUFF.
H.M. FORCES	SINGLE	(Third Class)	BLUE with broad PURPLE central band horizontally.
	RETURN		OUT: GREY. RET.: GREY with RED vertical Band.
DOG (in charge of owner)	SINGLE		GREEN.
	RETURN		GREEN with broad WHITE Central band horizontally.

Official Title		
BICYCLE, PERAMBULATOR or MAIL CART (accompanied by owner)	SINGLE	BUFF
	RETURN	OUT: GREEN with Vertical BLUE Band. RET.: GREEN with Vertical BLUE band overprint R.
GO-AS-YOU-PLEASE (Year 1937) 5*s*.	TWO DAYS availability within SEVEN of issue. Third Class. BLUE: with broad Central Vertical WHITE band. (Colours vary with week of issue.)	
HOLIDAY RUNABOUT	PERIOD (as stated on ticket) all-stations ticket for all-in payment. (Overwritten if for First Class.) Large card - GREEN.	
DIRECTOR'S PASS	GOLD MEDALLION: Obverse: shows Legs of Man. Reverse: 'Isle of Man Railway' (Gothic characters) and Official Number.	

IOMR and Manx Northern tickets had advertising matter on the backs in early years.
Colours for Third were those normally used elsewhere for Second (Thirds are usually Green/Buff but are not used in IOM.)
Child's tickets latterly denoted by 'Half-Snip' cut-out.

*Not issued: Monthly or 'Special Day Excursion' used as suitable. Overprint R - not done on early issues.
†*Singles*: Probably in practice, used on day of issue only. Early issues do not state 'Available on day of issue only.'
#Bicycle (etc.) excepted, i.e. MNR GREY.

ISLE OF MAN RAILWAY

DOUGLAS STATION—ATHOL STREET AND NORTH QUAY.

TIME TABLE for MONDAY, JULY 4th, 1938, and until further notice.

NOTICE.—The hours or times stated in the Company's Time Tables, Books, Bills, and Notices, are appointed as those at which it is intended so far as circumstances will permit that the trains shall depart from and arrive at the several Stations, but their departure or arrival at the times stated is not guaranteed, nor will the Company under any circumstances be held responsible for delay or detention, however occasioned, or any consequences arising therefrom. The right to stop the trains at any Station on the lines, although not marked as a stopping station, and to alter or suspend the running of any of the trains, is reserved.

This Time Table will Not Operate on Any Day that may require a Special Time Table.

DOUGLAS—PORT ERIN LINE.

STATIONS	Weekdays.				To PORT ERIN.										Sundays			
	2	4	6	8	10	12	14	16	18	20	22	24	26	28	2	4	6	8
DOUGLAS ... ... Depart	8 15	10 5	10 15	10 35	11 0	12 10	2 15	2 45	3 20	4 35	5 35	7 45	9 5	*11 0* *Saturdays Only.*	10 0	2 30	7 15	8 0
Port Soderick ... ... ,,	R	...	10 26	10 46	11 13	12 21	...	2 56	3 31	4 46	5 46	7 56	9 16	*11 11*	10 11	2 41	7 26	8 11
Santon ... ... ,,	R	...	10 34	10 54	..	12 29	...	3 4	3 39	4 54	5 54	8 4	9 24	*11 19*	10 19	2 49	7 34	8 19
Ballasalla ... ... ,,	8 40	...	10 42	11 2	11 28	12 37	2 40	3 12	3 47	5 2	6 2	8 12	9 32	*11 27*	10 27	2 57	7 42	8 27
Castletown ... ... ,,	8 45	...	10 46	11 7	11 33	12 43	2 45	3 18	3 53	5 8	6 8	8 18	9 38	*11 33*	10 33	3 3	7 48	8 33
Ballabeg ... ... ,,	R	...	...	...	...	...	...	R	R	R	...	R	R	R	R	R	R	R
Colby ... ... ,,	8 52	...	...	11 15	11 41	12 51	...	3 27	4 1	5 16	6 16	8 26	9 46	*11 41*	10 41	3 11	7 56	8 41
Port St. Mary ... ... ,,	8 58	10 43	...	11 22	11 48	12 58	2 58	3 34	4 8	5 23	6 23	8 33	9 53	*11 48*	10 48	3 18	8 3	8 48
PORT ERIN ... ... Arrive	9 0	10 45	...	11 24	11 50	1 0	3 0	3 36	4 10	5 25	6 25	8 35	9 55	*11 50*	10 50	3 20	8 5	8 50

	Weekdays.				To DOUGLAS.										Sundays.			
	1	3	5	7	9	11	13	15	17	19	21	23	25	27	1	3	5	7
PORT ERIN ... ... Depart	7 15	9 15	...	11 5	12 0	1 15	2 15	3 20	4 20	5 35	6 40	8 0	9 5	*10 5* *Saturdays Only.*	9 0	4 30	7 0	9 15
Port St. Mary ... ... ,,	7 18	9 18	...	11 8	12 3	1 18	2 18	3 23	4 23	5 38	6 43	8 3	9 8	*10 8*	9 3	4 33	7 3	9 18
Colby... ... ... ,,	7 23	9 23	...	11 14	...	1 23	2 23	3 28	4 28	5 43	6 48	8 8	9 13	...	9 8	4 38	7 8	9 23
Ballabeg ... ... ,,	R	...	...	...	...	R	R	...	...	R	...	...	...	...	R	R	R	R
Castletown ... ... ,,	7 33	9 31	10 55	11 23	12 16	1 33	2 33	3 38	4 38	5 53	6 58	8 18	9 23	*10 21*	9 18	4 48	7 18	9 33
Ballasalla ... ... ,,	7 39	9 36	11 1	11 29	12 22	1 39	2 39	3 46	4 44	6 1	7 4	8 24	9 31	...	9 24	4 54	7 25	9 39
Santon ... ... ,,	7 47	9 43	...	...	12 30	1 47	2 47	3 54	4 53	6 9	7 12	8 32	9 39	...	9 32	5 2	7 33	9 47
Port Soderick ... ... ,,	7 55	9 50	11 14	11 45	12 38	1 55	2 55	4 2	5 1	6 17	7 20	8 40	9 47	...	9 40	5 10	7 41	9 55
DOUGLAS ... ... Arrive	8 5	10 0	11 24	11 55	12 48	2 5	3 5	4 12	5 11	6 27	7 30	8 50	9 57	*10 50*	9 50	5 20	7 51	10 5

DOUGLAS—PEEL and RAMSEY LINES.

	Weekdays.					To PEEL and RAMSEY.												Sundays.					
		2	4	6	8	10	12	14	16	18	20	22	24	26	28	30	32	2		4	6	8	10
DOUGLAS ... ... Depart	*Bus*	8 15	...	10 0	10 10	10 40	11 0	12 5	...	2 30	3 35	4 30	5 35	6 40	7 40	9 5	*Saturdays Only.*	10 0	**Special Trains—Douglas dep. at 10 10 & 10 20 am. for Kirk Braddan.**	2 30	...	7 0	...
Union Mills ... ... ,,		8 22	...	...	10 17	...	11 7	12 12	...	2 37	3 42	4 37	5 42	...	7 47	9 12		10 7		2 37	...	7 7	...
Crosby ... ... ,,		8 29	...	...	10 24	...	11 14	12 19	...	2 44	3 49	4 44	5 49	...	7 54	9 19		10 14		2 44	...	7 14	...
St. John's ... ... Arrive		8 38	..	10 19	10 33	11 0	11 23	12 28	...	2 53	3 58	4 53	5 58	7 0	8 3	9 28		10 23		2 53	...	7 23	...
St. John's ... ... Depart	...	8 41	9 35	...	10 34	11 3	11 26	12 31	1 45	2 56	4 1	4 59	6 1	...	8 6	9 31		10 26		2 56	5 3	7 26	10 8
PEEL... ... ... Arrive	...	8 50	9 44	...	10 43	11 12	11 35	12 40	1 54	3 5	4 10	5 8	6 10	...	8 15	9 40		10 35		3 5	5 12	7 35	10 17
St. John's ... ... Depart	...	8 43	...	10 21	...	11 5	...	12 33	...	2 57	4 2	4 59	6 2	7 5	8 8	9 33		10 28		2 58	...	7 28	...
Peel Road ... ... ,,	...	...	...	...	...	...	...	R	...	R	R	R	R	...	R	R		R		R	...	R	...
St. Germain's ... ... ,,	...	R	...	...	...	...	...	R	...	R	R	R	R	...	R	R		R		R	...	R	...
Kirk Michael (Glen Wyllin) ... ,,	*8 10*	9 6	...	10 39	...	11 26	...	12 54	...	3 18	4 23	5 19	6 23	7 25	8 29	9 54	*10 15*	10 49		3 19	...	7 49	...
Ballaugh... ... ... ,,	*8 18*	9 14	...	...	...	11 34	...	1 3	...	3 26	4 31	5 28	6 31	7 33	8 37	10 3	*10 23*	10 57		3 27	...	7 57	...
Sulby Glen ... ... ,,	*8 24*	9 20	...	...	...	11 40	...	1 9	...	3 32	4 37	5 34	6 37	7 39	8 43	10 9	*10 29*	11 3		3 33	...	8 3	...
Sulby Bridge ... ... ,,	*8 27*	9 23	...	...	...	11 44	...	1 12	...	3 35	4 40	5 37	6 40	7 42	8 46	10 12	*10 32*	11 6		3 36	...	8 6	...
Lezayre ... ... ,,	...	...	...	...	...	...	...	R	...	...	R	...	...	...	R	R	R	R		R	...	R	...
RAMSEY... ... ... Arrive	*8 36*	9 32	...	11 0	...	11 53	...	1 21	...	3 44	4 49	5 46	6 49	7 51	8 55	10 21	*10 41*	11 15		3 45	...	8 15	...

	Weekdays.					To DOUGLAS.										Sundays.					
	1		3	5	7	9	11	13	15	17	19	21	23	25	27	1		3	5	7	9
RAMSEY... ... ... Depart	6 45	*7 40*	8 40	...	10 10	11 35	12 45	2 0	2 50	...	4 10	5 10	7 15	8 35	*9 45*	8 35	**Special Trains—Kirk Braddan dep. from 11-30 to 12 noon for Douglas.**	...	4 15	...	9 20
Lezayre ... ... ,,	R	...	R	...	...	...	R	R	...	...	R	...	...	R	R	R		...	R	...	R
Sulby Bridge... ... ... ,,	6 55	*7 52*	8 50	...	10 20	11 45	12 55	2 10	3 0	...	4 20	5 20	...	8 45	*9 55*	8 45		...	4 25	...	9 30
Sulby Glen ... ... ,,	6 58	*7 54*	8 53	...	10 23	11 48	12 58	2 13	3 3	...	4 23	5 23	7 28	8 48	*9 58*	8 48		...	4 28	...	9 33
Ballaugh... ... ... ,,	7 4	*8 2*	8 59	...	10 29	11 54	1 4	2 19	3 9	...	4 30	5 29	7 34	8 54	*10 4*	8 54		...	4 34	...	9 39
Kirk Michael (Glen Wyllin) ... ,,	7 12	*8 10*	9 7	...	10 38	12 2	1 12	2 27	3 17	...	4 38	5 37	7 42	9 2	*10 11*	9 2		...	4 42	...	9 47
St. Germain's ... ... ,,	R	*Bus*	R	...	...	...	R	R	...	...	R	...	R	R	*Saturdays Only.*	R		...	R	...	R
Peel Road ... ... ,,	R		...	...	...	...	R	R	...	...	R	...	R	R		R		...	R	...	R
St. John's ... ... Arrive	7 32		9 27	...	10 58	12 22	1 32	2 47	3 37	...	4 58	5 57	8 2	9 22		9 22		...	5 2	...	10 7
PEEL ... ... Depart	7 25	...	9 20	10 5	10 53	12 15	1 25	2 40	3 25	4 45	...	5 50	7 55	9 15		9 15		2 45	4 52	7 15	9 55
St. John's ... ... Arrive	7 34	...	9 29	10 14	11 2	12 24	1 34	2 49	3 34	4 54	...	5 59	8 4	9 24		9 24		2 54	5 1	7 24	10 4
St. John's ... ... Depart	7 37	...	9 32	...	11 5	12 30	1 37	2 54	3 40	4 55	5 5	6 2	8 7	9 29		9 27		...	5 5	...	10 10
Crosby ... ... ,,	7 47	...	9 42	...	11 15	12 40	1 47	3 4	3 50	...	5 15	6 12	...	9 39		9 37		...	5 15	...	10 20
Union Mills ... ... ,,	7 54	...	9 49	...	11 22	12 47	1 54	3 11	3 57	...	5 22	6 19	...	9 46		9 44		...	5 22	...	10 27
DOUGLAS ... ... Arrive	8 0	...	9 55	...	11 28	12 53	2 0	3 17	4 3	5 16	5 28	6 25	8 28	9 52		9 50		...	5 28	...	10 33

FOXDALE LINE.—Weekdays—St. John's...depart... 7 55 ... *(Bus)* *10 40* ... *(Bus)* *2 0* ... 5 10
Foxdale......arrive... 8 9 ... *10 50* ... *2 10* ... 5 24

Weekdays—Foxdale ......depart... 8 20 ... *(Bus)* *10 50* ... *(Bus)* *2 20* ... 5 35
St. John's ...arrive... 8 34 ... *11 0* ... *2 30* ... 5 49

R—Trains marked thus will stop at Station indicated "by request."

RETURN TICKETS to the Terminal Stations — **Port Erin, Peel** and **Ramsey** — are available for BREAK OF JOURNEY AT INTERMEDIATE STATIONS, going or returning, thus affording a Cheap and Ideal Day's Outing.

A Special Point should be made of Visiting the

NEW GLEN WYLLIN

(Kirk Michael Station). Everything for your amusement. There is no more delightful place to spend a day, afternoon or evening. Magnificent Motor Boating Lake. Sun and Sea Bathing.

SPECIAL TOUR TICKETS

You can travel ANYWHERE with the popular **GO-AS-YOU-PLEASE TICKETS,** issued by ISLE OF MAN RAILWAY—the Best and Cheapest way to see the Island. Similar Tickets are also issued by arrangement with ISLE OF MAN ROAD SERVICES, LTD., covering the Train and Bus Services combined. Full information and Tickets obtainable at all Stations and Offices of the Companies.

Special Booking and Enquiry Offices: At Villa Marina Colonnade, at Crescent Cinema, at Pier Buildings, and at Villiers Buildings, Douglas.

Douglas. A. M. SHEARD, Secretary and Manager

BUS STATION—Adjoining Market Place. DOUGLAS RAILWAY STATION—Athol Street and Top of Harbour

IOMR Timetable for 1938.

Timetables

A selection of timetables taken from publicity material serves as a reminder of times past. For those anxious for additional information - for a careful reading-between-the-lines of a timetable reflects the day-to-day story of a railway - the Railway Museum at Port Erin has among others:

October 1909; Whitsuntide 1914; July 1920; October 1924; 1947; 1954; 1955

There was differing opinion as to the validity of publishing joint tables for the three steam railways; the first MNR joint table of 1879 was headed ISLE OF MAN RAILWAY but became ISLE OF MAN RAILWAYS in November 1880. When a joint table was abandoned in August 1886 due to the IOMR refusing to add the Foxdale line, the MNR was obliged to issue a joint MNR/FR table (but the IOMR continued to use the plural title). The new table, thus forced on the MNR, gave MNR connections to Douglas but not the South Line.

Folders in red leather with gilt lettering first appeared from the IOMR and were imitated by the MNR later; they held booklets having tables, fares, conditions etc. for use in public places, ticket agencies, stations etc.

Pocket timetables. A joint IOMR/MNR example for 1899 is in the WEH-LYN Railway Records at the National Railway Museum and acknowledges the existence of the Foxdale system by according one line at the foot to two Up and two Down daily trains - there is no mention of Sunday working. The map on the cover *excludes* the Foxdale Line.

An unusual item was a IOMR table printed on a small disc of paper to fit inside the cover of a guard's pocket watch. (Narrow Gauge Railway Museum, Tywyn.)

As the tourist trade developed, an average of twelve trains each for the Peel and South Lines, and eleven trains on the North was adequate in summer. The cut-back since World War II included evening trains as visitors were back in their lodgings before 6 pm to partake of 'High Tea' (partly a habit and partly due to postwar rationing): this was acceptable to the IOMR as it brought economies and lessened overtime. In summer 1961 there were eight Up and six Down trains on the South Line, two Up and four Down on the Peel and three workings each way between St John's and Ramsey, daily. In addition, there was a working for school-children Kirk Michael-Ramsey, twice daily. Subsequent reductions are mentioned in Vol. II and these brought a daily train in winter down to one engine and one coach, working to Port Erin in the morning and Peel after noon. (Ramsey was closed in the winter, and served by Railway Bus.) Kirk Braddan apart, Sunday workings ceased with a single return train on the South Line in the afternoon in summer 1957, but the policy of the present time has looked upon Saturday closures with favour, and working on Sundays. In part, this is due to changing patterns in Sunday leisure. To be dogmatic about IOMR timetable procedures is impossible . . . It is pertinent to remember that in 1926, Specials apart, Douglas station dealt with forty-six booked trains - forty-seven on Saturdays; at that time trains left up to 11 pm and the station awaited the last from Peel at 11.21 pm.

The fast Down trains of 1936-38 are mentioned in Vol. I pp. 105-6; they were continued to the outbreak of World War II and there was a fast Up train on the South Line leaving Port Erin at 10.5 am, stopping at Port St Mary and Castletown only. Headboards were carried, COCK O' THE NORTH for Ramsey, and SOUTHERN BELLE for Port Erin.

ISLE OF MAN RAILWAY

NOTICE.—The hours or times stated in the Company's Time Tables, Books, Bills and Notices are appointed as those at which it is intended so far as circumstances will permit, that the trains shall depart from and arrive at the several Stations, but their departure or arrival at the times stated is not guaranteed, nor will the Company under any circumstances be held responsible for delay or detention, however occasioned, or any consequences arising therefrom. The right to stop the trains at any Station on the lines, although not marked as a stopping Station, and to alter or suspend the running of any of the trains, is reserved.

This Time Table will Not Operate on Any Day that may require a Special Time Table.

TIME TABLE for Wednesday, July 6th, 1949, and until further notice

DOUGLAS—PORT ERIN LINE.—WEEKDAYS SUNDAYS.

To PORT ERIN

STATIONS	4	6	8	10		12	14	16		18	20	22	24 SATURDAYS ONLY		2 (Sundays)	4 (Sundays)
DOUGLAS Dep.	8 25	10 10	10 40	11 40	...	2 15	3 10	4 10	...	5 45	6 45	8 5	9 0	...	2 35	7 15
Port Soderick .... "	R	...	R	...	...	R	R	R	...	R	....	R	R	...	R	R
Santon .... "	8 44	10 29	10 59	11 59	...	2 34	3 29	4 29	...	6 3	7 4	8 23	9 19	...	2 54	7 34
Ballasalla .... "	8 52	10 37	11 7	12 7	...	2 42	3 37	4 37	...	6 12	7 12	8 32	9 27	...	3 2	7 42
Castletown .... "	8 58	10 43	11 13	12 13	...	2 48	3 43	4 43	...	6 18	7 18	8 38	9 33	....	3 8	7 48
Colby .... "	9 6	10 51	11 21	12 21	...	2 56	3 51	4 51	...	6 26	7 26	8 46	9 41	...	3 16	7 56
Port St. Mary .... "	9 13	10 58	11 28	12 28	....	3 3	3 58	4 58	...	6 33	7 33	8 53	9 48	...	3 23	8 3
PORT ERIN Arr.	9 15	11 0	11 30	12 30	....	3 5	4 0	5 0	...	6 35	7 35	8 55	9 50	...	3 25	8 5

To DOUGLAS

STATIONS	1	5		7	9	11	13	15		17	19	21	23		1 (Sundays)	3 (Sundays)
PORT ERIN Dep.	7 10	8 40	...	10 25	11 45	1 0	2 0	4 10	....	4 25	5 30	7 0	7 50	...	4 25	9 0
Port St. Mary "	7 13	8 43	...	10 28	11 48	1 3	2 3	4 15	...	4 28	5 33	7 3	7 53	...	4 28	9 3
Colby .... "	7 18	8 48	...	10 33	11 53	1 8	2 8	4 20	....	4 33	5 38	7 8	7 58	....	4 33	9 8
Castletown .... "	7 28	8 57	....	10 42	12 2	1 17	2 17	4 30	...	4 42	5 47	7 17	8 7	....	4 42	9 17
Ballasalla ... "	7 37	9 3	...	10 48	12 8	1 23	2 23	4 38	...	4 53	5 53	7 23	8 13	....	4 48	9 23
Santon ... "	7 47	9 12	...	10 58	12 17	1 32	2 32	....	....	5 2	6 2	7 32	8 22	....	4 57	9 32
Port Soderick .... "	R	R	...	R	R	R	R	....	...	5 10	R		R	...	R	R
DOUGLAS Arr.	8 5	9 30	...	11 15	12 35	1 50	2 50	5 5	....	5 20	6 20	7 50	8 40	...	5 15	9 50

DOUGLAS—PEEL and RAMSEY LINES. WEEKDAYS

To PEEL and RAMSEY

STATIONS	2	4	6		8	10		12		14	16	18	20		22		24	B	26 SATURDAYS ONLY
DOUGLAS Dep.	...	8 25	9 5	....	10 15	10 45	...	12 0	...	2 15	3 30	4 17	4 35	...	5 40	...	6 45	B	9 0
Union Mills .... "	...	8 32	9 12	....	...	R	...	12 7	...	R	R	4 24	4 42	...	5 47	...	6 52	...	9 7
Crosby .... "	...	8 39	9 19	...	...	10 59	...	12 14	...	2 29	3 44	4 31	4 51	...	5 54	...	6 59	...	9 14
St. John's Arr.	...	8 48	9 28	...	10 35	11 8	...	12 23	...	2 38	3 53	4 40	5 0	...	6 3	...	7 8	...	9 23
St. John's Dep.	...	8 51	9 36	...	...	11 11	...	12 26	1 30	2 41	....	4 43	...	...	6 6	...	7 11	...	9 26
PEEL .... Arr.	...	9 0	9 45	...	...	11 20	...	12 35	1 39	2 50	....	4 52	...	...	6 15	...	7 20	....	9 35
St. John's Dep.	....	...	9 38	...	10 38	11 13	...	12 26	...	2 41	3 55	...	5 7	...	6 8	...	7 13	....	9 28
Peel Road .... "	....	...	...	...	...	....	...	...	...	....	....	....	....	...	....	...	...	....	...
St. Germain's .... "	....	...	R	...	...	R	...	R	...	...	R	...	R	...	R	....	R	....	R
Kirk Michael .... "	8 0	...	9 59	...	10 58	11 34	...	12 47	...	3 2	4 16	...	5 27	...	6 29	...	7 34	....	9 49
Ballaugh .... "	8 8	...	10 7	...	...	11 42	...	12 55	...	3 10	4 24	...	5 35	...	6 38	....	7 42	....	9 57
Sulby Glen ... "	8 14	...	10 13	...	....	11 48	...	1 2	...	3 16	4 30	...	5 41	...	6 43	...	7 48	....	10 3
Sulby Bridge .... "	8 17	...	10 16	...	...	11 51	...	1 6	...	3 21	4 33	...	5 46	...	6 46	...	7 51	....	10 6
Lezayre ... "	R	...	...	...	...	...	...	....	...	...	....	...	R	...	....	...	...	....	....
RAMSEY Arr.	8 27	...	10 25	...	11 20	12 0	...	1 15	...	3 30	4 42	...	5 55	...	6 55	...	8 0	...	10 15

To DOUGLAS

STATIONS	1		3	5	7		9		11	13	15	17	19		21	23 SATURDAYS ONLY	25 SATURDAYS ONLY
RAMSEY Dep.	6 45	....	7 30	...	8 45	...	11 40	...	12 35	1 45	...	4 5	5 15	...	6 20	....	8 35
Lezayre .... "	...	....	....	...	R	...	...	...	R	....	...	R	...	....	...	....	...
Sulby Bridge .... "	6 55	....	....	...	8 55	...	11 50	...	12 45	1 55	...	4 15	5 25	....	6 30	....	8 45
Sulby Glen .... "	6 58	....	....	...	8 58	...	...	...	12 48	1 58	...	4 18	5 28	....	6 33	....	8 48
Ballaugh .... "	7 4	....	....	...	9 4	...	...	...	12 54	2 4	...	4 24	5 34	....	6 39	....	8 54
Kirk Michael .... "	7 12	....	7 55	...	9 12	...	12 5	...	1 2	2 12	...	4 32	5 42	...	6 47	....	9 2
St. Germain's .... "	R	....	....	...	R	...	...	...	R	....	...	R	...	...	R	....	R
Peel Road .... "	R	....	....	...	...	...	...	...	R	....	...	R	...	....	...	....	...
St. John's Arr.	7 32	....	....	...	9 32	....	12 25	...	1 22	2 32	...	4 52	6 2	....	7 7	....	9 22
PEEL .... Dep.	7 25	...	....	8 5	9 25	10 20	12 15	...	1 15	2 25	4 30	...	5 55	....	7 0	8 0	....
St. John's Arr.	7 34	...	....	8 14	9 34	10 29	12 24	...	1 24	2 34	4 39	...	6 4	...	7 9	8 9	....
St. John's Dep.	7 37	...	....	8 16	9 37		12 27	...	1 27	2 40	4 42	5 2	6 7	...	7 12	8 12	....
Crosby .... "	7 47	...	....	8 26	9 47		12 37	...	1 37	2 50	4 52	5 12	6 17	...	7 22	8 22	...
Union Mills ... "	7 54	...	....	8 33	9 54	...	12 44	...	1 44	2 58	4 59	5 19	6 24	...	7 29	8 29	...
DOUGLAS Arr.	8 0	...	....	8 40	10 0	....	12 50	...	1 50	3 5	5 5	5 25	6 30	....	7 35	8 35	...

Kirk Braddan Open Air Service, Sunday Mornings—Trains to and from Braddan Bridge adjacent to the Church:
Douglas dep. 10 0 to 10 40
Braddan Bridge dep. 11 30 to 12 0—Fare 4d.

R—Request Halt.

B—Bus Service, Douglas (Market Place) dep. 8 0 p.m. for Kirk Michael, with connection to Ballaugh, Sulby, etc.

Douglas. A. M. SHEARD, Secretary & Manager.

Bus Service between Pier and Douglas Station in connection with Steamers.

IOMR Timetable for 1949.

Mining in the Island

The Island was heavily mineralised and in the past has produced substantial quantities of metalliferous types, mainly lead, silver and zinc, though copper and iron were also mined on a smaller scale. The relevant importance of the Island mines to others in England and Wales was high but extended detail is inappropriate here, sufficient to say that mining existed long before railways and the list of mines herein mentions only those which used the steam railways. Output apart, all mines required an inward supply of coal for the furnaces to heat the boliers and supply steam for hoisting and pumping; such power had at first come from water wheels; there were copious supplies of water in this respect.

The St John's & Foxdale Railway provided the most important rail link but only such Foxdale mines as were adjacent its terminus could avoid the slow and costly horse-and-cart haulage from workings to station. No figures are available to show tonnages each mine put on rail, only the Railway's Annual Returns showed the total minerals carried. The only direct reference to mining by the IOMR is in the Annual Report of 29th September, 1886.

Mining statistics first appeared in 1845 and by the time the Foxdale Railway was opened its mines were producing more than two-thirds of the Island's lead and silver tonnages. Foxdale reached its peak tonnages in the early 1890s; a doubtful policy of continuous expansion was carried out at the same time as prices were falling. Serious difficulties were experienced below ground and in consequence mining in the district ceased before the First War. The Isle of Man Mining Co. Ltd., the largest undertaking at Foxdale, liquidated in 1911.

Mines which used Foxdale station as the railhead included:*

Mine		*Map Ref.*	*Period*
1	Beckwith's	252779	*c.* 1832-*c.* 1880
2	Cross's	263780	*c.* 1832-1881
3	Dixon's†	269780	*c.* 1835-*c.* 1868
4	Upper Old Foxdale#	280781	pre 1828-*c.* 1902
5	Lower Old Foxdale†	283778	pre 1828-1829
6	Old Flappy#	281778	pre 1740-*c.* 1902
7	Maghie's	281774	1834-1880
8	Louisa#	288778	1831-*c.* 1902
9	Far Gin }		
10	New Foxdale }	300768	pre 1828-1883
12	Ballergy#	280787	1837-1926

*The above is a simplified list; for extended detail see INDUSTRIAL ARCHAELOGY OF THE ISLE OF MAN pp.68-87 (David & Charles). List also incorporates Paul Abell's notes from Manx Museum Ref. File B170 7x, and use of ISLE OF MAN, MEMOIRS OF THE GEOLOGICAL SURVEY, 1905 (S.W. Lamplugh).

†Closed before coming of the railway.

#Operated as one latterly.

Used level crossing on Peel Line at Ballacurry.

Mine		*Map Ref.*	*Period*
11	Townshend's (or Cornelly)	298796	1837-1886

The following mines had access to the railway if required:

Mine	*Map Ref.*	*Period*	*Station*
Ballacorkish	220700	1862-1910	Colby
Belle Abbey	224706	1876-1889	Colby
Langness	282660	1881-1913	Castletown

The Foxdale Mines

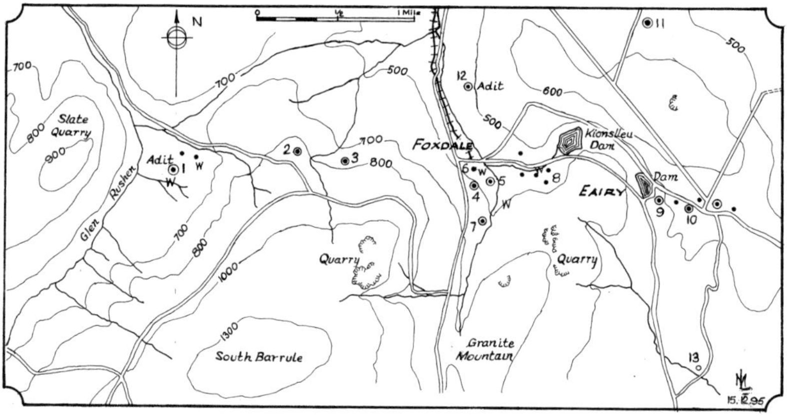

Appendix One

Acts of Tynwald concerning railways

Act of 1872	Isle of Man Railway Co. Ltd.	(Powers etc.)
1874	Isle of Man Railway Co. Ltd.	(Borrowing Powers)
1887	Isle of Man Railway Co. Ltd.	('Ltd.' to be dropped)
1874	Railways Refreshment Rooms.	(Licensing)
1876	Railways Refreshment Rooms.	(1874 Act repealed)
1878	Regulation of Railways.	
1885	Regulation of Railways.	(Surplus Lands)
1930	Railway Regulation Amendment.	(Rates & charges)
1967	IOMR & Railway Regulation.	(Special provisions & powers to sell)
1878	Manx Northern Railway Co. Ltd.	(Powers etc.)
1879	Manx Northern Railway Co. Ltd.	(1878 Act amended)
1888	MNR & Foxdale Railway Co. Ltd.	(Powers etc: 'Ltd.'to be dropped)
1890	Manx Northern Railway.	
1884	Foxdale Railway Co. Ltd.	(Powers etc.)
1904	IOM Railways.	(Purchase of MNR/FR by IOMR)

Among the conditions set forth in the above, may be cited:

Isle of Man Railway (1872 Act)
Speed over level crossings not to exceed 10 mph.
To safeguard animals on roadways adjoining the railway, a board fence to be erected between the two.
Mileposts to be erected every quarter-mile.
Passenger fares not to exceed 2*d*. per mile.
Postmaster General may require the railway to carry mail.
IOMR may lay down telegraph wires for their own use.
All accidents must be reported to the Governor. Steam locomotives must consume their own smoke.

Manx Northern Railway (1878 Act)
To make junction with the IOMR at St John's.
To erect signalling at St John's to IOMR satisfaction and control but at MNR expense.

Foxdale Railway (1888 Act)
Clearance under the Luke Bridge to be at least 14 ft.
Junction with the IOMR is forbidden.
Powers were granted to extend the railway to Ballasalla, Castletown (etc).
The bridge at St John's carrying the railway over the IOMR, to be erected to the satisfaction of the IOMR. In the event of disagreement, the Governor to act as referee.

Appendix Two

Locomotive Superintendents

(This post was established when that of General Superintendent was abolished; there was therefore no appointee until May 1876)

Henry R. Hunt	May 1876-January 1886	(1)
Joseph Sproat	February 1886-March 1912	(2)
James Bradshaw	April 1912-February 1929	(3)
Frederick Joseph Vaughan	February 1929-July 1946	(4)
Donald Shaw	August 1946-February 1976	(5)

(1) Notice of resignation August 1885; Joseph Sproat, Locomotive Foreman, 'to take his place for the time being'.

(2) Suffered a stroke 17th March, 1912, and died 'in office'. Had previously been employed by Maryport & Carlisle Railway.

(3) Came from Beyer, Peacock & Co. Ltd. Locomotive Foreman 1909. Promoted Acting Locomotive Superintendent 1911 during Sproat's illness prior to a stroke. Appointed Superintendent 17th April, 1912. Was retired on small pension following Oakhill collision on 15th November, 1928. He died on 31st December, 1937.

(4) Resigned suddenly on 31st July, 1946. Retained as consultant.

(5) Joined IOMR on 2nd October, 1922 as apprentice; became Works Foreman June 1930. Appointed Locomotive Superintendent etc. August 1946. Retired February 1976. Retained as consultant. Died July 1980.

Appendix Three

Isle of Man Railway - Island Directors after whom locomotives were named

No. 10	George Henry WOOD
No. 11	Dalrymple MAITLAND
No. 12	William A. HUTCHINSON
No. 13	Edward Thomas KISSACK

George Henry Wood of Oakley House, Derby Road, Douglas. Son of Thomas Wood of Highfield, Slaithwaite, near Huddersfield. Came to Island and became an accountant and insurance agent after employment in Harris & Adams, advocates. Great friend of Goldie-Taubman family, for which estate he acted as agent. Was sometime Coroner for Middle. Died 1925, age 89. His psychic powers were notable and he was something of a clairvoyant. (1)

Dalrymple Maitland of Brook Mooar, Unhills. His father was proprietor and Editor of the LIVERPOOL MERCURY. His mother's family owned a cloth manufactory and corn mill at Union Mills, businesses which he sold in 1890 on becoming Board member of IOMSPCL and IOM Banking Co. Board member of IOMR 1899-1919. Died 1919, age 71. (2)

William A. Hutchinson of The Groves, Marown. Born 1853 in the Island but was in business in Yorkshire until returned; was a Board member of IOM Banking Co., Chairman of IOM Fisheries Board. Captain of Parish of Marown. Board member of IOMR 1898-1909. Died 1909. (3)

Edward Thomas Kissack of Eyreton, Quarterbridge Road, Douglas. Born 1850, third son of James Kissack who owned a chain of grocery shops. By profession a dentist; he had a highly rewarding practice in Manchester. Retired to Douglas. Board member 1902-1927. Died 1928. (4) [Kissack is the only Manx surname to be carried by a Manx locomotive].

(1) Family history per Mrs John Crocker (nee Audrey Wood), a grand-daughter of G.H. Wood.

(2) See also MANX QUARTERLY No. 21 Vol. V, April 1920. (Portrait).

(3) See also MANX QUARTERLY No. 7. 1909, IOM EXAMINER ANNUAL 1905 p.37 (Portrait).

(4) See also SEED OF ISAAC (Rev. Rex Kissack) p. 178.
Family details per Rev. R. Kissack, Glen Mooar.

Appendix Four

Contents of Ramsey Workshop

As at 13th October, 1905 (verbatim)

Screwcutting Lathe, 9 in. centres
Foot Lathe, 5½ in. centres
Small planing machine
Small Gas Engine c. 2½ hp
Four bench vices (two each in Fitting & Joiner's Shop)
Bellows, anvil, hammer, Smith's hearth
Brazing machine and stand
Boring machine for locomotive cylinders
Joiner's wood boring machine
3 chain lifting blocks
15 ton hydraulic lifting jack
Old vertical boiler in bad order, with part of pump connected

Appendix Five

Governors 1863-1995

1863	Henry Brougham Loch
1882	Spencer Walpole
1893	Sir John West Ridgeway
1896	Lord Henniker
1902	Lord Raglan
1919	Maj. Gen. Sir William Fry
1926	Sir Claude H.A. Hill
1933	Sir Montague Butler
1937	Vice Admiral The Earl Granville
1945	Sir Geoffrey Rhodes Bromet
1952	Sir Ambrose Dundas Flux Dundas
1957	Sir Ronald Herbert Garvey
1966	Sir Peter Hyla Gawne Stallard
1974	Sir John Warburton Paul
1980	Rear Admiral Sir Oswald Nigel Cecil
1985	Maj. Gen. Laurence New
1990	Air Marshall Sir Laurence Alfred Jones

Value of Daily Traffic to IOMR (From off MNR and FR)

Thursday 1st June, 1899 - Sunday 18th June, 1899

Date		*Day*	*MNR Origin*			*FR Origin*		
			£	s.	d.	£	s.	d.
1st	June	Thursday	26	5	0	0	9	7
2nd	June	Friday	21	15	8	1	3	11
3rd	June	Saturday	112	8	8	15	15	8
4th	June	Sunday	8	9	6	-	-	-
5th	June	Monday	27	9	3	1	12	8
6th	June	Tuesday	24	3	6	1	15	2
7th	June	Wednesday	25	0	8	0	8	0
8th	June	Thursday	20	13	8	1	8	1
9th	June	Friday	18	6	8	0	10	0
10th	June	Saturday	38	6	6	3	3	10
11th	June	Sunday	9	4	3	-	-	-
12th	June	Monday	25	18	0	0	5	7
13th	June	Tuesday	24	19	6	0	3	4
14th	June	Wednesday	27	11	2	1	4	11
15th	June	Thursday	32	5	6	2	0	0
16th	June	Friday	21	8	9	0	3	3
17th	June	Saturday	43	9	1	1	22	11
18th	June	Sunday	7	13	5	-	-	-

It is assumed that the values represent income from all types of traffic combined. Note the increase in value on Saturdays; there are no Foxdale values for Sundays. There is provision for Waterfall takings, but none are recorded in this period.
(The ledger from which these extracts are taken was accessioned in the Manx Museum during 1995.)

Appendix Seven

Extracts from IOMR Train Books 1874 and 1879

Month ending 31 May 1874 (Douglas-Peel Line open)

Engine No.	*Miles*	*Enginemen's Wages*			*Cost per Train Mile*
1	1,786	£11	10s.	6*d.*	5.85*d.*
2†	15		1s.	11*d.*	-
3	2,231	£14	7s.	9*d.*	5.34*d.*

†No. 2 was on shunting only, after overhaul in the Workshop.

Month ending 31 August 1879 (Peel & South Lines open)

Engine No.	*Miles*	*Enginemen's Wages*			*Cost per Train Mile*	*Driver*
1	2,806	£13	17*s.*	11*d.*	3.79*d.*	Cain
2	2,769	£15	2*s.*	5*d.*	3.78*d.*	JBP
3	1,004	£1	1*s.*	5*d.*	6.67*d.*	Various
4	3,077	£17	18*s.*	9*d.*	3.60*d.*	Kendall
5	3,196	£21	16*s.*	10*d.*	3.97*d.*	Steels
6	824	£4	11*s.*	10*d.*	4.79*d.*	Various

Among other facts revealed should be noted; Costs per train mile lessen as experience / running-in continues: low mileages indicate an engine which has just been through the Works (or is about to be taken in): the allocation of one engine / one driver (the same names continue down the years).

These figures are taken from IOMR ledgers accessioned in the Manx Museum in 1995. To simplify the listed statistics, only sample extracts are quoted but they serve to show the detailed records kept by the office staff.

Appendix Eight

Manx Northern Railway

Cost of rolling stock at time of purchase

Listing by IOMR on 19th April, 1905

Item	£	*s.*	*d.*	
NORTHERN and RAMSEY	1,135	0	0	each
THORNHILL	1,272	0	0	
CALEDONIA	1,235	0	0	
First Class Six-wheeled	433	0	0	
Composite Six-wheeled	414	10	0	
Composite Bogie*	495	0	0	
Third Class Six-wheeled	339	0	0	
Third Class Saloon	360	0	0	
Passenger Brake Vans	154	0	0	
Goods Wagons Covered	64	5	0	
Goods Wagons (averaged)	44	7	0	
Cattle Trucks	61	6	8	

Total value of all stock £13, 127.

In addition there were two Third Class carriages so much damaged that they were turned into Trainmen's Shelters.

Cost of new couplings and alterations £151
Cost of making new carriage cushions.. £57

*Author's note: The valuation cites three vehicles under this heading, therefore the two MNR Hurst, Nelson coaches and the coach bought for the Foxdale line were averaged at £495 each.

Appendix Nine

Rolling Stock Survey

Compiled January 1992

This survey was made by Tony Beard with the co-operation of Colin Goldsmith, and later published in the MANX STEAM RAILWAY NEWS. Certain changes in 1993-94 appear in the chronologies of Vol. II to which reference should be made for completeness.

Locomotives

No. 1	SUTHERLAND	Withdrawn; extant Port Erin Museum.
No. 2	DERBY	Dismantled 1951; pony truck exists.
No. 3	PENDER	Withdrawn; left IOM on 12/9/79 for North West Museum of Science & Industry.
No. 4	LOCH	In service.
No. 5	MONA	Withdrawn; extant Douglas.
No. 6	PEVERIL	Withdrawn; extant Douglas.
No. 7	TYNWALD	Dismantled 1945; frame still exists.
No. 8	FENELLA	Withdrawn 1968.
No. 9	DOUGLAS	Withdrawn; extant Port Erin shed.
No. 10	G.H. WOOD	Withdrawn; exists (no boiler) Douglas.
No. 11	MAITLAND	In service.
No. 12	HUTCHINSON	In service.
No. 13	KISSACK	In service.
No. 14	THORNHILL	Withdrawn; privately preserved in IOM.
No. 15	CALEDONIA	Withdrawn; extant Port Erin Museum.
No. 16	MANNIN	Withdrawn; extant Port Erin Museum.

Railcars

Diesel Railcars Nos. 19 and 20 (ex-County Donegal Railways) extant, used only on permanent way trains.

Motorised Trolleys

Wickham	Ex-Queens Pier Tramway: was loaned to the Railway in February 1987.
Wickham	Two of these vehicles arrived in 1979/1980 and are understood to have been obtained (?) by William Jackson (then Chief Executive) from an Ordnance Depot. Extant Douglas carriage shed - not in use.
Simplex	Given by North West Museum of Science & Industry in 1980/1981 loaned to civil engineers Miller & Baird of Nottingham; later returned to the Island. By then re-gauged to 3 ft (was 2 ft 11½ in.). Extant Douglas carriage shed. Never used on IOMR.

Carriage Stock

F 1 Burnt St John's shed fire 1975.
F 2 Burnt St John's 1976.
F 3 Sold to Welsh Highland Railway.
F 4 Burnt St John's shed fire 1975.
F 5 Burnt St John's 1976.
F 6 Sold Mr Rampton.
F 7 Burnt St John's shed fire 1975.
F 8 Burnt Douglas 1970.
F 9 Extant Douglas.
F10 Extant Douglas.
F11 Extant Douglas.
F12 Scrapped November 1982.
F13 Burnt St John's shed fire 1975.
F14 Burnt St John's 1976.
F15 Extant Douglas.
F16 Burnt St John's shed fire 1975.
F17 Burnt St John's shed fire 1975.
F18 Extant Douglas.
F19 Burnt St John's 1976.
F20 Burnt St John's shed fire 1975.
F21 Sold to Welsh Highland Railway.
F22 Burnt St John's shed fire 1975.
F23 Scrapped February 1983. (a)
F24 Burnt St Johns shed fire 1975.
F25 Extant Douglas.
F26 Extant Douglas.
F27 Extant Douglas.
F28 Extant Douglas.
F29 Extant Douglas.
F30 Extant Douglas.
F31 Extant Douglas. (b)
F32 Extant Douglas. (b)
F33 Scrapped. (c)
F34 Burnt St John's shed fire 1975.
F35 Extant Douglas. (b)
F36 Extant Port Erin Museum.
F37 Sold Mr Rampton.
F38 Sold Mr Rampton.
F39 Extant Douglas.
F40 Scrapped Douglas 1977. (c)
F41 Extant Douglas.
F42 Burnt St John's shed fire 1975.
F43 Extant Douglas.
F44 Scrapped 1983. (c)
F45 Extant Douglas.
F46 Extant Douglas.
F47 Extant Douglas.
F48 Extant Douglas.
F49 Extant Douglas.
F50 Scrapped 1974. (c)
F51 Scrapped St John's 1968. (d)
F52 Scrapped St John's 1968. (d)
F53 Scrapped St John's 1968. (d)
F54 Extant Douglas. (e)
F55 Scrapped St John's 1968.(d)
F56 Scrapped St John's 1968.(d)
F57 Extant Douglas.
F58 Scrapped St John's 1968. (d)
F59 Scrapped St John's 1968. (d)
F60 Scrapped St John's 1968. (d)
F61 Scrapped St John's 1968. (d)
F62 Extant Douglas.
F63 Extant Douglas.
F64 Scrapped 1978. (c) (f)
F65 Scrapped 1973. (g)
F66 Extant Douglas. (h)
F67 Extant Douglas.
F68 Sold Mr Rampton.
F69 Scrapped Castletown 1968.
F70 Extant Douglas.
F71 Scrapped. (c)
F72 Scrapped St John's 1968. (d)
F73 Scrapped. (c)
F74 Extant Douglas.
F75 Extant Port Erin Museum.

N40 Sold Mr Rampton.
N41 Mess hut outside Douglas steam shed.
N42 Extant Port Erin Museum.
N43 Fired 1975.
N44 Fired 1975.
N45 Privately preserved in IOM.
N46 Fired 1975.
N47 Fired 1975.
N48 Scrapped prior to 1975.
N49 Fired 1975.
N50 Fired 1975.
N51 Sold Mr Rampton.

Notes:

(a) Coach body scrapped February 1983. Frame now used to carry equipment required for weed killing and fire train, numbered to correspond with former coach number.

(b) F31/35/32 (in this formation) were converted in 1980/1981 to form a special three-coach train for party hire (now known as 'The Bar Set'). F31/32 were gutted with new seats and tables fitted, the central partitions removed and corridor connections made with coach F35; the central partition was removed as were the seats in the 3rd Class section: replaced with a drinks bar and toilet. It is also fitted with its own generator to provide power, particularly for the lights. The external livery on all three coaches is red and white.

(c) Coach body scrapped. Frame used as a Runner and numbered to correspond with former coach number.

(d) Coach body scrapped. Frame sold 1974 to Festiniog Railway.

(e) Coach body scrapped.

(f) F64. Douglas end of coach body damaged by fire at Port Erin on 6th August, 1978 and later scrapped. Remaining half (formerly C1) survives but has been turned round and now sits on an 'M' wagon. The frame from F64 is now under F66. The frame now used as a Runner and fitted with drop sides.

(g) F65. Coach body scrapped. Frame converted into a ballast hopper.

(h) F66. Coach body refurbished in 1979 and placed on the frame from F64 and renumbered No. 1 for a short time (now reverted to F66). The frame from F66 is now numbered F64.

RUNNERS used for carrying rails sleepers, etc. are F33; F40; F44; F50; F64; F71; F73.

G Vans

G 1	Extant Douglas.
Gr12	Extant Port Erin Museum.
G19	Extant Douglas (still retaining vacuum brakes to run between railcars): now fitted with roof platform for use as a tree-lopper.

M Wagons

M69	Believed carrying the remaining half of coach body F64.
M70	Extant Douglas.
M78	Dismantled in Douglas workshops.

Well Wagon

Originally single 4-wheeled well wagon built 1936, lengthened in recent years and fitted with bogie trucks.

Crane

Breakdown crane supplied by Richard C. Gibbins sold by IOMR in 1974 to Manx Metals Ltd., leased back to Railway Society. Extant at Union Mills as an exhibit (part of the Railway Heritage Trail).

Ramsey Pier Truck

4-wheeled truck (formerly used to carry luggage on the pier tramway). Extant.

Rail Ballast Tamper

Obtained in 1980/1982; extant Douglas.

Appendix Ten

Stock List - January 1996

(as supplied)

Coaches

F9	In Service	Now with plate frame bogies ex F64
F10	In Service	Plate frame bogies ex F71
F11	In Service	Plate frame bogies ex F73
F15	In Service	
F18	In Service	
F25	Withdrawn	
F26	In Service	
F29	In Service	
F30	In Service	
F31	In Service	
F32	In Service	
F35	In Service	Now with plate frame bogies ex F65
F36	Port Erin Museum	Now with plate frame bogies ex ?
F39	In Service	
F41	Withdrawn	
F43	Withdrawn	
F45	In Service	
F46	In Service	
F47	In Service	
F48	In Service	
F49	In Service	
F54	In Service	
F62	Withdrawn	
F63	Withdrawn	
F66	In Service	Underframe changed with F64
F67	Withdrawn	
F70	Withdrawn	
F74	Withdrawn	
F75	Port Erin Museum	
N41	Mess Hut at Douglas	
N42	Port Erin Museum	(IOM Railway Society)
N45	Lezayre	(J. Edwards)
F27	Empress Van	
F28	Empress Van	
F64	One half of body in carriage shed	

Runners

F23	Weed spraying/Fire fighting
F 33	

Runners (continued)

F40	Bogies ex F12 - Original bogies now spares at Douglas
F44	
F50	
F57	Body scrapped December 1995
F64	Double 'M' wagon, originally under F66, bogies ex F9
F65	Ballast hopper, bogies ex F 35, brake work fitted
F71	Bogies ex F10
F73	Bogies ex F11

Vans

G1	
G19	
Gr12	Port Erin Museum

'M' Wagons

M69
M70

1 Well Wagon

Cranes

No. 2	Union Mills (IOM Railway Society)
No. 3	Taylor & Hubberd 30 cwt. steam (S.P. Carter). Built 1902 re-commissioned July 1994; originally standard gauge at Laxey Harbour.

Wickham Trolleys

W6/11-1	Type 27 built 30th May, 1956
W6/11-3	Type 27A built 10th February, 1961

Simplex

One Locomotive Type 40s

In Conclusion

There were times past when a railway company was fortunate if it found anyone to compile and publish its history. Anyone familiar with the pattern of things as they were would correctly have deduced that would-be authors were deterred by the enormity of research together with the time required and expense involved. Even having completed such an undertaking, there were few publishers who would show the same enthusiasm for a subject as a budding writer possessed. So the background to, and evolvement of, our larger railways remains to be written: true, along the shelves may be found titles covering the Great Western, the Great Central and the Midland Railway - together with others of lesser mileage - but there are obvious gaps which may never be filled.

Over fifty years ago the writer appeared to be surrounded by knowledgeable people who surely one day, were bound to fill that gap with erudite works on the London & North Western Railway, for instance. But it did not happen. Equally, there seemed to be enormous potential to investigate the lesser names which were just as vital to their users as were the Big Names.

To contemplate the challenge of small railways brings no less reward than a larger one, but the boy to whom the Isle of Man Railway brought such attraction that he has never lost it in almost three-score years, could hardly have imagined that he would one day be writing these final lines of a three-volume saga. Times bring changes, and what was written in the preface to Volume I is now tinged with more optimism and leads to cautious hope.

Gone from among us are some whose ambition lay in giving so much to an end they will now never see, but the goal has been reached.

So it is that:

> My thoughts went back to times long past, And I remembered forgotten years:'

(Psalm 77. v. 5)

and I found reward after all.

J.I.C.B.

Acknowledgements

The further assistance of the following during the preparation of this volume is gratefully appreciated

H.M. Attorney General's Office	-	Douglas
John Bowring	-	Librarian, Douglas Library
Roger Simms	-	Archivist, Manx Museum
Patrick Keef	-	Ross-on-Wye
Douglas Robinson	-	Bolton
George Hearse	-	Ramsey
Stan Basnett	-	Glen Vine, Marown
David Heaton	-	IOM Transport
Peter Craine	-	IOM Transport
John Smith	-	IOM Transport
George Lawson	-	IOM Transport
Brian Cottier	-	IOM Transport
Peter Kelly	-	Onchan

(IOM Transport is now IOM Railways: Manx Museum is now National Heritage Library.)

During the long drafting period we were greatly encouraged by the confidence, trust and enthusiasm shown in and to us by Robert Smith (Chief Executive) and all Headquarters' Staff of the Isle of Man Railways: this echoed in friendliness and help 'all along the line'.

Sadly, there came a time of great doubt and difficulty when my wife died unexpectedly, and the last volume had not even been commenced. Shortly beforehand, a set-back had left me incapacitated and all seemed lost. Throughout a dismal period, the support, encouragement and friendship of Jane Kennedy of The Oakwood Press, not less the welcome on setting foot in the Island once more, did much to restore my determination and bring events to their intended conclusion.

Sources

Primary

Government Office papers
Railways' Minute Books
The Tower Collection
Diary of G.H. Wood
Isle of Man Public Records Office

Secondary

Isle of Man Harbour Board
Castletown Commissioners
Attorney General's Chambers records
Isle of Man Land Registry
Royal Military School of Music
Wakefield Libraries
Derby Libraries
Glasgow District Libraries
Leeds Leisure Services
Sheffield County Council
Quiggin & Co. Ltd.
Bradshaw's Railway Manual (annual)
Field notes by R. Shepherd, Ian Macnab, L.T. Catchpole and Frank Hewitt
STEAM RAILWAY NEWS (IOMR Supporters' Association)

Newspapers

MANX SUN
ISLE OF MAN TIMES
ISLE OF MAN EXAMINER
PEEL CITY GUARDIAN
RAMSEY COURIER (now ISLE OF MAN COURIER)

Bibliography

STATUTES OF THE ISLE OF MAN	Manx Government
HISTORY OF THE ISLE OF MAN RAILWAY	Ian Macnab
ISLE OF MAN TRAMWAYS	F.K. Pearson
MANX NORTHERN RAILWAY	P. & P. Hendry
INDUSTRIAL ARCHAEOLOGY OF THE ISLE OF MAN	Various
ON THE ISLE OF MAN NARROW GAUGE	J.I.C. Boyd
ISLE OF MAN - PAST & PRESENT	George Woods
ISLE OF MAN - MEMOIRS OF A GEOLOGICAL SURVEY	G.W. Lamplugh
ISLE OF MAN	E.H. Stenning
THE ISLE OF MAN	John Quinn
BRITISH STEAM LOCOMOTIVE BUILDERS	James Lowe
A BIOGRAPHY OF RAILWAY ENGINEERS	John Marshall
THE LIVERPOOL OVERHEAD RAILWAY	C.E. Box
THE CENTENARY OF THE ISLE OF MAN STEAM PACKET CO. LTD.	P.W. Caine
ATLAS OF THE ISLE OF MAN	George Woods
THE DUMBELL AFFAIR	Connery Chapell
ISLAND LIFELINE	Connery Chapell
ISLE OF MAN: CELEBRATING A SENSE OF PLACE	Robinson & McCarroll
BIBLIOGRAPHICAL ACCOUNT OF WORKS RELATING TO THE ISLE OF MAN	William Cubbon
CAMPING IN THE ISLE OF MAN AT RAMSEY, BALLAHOT, KNOCKALOE, CASTLETOWN & PEEL BATTERY	Anon
HISTORY OF FOXDALE MINES - ORE & STONE MINING 1894 (Yn Lioar Manninagh ii 1892-4 Transactions)	KITTO
ISLE OF MAN EXAMINER (Annual)	
GEOLOGY OF THE ISLE OF MAN	G.W. Lamplugh
WITH HEART & SOUL & VOICE - 100 YEARS OF MANX MUSIC	Martin Faragher
THE MANX QUARTERLY	
FAMILY HISTORY OF KISSACKS OF THE ISLE OF MAN	Rex Kissack
THE MANX FAMILY TREE	
WEST COAST SHIPPING	M.K. Stammers
REGISTER OF DISSOLVED COMPANIES	
DIRECTORIES	Various including Brown's, Slater's, Thwaite's, Pigot's
JOURNAL OF THE MANX MUSEUM	

Index

Index to Maps and Plans